Visions for Racial Equality

Focusing on David Clement Scott, the head of the Church of Scotland mission in Malawi, who came to see Europeans as learners in Africa, this innovative book narrates the rise and demise of a unique vision for racial equality in nineteenth-century Africa. By immersing himself in the vernacular language and institutions, Scott developed a theology of reversals to pursue justice in race relations. It set him on a collision course with the Church, the colonial government, and the White commercial interests spearheaded by Cecil Rhodes. Harri Englund shows how Scott's struggle for justice was as much epistemic as it was political and spiritual – a vision for the future in which White and Black would thrive in their mutual recognition as co-knowers. From linguistic translation to conflicts over land and taxation, from slave trade to personal intimacies, *Visions for Racial Equality* weaves a rich tapestry of themes in the life and times of a little-known visionary.

HARRI ENGLUND is Professor of Social Anthropology at the University of Cambridge. A Fellow of the British Academy, he has three decades of research experience in southern and central Africa. He is the author of *From War to Peace on the Mozambique–Malawi Borderland* (2002), *Prisoners of Freedom: Human Rights and the African Poor* (2006) which was awarded the Amaury Talbot Prize, *Human Rights and African Airwaves: Mediating Equality on the Chichewa Radio* (2011), and *Gogo Breeze: Zambia's Radio Elder and the Voices of Free Speech* (2018).

Visions for Racial Equality

David Clement Scott and the Struggle for Justice in Nineteenth-Century Malawi

HARRI ENGLUND

CAMBRIDGE
UNIVERSITY PRESS

Shaftesbury Road, Cambridge CB2 8EA, United Kingdom

One Liberty Plaza, 20th Floor, New York, NY 10006, USA

477 Williamstown Road, Port Melbourne, VIC 3207, Australia

314–321, 3rd Floor, Plot 3, Splendor Forum, Jasola District Centre, New Delhi – 110025, India

103 Penang Road, #05–06/07, Visioncrest Commercial, Singapore 238467

Cambridge University Press is part of Cambridge University Press & Assessment, a department of the University of Cambridge.

We share the University's mission to contribute to society through the pursuit of education, learning and research at the highest international levels of excellence.

www.cambridge.org
Information on this title: www.cambridge.org/9781009077057

DOI: 10.1017/9781009076487

© Harri Englund 2022

This publication is in copyright. Subject to statutory exception and to the provisions of relevant collective licensing agreements, no reproduction of any part may take place without the written permission of Cambridge University Press & Assessment.

First published 2022
First paperback edition 2024

A catalogue record for this publication is available from the British Library

Library of Congress Cataloging-in-Publication data
Names: Englund, Harri, author.
Title: Visions for racial equality : David Clement Scott and the struggle for justice in nineteenth-century Malawi / Harri Englund.
Other titles: David Clement Scott and the struggle for justice in nineteenth-century Malawi
Description: [New York] : Cambridge University Press, [2022] | Includes bibliographical references and index.
Identifiers: LCCN 2021039273 (print) | LCCN 2021039274 (ebook) | ISBN 9781316514009 (hardback) | ISBN 9781009077057 (paperback) | ISBN 9781009076487 (epub)
Subjects: LCSH: Scott, David Clement, 1853-1907. | Church of Scotland–Missions–Malawi–History–19th century. | Race relations–Religious aspects–Christianity–History–19th century. | Malawi–Church history–19th century. | BISAC: HISTORY / Africa / General
Classification: LCC BV3625.N82 S368 2022 (print) | LCC BV3625.N82 (ebook) | DDC 266/.02341106897–dc23/eng/20211014
LC record available at https://lccn.loc.gov/2021039273
LC ebook record available at https://lccn.loc.gov/2021039274

ISBN   978-1-316-51400-9   Hardback
ISBN   978-1-009-07705-7   Paperback

Cambridge University Press & Assessment has no responsibility for the persistence or accuracy of URLs for external or third-party internet websites referred to in this publication and does not guarantee that any content on such websites is, or will remain, accurate or appropriate.

Contents

List of Figures		*page* vi
List of Maps		vii
Preface and Acknowledgements		ix
1	Introduction	1
2	Among the Wild Scotsmen	33
3	Champagne and Slaves	52
4	The Universal Vernacular	76
5	Frightful Libel upon Humanity	103
6	Rhodes Must Not Rise	132
7	A Future Foreclosed	163
8	Grief Never Wears Out	201
9	Liberal Translations	233
10	The Rest Is History	265
Bibliography		283
Index		302

Figures

1.1	David Clement Scott	*page* 24
2.1	Chief Kapeni's village, 1886	42
3.1	Chief Kapeni, 1886	60
5.1	The foundations ceremony, 1888	122
5.2	St Michael's and All Angels Church, 1926	124
5.3	St Michael's and All Angels Church, 2018	124
7.1	David Clement Scott and female missionaries	166
7.2	Harry Kambwiri Matecheta, Jeannie Chendetsa, and their child	171
8.1	Adam Currie and pupils	206
9.1	Alexander Hetherwick at his desk in Blantyre	234
10.1	Maganga House, 2018	266
10.2	Che Chamba, 2018	266

Maps

1 Malawi and the neighbouring countries *page* xv
2 Southern and central Malawi xvi

Preface and Acknowledgements

In the twenty-first century, rousing White people from the stupor of their racialized advantage and privilege has become one of the most urgent tasks in achieving racial equality. It is not enough to condemn White supremacy whenever it still tries to raise its ugly head. Activists and scholars insist that White people should also be disabused of their habit of regarding others as being of a certain race while considering themselves to belong to the human race *tout court*.[1] Educating White people begins with urging them to listen to racialized others speaking for themselves.

What White people will hear and how they might act upon their new learning should also be of interest to anyone advocating racial equality. This book presents a case of listening and learning from the nineteenth century. It issues a challenge to the twenty-first-century reader by taking as its central subject a White male Protestant missionary. How open are we to the possibility that this person has anything to offer as we contemplate the future of racial equality? My own thirty-year commitment to listen and to learn in central Africa, mostly in a vernacular language, has attempted to give primacy to Black over White in full awareness of the ways in which White colonial administrators, missionaries, and anthropologists have all too often directed the production of knowledge about this region. It did take some time to develop an interest in White missionaries. The more I have learnt of David Clement Scott's thought, however, the more convinced I have become of how rewarding an unbiased investigation into his struggle against prejudices could be.

Sent to re-establish the Church of Scotland mission in present-day Malawi in 1881, Scott fits uneasily into either of the two categories by which enlightened or unconventional Christian missionaries are often described: liberals and primitivists. Although liberalism as a

---

[1] Richard Dyer, *White*, 2nd ed., New York: Routledge, 2017.

philosophical orientation may be multifaceted enough to accommodate Scott, his thought was resolutely at odds with the central tenets by which liberal missionaries tended to understand human diversity at the turn of the twentieth century. Much as Black and White might share the same Christian faith, for these liberal missionaries their cultural differences were such that both were best left to develop themselves in their own manner. The flip side of this liberal toleration was racial segregation, a prospect Scott never tired of warning against. A primitivist impulse to marvel at African civilization, to the point of 'going native', never swayed Scott either. His was an orientation committed to the common humanity of Black and White, expressed in Christian idiom even as he faced mounting criticism from the Church of Scotland.

In Scott's theology of reversals, teacher became learner and had no monopoly over the meaning of Christianity. It was not a reversal of roles, as if various hierarchies could simply be wished away, but a *theology* of reversals for the way in which the figure of the risen Christ inspired Scott to envisage the race relations. The risen Christ was a stranger demanding the recognition of one's own limitations in understanding. In this vein, Africans confronted the Scottish missionary with knowledge that was not confined to their 'tribal' cultures but stood to enrich humanity as a whole. Christianity provided Scott with tools both to recognize common humanity and to reject some of the authoritative ways Christianity had come to be practised and disseminated. It is hard to think of a secular orientation that would in the twenty-first century achieve a similar degree of radical self-reflection. The discourse on human rights commends itself as the champion of common humanity, but having observed so-called human rights educators – Black and White – at work in Malawi, I am yet to discern a philosophy of reversals among its practitioners.[2] They made a sharp distinction between those who knew what human rights were and those who were ignorant about them. Alas, little was achieved when the gospel of human rights was spread with the righteous zeal of the unreflective missionary.

---

[2] Harri Englund, *Prisoners of Freedom: Human Rights and the African Poor*, Berkeley: University of California Press, 2006; Harri Englund, *Human Rights and African Airwaves: Mediating Equality on the Chichewa Radio*, Bloomington: Indiana University Press, 2011.

Even if the reader felt able to rise to the challenge of considering a nineteenth-century White missionary as an advocate of racial equality, impediments to understanding remain. Chief among them is David Clement Scott's lack of status among the intellectuals of his era, largely as a result of his writings being confined to scattered articles, sermons, and letters. His life was cut too short to allow for the tomes of theological and moral reflection that some missionaries produced after retirement. Yet this observation is only another aspect of the question of who might be admitted as a worthy contributor to discussions about racial equality. Contemporary intellectual history tends to prefer two kinds of approaches to the study of turn-of-the-twentieth-century responses to colonization and the empire, as illustrated by two of my Cambridge colleagues. Duncan Bell has, in his *Reordering the World*, shown in compelling detail the diverse 'ways in which *prominent thinkers* tackled the legitimacy of conquest and imperial rule'.[3] So prominent, if not canonical, are those thinkers – from John Stuart Mill to John Robert Seeley – that David Clement Scott, from his base in south-central Africa, would seem decisively peripheral in their company. Yet here is another challenge issued by this book: what more is there to be learnt if such a peripheral character is allowed to occupy the centre stage?

In *Insurgent Empire*, Priyamvada Gopal would seem to have confronted the centre–periphery distinction head on.[4] Reversals enter her analytical radar as a matter of exploring how the White British critics of the empire were influenced by protests and uprisings in Africa, Asia, and the West Indies. The end of the empire did not, in other words, come from the benevolence of the metropolitan colonizers – it required determined action by the colonized and principled dissent among the British intelligentsia. Laudable as this reversal of perspectives is – the colonized educating the colonizers – Gopal's roster of thinkers again leaves out figures such as David Clement Scott. Wary of over-represented topics in the study of anti-colonialism – such as Gandhi and Indian nationalism – Gopal nevertheless associates British dissent with high-profile metropolitan intellectuals, from journalists to members of parliament. The omission of an apparently minor figure

---

[3] Duncan Bell, *Reordering the World: Essays on Liberalism and Empire*, Princeton: Princeton University Press, 2016, 2, emphasis added.
[4] Priyamvada Gopal, *Insurgent Empire: Anticolonial Resistance and British Dissent*, London: Verso, 2019.

in the empire's periphery is not the main contrast to the present book. More important is to recognize the manner in which Scott learned his lessons. Immersed in vernacular worlds, Scott pursued reversals in the very ideas that had brought him to Africa. Long before Malawi's first anti-colonial uprising, Scott's vision for an interracial future proved too subversive to his White contemporaries.

Scott neither left behind tomes of scholarship nor became the subject of biographies. This is surprising, because biographies, particularly hagiographical ones, were a prominent feature of the turn-of-the-twentieth-century missionary enterprise. From within Scott's mission alone arose biographies with titles such as *A Hero of the Dark Continent*, devoted to his younger brother who predeceased him in Malawi, and *A Prince of Missionaries*, devoted to Scott's successor, Alexander Hetherwick.[5] 'Devotion' is the right word to use here, so idealized were their portrayals of missionary lives. Scott did receive adulatory obituaries from his long-standing associates upon his death in Kenya in 1907. Yet the absence of a biography bespeaks the controversies that engulfed him. Some of them were theological and political, and others intensely personal. It has not helped Scott's would-be biographers, the present author included, that his family disposed of many of his papers. The reasons remain unclear, but the tragedies that struck his first wife in Malawi and his second wife in Kenya, as described in this book, may give some clues.

The turn-of-the-century missionary biographies had a clear purpose: to celebrate self-sacrifice in order to galvanize support for the cause. What might be the purpose of a twenty-first-century biography about a nineteenth-century missionary? Moreover, does my enchantment with my biographical subject, already apparent in the preceding paragraphs, restate some of the hagiographical proclivity of the biographers one hundred years ago? Enchantment with the subject matter is hardly desirable in secular anthropology and history, but being inspired by it ought to be acceptable. After all, the challenge of this book is to persuade its predominantly secular readership to discover in Scott's Christian orientation a radical rebuttal of racial inequality. The purpose, as such, is to introduce some hard questions about the

---

[5] W. Henry Rankine, *A Hero of the Dark Continent: Memoir of Rev. Wm. Affleck Scott*, Edinburgh: William Blackwood and Sons, 1896; William P. Livingstone, *A Prince of Missionaries: The Rev. Alexander Hetherwick of Blantyre, Central Africa*, London: James Clarke and Co, 1931.

intellectual and political horizons of racial equality. Who can be admitted to participate in imagining those horizons? How to discern common humanity beyond the politics of racialized peoplehood?

***

The discovery and exploration of David Clement Scott's thought and the times in which he lived took me to archives and other sources unfamiliar to me from my previous research. The work required a period of dedicated study, which the Leverhulme Trust's three-year Major Research Fellowship generously supported. I am grateful for the risk it took to provide me with this degree of intellectual freedom. My work in the archives in Edinburgh was much enlivened by the many remarkable scholars at the University of Edinburgh who shared their insights with me. Gerhard Anders, George Karekwaivanane, Wolfgang Zeller, and their families, were particularly hospitable on several occasions. Another delight of this research was my return to Zomba. Wapulumuka Mulwafu extended a heartfelt welcome at Chancellor College, while Clement Mweso responded stoically to my requests to retrieve misplaced or lost files in the National Archives of Malawi. The Centre of Language Studies was again the place where I could find likeminded scholars with whom to explore the past and present of Chichewa expression. Alick Bwanali, Pascal Kishindo, and Ahmmardouh Mjaya were generous with their time. Andrew Cohen kindly facilitated the retrieval of material from the National Archives of Zimbabwe.

A quartet of historians enriched my thought beyond measure. Giacomo Macola's command of central Africa's historiography continued to guide and impress, while Markku Hokkanen, Emma Hunter, and Derek Peterson also challenged me on various aspects of my drafts. Discussions with Jake Richards about the historian's craft were formative. Tom Cunningham made valuable suggestions on the basis of his research on Scottish missionaries in Kenya. Patrick McKearney gave advice on theological matters. Kenneth Ross's essay was the first I read about David Clement Scott, and I thank him for his encouragement and insights. At various stages of this research, comments from, and conversations with, several scholars were critical to the development of my thought. Karin Barber, Susan Bayly, Jonathon Earle, Klaus Fiedler,

Judith Irvine, Deborah James, Christopher Lee, Isak Niehaus, and Anye Nyamnjoh set in train some of the ideas presented here.

The foundational work by John McCracken and Andrew Ross informs most pages of this book. Unfortunately, both had passed on by the time I embarked on this research. A pair of books about Malawi's history by two other scholars has often been on my mind in what now seems a rather uncanny series of events. I first visited Cambridge in 1987, the year when Cambridge University Press published *The Story of an African Famine: Gender and Famine in Twentieth-Century Malawi* by Megan Vaughan and *Magomero: Portrait of an African Village* by Landeg White. An undergraduate student in cultural anthropology at the University of Helsinki, I was interested in famines but wholly ignorant about Malawi. It is no exaggeration to describe discovering these two books in the Cambridge University Press bookshop as a life-changing moment, so entwined became my life and my research in Malawi over the following decades. What makes the life-changing moment look uncanny now is how Cambridge, along with Malawi, became unexpectedly a significant place in my own biography. Having been introduced to Malawi by historians, having written my own book on Malawi's history in Cambridge, being able to publish it with Cambridge University Press – it all gives an unusual sensation. While of no consequence to anyone else, it marks a personal milestone, the closing of a circle.

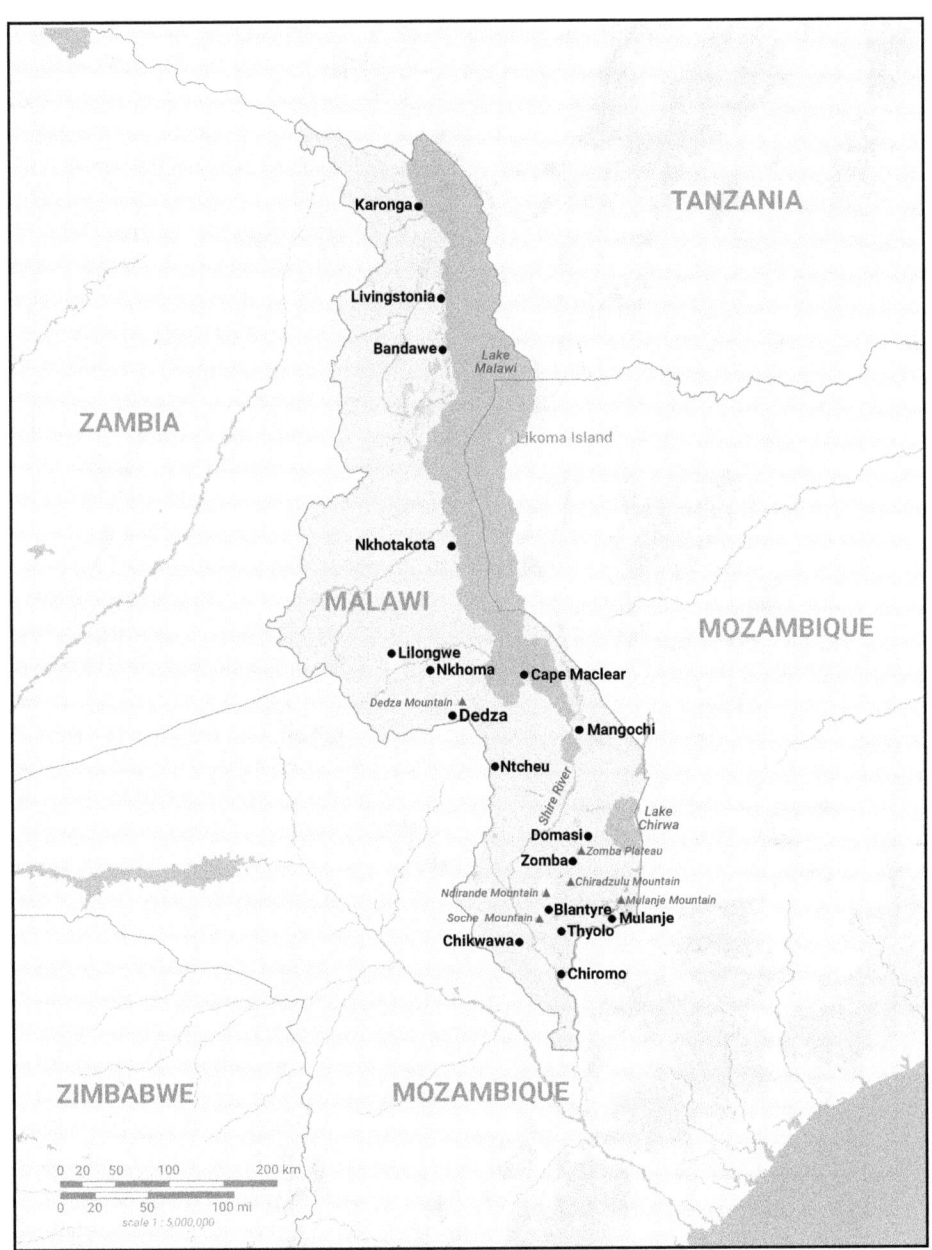

Map 1 Malawi and the neighbouring countries

Map 2 Southern and central Malawi

1 Introduction

'Africa is an education; here you come to school again.'[1] So was David Clement Scott known to advise European newcomers in the late nineteenth century when he led the Blantyre Mission in present-day Malawi. Many of the newcomers misunderstood him. It was not an education to prepare the European to rule over the African, or even to convert the African to Christianity. Scott's vision was of status reversals in which the newcomer, however powerful or wealthy, learned from those they had come to teach.

In another of his demands on the incoming European powers, Scott stated that 'Africa is an altar of sacrifice, and on this altar the powers have laid their vows'.[2] Here his impetus came from the international slave trade that had disrupted life in the region long before the arrival of his mission. British opposition to slavery had also been long-standing, from the early abolitionists to David Livingstone's description of the slave trade, inscribed in his tombstone at Westminster Abbey, as the 'open sore of the world'. By invoking sacrifice, Scott contested a discourse that had started to lose its radical tenor. The British were not the redeemers, for so heavy were their own burdens that they could atone for them only through sacrifice. Scott came to see Christ in the figures of the slave and Africa.

But in order to put down the slave trade you must have a proper doctrine of humanity, a true appreciation of the slave. Just as Christ took upon Him the form of a slave long ago, so He takes upon Him the form of Africa today. Africa bears the sins of the world's rulers. How long are we as a nation going to lay our selfishness, our meanness, our falsehood, our lusts, yea, and the whole burden of our sins upon this Lamb of God?[3]

---

[1] Alexander Hetherwick, *The Romance of Blantyre: How Livingstone's Dream Came True*, Edinburgh: Lassodie Press, 1931, 155.
[2] *Life and Work in British Central Africa* (*LWBCA*), June 1889.
[3] *LWBCA*, August–December 1897.

Scott saw in Africa what the Archbishop of Canterbury, some one hundred years later, came to interpret as the disciples' predicament: 'Jesus condemns the inadequacy of their earlier understanding: he is not what they have thought him to be, and thus they must "learn" him afresh, as from the beginning.'[4] The unrecognizability of the risen Christ profoundly unsettles the disciples' certainties; it subverts any reduction of Christ to a particular identity.

Africa as the risen Christ in Scott's thought likewise assaulted the prejudices that had long acquired the status of certainties in European ideas of Africa. For Scott, Africa may have been unrecognized, but it was not unknowable. It was not the Dark Continent, let alone a continent outside history as in Hegel's oft-cited fallacy.[5] Africa confronted Scott with the otherness of the risen Christ, an otherness that exposed the limits of the newcomer's learning.

The redemptive urge in Scott's thought outlines a different sense of sacrifice than the one missionaries have used to describe their vocation in the nineteenth and twentieth centuries. Inspired by the figure of Christ on the Cross rather than by the risen Saviour, they have seen self-sacrifice as a matter of forsaking the comforts of their homes in order to save souls in far-flung places.[6] While Scott had more than his share of personal misery in Malawi, the sacrifice he sought was of a different order. Already by his time, redemptive politics had assumed a pattern by which the redeemer would not pursue transformation in their own outlook.[7] 'The attack on slavery', an historian remarked in the mid-twentieth century, 'represented hatred of a concept rather than love of its victims'.[8] By the late nineteenth century, the anti-slavery campaign had become a mark of distinction that 'automatically placed

---

[4] Rowan Williams, *Resurrection: Interpreting the Easter Gospel*, London: Darton, Longman, and Todd, 2002 [1982], 75.
[5] G. W. F. Hegel, *The Philosophy of History*, trans. J. Sibree, New York: The Colonial Press, 1999; Kwame Anthony Appiah, *Lines of Descent: W. E. B. Dubois and the Emergence of Identity*, Cambridge, MA: Harvard University Press, 2014, 120–1; Tom C. McCaskie, 'Exiled from History: Africa in Hegel's Academic Practice', *History in Africa*, 46, 2019, 165–94.
[6] Peter Pels, *A Politics of Presence: Contacts between Missionaries and the Walguru in Late Colonial Tanganyika*, Amsterdam: Harwood, 1999, 52–5.
[7] Talal Asad, *Formations of the Secular: Christianity, Islam, Modernity*, Stanford, CA: Stanford University Press, 2003, 61–2.
[8] H. Alan C. Cairns, *Prelude to Imperialism: British Reactions to Central African Society 1840–1890*, London: Routledge & Kegan Paul, 1965, 140.

the British, as judges and deliverers, in the vanguard of the moral progress of the world'.[9]

Scott's sacrifice was as much epistemic as it was personal. By adopting the position of a learner, Europeans in Africa would come to revise and even reject some of their cherished ideas. After all, it was ideas, whether in the Christian idiom or not, that justified the colonial conquest. As Marlow's account in *Heart of Darkness* of the atrocities committed by European conquerors put it, 'What redeems [the atrocities] is the idea only…something you can set up, and bow down before, and offer a sacrifice to.'[10] For Scott, the idea that had brought him and other missionaries to Africa came to bear disquieting resemblance to a prejudice. When confronted with the powers of African languages to express spiritual, moral, and political ideas, the missionary was the one who had to question the sources and nature of civilization. At no point would Scott question Christianity itself. What made his sense of sacrifice particularly challenging was precisely the realization that the Christian civilization could be enriched by Africans who had barely been touched by missionary teachings. One of Scott's most startling maxims put it thus: 'The native may be saved without us, but we doubt if we here can be saved without the native.'[11]

Scott was not impervious to the vocabulary of his times, but 'native' – the only n-word he would use – appeared along with 'African' in his writings. Rather than becoming distracted by the nineteenth-century lexicon, the twenty-first-century reader may more profitably discern in Scott's vision a new kind of society in which Black and White would live together, 'not side by side but as one'.[12] Racial equality would not deracialize all differences, but it would be the principle by which justice would be sought and delivered in the new society. Scott's struggle for justice took place in a variety of domains, from language use to land tenure. Although not carried out in the name of gender equality, his promotion of girls and women was for some of his contemporaries almost as unsettling as his desire to learn from Africans. Not only did Scott include girls and women in the earliest cohorts of school children and so-called African deacons. He also oversaw new income-generating industries among both men and

---

[9] Ibid.
[10] Joseph Conrad, *Heart of Darkness*, London: Penguin Random House, 2019 [1902], 8.
[11] LWBCA, December 1891.   [12] Ibid.

women. Particularly controversial was his decision to send unmarried White women to work with an African man at a newly-established mission station.

Scott's vision was not curtailed by blind egalitarianism. He found in African chiefly authority food for thought, just as the missionary's efforts to learn from Africans never denied his capacity to teach them. Hierarchies would persist, but they revealed common humanity, not innate racial or cultural difference. It was common humanity as seen from a particular vantage point. Scott remarked on the campaign against slavery: 'The basis is wider than Protestantism, it is humanity, it is the Church of Christ.'[13] Far from being a view from nowhere, let alone the politically expendable 'bare life' that critics would theorize after twentieth-century atrocities,[14] common humanity was for Scott Christian humanity, inspired by the risen Christ. Its challenge to prevailing White prejudices lay in its reversals, in the possibility that the scope of Christian civilization could include those whom Europeans had relegated to the status of non-Christians, perhaps even to the condition of being less-than-human.

Whatever else it would have entailed in nineteenth-century central Africa, racial equality required the end of White domination in defining acceptable knowledge in racialized encounters. Epistemic justice was, in other words, the *sine qua non* of Scott's struggle for justice in various other domains. As understood by contemporary moral philosophers, epistemic justice corrects the wrongs committed when people are disregarded as knowers because of blanket presumptions about their sex, race, nationality, class, and so forth.[15] In their search for ethically and epistemologically robust responses to prejudice, some philosophers doubt whether epistemic justice demands a particular virtue, a stable disposition of character which, much like honesty, would serve as a bulwark against prejudice.[16] Few dispute, however, the contention that 'eradicating [epistemic] injustices would ultimately

---

[13] Ibid., August–December 1897.
[14] Giorgio Agamben, *Homo Sacer: Sovereign Power and Bare Life*, trans. D. Heller-Roazen, Stanford, CA: Stanford University Press, 1998.
[15] Miranda Fricker, *Epistemic Injustice: Power and the Ethics of Knowing*, Oxford: Oxford University Press, 2007.
[16] Benjamin R. Sherman, 'There's No (Testimonial) Justice: Why Pursuit of a Virtue Is Not the Solution to Epistemic Injustice', *Social Epistemology*, 30 (3), 2016, 229–50.

take not just more virtuous hearers, but collective social political change'.[17] Historical and anthropological study can take the contention forward by attending to epistemic justice as a *struggle* in specific political, racialized circumstances.

How David Clement Scott, the son of a middle-class Edinburgh family with no Christian calling until relatively late in life, came to pursue epistemic justice in central Africa deserves a study of the multiple historical currents that ran through these turbulent times. He was invited to re-establish the Church of Scotland's mission in 1881 after the first attempt had ended in violence and scandal. With his Scottish and African associates, Scott approached the task with such energy that his departure in 1898 would seem to have brought to a close a period of unmitigated success. Although the departure was ostensibly caused by ill health, Scott left the Blantyre Mission as a broken man, criticized, if not vilified, by influential figures in the Church of Scotland, the colonial administration, and the White settler class.

This book draws on the biographical method to illuminate the intricacies of Scott's struggle. Against 'Great Man' history, in which a White man single-handedly shapes the course of history, the biographical method, not least when deployed to explore Africa's missionary and colonial past, can reveal the subject's transformation through time.[18] It can uncover complexity and connection obscured by the reduction of persons to categories, such as 'missionary'.[19] The sources of Scott's struggle for justice were multiple and not reducible to his individual disposition as a 'virtuous hearer'. This book puts an emphasis on the influence of vernacular African thought and practice on his struggle. At the same time, despite its intermittent successes, the struggle was ultimately doomed as forces more powerful than his vision began to consolidate central Africa's colonial and capitalist capture. Yet in its very failure the twenty-first-century reader may find

---

[17] Fricker, *Epistemic Injustice*, 8.
[18] Lisa A. Lindsay, 'Biography in African History', *History in Africa*, 44, 2017, 11–26; Klaas van Walraven, 'Prologue: Reflections on Historiography and Biography and the Study of Africa's Past', in Klaas van Walraven, ed., *The Individual in African History: The Importance of Biography in African Historical Studies*, Leiden: Brill, 2020, 1–50.
[19] Isak Niehaus, *Witchcraft and a Life in the New South Africa*, Cambridge: Cambridge University Press for the International African Institute, 2013.

an opportunity to evaluate the ideas by which the horizons of racial equality are now envisaged.

The chapters that follow chronicle the developments from Scott's initial experiences of friendship and well-spoken deliberations among Africans to his immersion in the vernacular language, from his dismay at the newly-established administration's resort to warfare against defiant chiefs to his early criticisms of Cecil Rhodes's imperial designs. Several characters, African and European, appear along the way, not least Scott's successor Alexander Hetherwick and the leader of Malawi's first anti-colonial uprising, John Chilembwe. Between them, Hetherwick and Chilembwe embodied the directions race relations would take after Scott's vision for racial equality had been extinguished. White liberal paternalism and Black militant nationalism appeared as the only alternatives to White supremacy, both incompatible with Scott's visionary practice. It was visionary precisely because its work towards an interracial future found few parallels in the available approaches to race relations.

Missionary Positions

Despite being the subject of an extensive scholarly literature, Christian missions continue to attract spurious generalizations even among professional historians. To quote one of the most prominent, Eric Hobsbawm had in his magisterial history of colonial empires little time for them except to comment that Christian missions were 'something done by whites for natives, and paid for by whites'.[20] As the case of the Blantyre Mission shows, he also seemed to get the chronology wrong by asserting that 'colonial conquest opened the way for effective missionary action'. More mindful of the chronology in missionary and colonial enterprises in east and central Africa, another historian could nevertheless regurgitate some of Hobsbawm's attitude in the twenty-first century. For Roy Bridges, missionaries in the nineteenth century were 'unofficial imperialists', who 'did believe that it was their task to reorder African religion, politics, society, and economy in ways decided by them and for a good as defined by them'.[21]

---

[20] Eric Hobsbawm, *The Age of Empire 1875–1914*, London: Weidenfeld & Nicolson, 1987, 71.

[21] Roy Bridges, 'The Christian Vision and Secular Imperialism: Missionaries, Geography, and the Approach to East Africa, c. 1844–1890', in Dana L. Robert,

Although the call for including missionaries in anthropological studies goes as far back as 1928, it was not until the 1980s that they became the subjects of major African ethnographies.[22] The early overlap between anthropological and missionary enterprises may have accounted for this late recognition of missionaries as worthy subjects of study along with local people.[23] The long gestation of the anthropological interest did not, however, ensure subtlety about the variety of positions missionaries may have taken. Trends in social theory could take precedence over such subtlety, resulting in myopia about how missionaries had been represented in popular and academic thought previously. A specialist on missionary history, for example, came to describe the influential work by Jean and John Comaroff as breathing 'new life into the almost lifeless corpse of the missionary-as-imperialist'.[24] Building on the rediscovery of Antonio Gramsci's concept of hegemony in social theory to highlight both symbolic and material domination, they asserted that 'the southern Tswana had no alternative but to be inducted, unwittingly and often unwillingly, into the *forms* of European discourse'.[25] Both power and resistance to it came, in this perspective, to be locked in an embrace that was as tight as it seemed inexorable – the southern Tswana 'could not avoid internalizing the terms through which they were being challenged'.

By the early 2000s, other conceptual preoccupations had taken hold in anthropology. Among them was Bruno Latour's concept of purification, which Webb Keane put to use in his study of Calvinist

---

ed., *Converting to Colonialism: Visions and Realities in Mission History, 1706–1914*, Grand Rapids, MI: William B. Erdmans, 2008, 46.

[22] Isaac Schapera, 'Economic Changes in South African Native Life', *Africa*, 1 (2), 1928, 170–88; T. O. Beidelman, *Colonial Evangelism: A Socio-Historical Study of an East African Mission at the Grassroots*, Bloomington: Indiana University Press, 1982; Frederick Cooper, *Colonialism in Question: Theory, Knowledge, History*. Berkeley: University of California Press, 2005, 47–8.

[23] Patrick Harries, 'Anthropology', in Norman Etherington, ed., *Mission and Empire*, Oxford: Oxford University Press, 2005, 238–60.

[24] Norman Etherington, 'Introduction', in ibid., 4; Elizabeth Elbourne, 'Word Made Flesh: Christianity, Modernity, and Cultural Colonialism in the Work of Jean and John Comaroff', *American Historical Review*, 108 (2), 2003, 435–49; Brian Stanley, 'Conversion to Christianity: The Colonization of the Mind?', *International Review of Mission*, no. 366, 2013, 315–31.

[25] Jean and John Comaroff, *Of Revelation and Revolution: Christianity, Colonialism, and Consciousness in South Africa. Volume One*, Chicago: University of Chicago Press, 1991, 213.

missionaries in Indonesia.[26] For Keane, the missionaries 'had to know the false religion in order to combat it effectively, and the culture in order to convert people in accordance with, and thus with the support of, their particular way of living'.[27] Purification as a quintessentially 'modern' protocol to distil true from false marked little conceptual advance over hegemony, because in neither case would the anthropologists claim that the processes had been entirely successful from the missionary point of view. The question is, rather, whether concepts such as hegemony or purification – or epistemic justice, for that matter – get deployed to drive an intellectual agenda that is less concerned to explore the variety of missionary positions than to insert the study into an academic trend. The call for more subtlety about missionary positions by no means suggests modesty about the scope of issues to be raised. In David Clement Scott's thought, race relations and common humanity appeared in ways that demand a fresh look in the twenty-first century.

One reason why Scott's thought compels consideration – and why the variety of missionary positions must be recognized – is precisely the range of liberal, progressive and even Afrocentric standpoints that missionaries have taken in Africa in the nineteenth and twentieth centuries. Scott's is only one of those standpoints, easily overlooked if subtle (and not so subtle) differences are not acknowledged. His appreciation of vernacular thought and practice might seem primitivism to some, the position some missionaries took both to marvel at African culture and to bemoan aspects of it as obstacles to conversion.[28] Primitivism's more radical form was Afrocentrism that could lead to ostracism from the mission movement itself, such as when Johannes Winter from Germany began to live with his Sotho family in a straw house, or when Joseph Booth became a nineteenth-century advocate of African political independence.[29] For others, such as the Irish lay evangelist Charles Stokes who married the daughter of an African chief and was promptly dismissed by his missionary society,

---

[26] Webb Keane, *Christian Moderns: Freedom and Fetish in the Mission Encounter*, Berkeley: University of California Press, 2007.
[27] Ibid., 99.   [28] Harries, 'Anthropology', 246.
[29] Richard Elphick, *The Equality of Believers: Protestant Missionaries and the Racial Politics of South Africa*, Charlottesville, VA: University of Virginia Press, 2012, 64.

'Afrocentric' would be too refined an attribute.[30] An altogether more scholarly variety was the well-known case of John William Colenso, the Anglican bishop of Natal, who had by the mid-nineteenth century developed doubts about certain fundamentals of Christian doctrine.[31] That none of these standpoints describes Scott's vision calls for a closer look at the variety in missionary approaches to race relations.

In 1945, some half-a-century after Scott's departure from Blantyre, a pioneering missionary study of African thought was published. While anthropologists, notably E. E. Evans-Pritchard,[32] had by then discredited European ideas about Africans' deficient reasoning, *Bantu Philosophy* by Placide Tempels presented a missionary's respectful account of practical wisdom and what he called ontological ideas.[33] For the Catholic missionary in Congo, this ontology offered a window into 'the soul of the Bantu people'.[34] It is not so much the content of those ideas, as understood by Tempels, as the purpose of his study that is relevant to the question of epistemic justice. For the missionary's purpose was to know in order to civilize. The ontology identified by Tempels would 'serve as the starting point of a higher civilization',[35] but if it was not properly understood by the missionary or colonist, 'one [ran] the risk, while believing that one [was] "civilizing" the individual, of in fact corrupting him'.[36] Tempels was motivated here by the common European concern about the emergence of uprooted Africans, or *déracinés*, outnumbering 'fully civilized persons, or true *évolués*'.[37] The majority, however, remained 'under a light coating of white imitation', immersed in the ontology identified by Tempels. The missionary's knowledge was needed, because Africans had no method of presenting their ontology as a philosophy. 'It is we', Tempels asserted, 'who will be able to tell them, in precise terms, what their inmost concept of being is'.[38]

The respectful attitude that Tempels adopted betrayed him as the owner of superior knowledge. The respect he accorded to Africans

---

[30] Anna Luck, *Charles Stokes in Africa*, Nairobi: East African Publishing House, 1972.
[31] Jeff Guy, *The Heretic: A Study of the Life of John William Colenso 1814–1883*, Johannesburg: Ravan Press, 1983, 55.
[32] E. E. Evans-Pritchard, *Witchcraft, Oracles, and Magic among the Azande*, Oxford: Clarendon Press, 1937.
[33] Placide Tempels, *Bantu Philosophy*, trans. Colin King, Paris: Présence Africaine, 1959.
[34] Ibid., 20.   [35] Ibid., 113.   [36] Ibid., 17.   [37] Ibid., 19.   [38] Ibid., 25.

recognized their ways of knowing as specific to them, so much so that any 'higher civilization' that they might achieve would always be 'their own Bantu civilization, a stable and noble one of their own'.[39] Here, too, he subscribed to common twentieth-century, ostensibly liberal European views on how best to develop Africa. Segregation along racial lines was the logical conclusion of those views, although it came to define settler colonies more than Congo where Tempels worked. The South African-born Methodist missionary and one-time president of the Royal Anthropological Institute Edwin Smith had become aware of Tempels's study long before it was translated into English and pursued related ideas with regard to countries where White settlers were gaining prominence.[40] Already in the 1920s, he insisted on respect rather than pity as the attitude Europeans should adopt towards Africans.[41] Such an attitude would stimulate the African 'to develop his culture according to his own genius'. Tempels's premonition about uprooted Africans was anticipated by Smith's sense of confusion. 'The danger is', Smith wrote, 'that in the process of social revolution [the African] should lose his old moral restraints and gain no others'.[42] If 'thorough, out-and-out assimilation' was not possible because of White prejudices, segregation in a 'limited sense' had to be considered, with a view to allowing Africans 'to develop their own civilization on their own land'.[43]

The doctrine of separate development, as enshrined by the apartheid policies in South Africa after the 1948 elections, was one extreme to which segregation could be taken. It clearly was not what Tempels and Smith advocated, but their writings indicate the extent to which related ideas were in the air in the early twentieth century. Smith saw in 'tribalism' a source of admiration, if not envy, for Europeans, 'a solidarity that civilized communities find it hard to attain'.[44] Where it still existed, 'tribalism' had to be 'jealously safeguarded in the moral interests of the Natives'.[45] Those African Christians who had grown

---

[39] Ibid., 113.
[40] W. John Young, '"They Have Laid Hold of Some Essential Truths": Edwin W. Smith (1876–1957), A Wise Listener to African Voices', in Frieder Ludwig and Afe Adogame, eds, *European Traditions in the Study of Religion in Africa*, Wiesbaden: Harrassowitz, 2004, 201–2.
[41] Edwin W. Smith, *The Golden Stool: Some Aspects of the Conflict of Cultures in Modern Africa*, London: Edinburgh House, 1927, 94.
[42] Ibid., 215.   [43] Ibid., 186.   [44] Ibid., 214.   [45] Ibid., 215.

rather too zealous in condemning African ways of life represented failure rather than success in missionary work.[46] European missionaries were not to determine which form African Christianity would take but 'to lay the foundations securely and well'. Indeed, they were 'not a permanent factor in the life of Africa'. By 1946, Smith had discovered a phrase for the disposition he wanted to combat – 'cultural imperialism'.[47]

The liberal tone of Smith's thought could not conceal an epistemic order in which it was the European missionaries who had laid the foundations of Christian knowledge for Africans to build on. Despite his appreciation of what he called African religion, it was bound to appear inadequate and in need of missionary guidance.[48] For its part, Tempels's study became an inspiration for late-colonial African intellectuals despite his view that the ontology he described hardly merited the status of philosophy as understood in Europe.[49] The reputations that Tempels and Smith enjoy for their progressive ideas may be a measure of how rare an avowedly respectful attitude to Africans had become by the early twentieth century. At the same time, the idea that African civilization, 'African Christianity' included, should develop along its own lines issued no challenge to Europeans to learn from it, let alone, as David Clement Scott had insisted earlier, to recognize Christianity in those who had not even begun to live by its doctrines. At its most tragic, the idea emphasizing a unique ethnic or racial path to civilization travelled from early German missionary and colonial linguistics to the Nazi ideology and the apartheid policies.[50]

What the cases of Tempels and Smith demonstrate are some of the reasons why, as already mentioned, the figure of the missionary as an imperialist indeed is an 'almost lifeless corpse'.[51] Whatever the affinity between their ideas and those that came to underpin Nazism and apartheid, it of course made all the difference whether the ideas promoted self-determination or oppression among Africans. Yet such a

---

[46] Ibid., 281–2.
[47] Edwin W. Smith, *Knowing the African*, London: Lutterworth Press, 1946, 18.
[48] Young, 'They Have', 201.
[49] Stephen Howe, *Afrocentrism: Mythical Pasts and Imagined Homes*, London: Verso, 1998, 157.
[50] Sara Pugach, *Africa in Translation: A History of Colonial Linguistics in Germany and Beyond, 1814–1945*, Ann Arbor: University of Michigan Press, 2012, 191–2.
[51] Etherington, 'Introduction', 4.

qualification should not obscure fundamental differences between the epistemic attitudes that they and Scott adopted. The differences may be partly epochal and are bound to reduce, as such, any misconception of Scott as a lone genius. A shift in attitudes among nineteenth-century European missionaries in Africa has been observed by several historians. Already in the 1840s Cape Colony, James Reid of the London Missionary Society appeared 'old-fashioned' in his battle against racial prejudice within and without the church.[52] A new generation of missionaries became engaged in 'a rethinking of the initial promise of an interracial church, with a colour-blind career path for White and Black ministers and church officials as well as racially mixed congregations'.[53]

It was at the turn of the twentieth century when such rethinking became common. Surveying the shifting attitudes among Protestant missionaries in South Africa, Richard Elphick noted that 'the ideal of equality among Christians moved slowly to the margins of their minds. Once radical egalitarians, the missionaries had now become benevolent paternalists'.[54] In another example, for a period of thirty years in the mid-nineteenth century, Henry Venn steered the Anglican Church Missionary Society towards the establishment of an indigenous church in Africa, with Samuel Ajayi Crowther ordained in 1864 as the first African Anglican bishop.[55] Crowther's death in 1891 marked an end to this era as the Society failed to appoint an African successor to him. More broadly, Olufemi Taiwo has claimed that the turn of the twentieth century saw missionaries' egalitarian standpoint 'overthrown and supplanted by attitudes that questioned the viability of African agency, placed Africans at the bottom of the human ladder, and proceeded to treat them as if they were children'.[56]

---

[52] Elizabeth Elbourne, *Blood Ground : Colonialism, Missions, and the Contest for Christianity in the Cape Colony and Britain, 1799–1853*, Montreal: McGill-Queen's University Press, 2002, 344; Robert Ross, *The Borders of Race in Colonial South Africa: The Kat River Settlement, 1829–1856*, Cambridge: Cambridge University Press, 2014, 71.
[53] Elbourne, *Blood Ground*, 344. [54] Elphick, *The Equality*, 25.
[55] Kevin Ward, '"A Theology of Attention": The CMS Tradition at the End of the Colonial Era in Africa: Max Warren (1904–1977) and John V. Taylor (1914–2001)', in Frieder Ludwig and Afe Adogame, eds, *European Traditions in the Study of Religion in Africa*, Wiesbaden: Harrassowitz, 2004, 227.
[56] Olufemi Taiwo, *How Colonialism Preempted Modernity in Africa*, Bloomington, IN: Indiana University Press, 2010, 87.

The chapters that follow will chart some of the reasons for the epochal shift, not least the tightening grip of colonial and capitalist interests in the region, moderated by the paternalist instincts among Scott's successors who did not share his vision for an African Church. What makes Scott's trajectory different from a simple story of egalitarianism to paternalism is, as mentioned, his theology of reversals in an interracial African Church. He never advocated European withdrawal from Africa, but the European presence there had to be examined for the prejudices it was based on. Scott's struggle for justice sought moral, spiritual, political, and economic conditions for Black and White to live together, not how they might best follow their separate paths to civilization. Despite Isaac Schapera's call in 1928 to study White missionaries and Africans in the same social field,[57] research in this vein remains surprisingly sparse. 'The stories of black and white Christianity', Joel Cabrita observed 90 years after Schapera's call, 'tend to be told in parallel fashion – running alongside each other, but seldom intersecting'.[58] In Scott's struggle for justice, historians and anthropologists may find echoes of their own difficulties to keep Black and White within the same purview.

Culture versus Civilization

The appeal of Tempels's study among anti-colonial African intellectuals is only one example of how European ideas of African distinctiveness could convert into charters of African pride and self-determination. The notion of African religion is a case in point. Collaborations between specific missionaries and Africans were critical to its emergence, whether to contrast African religion with Christianity or to delve into its cosmological tenets.[59] The epochal shift at the turn

---

[57] Schapera, 'Economic Changes'.
[58] Joel Cabrita, *The People's Zion: Southern Africa, the United States, and a Transatlantic Faith-Healing Movement*, Cambridge, MA: Harvard University Press, 2018, 19.
[59] David Chidester, *Savage Systems: Colonialism and Comparative Religion in Southern Africa*, 1996; Jeff Guy, 'Class, Imperialism, and Literary Criticism: William Ngidi, John Colenso, and Matthew Arnold', *Journal of Southern African Studies*, 23 (2), 1997, 219–41; Joel Cabrita, 'Writing Apartheid: Ethnographic Collaborators and the Politics of Knowledge Production in Twentieth-Century South Africa', *American Historical Review*, 125 (5), 2020, 1668–97.

of the twentieth century, when some missionaries began to see their task as preserving local cultures while transforming local religions,[60] evolved in the twentieth century into a concerted effort by African scholars to give the study of African religion the legitimacy of an academic discipline. Few were more influential in this regard than the Kenyan scholar John Mbiti, who penned foundational studies at the Makerere University in Uganda. In his *African Religions and Philosophy*, first published in 1969, Mbiti acknowledged that Tempels had opened 'the way for a sympathetic study' of this subject while criticizing his approach.[61] Where Tempels and 'the fellow colonialists whom he addresse[d]' took an interest in this subject so as to 'civilize' Africans, Mbiti insisted that ideas such as the omniscient God were indigenous to Africa. His survey on a 'continental scale' gave this conclusion: 'African soil is rich enough to have germinated its own religious perception.'[62]

Mbiti's evocation of the soil recalls the blood-and-soil primordialism associated more with German thought than African polities. Yet his approach was not primordial enough for some, as the critique by his Makerere colleague Okot p'Bitek attests. To Mbiti's declaration in the opening pages of his study that 'I am by birth an African',[63] p'Bitek added the qualification that Mbiti 'was also a Christian theologian and a priest'.[64] It accounted for the nature of his works as 'more Christian than African'. p'Bitek, on the other hand, thought that there was nothing for the African scholar to 'justify' in the eyes of his White observers nor any need 'to show to the world', as Mbiti had done, that Africans had the idea of one God.[65] p'Bitek was, however, also a poet who wrote verse on the condescension that formally educated Africans showed to their less schooled compatriots.[66] For his part, Mbiti provided 'a theological justification for tyranny' in the early years of Idi

---

[60] Keane, *Christian Moderns*, 106.
[61] John S. Mbiti, *African Religions and Philosophy*, Second Edition, Oxford: Heinemann, 1989 [1969], 10.
[62] Ibid., 30.   [63] Ibid., 2.
[64] Okot p'Bitek, *African Religions in Western Scholarship*, Nairobi: Kenya Literature Bureau, n.d., 108.
[65] Ibid., 7, 47.
[66] Okot p'Bitek, *Song of Lawino & Song of Ocol*, Oxford: Heinemann, 1984 [1966, 1967].

Amin's murderous regime.⁶⁷ Much as their personal trajectories diverged, their views on the study of African religion outlined an aspect of the debates that anti-colonial and postcolonial African intellectuals were embroiled in. From the possibility of African philosophy to the uses of European and African languages in creative writing, the questions often revolved around the extent to which an indigenous African intellectual and artistic life was feasible in the shadows of European colonial occupation.⁶⁸

An epistemic straitjacket loomed in some of the responses to these conundrums. Valentin Mudimbe, himself a former Catholic seminarian, saw it as a matter of inexorable logic that 'the missionary [did] not enter into dialogue with pagans and "savages" but must impose the law of God that he incarnates'.⁶⁹ The pursuit of 'African autonomy' beyond the epistemic straitjacket has continued well into the twenty-first century to galvanize not only political but also intellectual efforts.⁷⁰ Epistemic justice is, from this perspective, a matter of epistemic freedom.⁷¹ It extends beyond the imperative of academic freedom to a recognition of diverse ways of knowing, and the ways in which Eurocentric knowledge has long marginalized or discredited that diversity. For the advocates of epistemic freedom, the postcolonial

---

⁶⁷ Derek R. Peterson, 'Reading John Mbiti from Uganda', *Africa Is a Country Blog*, https://africasacountry.com/2019/10/reading-john-mbiti-from-uganda, accessed 19 December 2019.

⁶⁸ Chinua Achebe, *Home and Exile*, New York: Anchor Books, 2000; Kwame A. Appiah, *In My Father's House: Africa in the Philosophy of Culture*, London: Oxford University Press, 1992; Paulin J. Hountondji, *African Philosophy: Myth and Reality*, Bloomington, IN: Indiana University Press, 1983; Valentin Y. Mudimbe, *The Invention of Africa: Gnosis, Philosophy, and the Order of Knowledge*, Bloomington, IN: Indiana University Press, 1988; Ngũgĩ Wa Thiong'o, *Decolonizing the Mind: The Politics of Language in African Literature*, London: James Currey, 1986; Kwasi Wiredu, *Cultural Universals and Particulars: An African Perspective*, Bloomington, IN: Indiana University Press, 1996.

⁶⁹ Mudimbe, *The Invention*, 47.

⁷⁰ E. S. Atieno-Odhiambo, 'From African Historiographies to an African Philosophy of History', in Toyin Falola and Christian Jennings, eds, *Africanizing Knowledge: African Studies Across the Disciplines*, New Brunswick: Transaction, 2002, 14.

⁷¹ Sabelo Ndlovu-Gatsheni, *Epistemic Freedom in Africa: Deprovincialization and Decolonization*, London: Routledge, 2018.

era presents the spectre of a 'cognitive empire' surviving the formal independence of formerly colonized countries.[72]

Attacks on that empire are naturally epistemic and political at once, but the quest for autonomy and self-determination retains some of the emphasis on primordialism that provided one influential standpoint among earlier generations of African intellectuals. African distinctiveness is *sui generis*, suppressed over the centuries by Eurocentric thought. It is difficult to avoid the impression of bearing witness to yet another appearance of the concept of culture that liberal missionaries and White supremacists have deployed to their own ends. 'The specificity of so-called African culture is not placed in doubt', Achille Mbembe has remarked on the calls to invert African inferiority.[73] 'What is proclaimed is the relativity of cultures in general.'

In David Clement Scott's vision for racial equality, reversals were not simple inversions. After all, as Franz Fanon put it, 'the man who adores the Negro is as "sick" as the man who abominates him'.[74] For Scott, the key concept was *civilization*, not culture. In 1893, for example, he described central African history before the European conquest as 'epic' in the vein of the northern sagas.[75] Culture was here the general human capacity to make history, not the basis for dividing humanity into mutually exclusive sub-sets in a manner analogous to the race concept.[76] Reversals were necessary for Europeans to adopt the stance of learners in Africa. Rather than marking a backhanded compliment to an inferior culture, the reversals sought permanent changes in exploitative race relations. Epistemic justice demanded mutual recognition between different knowers more than it did epistemic freedom in which antagonistic parties would survey one another from the position of relative autonomy. From Bible translation's renewal through African languages to 'convivial scholarship'

---

[72] Boaventura de Sousa Santos, *The End of the Cognitive Empire: The Coming of Age of Epistemologies of the South*, Durham, NC: Duke University Press, 2018.
[73] Achille Mbembe, *Critique of Black Reason*, trans. Laurent Dubois, Durham, NC: Duke University Press, 2017, 90.
[74] Frantz Fanon, *Black Skin, White Masks*, trans. Charles Lam Markmann, London: Pluto Press, 1986 [1952, 1967], 2.
[75] LWBCA, January 1893.
[76] Verena Stolcke, 'Talking Culture: New Boundaries, New Rhetorics of Exclusion in Europe', *Current Anthropology*, 36 (1), 1995, 1-24.

suspicious of all identity markers,[77] Scott's vision for racial equality may find more recent parallels elsewhere than in the calls for epistemic freedom. So entrenched, however, may the idea of cultural differences have become that Scott's vision demands a fresh stance of learning to be appreciated.

Vernacular Worlds

Scott's encounters with African concepts, institutions, and conflicts would prove to be utterly formative in his emergence as a champion of epistemic justice – indeed the *sine qua non* of his personal trajectory. In the light of the foregoing argument, however, it would be richly ironic to present those diverse sources as though they amounted to one coherent body of vernacular thought. In matters of cosmological and existential interest, newcomers to central Africa in the nineteenth century could observe, if their minds were sufficiently open to them, a variety of cults and movements, from territorial secret societies such as *nyau* (also known as *gule wamkulu*, 'the great dance') to village-based rain-calling cults to household-based cults of affliction, with female and male initiation ceremonies carried out in various forms across the region.[78] Some of the observations Scott made on this cosmological diversity informed the conceptual work for his dictionary, as subsequent chapters will show. Yet an approach to the diversity that would soon become dominant in missionary, administrative, and academic circles hardly concerned Scott. It was the tendency to see the vernacular worlds divided into ethnically discrete sections. If the diversity was not primarily ethnic or 'tribal' for Scott, how else could it be described for the twenty-first century reader?

---

[77] Lamin Sanneh, *Translating the Message: The Missionary Impact on Culture*, Maryknoll, NY: Orbis Books, 1990; Francis B. Nyamnjoh, *Drinking from the Cosmic Gourd: How Amos Tutuola Can Change Our Minds*, Bameda: Langaa, 2017.

[78] Elias C. Mandala, *Work and Control in a Peasant Economy: A History of the Lower Tchiri Valley in Malawi 1859–1960*, Madison, WI: University of Wisconsin Press, 1990, 152; J. M. Schoffeleers, *River of Blood: The Genesis of a Martyr Cult in Southern Malawi, c. A.D. 1600*, Madison, WI: University of Wisconsin Press, 1992; Victor Turner, *The Drums of Affliction: A Study of Religious Processes among the Ndembu of Zambia*, Oxford: Clarendon Press, 1968.

No doubt some of the institutions were, or at least became, markers of ethnic distinction, such as *nyau* for 'Chewa' and 'Mang'anja', and the *jando* male circumcision for 'Yao'. For historians, shorthands based on ethnic labels have also appeared irresistible when seeking some descriptive order in the tumult that was the late-nineteenth century south-central Africa.[79] What the Scotsmen called Blantyre was in a territory of Mang'anja smallholder farmers, who had after the 1820s felt increasingly harassed by Yao invaders, themselves connected to Swahili traders on the coast through a supply of slaves and ivory. Added to this mixture were the marauding troops of Ngoni, northwardly mobile offshoots of the troubles in South Africa and Swaziland that accompanied the development of the Zulu kingdom there. The shorthand description is not wrong in these bare outlines. Yet it says nothing about the people behind the ethnic labels. Without a view on what wealth, power, and security looked like in late-nineteenth century south-central Africa, it also says nothing about the reasons for their conduct.

That none of the ethnic labels had existed from the time immemorial is illustrated particularly clearly by David Livingstone's legacy in this regard. His expedition in the 1850s saw the rise of a new ethnic designation from the 112 porters who had been assigned to him by a paramount chief in Barotseland, Zambia's Western Province.[80] Livingstone rewarded them with cloth and firearms and thus unwittingly equipped them to emerge as major players in the local economy. Livingstone came to dismiss them after they had showed more propensity to kill elephants for ivory than to assist him.[81] In 1863 when the expedition was finally recalled, not one of them had remained with Livingstone. Around fifteen of these men settled in the Shire region and came to be known as Kololo ('Magololo' in some accounts). Only two of them were of the chiefly stock, while the rest had become subjects of the Barotse kingdom through capture and slavery. Equally armed by Livingstone, however, they soon 'assumed the air and bearing of those who had lately been lords over them'.[82] Livingstone had expected these

---

[79] John McCracken, *Politics and Christianity in Malawi 1875–1940: The Impact of the Livingstonia Mission in the Northern Province*, Cambridge: Cambridge University Press, 1977, 4–7.
[80] Mandala, *Work and Control*, 81. [81] Ibid., 306.
[82] Henry Rowley, *Africa Unveiled*, London: Society for Promoting Christian Knowledge, 1876, 177–8.

men to return to Barotseland, but the instability created by slave raiding and famine offered them an opportunity to develop into a major new polity.

The famine of 1862–63 was a major catalyst.[83] Until then, the Kololo newcomers had been too few in number to unsettle the patterns of authority in the Shire region. The local economy had also been linked to networks of trade that entailed a variety of crafts and goods in Mang'anja villages. Livingstone described how a 'brisk trade' would spring up in the villages when his expedition visited them.[84] While the visitors were offered a variety of food, villagers' capacity to produce non-agricultural goods was also evident to Livingstone in the smelting-houses, charcoal-burners, and blacksmiths that could be seen in virtually every village.[85] Iron, locally made salt, dried fish, and skins were the principal goods used to obtain other goods further afield. Rings, bracelets, and anklets, made of copper, brass, or iron, were commonly worn by women and men in a sharp contrast to the paucity of bodily adornment in the twentieth century. The Kololo newcomers rose to prominence when their guns could secure food and protection during the famine.[86] Their hunting and trading expeditions brought more guns, powder, and ivory on which to build an economic presence and political following. By the 1870s, the newcomers had dislodged Mang'anja chiefs and installed six independent chieftaincies.[87] The newcomers' Yao retainers were appointed headmen in some chieftaincies with the task of collecting tribute in food and labour for the chiefs.

When the salt and iron industries faced a collapse because of imported goods, the Kololo overlords added sesame to the ivory in their long-distance trade.[88] By the late 1890s, these goods had also faced a decline in demand, and the cultivation of maize grew to become a major component of the local economy, for both trade and subsistence, not least because of European settlers' preference for cultivating cash crops such as coffee, cotton, and eventually tobacco. Slavery, to be discussed further in the next two chapters, had a profound impact

---

[83] Elias C. Mandala, *The End of Chidyerano: A History of Food and Everyday Life in Malawi, 1860–2004*, Portsmouth, NH: Heinemann, 2005, 43.
[84] David Livingstone and Charles Livingstone, *Narrative of an Expedition to the Zambezi and Its Tributaries; and of the Discovery of the Lakes Shirwa and Nyassa, 1858–64*, London: Duckworth, 2001 [1865], 84.
[85] Ibid., 90.   [86] Mandala, *The End*, 43.
[87] McCracken, *A History of Malawi*, 41.   [88] Mandala, *The End*, 45.

on the local economy, but the area was not importing slaves in the manner of certain larger polities in central Africa, such as the Barotse kingdom.[89] The caravans that the Kololo overlords or their Yao retainers led to the east coast deployed captives as porters, some of whom had been obtained from the Ngoni in exchange for salt, while others had been the victims of raids into non-Kololo polities.[90] Guns, gunpowder, cloth, and alcohol were the principal items brought from the coast in return for ivory and captives. At the same time, the memories of having served 'the English' were kept alive and the reputation for being 'black Englishmen' made Kololo chiefs seek immediate association with the Scottish newcomers in the 1870s.[91]

While the core of the Kololo influence was in the Shire Valley rather than the Highlands where Blantyre was established, neither area warranted a description of clear-cut ethnic divisions. The association of the Yao identity with the slave trade and Islam, for example, would make missionaries and colonial administrators regard it more unfavourably than other ethnic labels – until, that is, their 'pacification' at the turn of the twentieth century would imbue them, in the imagination of some administrators, with the qualities of a 'martial race' destined for service in the colonial army.[92] That some Yao in the Shire Highlands could themselves be refugees fleeing the Ngoni had begun to dawn on the pioneering party of the Universities' Mission to Central Africa in the 1860s.[93] The real surprise to them was how little unity there could be among the Yao as a 'tribe', with animosities between some Yao chiefs quite as fierce as their attacks on Mang'anja villages. Indeed, Landeg White argues that 'Yao' was becoming 'very close to being a purely professional designation'.[94] He further points out that in the late nineteenth-century Shire Highlands, 'the relationship that came to

---

[89] John Iliffe, *The African Poor: A History*, Cambridge: Cambridge University Press, 1987, 57.
[90] Edward A. Alpers, *Ivory and Slaves in East Central Africa: Changing Patterns of International Trade in the Late Nineteenth Century*, London: Heinemann, 1975, 17.
[91] Mandala, *Work and Control*, 86–7.
[92] Risto Marjomaa, 'The Martial Spirit: Yao Soldiers in British Service in Nyasaland (Malawi), 1895–1939', *Journal of African History*, 44 (3), 2003, 413–32.
[93] Landeg White, *Magomero: Portrait of an African Village*, Cambridge: Cambridge University Press, 1987, 48.
[94] Ibid., 49.

matter was not that based on kin or "tribe" but that between patron and client, the protector and the protected'.

The arrival of the Ngoni bands had only reinforced the need for such a relationship. Despite sharing similar values attributed to cattle-keeping – and a similar aversion to firearms in preference for spears and arrows – no single centralized Ngoni state ordered the military campaigns that swept from South Africa across the region in the aftermath of the 1820s rise of the Zulu in Natal.[95] Different factions had settled in different parts of Malawi, Tanzania, and Zambia by the second half of the nineteenth century. Capturing people was a central way in which these factions expanded, but unlike the region's slave raiders, Ngoni chiefs and notables sought to incorporate these strangers into their polities instead of sending them to international slavery. A key feature of the 'snowball states'[96] was the opportunity they gave to new recruits to rise through the ranks to head their own groups of dependants. Yet it did little to create a sense of security in a region already in turmoil. When they did not attack villages, the Ngoni bands could cause havoc among smallholders by stealing their harvests.[97] While Yao and Kalolo may have instilled fear among those they tormented for slaves or subjects, some Yao – whatever the spread of Islam – would soon see the Blantyre Mission as a welcome sanctuary against Ngoni raids. At the same time, the shifting chiefly and commoner alliances also featured in Ngoni polities. Yao chiefs were as likely to clash with each other as with Ngoni chiefs. Their alliances, moreover, saw the Yao chief Mponda cooperating with the Ngoni chief Chikuse against his rival Makanjira. Makanjira, in turn, supported Chifisi, who had challenged Chikuse's claim to leadership in their Ngoni faction.[98]

In a world of shifting alliances, friendship could be more consequential than kinship – or indeed the relationship from which kinship would emerge. It indicated the tendency, as described by Max

---

[95] Harri Englund, *From War to Peace on the Mozambique–Malawi Borderland*, Edinburgh: Edinburgh University Press for the International African Institute, 2002, 40–5; Giacomo Macola, *The Gun in Central Africa: A History of Technology and Politics*, Athens, OH: Ohio University Press, 2016, 119–40.

[96] J. A. Barnes, *Politics in a Changing Society: A Political History of the Fort Jameson Ngoni*, London: Oxford University Press, 1954, 29.

[97] Duff Macdonald, *Africana: The Heart of Heathen Africa, Vol. II: Mission Life*, Edinburgh: John Menzies & Co, 1881, 24.

[98] McCracken, *Politics and Christianity*, 13.

Gluckman for Barotseland, 'to expand isolated transactions between strangers into multiplex associations that resemble[d] kin relationships'.[99] A barter relationship could grow from friendship into a blood-brotherhood with enduring obligations to protect one another.[100] The trajectory was attractive in nineteenth-century central Africa, where such friendship could ensure safe travel in pursuit of long-distance trade. Indeed, the Kololo porters recruited by Livingstone drew on these kinds of arrangements when they accompanied him across political boundaries and were able, among other things, to exchange cattle for canoes.[101] On a smaller spatial scale, and yet also to facilitate travel, Mang'anja villagers made a distinction between the ordinary friendship of *bwenzi* and the friendship of *shamwali* based on extensive food transactions.[102] The poor had little prospect of developing their *bwenzi* into a *shamwali* and were deprived, as such, not only of the protection it provided but also of the camaraderie while enjoying the pleasures of life. Patterns of friendship exclusive to women have also been recorded for southern Malawi.[103] It was, as will be seen, friendship that began Scott's journey to epistemic justice and gave conceptual inspiration to his translation of the Scriptures.

Another feature of central African social life that exerted a profound influence on Scott was the *mlandu* process of deliberating on disputes. In his dictionary, Scott described the concept, whose plural form is *milandu*, as 'the most characteristic word of African politics; itself a charter of limited government, and appeal to right and sufficient reason'.[104] It was an apt concept in social life in which customs and rules were not so much abstractions as subject to modification in historical time. *Mlandu* would confound the colonial administrators

---

[99] Max Gluckman, *The Ideas in Barotse Jurisprudence*, Manchester: Manchester University Press, 1972 [1965], 173.
[100] Max Gluckman, *The Judicial Process among the Barotse of Northern Rhodesia*, Manchester: Manchester University Press, 1955, 17.
[101] Gluckman, *The Ideas*, 174.   [102] Mandala, *The End*, 55.
[103] Megan Vaughan, 'Which Family?: Problems in the Reconstruction of the History of the Family as an Economic and Cultural Unit', *Journal of African History*, 24 (2), 1983, 275–83.
[104] D. C. Scott, *A Cyclopaedic Dictionary of the Mang'anja Language Spoken in British Central Africa*, Edinburgh: Foreign Mission Committee of the Church of Scotland, 1892, 361.

keen to codify a 'customary law'.[105] At the heart of the confusion was the administrators' search for rules that could be applied across diverse cases, while the rules and customs that litigants brought to bear on their arguments are best seen as resources to be deployed in disputes. Although litigants and judges could evoke precedents and exemplary behaviour, the principles in this sort of deliberation were, in Gluckman's words, 'elastic': 'They [could] be stretched to cover new types of behaviour, new institutions, new customs, new ranges of leeway.'[106] It was the well-spoken reasoning and the unhurried hearing of all parties, whether male or female, that impressed Scott, who would soon after arrival in Blantyre start appearing at *mlandu* hearings alongside chiefs such as Kapeni and Mpama.[107] *Mlandu* introduced him to local modes of diplomacy, to skills and sensibilities that would serve him well as he embarked on reviving the Blantyre Mission amid turmoil and hostility near and far.

The *mlandu* hearings were also indispensable to Scott's education in vernacular idioms, many of which would spark his philosophical and theological interests and move him to insist that Chimang'anja be used in sermons for both Black and White congregants. It is an open question whether his vision for an interracial African Church would have been different had he worked in one of those areas of Africa where missionaries faced a mosaic of mutually unintelligible language forms. What Scott called Chimang'anja was a language form of extensive geographical reach and gradual, rather than abrupt, transformations into forms no longer mutually intelligible. Scott was able to cherish a capacious and expansive language without any of the concerns to prove the primacy of one form over another that would exercise Africans and Europeans alike in the twentieth century.[108] Other names would become more established in official use, such as Chinyanja and Chichewa, and ethno-linguistic affiliations would obscure the origins of names such as Chimang'anja and Chinyanja in the association of their speakers with Lake Malawi and its rivers rather than with an ethnic identity. The twenty-first century consensus among

---

[105] Martin Chanock, *Law, Custom, and Social Order: The Colonial Experience in Malawi and Zambia*, Cambridge: Cambridge University Press, 1985, 75–6.
[106] Gluckman, *The Judicial Process*, 160.   [107] Chanock, *Law*, 80.
[108] T. Price, 'Nyanja Linguistic Problems', *Africa*, 13 (2), 1940, 125–37; M. G. Marwick, 'History and Tradition in East-Central Africa through the Eyes of the Northern Rhodesian Cewa', *Journal of African History*, 4 (3), 1963, 375–90.

Figure 1.1 David Clement Scott. Reproduced with the permission of the National Library of Scotland and the Church of Scotland World Mission Board

linguists that these names belong to 'a family of dialectical variants' would have been acceptable to Scott.[109] Nor would he have had qualms about its openness to influences from a range of other languages, including English, Portuguese, Arabic, and regional languages such as Chiyao, Chitumbuka, and Swahili. As will be seen in Chapter 4, one of Chimang'anja's attractions to Scott was its vitality as a changing, living language.

Knowing David Clement Scott

The bare outlines of Scott's life include his birth in 1853, his arrival in Blantyre in 1881 and final departure in 1898, followed by missionary work in Kenya from 1901 until his death in 1907 (Figure 1.1). His first wife was Isobel Bowie, who died in 1895 and left behind two daughters, Margery and Isobel. Edith Ruffelle was Scott's second wife,

---

[109] Steven Paas, *Johannes Rebmann: A Servant of God in Africa Before the Rise of Western Colonialism*, Bonn: VTR/VKW, 2011, 255.

who lost her infant child shortly before their departure from Blantyre and died in Kenya in 1902. Scott's struggle for justice suffered devastating blows not only because of the multiple challenges mounted against it by a variety of White interests. In addition to his diplomacy and friendship with Africans, he had also been supported in Blantyre by his Scots 'clan' who were either related to him through kinship and marriage or had been inspired by him to join the Mission.[110] They included his own brother and his first wife's brother and sister, all three of whom shared some of Scott's vision but all of whom would perish before he left Blantyre.

Both the Scotts and the Bowies emanated from Edinburgh's middle class. Isobel Bowie's father had been the secretary of the Philosophical Institution, while David Clement Scott's father was a chartered accountant. His mother appears to have been a greater influence in matters of morality and spirituality. In a rare reference to his parents, Scott wrote in a private letter shortly after Isobel's death in 1895 that the memory of his mother's 'elasticity of nature' helped him in his bereavement.[111] An English woman who passed away in 1883,[112] Mary Jane Bancks had in her final years been described by her minister as 'one of the most spiritual women' he had known.[113] She also took a keen interest in her children's development and read with them, among others, *Missionary Evenings at Home*.[114] The family was not, however, particularly pious or one that incubated missionary zeal. Scott himself followed his father's footsteps and worked in an insurance company after completing his education in the Royal High School.[115]

---

[110] Andrew C. Ross, *Blantyre Mission and the Making of Modern Malawi*, Blantyre: Christian Literature Association of Malawi, 1996, 24, 159.
[111] David Clement Scott to James Robertson, 27 May 1895, EUL, Special Collections, Gen. 717–10.
[112] Statutory Registers: Deaths in 1883, retrieved from scotlandspeople.gov.uk
[113] W. Henry Rankine, *A Hero of the Dark Continent: Memoir of Rev. Wm. Affleck Scott*, Edinburgh: William Blackwood and Sons, 1896, 1.
[114] James Robertson, *In Memoriam: David Ruffelle Scott D.D.*, Edinburgh: William Blackwood and Sons, 1907, 1, *Nyasaland and Kikuyu Vol V: 1906–08*, Centre for the Study of World Christianity, University of Edinburgh.
[115] A. H. Charteris, *In Memoriam: David Ruffelle Scott*, Edinburgh: R & R Clark, 1907, 1, *Nyasaland and Kikuyu Vol V: 1906–08*, Centre for the Study of World Christianity, University of Edinburgh; Markku Hokkanen, '"Christ and the Imperial Games Fields" in South-Central Africa – Sport and the Scottish Missionaries in Malawi, 1880–1914: Utilitarian Compromise', *International Journal of the History of Sport*, 22 (4), 748.

Scott did not leave behind a memoir of his life and times. Insights into his path to the missionary vocation are as fragmentary as they are sparse. They include a comment he made towards the end of his life in a conversation with a young missionary colleague in Kenya. Scott told John William Arthur that an 'old nurse' had inspired his conversion, but 'for years' he had fought his own doubts about his vocation.[116] So unrelenting was the growing conviction, however, that Scott declined a high promotion in the insurance company and decided to enter the University of Edinburgh to study the Arts and Divinity.[117] While the information on Scott's conversion is sparse, the references to his brilliance at the university abound.[118] When he had enrolled on A. H. Charteris's Divinity class in 1879, he emerged as the 'first man' in the final examinations in two successive years. Other eminent scholars also noticed his unusual enthusiasm and ability, including Henry Calderwood, Professor of Moral Philosophy, and Alexander Campbell Fraser, Professor of Logic and Metaphysics.

Just as Scott left few traces of his path to conversion, so too are his own reflections on his intellectual influences largely absent from the historical record. The programme for graduation in the Arts that he took in 1877–78 lists canonical works in Moral Philosophy, such as Plato's *Republic*, Aristotle's *Ethics,* and Kant's *Metaphysics of Ethics*, and studies by Berkeley, Hume, and Locke in Metaphysics.[119] 'Prose composition' and translation in Latin and Greek were also included in the degree, while Hebrew awaited Scott when he enrolled on the Divination course, along with subjects such as Systematic Theology, Church History, and Biblical Criticism.[120] James Robertson, who had graduated with Scott in the Arts in 1878[121] and would remain a close friend throughout his life, indicated in Scott's obituary that erudition never displaced an independent, inquisitive mind.[122] Great doctrines fascinated Scott, but 'he seemed to hold them and connect them

---

[116] John William Arthur to his mother, 4 June 1907, EUL, Coll-207.
[117] Charteris, *In Memoriam*, 4.
[118] Ibid.; Robertson, *In Memoriam*, 2; Andrew C. Ross, 'Scott, David Clement Ruffelle', in Gerald H. Anderson, ed., *Biographical Dictionary of Christian Missions*, New York: Simon & Schuster, 1998, 608.
[119] *The Edinburgh University Calendar 1877–78*, Edinburgh: James Thin, 1877, 120–1.
[120] *The Edinburgh University Calendar 1878–79*, Edinburgh: James Thin, 1878, 152–3.
[121] Ibid., 128.   [122] Robertson, *In Memoriam*, 2–3.

together in a manner of his own'. Robertson was not alone in describing Scott's thought as 'mystical', and when Scott spent a few summer months as an apprentice missionary in the Shetlands, he is said to have stunned the parishioners. Charteris's language may have been hyperbolic had it not reported a Shetland islander's own words – Scott's departure was a scene 'like that which we associate with St Paul's leave-taking at Miletus'.[123]

Superlatives also describe Scott's sporting success. Among other achievements, he won a 'foot race' open to all British universities 'so thoroughly that he had time to look behind him and see how the others were coming on'.[124] Later in central Africa, Scott's 'strong, handsome, muscular frame' represented for his successor Alexander Hetherwick one reason why he could become 'a leader and a hero' among some Africans.[125] Indeed, sports were an important mode of engagement with Africans in the Blantyre Mission, principally cricket for Scott and football for his brother, with Europeans and Africans taking together to the playing fields as they would in Scott's vision for the African Church.[126] Physical appearance overall seemed closely related to character-building in Scott's thought, as his attention to cleanliness and clothes suggests.[127] One of the many complaints that some Europeans made against his practice in Blantyre was his wearing white rather than black in church, while the loose white 'Arab' shirts worn by the choir struck the critics as surplices and, as such, evidence of high-churchism.

The criticisms of Scott's politics and liturgy in Blantyre did not feature in his obituaries. Nor were his final, fraught years there entirely denied of recognition in Edinburgh. In 1896, the University of Edinburgh bestowed on him the honorary degree of Doctor of Divinity, largely to mark his scholarship for the Chimang'anja dictionary.[128] 'To an ordinary man', Charteris eulogized after Scott's death, the dictionary 'might have been the work of a life-time: it was a mere episode in the strenuous career of David Scott'.[129] Yet the positive tone in the obituaries could not mask a lack of growth even among

---

[123] Charteris, *In Memoriam*, 5.   [124] Ibid., 4.
[125] Hetherwick, *The Romance*, 35.   [126] Hokkanen, 'Christ', 748–9.
[127] Robertson, *In Memoriam*, 7.
[128] *The Edinburgh University Calendar 1896–97*, Edinburgh: James Thin, 1896; Robertson, *In Memoriam*, 10.
[129] Charteris, *In Memoriam*, 10.

Scott's life-long supporters. His initial ambition had been to be sent to India, where the Church of Scotland had established a mission long before central Africa. The obituaries repeated the distinction that had been drawn at the beginning of Scott's career. His friends and teachers had thought that 'his genuine talent for high mental speculation and his vision of God in Christ might be expected to captivate the finer Hindoo spirits'[130] and that 'the subtlety of his thought and his general refinement of nature seemed specifically to fit him to meet and win the Indian mind'.[131] The consensus was that he would be 'wasted on savages'[132] – 'to send him to the barbarians of Africa was said to be using a razor to cut blocks'.[133] While Scott may not have been a fully-fledged champion of epistemic justice when he entered Africa, there is no evidence that he drew the distinction between Africa and India in quite this way. It is a bitter irony that his obituary-writers seemed to take no notice of what Scott's evolving vision had done to the distinction itself.

Much as the Scottish Enlightenment may have settled the question of humanity's equal capacity for moral and intellectual development,[134] such an irony shows the extent to which abstract principles could not prevent epistemic injustice. When Scott's vision came to be shared, or even understood, by so few, it is imperative to allow his own words to inform the following chapters. They can be found in disparate sources scattered across various archives, primarily in Edinburgh, Harare, London, and Zomba. His correspondence includes the letters he wrote throughout his Blantyre years to James Robertson, the friend he had made as a university student and who led the Whittinghame Parish for many years. The correspondence also involves various other figures within the Church of Scotland, the Livingstonia Mission, and the British government. Of particular value are Scott's numerous contributions to the Blantyre Mission's periodical *Life and Work in British Central Africa*, the few pamphlets and sermons that survive, and of course his dictionary and the translated Gospels.

---

[130] Ibid., 6.   [131] Robertson, *In Memoriam*, 3.   [132] Ibid., 4.
[133] A. B. W., 'A Great Missionary: The Late Rev. D. C. Ruffelle Scott, D.D.', *The Church of Scotland Forty-Seventh Quarterly Paper*, January 1908, 2, *Nyasaland and Kikuyu Vol V: 1906–08*, Centre for the Study of World Christianity, University of Edinburgh.
[134] Colin Kidd, *The Forging of Races: Race and Scripture in the Protestant Atlantic World, 1600–2000*, Cambridge: Cambridge University Press, 2006, 120.

Tranquil retirement in which to write volumes of personal and theological reflections, as was the fortune of some missionaries, did not occur to Scott. Nor did he become the subject of a biography as his brother did, among other Blantyre missionaries.[135] Andrew Ross, the author of the best available history of the Blantyre Mission,[136] may have written the biography in the late twentieth century had he not found that Scott's family had destroyed his personal papers.[137] Indeed, passing mentions in his contemporaries' writings of, for example, a diary that Scott kept for his sister in his final years can only indicate how limited the available sources are for a full-blown biography.[138] Yet such is not the task of the present study. Scott's surviving words are voluminous enough to warrant, when combined with perspectives on African and European thought and politics more generally, a biographical approach to what the struggle for justice became for someone who saw Africa as the risen Christ.

The Rise and the Fall

This book presents a broadly chronological account of the rise and fall of Scott's vision. The chapter that follows this introduction, *Among the Wild Scotsmen*, outlines the scene he entered in 1881. Scott faced a legacy of violence and contempt that the first contingent of Scotsmen had left in Blantyre, ill-equipped as they had been to address the turbulent circumstances of nineteenth-century central Africa. Their high-handed interventions into the slave trade betrayed their failure to distinguish between different forms of dependence and to see in chiefly authority an opportunity to learn. *Champagne and Slaves* describes how Scott seized this opportunity as a result of personal experiences. One formative encounter was with the African evangelist William Koyi, who inspired far-reaching reflections on friendship, an idiom that would prove salient in the turbulent circumstances more

---

[135] Rankine, *A Hero*; W. P. Livingstone, *A Prince of Missionaries: The Rev. Alexander Hetherwick of Blantyre, Central Africa*, London: James Clarke and Co, 1931; William Robertson, *The Martyrs of Blantyre: Henry Henderson, Dr. John Bowie, Robert Cleland*, London: John Nisbet and Co, 1892.
[136] Ross, *Blantyre Mission*.
[137] Kenneth Ross, personal communication, 10 February 2018.
[138] Charteris, *In Memoriam*, 19.

broadly. This chapter also describes how the African arts of diplomacy and deliberation informed Scott's development into a champion of epistemic justice. An early step in that journey was a pamphlet on the curse of Ham which he wrote in 1882 to start organizing his ideas of service, leadership, and reversals in race relations.

The Universal Vernacular presents an account of Scott's language ideology as the key component of his evolving vision for an interracial African Church. The equivalence he saw between Chimang'anja and Greek and Hebrew was not the patronizing act of allowing a 'primitive' language a role in translating the Scriptures. On the contrary, it celebrated Chimang'anja's capacity to let the whole humanity flourish in it, whatever the religious persuasion. A detailed look at Scott's work on the dictionary and on translating the Gospels reveals important aspects of the influence that vernacular thought had on his vision. *Frightful Libel upon Humanity* begins to indicate the depth of resistance that Scott's vision was bound to face. Henry Drummond, an academic and popular writer who spent ten months in central Africa in the early 1880s, published an account whose derogatory remarks on Africans Scott regarded as 'frightful libel upon humanity'. On the other hand, a scheme for repatriating people of African descent to central Africa also attracted his criticism for its assumption of Black exclusiveness. This chapter discusses further how Scott never came to renounce Christianity and how he approached those customs that did seem to him to be incompatible with Christianity.

Rhodes Must not Rise introduces the political and economic forces that led to the undoing of Scott's vision. Although the Blantyre missionaries had desired the arrival of the British administration as a buffer against the continuing Portuguese and Arab encouragement of the slave trade, they soon became the new administration's fiercest critics. One reason was its blatant disregard for the arts of diplomacy and deliberation when it embarked on a series of minor wars to 'pacify' the chiefs who did not succumb to its regime of taxation. Scott led the protests against these tactics, as he did against the land concessions that the administration pursued with local chiefs. He also became one of the earliest critics of Cecil Rhodes's attempts to acquire land and influence in the region. The chapter details the direct contacts that Rhodes had with British officials, Scott's attacks on them and on the racial thought that pervaded Commissioner Harry Johnston's book about central Africa.

Despite the financial, theological, and political pressures put on the Blantyre Mission by White people in both Scotland and central Africa, Scott's leadership initiated a number of practices on the ground, such as schools for both boys and girls, an apprenticeship programme, a printing press, and what Scott called the 'African deaconate'. Women, both European and African, also assumed unprecedented responsibilities in the life and work of the Mission. *A Future Foreclosed* narrates these innovations and the roles played by Scott's African interlocutors to demonstrate what was lost and what endured when he resigned in 1898. *Grief Never Wears Out* casts the impending doom in an even more personal mould by describing the toll that disease and death at the Mission took on Scott. These most intimate aspects of Scott's experience appear in the chapter along with the Commission of Inquiry that was set up to investigate the allegations made by some of his European adversaries. The chapter ends with an account of Scott's final years in Kenya, where he failed to pursue a vision similar to the one he had in Malawi.

After Scott's departure, Alexander Hetherwick became the head of the Blantyre Mission, having served there since 1883. Hetherwick, who was not a part of Scott's 'clan', was a paternalistic liberal where Scott was a visionary. In *Liberal Translations*, their contrasting language ideologies reveal key aspects of their differences, such as Hetherwick's conviction that the vernacular belonged to 'a people' rather than to humanity and that it lacked the capacity to express Christianity to the extent that Scott had envisaged. Hetherwick's work of translation shows his language ideology in practice, while the changes he oversaw at the Mission included the deepening regulation of all aspects of life and, above all, the separation of congregations along racial lines. The chapter considers the responses by Hetherwick and other Europeans to the 1915 rising led by Mission-schooled John Chilembwe as final examples of how obsolete Scott's vision had become.

The Rest Is History reconsiders Scott's vision in the new Millennium. Not even his name is remembered where the church he designed still stands. More than a century of colonial and postcolonial policies has elevated the status of the English language while fuelling most recently ethno-linguistic revivalism in Malawi. Beyond Malawi, race and culture continue to be major justifications for exclusion and identification. Countervailing ideas also exist, such as the *Ubuntu* concept popularized in post-apartheid South Africa, but a key conclusion of this book is to historicize racial prejudice and its alternatives. Not only do they assume varied forms across history, struggles against racial prejudice also reveal what visions for a better future the imagination makes available in different epochs. Humanity, for Scott, was as undivided as it was beset by inequalities. The risen Christ gave him the figure to address this predicament. It allowed him to approach the racialized stranger as a friend and a co-knower. It sought epistemic justice in a world of blatant racial prejudice. In the new Millennium, doing epistemic justice to his vision is to imagine anew racial equality.

2 Among the Wild Scotsmen

A triple-thonged rhinoceros-hide whip became an instrument of the Church of Scotland's first African venture.[1] Once its pioneering characters – a band of Scottish artisans led by a civil engineer – had assumed the right to administer justice, corporal punishment was never far from their disciplinary methods. 'Nine dozen lashes' – another way of saying that the number of strokes ran beyond 100 – were inflicted on thieves and other offenders among the Mission's African neighbours.[2] Duff Macdonald, the first clergyman to join the Mission two years after the initial party had arrived in 1876, mixed remorse with self-justification in his remarks on flogging.[3] The nine dozen lashes administered on a thief's body were divided into five dozen on the first day and, after a three-day hiatus, four dozen on the second occasion. 'The flogging was nothing like the flogging which used to be for British sailors and soldiers', Macdonald explained. 'Some skin only came off on the second day.'

Macdonald was writing his two-volume opus *Africana* when scandal and atrocity had become associated with the Blantyre Mission, causing considerable uproar in Scotland. For it was not only floggings but also an execution that the Scotsmen unleashed on Africans. The wildest of the Scotsmen would hardly have done their nation proud anywhere in the world, reminiscent as they were of 'the mercenaries from Scotland who [had] played such a role in the Swedish and German armies of the seventeenth century'.[4] The brutality among the

---

[1] A. J. Hanna, *The Beginnings of Nyasaland and North-Eastern Rhodesia 1859–95*, Oxford: Clarendon Press, 1956, 29; John McCracken, *A History of Malawi 1859–1966*, Oxford: James Currey, 2012, 47, gives the material as buffalo hide.
[2] Andrew C. Ross, *Blantyre Mission and the Making of Modern Malawi*, Blantyre: Christian Literature Association of Malawi, 1996, 54.
[3] Duff Macdonald, *Africana: The Heart of Heathen Africa, Vol. II: Mission Life*, Edinburgh: John Menzies & Co, 1881, 34.
[4] Ross, *Blantyre Mission*, 20.

more pious Scotsmen owed a great deal to their lack of preparation for the turbulent conditions under which they would find themselves. Violence was not their prerogative in nineteenth-century central Africa. Wittingly or not, they threw themselves into the turmoil of trade in slaves and ivory, of invasion and exile. At the same time, there were ever-shifting political constellations as local chiefs vied for followers, security, and largesse in the threats and opportunities presented by a myriad of African, Arab, and European agents on the scene. The early Blantyre Mission responded to violence not only with violence but also with the humanitarian impulse to shelter refugees. Its undoing lay both in this humanitarian impulse – for which its material means were as inadequate as was its political acumen – and in the brutality of floggings and execution.

Varieties of Slavery

The second half of the nineteenth century saw in central Africa a rapid increase in trade whose most notorious cargos were human beings.[5] For different reasons, as mentioned in the introduction, Ngoni and Yao polities expanded by capturing people, while the growth of Swahili trading from the east coast was largely driven by the international market for slaves. The Yao involvement built on the patterns of long-distance trade established in the eighteenth century, when the principal goods had been salt and ivory.[6] While the Ngoni expansion had little direct association with the international slave trade, it increased the risk of unfreedom, especially among women, whose kin were often helpless to stem their capture.[7] Slavery expanded as a social institution as the pool of the people at risk of capture increased with the growing demand. It was so profound and widespread as an institution across Africa that scholarly debates on slavery show no sign of abating.[8] The multiple agents involved in slave raiding and trade

---

[5] Martin Chanock, *Law, Custom, and Social Order: The Colonial Experience in Malawi and Zambia*, Cambridge: Cambridge University Press, 1985, 163.
[6] Edward A. Alpers, *Ivory and Slaves in East Central Africa: Changing Patterns of International Trade in the Late Nineteenth Century*, London: Heinemann, 1975, 17.
[7] Chanock, *Law*, 163.
[8] Suzanne Miers and Igor Kopytoff, eds, *Slavery in Africa: Historical and Anthropological Perspectives*, Madison, WI: University of Wisconsin Press, 1977; Frederick Cooper, 'The Problem of Slavery in African Studies,' *Journal of*

present one cause for continuing debate, as does the application of the term 'slavery' for both domestic arrangements among some Africans and the fate of those who became commodities in the international trade.[9] Perhaps the most contentious question of all is whether some descriptions of this variety have represented certain forms of slavery as overly benign.

The challenge that central Africa in the late nineteenth century poses to these debates is that, unlike in American slave societies, the line between slavery and freedom was not always sharply drawn. 'Slavery and freedom', John Iliffe has written, 'were extreme points of a spectrum of rights in people: chiefs in subjects, patrons in clients, husbands in wives, parents in children'.[10] Degrees of dependence found expression in languages, and compensation for crime or other transgression could send people to slavery as much as capture and trade did. Self-enslavement made the line between slavery and freedom very thin indeed. David Livingstone famously described his encounter with Chibanti, a free man who had sold himself to a relatively benevolent Portuguese master, for he was 'all alone in the world, had neither father nor mother, nor any one else to give him water when sick, or food when hungry'.[11] Chibanti was paid enough for selling himself to buy slaves of his own and to begin, in due course, the business of transporting people on the Zambesi River, including Livingstone. Such tales of self-enslavement as a means of advancement were not exceptional.[12]

African History, 20 (1), 1979, 103–25; Claire Robertson and Martin Klein, *Women and Slavery in Africa,* Madison, WI: University of Wisconsin Press, 1983; Sean Stilwell, *Slavery and Slaving in African History,* Cambridge: Cambridge University Press, 2014; Gwyn Campbell, 'Bondage', in Gaurav Desai and Adeline Masquelier, eds, *Critical Terms for the Study of Africa,* Chicago, IL: University of Chicago Press, 2018, 40–55; Benedetta Rossi, 'Dependence, Unfreedom, and Slavery: Towards an Integrated Analysis,' *Africa,* 86 (3), 2016, 571–90.

[9] Igor Kopytoff and Suzanne Miers, 'African "Slavery" as an Institution of Marginality,' in Suzanne Miers and Igor Kopytoff, eds, *Slavery in Africa: Historical and Anthropological Perspectives,* Madison, WI: University of Wisconsin Press, 1977, 3–81.

[10] John Iliffe, *Honour in African History,* Cambridge: Cambridge University Press, 2005, 120.

[11] David Livingstone and Charles Livingstone, *Narrative of an Expedition to the Zambezi and Its Tributaries; and of the Discovery of the Lakes Shirwa and Nyassa, 1858–64,* London: Duckworth, 2001 [1865], 41.

[12] Iliffe, *Honour,* 125.

The region where the Blantyre Mission came to be located had not seen the formation of a distinct class of oppressed people who would supply slaves for the international market.[13] Henry Rowley, a member of the initial Universities' Mission to Central Africa, observed in Mang'anja villages that no obvious differences in occupation existed between those who were free and those who lived in servitude.[14] He perceived a 'purely patriarchal aspect' to the way in which masters would call those in bondage not slaves but children and were themselves called fathers rather than masters. At the same time, as he remarked wryly, 'the Manganja [sic] were most ingenious in devising means for the forfeiture of their own freedom'. Servitude could await those found guilty of some crime or transgression, while chiefs could be persuaded to sell troublesome subjects to slave traders coming from afar. The different degrees of dependence could also result in rather sudden reversals of status – for instance, the person living in servitude could be redeemed by his or her kin.[15] Matters assumed a more sinister aspect when some captives disappeared without a trace. Yao traders struck deals with Mang'anja chiefs to carry away slaves in the dead of night to avoid commotion in villages.[16]

Livingstone's remark that 'the Manganja [sic] chiefs sell their own people' alluded to the widespread pattern by which the pool of potential slaves, rather than mere subjects living as their masters' 'children', increased in tandem with demand in the late nineteenth century. Slaves were captured and traded for cloth and guns across a wide area in the interior, among others from Chewa chiefs in central Malawi, who preferred Yao as slave traders to the Portuguese or their agents for the better price that Yao appeared to offer. As traders, Yao came to rely on Mang'anja for a substantial proportion of their foodstuffs, and as the trade in slaves and ivory brought them military superiority, Yao chiefs made Mang'anja their subjects or drove them further into the Shire Valley.[17] The headquarters of major Yao chiefs such as

[13] Elias C. Mandala, *Work and Control in a Peasant Economy: A History of the Lower Tchiri Valley in Malawi 1859–1960*, Madison, WI: University of Wisconsin Press, 1990, 33.
[14] Henry Rowley, *Africa Unveiled*, London: Society for Promoting Christian Knowledge, 1876, 174–5.
[15] William Percival Johnson, *Nyasa, the Great Water: Being a Description of the Lake and the Life of the People*, London: Oxford University Press, 1922, 23.
[16] Livingstone and Livingstone, *Narrative*, 98.
[17] McCracken, *Politics and Christianity*, 6.

Makanjira, Mataka, and Mponda became caravan towns, where slaves were assembled into large numbers and driven to the coast. Towards the end of the nineteenth century, trade and the organization of caravans were increasingly in Arab hands even in the interior, although Yao remained important intermediaries.

The Arab involvement arose from the growing importance of the Omani dynasty in east Africa.[18] It had engaged in trade with the Swahili people since the early eighteenth century, and in 1839 it moved its capital from Oman to Zanzibar. In the early 1860s, 19,000 slaves, most of them from the Malawi region, were reported to pass through Zanzibar, while the coastal port of Kilwa appeared to be exporting more than 22,000 slaves per year in the mid-1860s. They were destined to become agricultural slaves on the clove plantations of Zanzibar and Pemba and, eventually, the grain plantations of Mombasa and Malindi. Arab stockades were a feature of the landscape that the Blantyre missionaries came to know in the last decades of the nineteenth century. Of more enduring significance was the association of Yao identity with Islam, with twelve Qur'anic schools at Mponda's headquarters alone in 1891.[19] Islam as a popular religion was gaining ground at the precise moment when the long-distance trade was coming to an end. By Islamizing the Yao rites of passage, chiefs and Muslim teachers sowed the seeds of a new religion before the Scottish missionaries had been able to introduce their own.

The non-African agents on the late-nineteenth-century scene were hardly any less diverse than the African ones. As Rowley observed in Zanzibar, the general epithet 'Arab' masked the presence of a range of people from Asia, the Middle East, and Europe: among others, Comoro islanders, 'Persians', Indians, and multiracial people, including the descendants of long-established Yemeni and Indian merchants who had had children with African women.[20] The historical depth of this presence led a twentieth-century scholar to trace the roots of poverty in east-central Africa to a pattern of extractive international trade 'established by Arabs by the thirteenth century, seized and extended by the Portuguese in the sixteenth and seventeenth centuries,

---

[18] Stilwell, *Slavery and Slaving*, 170; Jonathon Glassman, *War of Words, War of Stones: Racial Thought and Violence in Colonial Zanzibar*, Bloomington, IN: Indiana University Press, 2011, 27–39.

[19] McCracken, *A History of Malawi*, 101.

[20] Rowley, *Africa Unveiled*, 189–90.

dominated by Indians in the eighteenth century, and finally commanded by a complex admixture of Indian, Arab, and Western capitalisms in the nineteenth century'.[21] As subsequent chapters show, the Portuguese were the Blantyre Missionaries' main non-African adversaries at first. Their cruelty as slavers and slave-owners was well publicized by British missionaries of various denominations, including Rowley, who reported on witnessing brutal punishments unleashed on African slaves by their Portuguese and biracial masters.[22] 'The most vile effects of slavery amongst the Portuguese in Africa', he added, 'will not bear publication'. Slavery was to continue as the principal method of acquiring labour in Portuguese Africa at least until 1911.[23] The forced labour that it developed to would eventually make Africans flee into the British protectorate to scarcely more favourable conditions on European-owned estates.[24]

A Mission Mired in Ignorance

As the Blantyre missionaries were to discover, fleeing into new relations of dependency was a common way of escaping abusive masters. Under the violent circumstances, personal autonomy would have meant perilous isolation – for both subject populations and their rulers. Among some chiefs, the prospect of access to guns and consumer goods also attracted them to the Scotsmen. The relationship proved to be a tense one, however, and one of its low points came with the murder of Chipatula, a major Kololo chief, by George Fenwick in 1884.[25] By then, Fenwick, an artisan-turned-trader of violent disposition, had been dismissed from the Mission that had brought him to Blantyre in 1876. The murder and its fraught aftermath, discussed in the next chapter, show how the tensions emanating from the Kololo expansion continued into the period of the reformed Blantyre Mission under David Clement Scott. A glimpse into their personal consequences can also be gained from Harry Kambwiri Matecheta's memories of attending the mission school. Matecheta, who became one of

---

[21] Alpers, *Ivory and Slaves*, 267.   [22] Rowley, *Africa Unveiled*, 186–8.
[23] Stilwell, *Slavery and Slaving*, 190.
[24] Landeg White, *Magomero: The Portrait of an African Village*, Cambridge: Cambridge University Press, 1987, 87–8.
[25] Mandala, *Work and Control*, 86.

the first African deacons taught by the Mission, began attending the school in 1884 but found it hard to stay there because of harassment by Kololo children.[26] Name-calling went both ways, and Matecheta, the son of a Yao, showed insubordination towards the sons of chiefs by engaging in physical fights with them.

The Scotsmen inserted themselves into the turbulent conditions equipped with little more knowledge about the local circumstances than what the legend of David Livingstone had disseminated in Britain. Indeed, British knowledge about the region, deprived of translations of Portuguese studies such as Antonio Gamitto's *King Kazembe*,[27] had until recently been 'virtually nil'.[28] Livingstone's Zambesi mission generated observations on the botanical, geographical, and anthropological aspects of the region, publicized through letters and Livingstone's study *Narrative of an Expedition to the Zambesi*, published in 1865.[29] It is unlikely that the original Blantyre party had pored over such studies to any great extent, although Macdonald's two-volume opus *Africana* made a substantial contribution upon its publication in 1882. What the Blantyre missionaries were hardly predisposed to recognize were the political and spiritual dilemmas that had contributed to turbulence in the region for decades, if not centuries, before their arrival. Kololo chiefs, for example, had sought to suppress rain shrines, centred on the figure of Mbona, because of their potential to advance forms of authority beyond their control.[30] The rise of Islam as a popular religion, however, did little to change the patterns of marriage, divorce, and inheritance. Their matrilineal features were shared widely irrespective of ethnic labels, so much so that even Ngoni chiefs and notables, for all their kinship to the patrilineal Nguni polities, surrendered themselves to the modes of

---

[26] Harry Kambwiri Matecheta, *Blantyre Mission: Nkhani za ciyambi cace*, Blantyre: Hetherwick Press, 1951, 6; translated as Harry Kambwiri Matecheta, *Blantyre Mission: Stories of Its Beginning*, trans. Thokozani Chilembwe, Berlin: Wichern-Verlag, 2016, 28.
[27] Antonio C. P. Gamitto, *King Kazembe and the Marave, Cheva, Bisa, Bemba, Lunda, and Other Peoples of Southern Africa*, trans. Ian Cunnison, Lisbon: Junta de Investigações do Ultamar, 1960.
[28] McCracken, *A History of Malawi*, 43.
[29] Livingstone and Livingstone, *Narrative*.
[30] J. M. Schoffeleers, *River of Blood: The Genesis of a Martyr Cult in Southern Malawi, c. A.D. 1600*, Madison, WI: University of Wisconsin Press, 1992, 92–116.

marriage, inheritance, and language among the people they had ostensibly conquered.³¹

The British ignorance of the region in the mid-nineteenth century was matched by the government's indifference towards establishing a presence there. During the years leading up to 1891, it was the Blantyre missionaries who were the most vocal of the British missionaries to demand such presence. Yet Anglicans rather than Scottish Presbyterians had been the first to respond to Livingstone's call for missionary work in south-central Africa. For all his Scottishness, Livingstone had given his famous lectures in 1857 in Cambridge and Oxford rather than in Edinburgh or Glasgow.³² The Universities' Mission to Central Africa, an Anglican society, had its short-lived operation in the southern Malawian village of Magomero between 1861 and 1863. It was brought to an end by similar ineptitude to face the region's refugee crisis as would haunt the Blantyre missionaries.³³

The Free Church of Scotland and the Church of Scotland, split in 1843, sent out their members to central Africa around the same time in the 1870s and cooperated on various occasions while developing distinct missions. Their decisive moment came with Livingstone's funeral in 1874, not as a sudden upsurge of enthusiasm across their parishes but as an initiative taken by a few committed individuals.³⁴ Backed by a committee of Glasgow businessmen, the Free Church had a somewhat speedier start, bringing its mission to the shores of Lake Malawi before settling in northern Malawi as Livingstonia. In the Church of Scotland, John Macrae took on the task of chairing an African Mission Committee but found his personal enthusiasm to be somewhat less infectious than he might have hoped for. In 1875, he had to defend the very notion of an African mission against the suggestion that the needs of India and Scotland were enough for the Church.³⁵ Calls for volunteers to join such a mission were also falling on deaf ears.

---

[31] Harry W. Langworthy, 'Central Malawi in the 19th Century', in R. J. Macdonald, ed., *From Nyasaland to Malawi: Studies in Colonial History*, Nairobi: East African Publishing House, 1975, 1–14.
[32] McCracken, *A History of Malawi*, 45.
[33] Owen Chadwick, *Mackenzie's Grave*, London: Hodder and Stoughton, 1959; White, *Magomero*, 3–70.
[34] McCracken, *A History of Malawi*, 44–46; Ross, *Blantyre Mission*, 39–41.
[35] Ross, *Blantyre Mission*, 19.

Blantyre Begins

Henry Henderson stepped forward in 1875, seasoned by his twelve-year residence in the Australian 'bush', where he had selected sites for sheep stations and ranches.[36] He sailed for Africa with the Free Church party when other volunteers were not even being considered by Macrae's committee. A conventional account sees Henderson single-handedly selecting the site for Blantyre 'almost on the very spot on which [Livingstone] had cherished dreams of a Mission and a Colony of his own countrymen'.[37] He was guided, so another early description enthused, by 'the Divine hand' and 'chose a pleasant, well-wooded spot' in 'a cool and picturesque plateau'.[38] An account less focused on Henderson described how the 'weary and feverish' Church of Scotland party that finally joined him in October 1876 preferred to remain 'where they had happened to spend the night' rather than proceeding to the hotter climes of Magomero that Henderson had intended as the Mission's site.[39] That Magomero ever featured in Henderson's considerations has been disputed by historical scholarship.[40] In any case, what all such accounts fail to recognize is the African involvement in this pioneering phase.

Unable to speak any local language, Henderson depended on an African guide to find his way in the tumultuous circumstances. Tom Bokwito (sometimes spelled as Boquito or Mbakwito) – a nameless 'lad' in an early account of Blantyre's origins[41] – had served the Free Church missionaries before he was assigned to assist Henderson in his search for a mission site.[42] One of the surviving captives released from a slave gang by Livingstone in 1861, Bokwito led Henderson to his ancestral home, now devastated by slave raiding and warfare. They

---

[36] William P. Livingstone, *A Prince of Missionaries: The Rev. Alexander Hetherwick of Blantyre, Central Africa*, London: James Clarke & Co., 1931, 16; Ross, *Blantyre Mission*, 19.
[37] Alexander Hetherwick, *The Romance of Blantyre: How Livingstone's Dream Came True*, Edinburgh: Lassodie Press, 1931, 22.
[38] Livingstone, *A Prince of Missionaries*, 16.
[39] William P. Livingstone, *Laws of Livingstonia*, London: Hodder and Stoughton, 1921, 106; Hanna, *The Beginnings of Nyasaland*, 22.
[40] Ross, *Blantyre Mission*, 42–3.   [41] Livingstone, *A Prince of Missionaries*, 16.
[42] John McCracken, '"Marginal Men": The Colonial Experience in Malawi,' *Journal of Southern African Studies*, 15 (4), 1989, 338–42; Ross, *Blantyre Mission*, 41–3.

Figure 2.1 Chief Kapeni's village, 1886. Reproduced with the permission of the National Archives of the United Kingdom

found abandoned villages, but Bokwito, himself taken ill, eventually found some of his relatives, who cared for him for three weeks. Henderson spent the time getting to know Chief Kapeni and the surrounding mountains of Ndirande, Michiru, and Soche (Figure 2.1). The chief remembered his earlier encounters with the English with some fondness, and it was in his neighbourhood, on a ridge stretching southward from Ndirande, that Blantyre was established. The next chapter considers Kapeni's own interests in encouraging the settlement.

Bokwito left Blantyre and returned to Livingstonia in September 1878, having helped Macdonald in his first fledgling attempts at learning Chiyao. Bokwito would thus have seen what irked Henderson after the Scottish party had joined them: their 'lethargy and depression' that Henderson felt was beyond his authority to correct.[43] While waiting for Edinburgh to send an ordained minister, he appealed to Livingstonia for help. It came in the form of James Stewart, who was

[43] Ibid., 44.

in the region to spend his holiday from the Public Works Department of the Government of India.[44] He did put the Scotsmen and their African dependants to work and saw some success in gardening and the building of houses and roads. Thus began the Blantyre Mission, led by a civil engineer who was not a member of the Church of Scotland and composed of a medical doctor (T. Thornton Macklin), gardeners (John Buchanan and Jonathan Duncan), and joiners and carpenters (George Fenwick, William Milne, and John Walker).[45]

When the 28-year-old Macdonald arrived with his wife in 1878, the gardening and construction work would be complemented by sermonizing and a fresh start in schooling. At first, however, the young couple had to adapt to their new abode:

Blantyre, although highly praised at home, did not possess many attractions for the newcomer. On our first introduction to the manse we perceived that it contained two rooms. In the larger of these there was nothing but a huge table... The smaller room we may describe as a bedroom, though when we were first ushered into it, it contained neither bedstead nor bed, and boasted only one small chair of the rudest description. In our hut there were two doors, but neither of them had a lock, and one had no fastening at all. When we learned that thieves and wild beasts were frequent visitors, we began to barricade doors and windows with chairs, books, and buckets.[46]

Along with 'thieves and beasts' persisted smaller nuisances such as rats and ants of various types. When schoolchildren were given a free afternoon in 1879 to hunt for rats, the tally of dead rats was 168.[47] In the minister's manse, 'an apology for a cupboard' had had its legs placed in water to prevent ants from reaching food.[48] Alas, 'these insects made a bridge over the bodies of their drowned companions and covered our breakfast fowl in such numbers that the fowl itself actually could not be seen'.

The Blantyre Atrocities

It was the atrocities committed on human beings that gave the early years an altogether more sinister aspect. Before Macdonald's arrival, Stewart had grown so incensed about frequent pilfering that he decided

---

[44] Ibid., 45. [45] Ibid., 19. [46] Macdonald, *Africana*, 73–4.
[47] Hanna, *The Beginnings of Nyasaland*, 28. [48] Macdonald, *Africana*, 76.

to make an example of the first thief he caught.[49] A man was caught in the act in February 1878, but Africans working at the station had advised the Scotsmen to surrender the man to the Kololo chief whose subject he was. Instead, with the threat that they would lose their wages, African workers were ordered to flog him over two occasions, and salt and water to be administered on his wounded back between the floggings. When a British Commissioner came to investigate the incidents in 1880, Fenwick, the eventual murderer mentioned above, traced in his witness statement to this flogging the introduction of the Mission's most vicious instrument: 'At first the instrument used was a hammock clue, but Mr Stewart said it was not half heavy enough, and substituted for it a whip made of several ropes mounted on a stick, with knots at the end of each rope.'[50]

More was to come before a word about the Blantyre atrocities had reached the British Consul in Mozambique through Andrew Chirnside, a Fellow of the Royal Geographical Society visiting the area.[51] Although Macdonald assumed the Mission's formal leadership, he did little to control the tempers among the Scottish artisans. In February and March 1879, a whole series of atrocities were committed.[52] Opportunities for Africans to help themselves to European goods had greatly increased with the erection at the Mission of a storehouse belonging to the Livingstonia Central Africa Company.[53] Subsequently known as the African Lakes Company, it was established by the Scottish brothers John and Frederick Moir, but short of staff and capital, they relied on the Blantyre missionaries to check goods in and out. Among other incidents, a man was convicted of throwing away a box of tea he had been told to carry to Blantyre, but the floggings he received for his crime were so severe that he died. A considerable psychological, as well as physical, pain must have been inflicted on the man who had been wrongly convicted of stealing beads from the Mission. It transpired that John Moir had removed the beads from the man's load but had neglected to include a note to that effect for his compatriots at the Mission.[54] Before this oversight was

---

[49] Hanna, *The Beginnings of Nyasaland*, 26.   [50] Ibid.
[51] Ibid., 31–2; Andrew Chirnside, *The Blantyre Missionaries: Discreditable Disclosures*, London: Ridgway, 1880.
[52] McCracken, *Politics and Christianity*, 65; Ross, *Blantyre Mission*, 54–5.
[53] Hanna, *The Beginnings of Nyasaland*, 22–3; Ross, *Blantyre Mission*, 54.
[54] Hanna, *The Beginnings of Nyasaland*, 29.

discovered, the convict had been subjected to a vicious schedule of floggings, the final series taking place by a grave and ending in the man being freed after most of the skin on his back had come off. The anguish caused by this procedure was exacerbated by forcing him a little earlier to witness the Mission's first execution. Two thieves had been caught, but when one of them managed to escape while the Scotsmen deliberated on the merits of the death penalty, it was decided to execute the remaining offender without further delay.[55] Macdonald offered him words of God on the graveside, followed by a clumsy display of firing skills by a squad of African workers.

In his subsequent reflections, Macdonald put forward remorse and excuse in equal measure. Having realized that 'the Mission (although this did not appear at the outset) was wrong in assuming that it had a right to inflict any punishment at all',[56] he none the less gave some consideration for the circumstances under which the Mission took its first steps. The thefts could deprive the Scotsmen of clothes and goods that took several months to replace, while imprisonment would become impractically long if it was to be proportionate to the value of stolen property. Besides, 'if [the African] had to do no work, to be housed and cared for by Europeans, would be the acme of enjoyment to him'.[57] On the whole, Macdonald reasoned, the Mission pursued a more 'lenient treatment' of offenders than what the 'native law' stipulated in similar situations. 'By the native law of the district', Macdonald reported, 'a thief puts himself beyond the pale of human rights, and becomes liable to be treated as a leopard'.[58]

What made the subject *human* in Macdonald's allusion to 'human rights' may have been a more apposite question than he was able to address. In the absence of evidence on the actual extent of pilfering and its motives, it can only be assumed that the arrival of clothes and goods with the Scotsmen may have presented to Africans fresh opportunities to pursue ambitions previously associated with long-distance trade. Those ambitions – more likely than not to deploy the acquired goods in further exchanges – found their purpose in the value placed on the relations of dependency. Human beings, as discussed above, could exercise their freedom in so far as they were persons tied to others whose protection and guidance were the best buffer against dangerous

---

[55] Ibid., 28–9.   [56] Macdonald, *Africana*, 43.   [57] Ibid.
[58] Macdonald, *Africana*, 42.

isolation. When the Scotsmen, chastised by the Commissioner sent out to investigate the incidents, did experiment with confinement as a method of punishment, they found village headmen rather unreliable wardens. 'Any headman performed this task with great zest when the offender was an alien', Macdonald observed, 'but when obliged to confine one of his own people (his "brothers"), he grumbled very much'.[59] That 'an alien' may not have been fully human until he or she became one of the headman's own people suggested a philosophy of punishment that Macdonald was unable to discern.

The Blantyre Asylum

The Scotsmen were themselves increasingly drawn to the condition of interpersonal dependency. Their dependency on African interpreters and guides was inevitable, but the artisans, as Macdonald was to discover with some dismay, quickly developed a taste for a whole army of personal attendants. Not only did the gardening and construction work bring hundreds of workers to the Mission, each artisan also 'had one or two black butlers, not to speak of cooks and clothes-washers!'[60] In what Macdonald took to be 'an unfortunate interpretation of the servility of the African', some Scotsmen tended to think that 'the more they kicked [the African worker] the more they were respected'.[61] The zeal to proselytize seemed secondary to establishing personal fiefdoms based on violence and the acquisition of land from chiefs attracted to clothes, alcohol, and other presents. After the Mission was recalled in 1881, some of the Scotsmen stayed in the area of their own accord. They opted for the prospect that Macdonald had found among them when he first arrived – 'they would find it better to become traders and chiefs among natives'.[62]

The brutality of their methods should not cloud what the Scotsmen held in common with many Britons back home: the opposition to slavery and international slave trade. The British Parliament had passed the Abolition Act in 1807, but the increasing missionary interest in the late nineteenth century was partly spurred by reports about the continuing scourge of slave trade in Africa.[63] Livingstone had seen in free trade a means by which the evil traffic in people could be brought

---

[59] Ibid.   [60] Ibid., 82.   [61] Ibid., 84.   [62] Ibid., 82.
[63] Kevin Grant, *A Civilised Savagery: Britain and the New Slaveries in Africa, 1884–1926*, New York: Routledge, 2004.

to an end.[64] His famous coupling of Christianity and commerce partly inspired the establishment of the African Lakes Company as the organ of 'legitimate trade' in the region.[65] Along with Christianity and commerce stood a nineteenth-century humanitarianism. For all their inclination to inflict physical and psychological pain on Africans, the Blantyre pioneers – 'other than Walker and Fenwick', as their foremost academic historian specifies[66] – showed themselves capable of humanitarian compassion. The medical doctor amongst them, Thornton Macklin, expressed it in this way in a letter in 1878:

> The Mission in its civil and social aspects is making reasonable and satisfactory progress. As an asylum for the poor, persecuted slaves, Blantyre is becoming known and prized. We have now six fellow-creatures rescued from the lash of the slave driver, and miseries worse than death. And this in turn, prepares them for giving a ready reception to the free offers of the greater emancipation, salvation by grace through Jesus Christ our Lord. My present circumstances give a new emphasis to the old law of the city of refuge. Just think of the poor, fainting woman bearing her child, fleeing for her life, but sustained by the hope that if only she can reach the British flag, which already she sees fluttering in the evening breeze, her child shall live and herself be free.[67]

Blantyre – 'the asylum for the poor, persecuted slaves' – thus acquired dependants whose increasing numbers could be taken as evidence of the spread of the Gospel, while 'the children of these refugees became the main hope of the school'.[68] It was humanitarianism in a specifically Christian and British style, one whose own politics of dependency would receive a far more thoughtful interpretation from David Clement Scott. In the meantime, the Blantyre missionaries – unable to discern gradations of dependency or to distinguish between domestic slavery and international slave trade – would become unmanageably embroiled in all manner of grievances.

The End of the Beginning

Macklin had already in 1877 described how a young man known to the Mission had returned there to seek asylum from a man who

---

[64] David Livingstone, *Missionary Travels in South Africa*, London: John Murray, 1857, 28.
[65] Hugh W. Macmillan, *The Origins and Development of the African Lakes Company, 1878–1908*, Doctoral Dissertation, University of Edinburgh, 1970.
[66] Ross, *Blantyre Mission*, 50.   [67] Macdonald, *Africana*, 32.   [68] Ibid., 29.

claimed to be his father.[69] He said, Macklin reported, that 'he was not the man's son, but a slave, and had been bought some years ago'. When the man came looking for him, Macklin pronounced these confident words: 'He is not your son, but a slave, and he has my protection, and is now free.' Aware of the wider impact of his words, Macklin explained that 'all this took place in public before a great many Yao men. The man said he did not wish to be an enemy, but that the boy was his. I told him we gave him his freedom and English protection'.

With characteristic hindsight directed at a scandalized readership, Macdonald assured his readers that he had put 'a remorseless logic in the place of mercy' when he took on the formal reins of the Mission.[70] He had applied it even to the 'unspeakably sad' case of the widow with six children.[71] One of Chief Kapeni's headmen had had the woman's oldest daughter killed as compensation for the death of his own son who had been playing with one of the widow's sons. The headman did not stop there but demanded the widow and her children as his slaves, a demand that Kapeni granted him. The woman fled to Blantyre with all her children, but Macdonald's 'remorseless logic' compelled him to rule that 'the Mission [had] nothing to do with this case of Kapeni's at all'. Macdonald's representation of the case revealed its dual audience – Chief Kapeni as the Mission's influential neighbour on one hand, and Macdonald's compatriots in Scotland on the other.

The same remorseless logic brought an end to the humanitarian impulse to protect more refugees. Chirnside, the visitor whose exposé would cause a stir back home, had his sleep disturbed in 1879 by the cries of those who were forced by the Blantyre missionaries to return to slavery or death.[72] It was his account of the execution and severe floggings that made the Church of Scotland act by sending Dr James Rankin of Muthill Parish and Alexander Pringle, an Edinburgh lawyer, to investigate the allegations.[73] Macdonald's private diary indicates that the Blantyre missionaries had initially hoped that the duo would rescue rather than reprove them. 'We perhaps expected too much', Macdonald wrote to himself in October 1880.[74] His 'disappointment'

---

[69] Ibid., 28.   [70] Ibid., 202.   [71] Ibid., 201–2.
[72] Chirnside, *The Blantyre Missionaries*; Ross, *Blantyre Mission*, 57.
[73] Ibid., 56; Hanna, *The Beginnings of Nyasaland*, 32; McCracken, *Politics and Christianity*, 66.
[74] Duff Macdonald Diary, 13 October 1880, NLS, Acc 7548/D79.

with the commissioners was caused by their own inability to manage the relations with Africans: 'We looked at first upon the Commission as having knowledge of the native mind and as being in a position to take some responsibilities upon them.' Not that the commissioners were content merely to observe the Mission. When Pringle took it upon himself to dismiss two girls from school for 'disobedience to Miss Pithie' (the future wife of Fenwick and later Hetherwick), Macdonald told his diary that it seemed 'a rather heartless procedure to the two heathen girls' and put him 'personally to some difficulty with their parents'.[75] A few days later, Macdonald's final entry conveyed mild panic over the direction that the investigation had taken. Rankin had demanded that the diary 'be given up for the purposes of investigation'.[76] Macdonald felt it necessary to close the diary by asserting that 'many of the statements in it are of a thoroughly private and *privileged* and confidential character and the writer did not intend that they should be used publicly in any way'.

In March 1881, Rankin and Pringle presented their findings to the General Assembly, where the decision was taken to dismiss Macdonald, Buchanan, and Fenwick. It came on the heels of unfavourable press coverage in Britain, with even the Foreign Office expressing interest in the controversy, while the old antagonism between the Church of Scotland and the Free Church reappeared. Rankin and Pringle put the blame for floggings on Stewart's shoulders, suggesting that he had brought to Blantyre 'the well-known practice at Livingstonia'.[77]

The Free Church responded by issuing a statement that reproduced the instructions with which it had equipped its own pioneering party in 1875.[78] They had prohibited any attempt to stop the slave trade by stating in no uncertain terms that 'active interference initiated on your side is in no case, and on no account whatever, to be resorted to'. The instructions urged the missionaries to observe 'conciliation, forbearance, and patient endurance', although as the response to the Blantyre controversy indicated, the instructions 'could not possibly meet the

---

[75] Ibid., 15 October 1880. [76] Ibid., 19 October 1880.
[77] McCracken, *Politics and Christianity*, 68.
[78] *Statement of Foreign Missions and Livingstonia Committees Relative to Reports on the Blantyre Mission of the Established Church of Scotland Which Were Submitted to Commission of Its General Assembly on 2nd March 1881*, Edinburgh: Free Church of Scotland, 1881.

requirements of every case which may occur'. The response gave an account of floggings in Livingstonia that appeared so few and sporadic as to absolve Livingstonia of any blame for the Blantyre atrocities. In one case, an unsupervised artisan had used a leather strap to punish a man for 'an attack on the women of the station for indecent purposes', while in the second case, based on 'hearsay', lashes were inflicted on a man who had 'committed the crime of rape on a girl of tender years'. Upon hearing about the floggings in Blantyre, the Free Church reported to have repeated its instructions to the Livingstonia Mission to forbid corporal punishment and to deploy deportations instead.

While the dispute between the two churches would subside and left no permanent damage on the missionary relations in central Africa, the investigations by Rankin and Pringle led the General Assembly to dismiss not only staff in Blantyre but also Macrae's sub-committee in Edinburgh.[79] As Macdonald was to demonstrate in his book, the sub-committee had clearly encouraged the Blantyre missionaries to exercise civil jurisdiction and to take the first steps towards establishing a colony.[80] Their moral or spiritual right to rule compromised by the revelations, the Blantyre missionaries also found themselves potentially in breach of British law. No British subject had the prerogative to establish colonies of the kind that Blantyre was becoming. Moreover, where there was no government recognized by Britain, British subjects committing crimes would be answerable to British courts.[81] The humanitarian impulse, however, would continue to trouble such legal arguments. Macklin refused to return from a holiday at home when he realized that slaves would no longer be protected by the Mission. He was replaced by another medical doctor in 1880 for the final months of Macdonald's tenure.[82]

Matecheta, eventually one of the first African deacons mentioned earlier, had learned Macdonald's nickname without ever meeting the man.[83] Macdonald lived in the memory of Blantyre's Africans as *Maso Mwamba*, the one whose eyes were fixed upwards to high heavens. If it alluded to the missionary's detachment from earthly concerns, it hardly did justice to the dilemmas he wrestled with as a young minister with

---

[79] Ross, *Blantyre Mission*, 61.   [80] Macdonald, *Africana*, 41–2; 208–10.
[81] Hanna, *The Beginnings of Nyasaland*, 31.   [82] Macdonald, *Africana*, 204.
[83] *Blantyre Mission: Nkhani za ciyambi cace*, 2; Matecheta, *Blantyre Mission: Stories of Its Beginning*, 25; see also L. M. Bandawe, *Memoirs of a Malawian*, Blantyre: Christian Literature Association of Malawi, 1971, 72.

little authority over the Scotsmen who had arrived before him. Indeed, one of the reforms to support the Church of Scotland's next venture in Blantyre was to buttress the head of Mission as its sole leader. Although somewhat exonerated by the General Assembly's apportioning of blame on the Edinburgh sub-committee as well as on the Blantyre Mission, Macdonald receded into an undistinguished career in the Church.[84] Yet more than his nickname would persist from the first Mission in Blantyre. The new head would have to live with its legacy in the form of those Scotsmen who had opted to stay, whether as the Mission staff, such as Henderson and Duncan, or as planters (Buchanan) or traders (Fenwick). Even more important was the legacy of a small number of committed Africans at the Mission, including Joseph Bismarck, Rondau Kaferanjira, and Donald Malota, all of whom would play a formative role in the new head's personal development.[85]

It would fall upon David Clement Scott to undo the violent legacies of the first Blantyre Mission. 'The Hour called for the Man, and in the Providence of God the call was answered', Alexander Hetherwick would much later eulogize about his predecessor,[86] never mind that the direction he in turn took diverged from Scott's vision. The dilemmas of freedom and dependency, deliberation and violence, and doctrine and pragmatism would be addressed in different ways under the three early heads of the Blantyre Mission: Macdonald, Scott, and Hetherwick. Only in Scott's case did these dilemmas lead to a quest for epistemic justice.

---

[84] George Shepperson, 'Introduction,' in Duff Macdonald, *Africana: The Heart of Heathen Africa*, London: Dawsons of Pall Mall, 1969, 8.

[85] Ross, *Blantyre Mission*, 68.   [86] Hetherwick, *The Romance of Blantyre*, 32.

3 | Champagne and Slaves

The investigations into the Blantyre atrocities, led by James Rankin, did not result only in the dismissal of some members of the Mission and the sub-committee in Edinburgh. They also came near to depleting the Mission's supply of wine. 'Dr Rankin found he could not do without it', David Clement Scott wrote in his first letter from Blantyre to his close friend in Edinburgh, Reverend James Robertson, a minister in the Whittinghame Parish.[1]

Writing a month after his arrival in 1881, Scott described the physical and mental strain that travel to central Africa had put on him, his wife Isobel Scott as well as on Dr and Mrs Dean, the physician who had replaced Dr Macklin. Scott had himself had 'a fever for a month more or less', while Dr Dean 'was very far gone with sun stroke in the Red Sea'. Scott had requested the committee in Edinburgh to send more champagne, because 'it has simply been life to [Mrs Dean]', who was causing much anxiety for her weakness. Scott admitted that it had a similar effect on him and his wife, 'even in strength after fever when great sinking comes on'. 'Wine, chiefly champagne, is God's gift indeed.' Scott's plea for replenished supplies voiced psychological anguish: 'I'm a teetotaller, but this would keep me from teetotal madness.' A vital ingredient in the missionaries' well-being had all but vanished.

Frustrated with the Edinburgh committee's tardiness in addressing his request, Scott sought help closer to Blantyre. His early correspondence with Robert Laws, the strongman of the Livingstonia Mission, contained similar pleas for champagne. 'We are in great need', Scott explained his request for Laws to 'send us down some bottles of champagne'.[2] He asked Laws to determine the quantity available and

---

[1] David Clement Scott to James Robertson, December 1881, EUL, Gen. 717-10.
[2] David Clement Scott to Robert Laws, 12 December 1881, Foreign Mission Committee, NLS, Ms 7902.

assured him that 'we can arrange as to payment'. The request appears to have been favourably received, because two months later Scott thanked Laws for 'the kind answer to my request for wine'.[3] Despite the policy of the African Lakes Company to refuse trading in alcohol,[4] the Moir brothers had delivered these goods to Blantyre, as they did for so much else consumed by the missionaries.

Alcohol would not feature in Scott's subsequent correspondence, but the emphasis he gave it in the early letters indicates some of the pressures even this would-be visionary felt upon his first arrival in Africa. Yet his turn towards matters of epistemic justice would not take long to appear. His personal experiences of Africans entrusted with responsibilities in the missionary encounter, of people fleeing slavery and abusive masters, and of well-spoken deliberations in chiefly courts all piqued his political and theological imagination. Only a year after his arrival, Scott was already drafting profound reflections on how the curse of Ham, conventionally thought to impair the Black race, could be better interpreted to demand reversals in race relations.

As mentioned in the introduction, any impression of a lone genius must be avoided, and one way of ensuring it is by recognizing African interests in the missionary encounter. Elsewhere in central Africa, chiefs placed missionaries ritually below themselves to temper the missionaries' own chiefly qualities.[5] Chief Kapeni's enthusiasm to have the 'English' secure peace and safety in his territory is an example of chiefly manoeuvring at the Blantyre Mission.[6] People fleeing slavery, on the other hand, were no dupes either, despite a recent verdict that former slaves attracted to Christian mission stations in Africa 'had not yet developed decolonial or anti-colonial consciousness necessary for tearing away from colonialism and Christian missionary thought'.[7] In

---

[3] Ibid., 16 February 1882, Foreign Mission Committee, NLS, Ms 7903.
[4] Hugh William Macmillan, *The Origins and Development of the African Lakes Company: 1878–1908*, PhD Dissertation, University of Edinburgh, 1970, 212–13.
[5] Gwyn Prins, *The Hidden Hippopotamus: Reappraisal in African History: The Early Colonial Experience in Western Zambia*, Cambridge: Cambridge University Press, 1980, 165.
[6] John McCracken, *Politics and Christianity in Malawi 1875–1940: The Impact of the Livingstonia Mission in the Northern Province*, Cambridge: Cambridge University Press, 1977, 41.
[7] Sabelo Ndlovu-Gatsheni, *Epistemic Freedom in Africa: Deprovincialization and Decolonization*, London: Routledge, 2018.

their search for dependencies that would offer both protection and prosperity, former slaves co-constructed knowledge with missionaries about the historical predicament that they to some extent shared. Scott proved himself uncommonly alert to such co-construction of knowledge.

From a Novice to a Knower

Unlike his predecessor Duff Macdonald, who had described his primitive dwellings at some length, Scott did not appear to have been taken aback by the housing conditions that awaited him in Blantyre. It was the status of Blantyre as a 'churchless mission' that preoccupied him from the start.[8] For now, he had to contend with a place of worship 'built of long staves with couples also of small trees, crossed with bamboo and thatched and walled with grass'. The only mention in the first letter to his friend of the house where he lived was in brackets and came with the warning that 'this is hardly to be made public'. George Fenwick and John Walker, two of the notoriously violent artisans in the pioneering party, had held alcohol-fuelled sessions with Chipatula, a Kololo chief, in the very house that now served as the missionary's residence. The language used on such occasions, Scott reported, had been 'fearful'.

The chief had taken a liking to Fenwick and Walker not only because of the brandy with which they plied him but also because they were 'war-men'. 'In such friendship', Scott observed, 'there can be no real friendship'. A troubling state of affairs had descended upon the diplomatic relations that the Mission depended on. Fenwick and Walker had 'lowered to a very great extent the Kololo chiefs' appreciation of the English', while 'the chiefs [begged] now with great audacity'. 'You can't love a man from whom you are trying to get as much as possible.'

Scott's insight into the deteriorating relations between the chiefs and the Europeans apportioned equal blame to both sides. Here his understanding revealed a sensibility that was in marked contrast to how the chiefs' apparent greed and duplicity had been received by Scott's compatriots. Macdonald had called the chiefs 'sneaking beings' and

---

[8] Scott to Robertson, December 1881.

'a perfect nuisance'.[9] 'They put themselves on the footing of beggars', Macdonald concluded, 'and the most unpretentious of the Europeans had to treat them as such'. In one of the first signs that he would be able to seek reversals in the missionary encounter, Scott had already before his departure for Africa come to doubt the integrity of the pioneering party. He had taken part in the farewell meeting for the artisans at St. George's Church but had come away disappointed.[10] The artisans were 'not joined to the spirit of the meeting', and Scott quoted a fellow member of the audience as having told him that 'these men don't know for what they are going'. Scott's own verdict was devastating: the artisans were 'without profession of Christian life or missionary spirit, and not even good workmen'.

Scott's thoughts on the task ahead of him would evolve rapidly from these initial impressions. In his first letter to Robertson, he was sharply critical of 'ritualism' in church life – a charge that would later be levelled against him by the authorities in Edinburgh. 'One has to guard against that hollow ritualistic priestliness on the one hand and irreverence on the other', Scott wrote. He had already noted the importance of 'medicine' to ritual life, such as in the precautions taken in warfare, but *manguala*, as Scott rendered *mankhwala* at this point, could not be taken as the missionary's prime mode of interaction with Africans. 'Ritualism', Scott felt, 'would simply aid their superstition, give one a medicine-man character, and leave their life untouched'. The 'medicine-man character' was, of course, a resource for many Christian missionaries in Africa to attract adherents to their otherwise alien practices. Scott echoed here little else than the conventional view that pitted Christianity against superstition. By contrast, a decade later, he would conclude the entry for *mankhwala* in his dictionary with these words: 'Nowhere, however, is there found the thick darkness which one is taught to look for – in fact the darkness is no more impenetrable than it is in civilised lands, and the same desideratum has its full effect, namely, a true man to needy man.'[11]

---

[9] Duff Macdonald, *Africana: The Heart of Heathen Africa, Vol. II: Mission Life*, Edinburgh: John Menzies & Co, 1881, 83.
[10] Scott to Roberts, December 1881.
[11] D. C. Scott: *A Cyclopaedic Dictionary of the Mang'anja Language Spoken in British Central Africa*, Edinburgh: Foreign Mission Committee of the Church of Scotland, 1892, 315–16. Scott's entry rendered the word as *mankwala*.

Divine Friendship

The first journey to Blantyre had already begun to teach Scott other lessons than those that asked the missionaries to look for 'thick darkness'. Whatever its tribulations that called for the replenishment of the Mission's champagne supplies, the journey had also given him his first insight into the responsibilities with which Africans could be entrusted. To mark his appreciation, he enclosed a cheque of £5.00 in his letter to Laws a month after his arrival.[12] It was to be paid to William Koyi, who had accompanied Scott's party on its way to Blantyre and had accepted Scott's invitation to spend a few days with him afterward. Scott reported to Laws to have enjoyed his company and conveyed how impressed he had been when, upon Moir's orders, Koyi had taken charge of the boats they were travelling on. 'This suggested some small gift', Scott observed, 'but the esteem in which I hold him is the main cause of my desire to give him this'.

Koyi was a South African Xhosa, one of the four who had in 1876 left for the Livingstonia Mission to volunteer there as catechists.[13] They were students or recent graduates of the Lovedale Missionary Institution in the Eastern Cape, where the Scottish missionary presence since the early 1820s had resulted in the opening of the school in 1841. A multiracial institution and, after the opening of a girls' school in 1868, a mixed educational facility offering teaching at both school and college level, Lovedale attracted the vast majority of its pupils from the Eastern Cape. Koyi and his colleagues had responded to Laws's call for 'native catechists', who would assist Livingstonia as artisans and evangelists. Koyi and one of his cohort, Mapassa Ntintili, had also been sent from Livingstonia to assist the first Blantyre Mission when its troubles had come to Laws's attention.[14] The journey that Koyi made with Scott was his second to Malawi, having returned to Lovedale in 1880. Until his death in 1886, Koyi was to grow into a major asset in Livingstonia's efforts to settle among the northern Ngoni. His legend would live on in the names he was given by his Ngoni hosts, such as *Mtusane* (a bridge-

---

[12] Scott to Laws, 12 December 1881.
[13] T. Jack Thompson, *Touching the Heart: Xhosa Missionaries to Malawi, 1876–1888*, Pretoria: University of South Africa Press, 1999, 6–30.
[14] Ibid., 61–2.

builder or a peacemaker) and *Umteteleli* (an advocate or a dispute counsellor).[15]

While Koyi's new Scottish colleague W. A. Elmslie praised his work, he added to the praise these ominous words in a letter to Laws in 1885: 'There is a danger in knowing the people too well and while Koyi is invaluable here there is not that respect shown to him which should be and which is a factor in raising the people from their low condition.'[16] Elmslie, the future author of *Among the Wild Ngoni*,[17] was to step up his rhetoric against the Lovedale evangelists and, after Koyi's death, they were no longer welcome at Livingstonia.[18] In a sharp, though unacknowledged, contrast to the vision Scott was pursuing at the same time in Blantyre, Elmslie insisted that 'the whole bearing of a European is more to the purpose of raising the natives than a Kaffir'.[19] He had thought that George Williams, another Lovedale evangelist, could work well 'along with a white man',[20] but Elmslie's attitude hardened even further when he noticed the rapport Williams had achieved with villagers.[21] Evidently jealous of this rapport, Elmslie felt that African evangelists lacked 'the moral or mental attainments that go to the formation of a sound character'.[22] Scott, by contrast, had caught his first glimpse of the poise with which an African could discharge a major responsibility. The £5.00 token of his esteem was more than a Lovedale evangelist's monthly salary had been while working for the Blantyre Mission a couple of years earlier.[23]

So profound was the impression Koyi left on Scott that he was moved in his first letter to Robertson to extol the virtues of friendship.[24] Scott wrote about 'a Christian kaffir staying with us for a short time and going to Livingstonia mission' when 'your friendship came into my mind and stood on one side as a living thing'. The encounter appeared to have brought Scott to John 6:57: 'As the living

---

[15] Ibid., 118–19; T. Jack Thompson, *Ngoni, Xhosa, and Scot: Religious and Cultural Interaction in Malawi*, Zomba: Kachere Series, 2007, 71–2.
[16] McCracken, *Politics and Christianity*, 191.
[17] W. A. Elmslie, *Among the Wild Ngoni*, Edinburgh: Oliphant, Anderson & Ferrier, 1899.
[18] W.A. Elmslie to Robert Laws, 28 February 1887, NLS, Ms 7890.
[19] Ibid., 7 January 1887.   [20] Ibid., 14 March 1887.
[21] Ibid., n. d., NLS, Ms 7891.   [22] Ibid., I July 1888.
[23] Thompson, *Touching the Heart*, 61; McCracken, *Politics and Christianity*, 190.
[24] Scott to Robertson, December 1881.

Father hath sent me, and I live by the Father: so he that eateth me, even he shall live by me', in which he underlined the words 'living', 'I live by the Father', and 'eateth me'. 'I felt the human illuminated the Divine', he went on to comment, 'and yet the explanation of the human arose from the contact of that verse with the existence of the friendship'. Scott allowed himself here to get absorbed in the vitalism of friendship as the lived consequence of 'the great eternity of the Living God'. His reflections indicated the propensity, evident throughout his missionary career, to move effortlessly from the mundane to the metaphysical in the same text and to emphasize the *living* character of all things important to his mission, whether the Church itself or every human being regardless of race as the living image of the Divine. Above all, although not brought into explicit comparison in the letter, the friendship he found in Koyi no less than in Robertson was something very different from the 'friendship' between the Scottish artisans and duplicitous chiefs that he had so disparagingly commented on earlier in the letter.

The divinely ordained friendship across the races found its test in the actual responsibilities with which Scott as the Mission's head would entrust Africans in the years to come. For the question of responsibilities to arise, there had to be practical schemes to pursue. Here Scott put himself on a collision course with Rankin, whose recommendation for the new Blantyre Mission had been to relinquish its industrial nature.[25] Pringle, Rankin's co-investigator of Blantyre's troubles, had even asserted that 'the natives in that particular part of Africa stand in no special need of anything but Christianity and education'.[26] The recommendation was to reverse the situation in which, according to Macdonald, 'although evangelistic work was not neglected, the secular side of the Mission was by far the more important'.[27] Infrastructural, agricultural, and jurisdictional work would fall outside the Mission's core remit. Yet not for the last time, Scott chose to ignore the recommendations and decrees issued from Edinburgh. Propelled by his vision of friendship and service, he embarked on a wide-ranging programme with evolving subtlety unseen in the Mission.

---

[25] Andrew C. Ross, *Blantyre Mission and the Making of Modern Malawi*, Blantyre: Christian Literature Association of Malawi, 1996, 64.
[26] McCracken, *Politics and Christianity*, 67.   [27] Macdonald, *Africana*, 31.

A Friend of Chiefs

The mode of temporal rule that Scott began to pursue was based on what he was learning in central Africa. The concept of *mfumu* (chief) inspired far-reaching reflections on political power in his magisterial dictionary published in 1892: 'With all his seeming power, the chief is hedged in as much as, perhaps more than, the most constitutional minister in the most civilised states; his wealth is merely a greater power of distribution, for his personal state is not extravagant; he does not live for "self-aggrandisement"; ordinary hereditary chiefs have several but not enormous numbers of wives.'[28] Note that these reflections did not outline the features of chiefly authority with a view to appropriating them for colonial rule, as would become the urge for administrators decades later under the policy of indirect rule. Nor did Scott describe the institution of the chief as though it belonged to a primitive society distinct from his own. The chief was as much of the contemporary world as political leaders in Europe were and, moreover, compared favourably to 'the most constitutional minister in the most civilised state'.

Scott's pointed comparisons did not, of course, take into account complex social processes on the ground. Blantyre had been established in the territory of the Yao chief Kapeni, not because of Henry Henderson's unique insight but because different interests made it a plausible site for the new mission. As described in the previous chapter, Henderson depended on Tom Bokwito to find his way, and Bokwito's convalescence among relatives near Kapeni's village proved crucial to the decision to establish the Mission there. The three-week stay resulted in Kapeni's offer of a site where a village had once been before it had been destroyed by a Kololo raid (Figure 3.1).[29] Kapeni also arranged a large number of porters to carry the Blantyre pioneers' belongings after their boat had moored at the river. Far from announcing the era of Scottish sovereignty in the Shire Highlands, their declaration of Blantyre threw them into a morass of authority and dependence.

Duff Macdonald's impression was that Kapeni was the 'Lord Superior of this district'.[30] The corollary of the 'greater power of

---

[28] Scott, *A Cyclopeadic*, 347.   [29] Ross, *Blantyre Mission*, 42–3.
[30] Duff Macdonald Diary, 27 November 1879, NLS, Acc 7548/D79.

Figure 3.1 Chief Kapeni, 1886. Reproduced with the permission of the National Archives of the United Kingdom

distribution' by which Scott defined chiefly authority was the power to collect tribute from subjects and lesser chiefs. For example, Mtaja had before the Scotsmen's arrival earned a following through involvement in the ivory trade but paid tribute to Kapeni as his superior.[31] The Scotsmen hardly bought freedom when they paid for the land Kapeni had allocated to them, first in 1876 and then in 1885, after the succession into the role by a new Kapeni.[32] Their total landholding as a mission was two and a half square miles.[33] Although Scott would use the phrase 'land-grabbing' for Europeans' manoeuvres in the 1890s, the initial land deal saw the missionaries enter a complex relationship

---

[31] W. H. Rangeley, 'Early Blantyre', *The Nyasaland Journal*, 7 (1), 1954, 37.
[32] Ibid., 41.
[33] Adrian Hastings, *The Church in Africa, 1450–1950*, Oxford: Clarendon Press, 1994, 427.

of interdependence. It represented, in a historian's words, 'a large African investment rather than a large European robbery'.[34]

The African Lakes Company had the policy of not paying chiefs any regular tribute,[35] informed by the somewhat illusory notion that 'we are not dependent'.[36] The Blantyre missionaries, by contrast, found themselves under the constant obligation to accommodate chiefly prerogatives, whether by giving presents or by providing work and schooling for their subjects. The scene shared the broad outlines of similar situations across Africa where the first Christian converts came from the chiefly stock, an insight from African history that historians of Christianity in Europe have also found suggestive.[37] Yet as has been seen, the relations deteriorated during Macdonald's leadership partly because the Scotsmen mistook for begging their expectations of continued payments. The ensuing problems with pilfering resulted in the brutal punishments described in the previous chapter as chiefs saw little reason to intervene on the Scotsmen's behalf. Nor did Scott's arrival smoothen all friction despite the determination with which he sought to learn from African modes of diplomacy and deliberation. The question of conversion, on the other hand, appeared to him somewhat secondary to the practical and philosophical work that he set himself, as Chapter 7 will show.

From Kapeni's point of view, it was not only the payments or the promise of a new religion that drove his interest in having 'the English' in his territory. Their guns and presence also promised security against Ngoni raids. As relations improved under Scott's leadership, Kapeni and Mpama, another nearby chief, became go-betweens when Scott sought contact with hostile chiefs.[38] The improving relations also required chiefs such as Kapeni and Mtaja to stay clear of the coastal trade in slaves.[39] Neither of them, however, became a subordinate to the Mission. It was richly symbolic, as well as strategic, for Kapeni to place the Mission geographically below him as he maintained his headquarters high on the Soche Mountain. Mtaja, on the other hand, was so impressed with the African Lakes Company's two-storey

---

[34] Ibid.   [35] Macmillan, *The Origins*, 207–8.
[36] Frederick T. Morrison Diary, 13 February 1884, EUL, Coll-443.
[37] N. J. Higham, *The Convert Kings: Power and Religious Affiliation in Early Anglo-Saxon England*, Manchester: Manchester University Press, 1997.
[38] Ross, *Blantyre Mission*, 69.   [39] Ibid., 88.

building that he had one built for himself.⁴⁰ The host of noisy, alcohol-fuelled festivities that irked Europeans, Mtaja was not their lackey. His building project was more likely to be a way of asserting mutuality with Europeans than an act of imitation.

It was mutuality that Scott pursued in his approach to chiefly authority – mutuality that he, in turn, learnt from a range of vernacular practices. Yet the actual circumstances in which he first encountered chieftaincy were marred, as mentioned, by the low esteem in which some Kololo chiefs had begun to hold 'the English'. The brazen displays of their assumed superiority had made the artisans seem decidedly less distinguished than David Livingstone's pioneering party. Scott's early understanding of deteriorating relations with chiefs proved prescient as George Fenwick's behaviour threatened to bring the Europeans further into disrepute. Fenwick had long been a nuisance to Europeans and Africans alike. Macdonald recorded in his diary in 1880 that Henderson had urged his 'immediate dismissal' for 'striking the natives and going about swearing'.⁴¹ Another diary entry noted that Fenwick had beaten 'for nothing' Rondau Kaferanjira, one of the Mission's first African stalwarts.⁴² By 1883, Fenwick had been dismissed not only from the Mission but from the African Lakes Company whose employee he had become in the wake of the Blantyre atrocities.⁴³ Working as an independent trader, he brought from the coast, among other things, spirits that the Company had refused to deal in.⁴⁴ It was in a dispute over payment in 1884 that Fenwick shot the Kololo chief Chipatula dead and was soon speared to death himself on the island in the Shire river where he had fled.⁴⁵

The aftermath saw the race relations around Blantyre reach a new low as Fenwick's head was displayed on a stake at Chipatula's headquarters and Ramakukan, the senior Kololo chief, demanded Elizabeth Fenwick, the 'Miss Pithie' mentioned in the previous chapter, as compensation along with his goods.⁴⁶ Before these developments, the message had reached Blantyre asking all Chipatula's dependants to

---

⁴⁰ Rangeley, 'Early Blantyre', 38–9.   ⁴¹ Macdonald Diary, 27 January 1880.
⁴² Ibid., 12 October 1880.   ⁴³ Morrison Diary, 1 February 1883.
⁴⁴ Macmillan, *The Origins*, 154.   ⁴⁵ Ibid., 202.
⁴⁶ John McCracken, 'Class, Violence, and Gender in Early Colonial Malawi: The Curious Case of Elizabeth Pithie', *The Society of Malawi Journal*, 64 (2), 2011, 7–8.

leave the school.[47] A piece of intelligence suggested that Africans 'were going to make war on all the English', but remarkable in all this tumult was the stance adopted by Scott. While his compatriots working for the Company were preoccupied with erecting barricades against the feared attack, with about forty loaded guns at the ready and informants stationed outside Blantyre, Scott declined to participate in any military effort and announced that the Mission would rather relocate itself.[48] No attack ensued, nor did Fenwick's widow suffer the fate threatened by Ramakukan, but Scott's principled response indicated more than unwillingness to be drawn into a conflict that had nothing to do with the Mission. It came as he was learning his formative lessons in diplomacy and deliberation through his study of chiefly authority. By 1891, it would mature into the conviction that 'we in the country are with the chiefs as *associated chiefs* under arrangements of associated co-occupation'.[49] Mutuality, not antagonism, was the key lesson Scott was drawing from his engagement with chiefs.

A Deluge of Dependants

Refugees fleeing slavery presented one of Scott's early challenges, not least because of the strain they had caused in the relations between Chief Kapeni and the Blantyre pioneers. In his first letter to Robertson, Scott observed that 'no less than three villages, one of very considerable size, have grown up from the coming in of fugitive slaves'.[50] While as passionately opposed to slave trade as some of the Scotsmen in the pioneering party, Scott saw more clearly than any of them the need to discern variable fates in the condition of being a slave. Those who were captured to be taken in caravans to the coast had to be distinguished from domestic slaves in the Mission's surrounding villages. The latter could have become slaves in a variety of ways – such as through crime or by being offered as compensation for some transgression by their kin – but crucial in Scott's interpretation was the role played by chiefs. 'Each chief knows all his people by name', he wrote, 'just as a shepherd knows his sheep'. A slave escaping one chief would seek refuge with another chief – there could be no freedom in

[47] Morrison Diary, 20 February 1884.   [48] Ibid., 23 and 24 February 1884.
[49] David Stuart-Mogg, 'The Rev. David Clement Scott and the Issue of Land Title in British Central Africa', *The Society of Malawi Journal*, 57 (2), 2004, 30.
[50] Scott to Robertson, December 1881.

meaningless and dangerous autonomy. Scott's insight was to see in the Mission, and particularly in the person of its head, a kind of chief among other chiefs.

'Blantyre of course was a powerful place', Scott pointed out with regard to the Mission's incursions into local politics and its control over large supplies of calico, the main currency. He added a greater dose of diplomacy to the practice that Macdonald had begun in 1880.[51] It was to appease the chiefs who claimed the refugees by paying them compensation while declaring that the Mission would not accommodate any more fugitives. Both ethical and pragmatic imperatives drove Scott's decision. 'If we were to send some away, just now', he wrote, 'we would give them up to be murdered.'[52] On the other hand, to disperse the villages, which the refugees had made their home through marriage and other signs of normalcy, would also have required enormous effort. The refugees would, instead, work for the Mission to cover the ransom it had paid.[53] They would become dependants of the Mission, not individuals unattached to any figure of authority. In the turbulent times of the late nineteenth century, they hardly desired anything else than the freedom in being attached to a right kind of guardian.

Although eventually reduced, the flow of people claiming to be fleeing from abusive masters or slave-traders did not come to an abrupt end with such a policy. For years to come, the missionaries would notice that these former refugees were 'harbouring and concealing their runaway friends'.[54] Yet the Blantyre Mission was at no point a missionary colony of freed slaves, as was the case for certain missions in Kenya,[55] and Scott's remark that 'we have a strange mixture in the villages'[56] indicated that the Mission was never cut off from its surrounding villages, the vast majority of which were by no means occupied by fugitives alone. A corollary of the Mission's immersion in the society where it found itself was the popular expectation that Scott served his subjects as their chief. Indeed, rather than subjecting Africans to him as a European magistrate, Scott embraced local modes of disputing and diplomacy. At the same time, he saw little distinction

---

[51] Ross, *Blantyre Mission*, 60. [52] Scott to Robertson, December 1881.
[53] Alexander Hetherwick, *The Romance of Blantyre: How Livingstone's Dream Came True*, Edinburgh: Lassodie Press, 1931, 39.
[54] Ibid., 54. [55] Ross, *Blantyre Mission*, 60.
[56] Scott to Robertson, December 1881.

between the theocratic and temporal aspects of rule, a distinction that had already been made at the Livingstonia Mission and that would become a pressing one with the arrival of the British colonial administration in the early 1890s.[57]

Diplomacy and Deliberation

An immediate test of Scott's understanding of chiefly authority and diplomacy was put to him by two Yao chiefs who had remained hostile to the Mission. One of them was Mitochi, who ruled some twenty miles away in Chiradzulu.[58] His subjects had, among other things, attacked the Mission's carriers and plundered their loads. Scott's response to this hostility, whose origins lay in the time before his arrival, was to seek an audience with Mitochi. Chiefs Mpama and Kapeni were able to convince him to grant such an audience. As Hetherwick came to describe it in some detail, Scott went to the meeting with his wife Isobel Scott so as to show that his intents were peaceful. They found the village eerily quiet, 'not a woman to be seen – an unfriendly situation'.[59] After a long while, the chief came out of his house and sat in silence. The Scotts offered an exchange of greetings and presents, and a friendship between him and Mitochi slowly emerged. By the time when the chief died, the friendship had matured to the point that the Mission gave his subjects, on their request, a coffin in which to bury him.

Less successful was Scott's attempt at diplomacy with the other hostile Yao chief, Chikumbu, 'a notorious slaver and the disturber of the peace of the white neighbourhood'.[60] Yet it was not only the Europeans who were inconvenienced by Chikumbu. His aggression was such that other Yao chiefs, Mkanda and Kapeni at the helm, conspired with the Kololo chief Kasisi to drive him out to Mulanje, where he posed little difficulty to Blantyre but would later become a nuisance again when the Mission established an outpost there.[61] At any rate, Scott's approach to diplomacy was already dawning on him a month after his first arrival in Blantyre. 'These things must be learned

---

[57] McCracken, *Politics and Christianity*, 164–5.
[58] Hetherwick, *The Romance of Blantyre*, 39–40; Ross, *Blantyre Mission*, 69.
[59] Hetherwick, *The Romance of Blantyre*, 39–40.   [60] Ibid., 40.
[61] Ross, *Blantyre Mission*, 69–70.

through the slow understanding of the African', he wrote to Robertson.⁶² 'Intuition is very quick but understanding very slow.'

The patient study of African modes of disputing and diplomacy was nowhere more handsomely rewarded than in Scott's involvement in the deliberations known as *milandu* (sing. *mlandu*). His dictionary defines *mlandu* as 'a meeting for discussion of some claim or right, lawsuit, or quarrel; a speech or debate, a legal case' and states, as mentioned in the introduction, that 'it is the most characteristic word of African politics; itself a charter of limited government, and appeal to right and sufficient reason'.⁶³ *Mlandu* set the standard for well-argued disputes: 'There are few finer experiences than a well-spoken native *mlandu*, and only adepts in the native tongue have any idea of the woful [*sic*] difference between a European's partial vision of a case and the clear solid constitutional grip of a cultured native.'⁶⁴ Such words convey more than a pragmatic interest in finding a local institution through which to extend mission influence. *Mlandu* came to signify for Scott a confluence of his various political, moral, spiritual, and linguistic preoccupations. By participating in and, from early on, conducting *milandu*, Scott immersed himself in a language of deliberation and adjudication that taught him idioms in which to cast his own sermons.⁶⁵

The first few years of Scott's leadership in Blantyre saw *mlandu* constantly threatened by *nkhondo* – 'war'. During a particularly intense episode in 1883, he had advised the Europeans to have their 'guns cleaned in readiness for any emergency'.⁶⁶ Yet his public intervention was to appeal to *mlandu* instead of escalating hostilities. Hetherwick had witnessed the mounting tension among his very first impressions of Blantyre that year.⁶⁷ The immediate reason had been the fatal stabbing that a man from the Mission's nearby village had inflicted on the member of a village some distance away. The man had gone there to join a beer party, but a quarrel had erupted with lethal consequence. An excited messenger came to interrupt Hetherwick's first lunch with the Scotts and announced that furious men were shouting the ominous words of '*nkhondo, nkhondo!*' Historical referents became immediately clear to Hetherwick, who was told that their brandishing of spears and shields evoked their earlier subjugation by the Ngoni – they 'had learned something of the methods of their old

---

⁶² Scott to Robertson, December 1881.
⁶³ Scott: *A Cyclopaedic Dictionary*, 361.   ⁶⁴ LWBCA, November 1894.
⁶⁵ Ross, *Blantyre Mission*, 71.   ⁶⁶ Morrison Diary, 20 September 1883.
⁶⁷ Alexander Hetherwick, 'My First Day in Blantyre', NAM, AHE 1-1.

masters'. The deceased man's villagers, on the other hand, were appearing on the scene armed with guns that their historical connection to the slave caravans had supplied.

Into this explosive situation rushed Scott with little else than words to offer. He, with Hetherwick in tow, found the aggrieved men already advancing in 'the Zulu battle formation of the crescent' but called them to a halt and gathered the men around an anthill for deliberation.[68] It was conducted in what was then 'an unknown tongue' to Hetherwick, but despite 'grumblings and mutterings' after Scott had finished, both parties agreed to come to the Mission on the following day for further deliberations. The *mlandu* lasted for two days, concluded by a compensation payment by the murderer's village of cloth, brass wire, beads, and other items. Although no record of the verbal exchanges exists, Scott's intervention was likely to consolidate his reputation as a chief among chiefs.

As a learning process, diplomacy had its moments of difficulty and failure as well as success. A particularly protracted – and risky – diplomatic effort concerned the Ngoni chiefs. The Maseko faction had settled in Dedza and Ntcheu in present-day central Malawi, but the Shire Highlands had been the target of their raids before the coming of the Blantyre Mission and rumours of further raids showed no signs of abating.[69] Scott had from the beginning wanted to meet their chief but had found no intermediaries to broker such a meeting. The opportunity availed itself in 1884 when his visit to a Kololo village brought him into the company of an Ngoni headman who was in the village for a regular exchange of goats for salt.[70] This low-ranking notable was able to secure the necessary introduction to Chief Chikuse, and Scott set off on a two-week journey, again with Isobel Scott to convey the peaceful intent. Accounts vary as to whether Scott was able to meet the chief or only the chief's mother, 'a very much more important personage than his son', according to Hetherwick.[71] In any case, the Scotts stayed for a few days and left after an exchange

---

[68] Ibid. [69] Hetherwick, *The Romance of Blantyre*, 50–1.
[70] Harry Kambwiri Matecheta, *Blantyre Mission: Nkhani za ciyambi cace*, Blantyre: Hetherwick Press, 1951, 2; translated as Harry Kambwiri Matecheta, *Blantyre Mission: Stories of Its Beginning*, trans. Thokozani Chilembwe, Berlin: Wichern-Verlag, 2016, 25.
[71] Hetherwick, *The Romance of Blantyre*, 51; Matecheta, *Blantyre Mission: Nkhani za ciyambi cace*, 3; Matecheta, *Blantyre Mission: Stories of Its Beginning*, 25; Ross, *Blantyre Mission*, 78–9.

of presents had inaugurated a lasting friendship. However, they had also noticed clear signs of the *impi* – the war party – being prepared for raids and returned to Blantyre in a nervous state.

The tension intensified rapidly across the Shire Highlands, with some of the villages becoming deserted as their men fled to nearby hills while hundreds of women and children took refuge in the Mission. Convinced that the Mission would not be attacked, Scott tried to persuade more people to enjoy temporary shelter there, but rumours had also begun to implicate it in the coming mayhem. The friendship between Scott and Chikuse had sowed the seed of suspicion that the Mission could pass people on to the Ngoni as captives.[72] When they came, the raids indeed spared the Mission, and Hetherwick's carriers who had come across the *impi* were sent by the disciplined warriors back to Blantyre with their loads intact.[73] The villages were less fortunate, their granaries and other food stores looted and burned, while those who had not fled, especially women, were taken away as captives. As the raiders showed no sign of leaving the area after several days of turmoil, Scott went with Henderson to persuade them to return home. Their lengthy reasoning with the Ngoni notables produced the promise of withdrawal in ten days, a promise that was duly kept. Hetherwick contended that they left with 'eight hundred captives in slave sticks' but also noted that 'this was the last great Ngoni raid in the Shire Highlands'.[74] As he added, 'the next time the Angoni appeared in Blantyre it was to tramp the clay for the bricks that were made to build the Blantyre Church'. There could be no more striking sign of the peace than this coming together of previously hostile neighbours to build a church.

Seen from the perspective of the villagers taken as captives in 1884, Scott's friendship with Chikuse brought few diplomatic rewards. Yet the growth of trust across the various divides could only be gradual if it was to avoid the ill-conceived measures taken by the Blantyre pioneers. On the other hand, not all of Scott's interventions sought harmony with chiefly prerogatives. One of his first decisions after arrival was to close the Mission school. He did so 'under disciplinary preparation', which included sending away the bulk of the male boarders – the sons

---

[72] Matecheta, *Blantyre Mission: Nkhani za ciyambi cace*, 3; Matecheta, *Blantyre Mission: Stories of Its Beginning*, 25.
[73] Hetherwick, *The Romance of Blantyre*, 51; Ross, *Blantyre Mission*, 79.
[74] Hetherwick, *The Romance of Blantyre*, 52.

of Kololo chiefs with their attendant slaves.[75] They were asked to return after a few months, but without their slaves. The pupils were 'to attend on themselves, to clean out and keep tidy their own dormitories, to set out their own meals and their own plates'.[76] A 'rebellion' first ensued after these dictates, but Scott's 'strong personality' is said to have overcome 'all their objections'.[77]

Scott certainly put a good deal of effort in bonding with his pupils, as can be seen, for example, from the account of Hetherwick's hectic first day in Blantyre. After lunch, it involved dissuading the abovementioned Chipeta villagers from starting a war and it ended with 'a visit to the dormitories and a chat with the boys sitting round their fires'.[78] Scott pursued bonding, not bondage, and was not averse to borrowing from both African and European traditions in his quest. A practice 'very far from typical of the Victorian mission stations' allowed the boarders to gather for dances and games on the nights when the moon was full, much as they would have done in their villages.[79] On the other hand, he also initiated weekly tea-parties at his residence, where the school's senior boys and senior girls would get accustomed to mixing with White people while Scott himself would seek to learn more about these youngsters' ideas and feelings.

God Saves Us by Our Very Curse

Such practical, even mundane measures never distracted Scott from his philosophical and theological reflections on the purpose of his mission. His translation and lexical work, along with extensive correspondence, and the articles and comments he wrote for the Mission's newsletter from 1888, formed the bulk of Scott's written output. Yet as early as November 1882 he enclosed a manuscript with his letter to Robert Laws in Livingstonia.[80] 'I have attempted a sort of eight-page pamphlet', Scott described his effort. Entitled 'Ham Shall Be His Servant', the manuscript took the curse of Ham in Genesis 9 as its vantage point on a somewhat elliptical set of reflections and statements brought together

---

[75] David Clement Scott to Robert Laws, 3 May 1882, Foreign Mission Committee, NLS, MS 7903.
[76] Hetherwick, *The Romance of Blantyre*, 41.   [77] Ibid.
[78] Hetherwick, 'My First Day.'   [79] Ross, *Blantyre Mission*, 75.
[80] Scott to Laws, 14 November 1882, Foreign Mission Committee, NLS, Ms 7903.

by a question of service and leadership.[81] It was a theme that Scott revisited, in a sermon delivered in Scotland in 1901, nearly two decades later and three years after his tenure in Blantyre had ended.[82]

The biblical story about the curse of Ham had acquired long before Scott's reflections dubious fame as a divinely sanctioned explanation for racial differences and slavery. At the core of the story were the separate ways in which the fortunes among Noah's sons would develop, culminating in the idea of blessed and cursed lineages in the human condition. Noah had, after drinking too much wine, collapsed unconscious, his private parts exposed. His son Ham had gossiped about it to his brothers Shem and Japhet, who had dutifully covered their father. After coming to his senses, Noah grew furious with Ham and pronounced the line of his son Canaan, Noah's grandson, cursed and henceforth servants of Shem, Japhet, and their descendants.

Although Genesis is silent on skin colour, the earliest association of Black skin with servitude in the context of Noah's story has been found in Syriac, Arabic, and Ethiopic texts a thousand years before Christian missionary work by Europeans in Africa had even been conceived.[83] In the early modern world, the difference between the lineages was less a matter of skin colour than the subject of sacred history.[84] In these debates, Ham was the father of idolatry, not necessarily the dark-hued victim of a curse whose descendants were condemned to serve those of the fair-skinned Shem and Japhet. While serious theologians would note that the curse had befallen Canaan's descendants and not the whole of Ham's lineage, such subtleties increasingly gave way to racialist perspectives on enslavement as a *black* condition at the dawn of the nineteenth century. Although 'the Bible was grist to the racialist mill'[85] in the nineteenth-century intellectual life in Europe and America – and would survive into the twentieth century most notably

---

[81] David Clement Scott, 'Ham Shall Be His Servant', Manuscript, NLS, Ms 7903.
[82] Rev, D. C. Ruffelle Scott, *'Living Stones': Sermon upon the Church of Scotland Blantyre Mission, British Central Africa*, Edinburgh: William Blackwood and Sons, 1901.
[83] Edith R. Sanders, 'The Hamitic Hypothesis: Its Origins and Functions in Time Perspective', *Journal of African History*, 10 (4), 1969, 521–32; David M. Goldenberg, *Black and Slave: The Origins and History of the Curse of Ham*, Berlin: De Gruyter, 2017, 76–9.
[84] Colin Kidd, *The Forging of Races: Race and Scripture in the Protestant Atlantic World, 1600–2000*, Cambridge: Cambridge University Press, 2006, 74–5.
[85] Ibid., 168.

through the apartheid-era theologians in South Africa[86] – Scott was also heir to the Scottish Enlightenment which had provided an intellectual justification for Christian missions in its insistence on the unity of humankind.[87] On the other hand, the Enlightenment did not suddenly embrace non-European civilizations.[88] The curse of Ham continued to circulate as a legend stigmatizing people of African descent. Scotland's premier poet, Robert Burns, had written these lines in the eighteenth century, still delivered from Presbyterian pulpits a century later: 'How graceless Ham leugh at his Dad / Which made Canaan a n*****.'[89]

Scott and his contemporaries in Blantyre left few clues as to what literary resources they may have drawn upon to reflect on their tasks ahead. In the absence of scholarly or literary citations, Scott's own writings must speak for themselves. They do so with some difficulty, because such are his scope and style in 'Ham Shall Be His Servant' that the contemporary reader may well sympathize with the bewilderment felt by the Aberdeen elder who had listened to Scott preaching, as quoted by Hetherwick: 'God forbid that I should presume to understand him.'[90] Nevertheless, the manuscript's theologically and politically daring intent becomes apparent once the reader revisits its second line in the light of what Scott asserts elsewhere in his pamphlet: 'The officer must learn from the soldier; in fact to lead at all must be as the soldier.'[91] The manuscript is a meditation on leadership as service, and the descendants of Ham (or Canaan, as Scott specifies in his 1901 text[92]) are the ones to teach those of Japhet. Beyond the anachronistic language of the Kaffir is thus Scott's apparent acceptance of the racialized reading of the curse of Ham. Yet this conventional reading is precisely the ground against which Scott's thoughts on the Christian mission in Africa can show their radical intent. 'Ham's children', Scott states, 'have groaned in slavery, as a race have groaned in bondage'. Scott proceeds to declare that 'bondage is not service', before issuing a striking reversal that biblical argument also allows for.[93]

---

[86] Ibid., 40.   [87] Ibid., 120.
[88] John H. Zammito, *Kant, Herder, and the Birth of Anthropology*, Chicago, IL: University of Chicago Press, 2002, 18.
[89] Cited in Kidd, *The Forging*, 40.
[90] Hetherwick, *The Romance of Blantyre*, 34.
[91] Scott, 'Ham Shall Be His Servant.'   [92] Scott, *'Living Stones.'*
[93] Scott, 'Ham Shall Be His Servant.'

Our position is this that if we but receive the true attitude of a servant we shall most intelligently deal with Africa, and most helpfully bring about that most blessed truth 'the last shall be first;' for Ham's service really understood and really accepted will place the crown of glory upon its head. God saves us by our very curse; in the acceptance of that curse we bring forth Christ.

The last shall be first: the reversal that has long inspired Christian critiques of power may be the main reason why Scott's text can confound its reader. For it is not a simple reversal of roles that he has in mind in the relationship between the European missionary and the African subject. Towards the end of his pamphlet, Scott describes the relationship as 'always that of sonship, and the master has to be the father, and yet is one of equality as well because you find not an undeveloped mind given to you to develop, but a developed though receptive mind'. Just as the bondage suffered by the African is no service at all, so too is the idea of a race condemned to an inferior intellectual–moral condition an anathema to the service that the missionary is called upon to render. It is an idea entirely at odds with the figure of the risen Christ – the figure, so prominent in Scott's writings on race and slavery, that confronts the Christian with an incessant need to learn.

In this theology of reversals, the prying gaze must always be returned to the party with greater representational power in the encounter. Europe is by no means without its own predicaments: 'All Europe's questions of labour and payment, master and servant, will be understood in the Christian contact of Europe with Africa.' In the reversals that this encounter can entail, it is the European who stands to be saved as much as the African does. In due course, such thoughts will mature into progressively more striking maxims, above all the one in 1891: 'In God's great wisdom the native may be saved without us, but we doubt if we here can be saved without the native.'[94]

In the meantime, 'God saves us by our very curse' is challenging enough as a maxim.[95] Scott appears to be claiming that the curse has afflicted the descendants of Japhet no less than those of Ham. Europe may have acquired power and wealth, but it is only by surrendering it all that Europeans can 'receive this new gift from God, this servant relationship, precious and full of blessing'. 'Has Japhet not been the prodigal?' is the rhetorical question that leads Scott to assert that 'only

[94] LWBCA, December 1891.   [95] Scott, 'Ham Shall Be His Servant.'

when we lay down our power at God's feet do we really possess it'. Rather presciently for someone writing before the worst of the European scramble for Africa, Scott insists that 'the possession which God gives us is not land and gold, but ability to love and the possession of truest relationships'. The relationship of service marks nothing less than 'the uniting to Japhet of Ham'.

In his 1901 text, Scott reiterates some of these points but goes further in his reflections on ownership.[96] The sentence 'Ham shall be his servant' is followed by the spirited statement that 'it is the servant who *possesses* the beautiful land'.[97] By then, Scott will have sparked controversy over his views on Cecil Rhodes's imperialistic designs and on White settlers' attitudes. Yet a message of humility was already in the conclusion to the pamphlet in 1882: 'Africa will make you humble when you feel its excellent greatness.'[98] By the same token, the question is how the power to rule is to be exercised: 'Still more will you be humbled when God says "rule it".' Equality and hierarchy depend on one another in the complex relationship of service, as Scott's evocation of 'sonship' had already indicated. Those listening to his sermon in Scotland in 1901, however, were given no ambiguity as to why humility would be required of Europeans in Africa:

The great Kaffir race, which *possesses* Africa along its mountain-chains and plateaux from Ethiopia to the Cape, and which spreads in the Negro into Nigiritia, has a deep sense of rule and authority, of religion and personal liberty. Its monarchy is twentieth century in character; its religion is the worship of one God; its personality far more exacting in politeness, mutual respect, recognition of the duties of the friendship and of every relationship in life, than our own; its home-ties deeply and pathetically real, and bereavement rends its heart with a sorrow understood only of a few.[99]

By thus returning the gaze from Africa to Europe, and specifically to Scotland, Scott made his mark on the Church of Scotland's raison d'être in Africa. His reflections came in the form of sermons, pamphlets, newsletter articles, a dictionary, and personal and official correspondence, never in the weighty tomes of scholarship that some European missionaries produced on the basis of their exposure to new lands. Nor is there a hint of scepticism about the Bible as a source of inspiration. Scott was no John William Colenso (1814–1883), the

---

[96] Scott, *'Living Stones.'*   [97] Ibid., 8.   [98] Scott, 'Ham Shall Be His Servant.'
[99] Scott, *'Living Stones,'* 5–6.

Anglican bishop of Natal who came to doubt the historical veracity of the Old Testament.[100] While there is no indication of direct influence, Scott's approach to missionary work was compatible with Colenso's precept 'to understand the concrete living situation in which the issue under consideration evolved, before passing judgement, and not blindly invoke dead dogmas'.[101] Yet for all its elevated language, Scott's was a practical philosophy, developed partly in response to what he considered to be the admirably practical orientation to religion among Africans.

Imperceptible Advance

In 1885, Scott was able to write to Robertson that 'the native character here is very strong'.[102] He went on to comment that 'they feel no difficulty in the miraculous, not because they are nature's priests but because they are so practical. They quite accept civilization, little as they can explain it, and seem to reap more benefit than those do at home who are as little masters of the materials of civilization and yet try to receive it without the God who made it'. Practical dispositions called for practical purposes, such as coming together in church service no less than in the work of building and deliberation, among others. Just over three years old in his position, Scott was also moved to reflect on the difference those years had made on his own outlook: 'Three years have imperceptibly produced the greatest advance in one's views of what missions are, so imperceptibly that one hardly realizes that it was not plain to one all before.' The novice in Africa preoccupied to replenish the supply of champagne and to avoid ritualism was transforming into a missionary radically different from anyone before or after him in Blantyre.

The undoing of Scott's vision that subsequent chapters will chronicle partly derived from the failure of other Scotsmen around him to experience a similar 'imperceptible advance'. A glimpse into what it may have been like to sit in Scott's congregation in the early years of his leadership can be gained from the diary of Frederick Morrison, the young Glaswegian carpenter employed by the African Lakes Company.

---

[100] Kidd, *The Forging*, 152; Jeff Guy, *The Heretic: A Study of the Life of John William Colenso 1814–1883*, Johannesburg: Ravan Press, 1983.
[101] Ibid., 73.   [102] Scott to Robertson, 5 January 1885.

A pious member of the Blantyre congregation, he on more than one occasion had to wonder whether it was him or Scott who was making the gospel incomprehensible. In February 1884, Morrison reported that the attendance at the English service was 'very good' but that 'Mr Scott was very much at sea (apparently) in his discourse. I don't know what is the matter with him just now, but he is not preaching as he used to.'[103] The following month brought more doubt and discomfort: 'Mr Scott gave us another of his lectures on I don't know what...I am sorry thus to speak of Mr Scott's addresses, because previous to this I used to like him so well. Is it a change in me or a change in him, oh God search my heart and let me see, but still let me delight to hear of Jesus.'[104] Previously in 1883, Hetherwick, a newcomer to Blantyre, had compared favourably with the Mission's leader. Scott's sermon 'had not the nice simple ring about it that Mr Hetherwick's discourse had'.[105]

Hetherwick himself came to describe Scott as 'seeing visions of men and things that few could see save himself'.[106] He also recalled that Isobel Scott had been her husband's fiercest editor, who would read his English sermons before he had delivered them and excised from them with particular vigour anything from the Book of Revelation and that had the word 'Heavenlies'.[107] Yet Scott's visionary practice had an empirical basis. Dependency, diplomacy, and deliberation rather than dreams informed Scott's political, theological, and moral reveries.[108] Hetherwick called his approach an 'African apprenticeship' in which Scott 'was fond of saying, "one went to school again"'.[109] That few of his compatriots were equally inclined to go to school sowed the seeds for other conflicts to take root, such as those over land and labour. From the *milandu* deliberations to translation and lexical work, language was the key domain in which the practical and the philosophical became one in Scott's thought. It was humanity's common heritage and, in its central African inflection, inspired another critical look at what one's own civilization had become.

---

[103] Morrison Diary, 3 February 1884. [104] Ibid., 2 March 1884.
[105] Ibid., 18 November 1883. [106] LWBCA, September–October 1907.
[107] Hetherwick, *The Romance of Blantyre*, 37.
[108] Compare Jonathon L. Earle, 'Dreams and Political Imagination in Colonial Buganda', *Journal of African History*, 58 (1), 2017, 85–105.
[109] Hetherwick, *The Romance of Blantyre*, 46.

4 | *The Universal Vernacular*

Towards the end of his tenure in Blantyre, David Clement Scott was moved to declare Chimang'anja 'a broad language, and the people a broad people. To be broad enough for Mahomet and Christian Missionary, and with room for more, is surely enough!'[1] Rather than being a parochially ethnic language, let alone a primitive language without any prospect of development, the vernacular was not only resourceful but so capacious as to give expression to different world religions – *with room for more*. It was the most immediate source of Scott's evolving thought on race relations. His reflections on friendship, chiefly authority, and the *mlandu* deliberations all prepared the ground for profound revisions to the missionary vocation. No domain, however, afforded a more searching perspective into epistemic justice than the vernacular language.

The effects of the vernacular on Scott's thought illustrate how language ideologies – common assumptions about what language is and how human linguistic diversity should be understood – can reveal varied ideas about the human condition more generally.[2] It is a truism that language ideologies played an important role in how both missionary and colonial encounters unfolded. Language learning and translation work were the *sine qua non* of much missionary effort in the nineteenth century, while the control of communications was virtually as important to colonial regimes as was the use of force.[3] Within these grand historical processes, strikingly different possibilities can be discerned if one cares to look hard enough.

---

[1] *Life and Work in British Central Africa* (LWBCA), April 1897.
[2] Kathryn A. Woolard and Bambi B. Schieffelin, 'Language Ideology', *Annual Review of Anthropology*, 23, 1994, 55–82.
[3] Johannes Fabian, *Language and Colonial Power: The Appropriation of Swahili in the Former Belgian Congo 1880–1938*, Berkeley: University of California Press, 1986; Joseph Errington, *Linguistics in a Colonial World: A Story of Language, Meaning, and Power*, Malden, MA: Blackwell, 2008.

To begin with, Scott's language ideology contrasted with a reading of the Bible that became dominant in Africa and elsewhere during European colonialism – that it is an historical narrative in which to situate one's own salvation as a people.[4] Scott's language ideology was an alternative to the agenda attributed to much linguistic work by Christian missionaries in Africa, namely that 'language, ethnicity, and territory were supposed to coincide'.[5] In several instances, missionaries sought to standardize distinct languages out of diverse speech forms.[6] Rather than codifying a sense of peoplehood through his work of translation, Scott appears to have drawn upon the equally salient imaginary by which 'Christianity tends to emphasize a universal rather than a territorial or ethnic-based sense of community'.[7] Among the turn-of-the-century missionary translators in Africa, it was a minority view.[8]

Considered in practical rather than philosophical terms, Scott's translations could not provide one coherent narrative for peoplehood simply because they presented the Scriptures in pieces rather than as a whole. Industrious as he was, translating the entire Bible was not one of Scott's achievements. His published translations of the Scriptures were the Gospels of Matthew and Mark in 1892, Luke and John in 1893, and Ephesians, Philippians, and Colossians in 1894.[9] Only at the turn of the century, after Scott's departure, did his successor Alexander Hetherwick convene a committee to translate the entire

---

[4] Adrian Hastings, *The Construction of Nationhood: Ethnicity, Religion, and Nationalism*, Cambridge: Cambridge University Press, 1997, 195–6; Joel Cabrita, *Text and Authority in the South African Nazaretha Church*, Cambridge: Cambridge University Press for the International African Institute, 2014, 70–1; J. D. Y. Peel, *Religious Encounter and the Making of the Yoruba*, Bloomington, IN: Indiana University Press, 2000, 279–83.

[5] Judith T. Irvine, 'Subjected Words: African Linguistics and the Colonial Encounter', *Language and Communication*, 23 (4), 2008, 338.

[6] Patrick Harries, 'The Roots of Ethnicity: Discourse and the Politics of Language Construction in South-East Africa', *African Affairs* 87 (346), 1988, 25–52; Judith T. Irvine, 'Mastering African Languages: The Politics of Linguistics in Nineteenth-Century Senegal', *Social Analysis* 33, 1993, 28.

[7] Bambi B. Schieffelin, 'Christianizing Language and the Displacement of Culture in Bosavi, Papua New Guinea', *Current Anthropology*, 55, 2014, S228.

[8] Emma Wild-Wood, 'Bible Translation and the Formation of Corporate Identity in Uganda and Congo 1900–40', *Journal of African History*, 58 (3), 2017, 489–507.

[9] Kenneth R. Ross, *Gospel Ferment in Malawi: Theological Essays*, Gweru: Mambo Press, 1995, 110.

Bible into what the translators called Union Nyanja (see Chapter 9). Yet Scott's other major achievement in linguistic scholarship, *A Cyclopaedic Dictionary of the Mang'anja Language Spoken in British Central Africa*, published in 1892, was driven by such philosophical verve that it left little doubt about the vernacular's capacity to evoke sentiments and ideas of universal scope.[10] It attracted contemporary criticism for its speculative passages, but few questioned then or since its foundational status as a work in vernacular thought, whether the language is named Chimang'anja, Chinyanja or Chichewa. Crucially, the philosophical and the practical also came together in the vision he held for an African Church in which Africans and Europeans would worship together, their communication with one another and with the divine carried by the African vernacular.

The English language, whether in Bible translation or in preaching, offered Scott little inspiration for his vision. Although Africans in the Blantyre Mission schools were taught English, much would take place before it acquired a superior status, as it did across much of the colonial world.[11] Nor was Scott's veneration of the vernacular simply another version of the common Protestant penchant for 'native' languages, however limited the numbers of their speakers were.[12] Chimang'anja and its closely related language forms were 'a broad language' for both philosophical and historical reasons.

The language form Scott chose to study confounded the distinctions commonly drawn in missionary and colonial encounters between 'vehicular' and 'native' languages, or between 'trade' and 'heart' languages.[13] As discussed in the introduction, spatial mobility and political turbulence were matched by an assemblage of mutually intelligible language forms. Out of them would the names Chimang'anja,

---

[10] D. C. Scott, *A Cyclopaedic Dictionary of the Mang'anja Language Spoken in British Central Africa*, Edinburgh: Foreign Mission Committee of the Church of Scotland, 1892.

[11] Ali A. Mazrui, *The Political Sociology of English Language: An African Perspective*, The Hague: Mouton, 1975; Alastair Pennycook, *English and the Discourses of Colonialism*, New York: Routledge, 1998.

[12] Errington, *Linguistics*, 95–6.

[13] Ibid., 124; Courtney Handman, 'Speaking to the Soul: On Native Language and Authenticity in Papua New Guinea Bible Translation', in Miki Makihara and Bambi B. Schieffelin, eds, *Consequences of Contact: Language Ideologies and Sociocultural Transformations in Pacific Societies*, Oxford: Oxford University Press, 2007.

Chinyanja, and Chichewa get codified as 'languages' when the twentieth century beckoned. Scott's language ideology, by contrast, was not detained by the concerns over choosing between one variant or another that would eventually spark debate.[14] He collected material for his dictionary from a range of people, some of whom were immigrant labourers at the Mission or refugees fleeing slavers or abusive masters, while he also pursued further linguistic work when he visited areas west of the Shire Valley. Not only were the 'broad people' spatially dispersed. Their 'broad language' could also accommodate such variety of thought that the whole humanity could flourish in it.

Duff Macdonald, Scott's predecessor as the head of the Blantyre Mission, had chosen Chiyao as the subject of his linguistic studies. As is discussed below, some of Scott's closest language consultants and co-workers in the Mission were also Chiyao speakers. Multilingualism was, therefore, a feature of the social world more than his high regard for Chimang'anja may have acknowledged. The wide geographical reach of its language forms may have attracted Scott to Chimang'anja as an aspect of his trust in the universal capabilities of the vernacular. Yet one would not have needed to go further than the Livingstonia Mission's sphere in northern Malawi to find a rather different linguistic situation. The missionaries' early correspondence bemoaned the difficulties of settling on one language, such as when W. A. Elmslie wrote to Robert Laws in 1887 that the varieties of Chitonga, Chingoni, and Chitumbuka spoken in different districts entailed 'a large amount of talk' that he could not understand.[15] The missionaries had attempted to use Chinyanja as the vehicle of Christian teaching, but had found that many people 'utterly refused it'.[16] While Elmslie had urged in 1887 the reduction of 'the number of languages which make a great barrier in spreading our work', Laws drew a somewhat brutal conclusion decades later: 'The sooner many of these different languages become extinct, the better for the peace, the prosperity, and the advancement of the country and its people.'[17]

What escaped the early Livingstonia missionaries was the possibility that the refusal to use a particular language form was not necessarily

---

[14] T. Price, 'Nyanja Linguistic Problems', *Africa*, 13 (2), 1940, 128.
[15] W. A. Elmslie to Robert Laws, 6 June 1887, NLS, MS 7890.
[16] Robert Laws, *Reminiscences of Livingstonia*, Edinburgh: Oliver and Boyd, 1934, 133.
[17] Ibid., 134.

caused by a failure to understand it. As Leroy Vail has pointed out, the tendency in central Africa has been 'for languages to shade off gradually into other languages through a series of dialectical gradations'.[18] A whole host of political reasons, including competition over mission resources, have provoked ethno-linguistic distinctions in a region marked by histories of migration and intermingling.[19] Scott's language ideology may have been less attuned to these histories than to a vision of the vernacular as the common heritage of humanity. Yet its effect was to demand epistemic justice in an encounter in which many Europeans' attitude to learning the vernacular was purely instrumental.

The United Worship of African and European

The depth of linguistic prejudice that Scott detected in many of his European compatriots received a sarcastic remark in 1895. He confessed in the Mission magazine that he had been 'much amused' by the description of Chimang'anja by an unnamed 'brother Missionary more than a hundred miles from Blantyre'.[20] The description had identified Chimang'anja as a 'barbarous language'. 'We can only ascribe his opinion', Scott commented, 'to either ignorance or that apotheosis of Swahili which is fashionable in certain quarters'. One interpretation of Scott's comment would see in it rivalry between missionaries over the languages in which to pursue their vocation among Africans. Yet Scott's defence of Chimang'anja was more sober than this interpretation would suggest: 'The Mang'anja language, like any other language, is just what one's knowledge of it is – nothing or everything.' For all his appreciation, if not veneration, of the vernacular, Scott considered Chimang'anja 'like any other language', willing to open its treasures to anyone who studied it.

'It is in Mang'anja', Scott told his friend in Scotland in 1890, 'that I often get most insight and even material for my English sermons'.[21]

---

[18] Leroy Vail, 'Religion, Language, and the Tribal Myth: The Tumbuka and Chewa of Malawi', in J. M. Schoffeleers, ed., *Guardians of the Land: Essays on Central African Territorial Cults*, Gweru: Mambo Press, 1979, 210.

[19] Jan Vansina, *Kingdoms of the Savanna: A History of Central African States Until European Occupation*, Madison, WI: University of Wisconsin Press, 1966.

[20] LWBCA, May 1895.

[21] David Clement Scott to James Robertson, 16 June 1890, EUL, Gen. 717-10.

Scott described a particularly moving occasion during the Chimang'anja service when he had realized the breakthrough in communication he had achieved. 'I never was able to preach more simply nor more freely', and so intense seemed the attention given to his sermon by the women, men, girls, and boys in his congregation that 'I had to stop at the end for fear of breaking down solely through the solemnity of the feeling'. Such personal, visceral experiences indicated that the lofty ideals in Scott's language ideology were far more than mere philosophical speculation. They also compelled him to recognize the limits of the English language in his vision for the African Church.

Scott's intent was to ensure not only his own progress in learning the vernacular but to convince all White people of the rewards as well as the necessity of acquiring fluency in it. He ended an article in the Mission magazine with the words, 'India demands that her missionaries, traders, politicians, and even soldiers, know the native language; it is even more necessary here'.[22] In the early 1890s, Scott conducted Chimang'anja classes for Europeans on Thursday evenings after service.[23] To encourage attendance, the Mission magazine proposed to run monthly competitions in which the best answers to a series of questions in Chimang'anja would be given monetary prizes. Little was said of this proposal subsequently, but the domain in which Scott could pursue his vision was the Church itself. In a letter to his friend in Scotland, Scott stated in 1889 that 'the Church must be a European-native church'.[24] With the words 'the native language' underlined, he reported that 'I have proposed a native Church for European and native in *the native language* for Sunday morning services – and am just waiting to see it gather shape and approval and definite promise of success'. In 1890, the Mission magazine carried the following notice.

It is proposed sometime to change the morning English Service into a Native one; the hymns and service book will be worthy of the dignity of the united worship of Native and European; the translation of the Bible will be well and carefully done, and the address studied and prepared just as in English. The lessons and sermon will be easily followed by almost all the Europeans; and the benefit of worship in clear Mang'anja will be felt by all. The all important communion of Native and European in one worship before God will elevate

---

[22] LWBCA, November 1894.   [23] Ibid., November 1892.
[24] Scott to Robertson, 10 May 1889.

all who take part; and the founding of the Native Church in this land will be fostered by a civilization Christian in deed as well as in name.[25]

Far from being the exclusive property of its 'native' speakers, and a tool appropriated by missionaries, the vernacular offered spiritual rewards to everyone. In 1891, the Mission magazine stated that 'we would gladly welcome the help and co-operation of the Europeans in the neighbourhood at the 8.30 Sunday morning native service. By their very presence joining in our prayers and praise they would aid the work of the Mission more than we can express'.[26] The unity of race and spirit, even when evoking the racialized hierarchies perpetrated by Scott's audience, was palpable in the expectation that 'some might even bring with them their servants and dependants or even their villagers'. The benefits of the new practice would be mutual: 'The spiritual life of the European will be increased by the presence of the native, and the native will be encouraged and strengthened by the presence at his worship of his employer or his master or his ruler.' More precisely, language learning and use in the Church would be one way of achieving the unity that the prosperity of all demanded. By the end of 1891, when the protectorate had been formally established, Scott was compelled to elaborate on his vision.

We are working here for the unity of the Church European and African. It has been the aim of the Mission during all those past years to bring and keep together the two parts of the Church – native and foreign. It would be a great blow to the Church of Christ should there arise in the future such a severance as we confess exists in the Colony between the native and European portions of it. Both portions will greatly increase as time goes on. We long to see them increasing together – not side by side but as one.[27]

Scott went on to state that 'the prosperity of the European and of the native are one. We mutually depend on each other. The interests of both are similar. Both will suffer or both will prosper together. The interests of labour and of trade bind us together. To administer the country justly for the native is to administer it also justly for the European'. By a cruel historical twist, it was exactly ten years later, in 1901, and under Hetherwick's leadership, that for the first time in Blantyre, two congregations were formed, one European and the other

[25] LWBCA, May 1890.   [26] Ibid., December 1891.   [27] Ibid.

'native'.[28] Scott's vision (and practice) of interracial worship was consigned to history.

Diversity's Dictionary

From the outset, careful lexicographical work was one of Scott's priorities in Blantyre. His early correspondence contains comments on language learning that stressed the easy availability of the vernacular for the interested student. Pointing out that Chimang'anja was written phonetically, Scott wrote to his friend in Scotland that the language was 'easily mastered'.[29] Although he reported to have 'printed the syllables which include all the sounds in the language', it is not clear whether he had consulted existing word lists and descriptions. He was likely to have consulted the grammar and word list compiled by Alexander Riddel, a Presbyterian missionary at Cape Maclear in 1880. It was based on the work of another missionary, Johannes Rebmann, entitled *Dictionary of the Kiniassa Language*, printed in 1877 but circulated as a manuscript before then.[30] Yet even if he consulted these studies, Scott would not have been able to achieve his dictionary of an entirely different scope without extensive fieldwork and frequent collaboration with particular speakers.

Just as Scott made few references to existing resources in Chimang'anja or Chinyanja, he neglected to acknowledge his Malawian collaborators in his dictionary and translations. Hetherwick, on the other hand, ended his preface to the new edition of the dictionary by singling out Che Ndombo, 'Headman, Christian, Linguist, and Leper; on whose familiarity with various African tongues both [Scott and Hetherwick] were privileged to draw'.[31] Yet Scott came under criticism by Europeans precisely for collaborating rather too closely with Africans, entrusting them with responsibilities as 'deacons' for example, whose names he was pleased to publicize

---

[28] Andrew C. Ross, *Blantyre Mission and the Making of Modern Malawi*, Blantyre: Christian Literature Association of Malawi, 1996, 178–9.
[29] Scott to Robertson, 5 January 1885.
[30] Steven Paas, *Johannes Rebmann: A Servant of God in Africa before the Rise of Western Colonialism*, Bonn: VTR/VKW, 2011, 258.
[31] Alexander Hetherwick, 'Preface', in D. C. Scott, *Dictionary of the Nyanja Language*, edited and enlarged by Alexander Hetherwick, London: Lutterworth Press, 1929, vii.

(see Chapter 7).[32] In his linguistic work, he took Nacho Ntimawanzako with him on a two-year visit to Scotland in 1885–7, when much of the desk work on the dictionary was carried out.[33] The other African on this visit was Mungo Chisuse, a close associate of Scott's throughout his tenure at Blantyre. Both men attended classes at Stewart's College in Edinburgh.[34] The nature of Scott's relationship with them was clearly collaborative to the extent that he gave back as well as received in the relationship. Baptized in Blantyre only after their return, Ntimawanzako and Chisuse had their expenses in Scotland paid by Scott.

Ndombo and Chisuse were speakers of Chiyao as much as Chimang'anja, two language forms already sufficiently distinct to be regarded as such by Africans in the nineteenth century. The involvement of some Yao chiefs in slave raiding and Islam was bound to heighten the distinction (see Chapter 3). Scott himself was not averse to drawing it. 'Hetherwick's mission is Yao; mine is Mang'anja', he affirmed in 1885, alluding to Hetherwick's newly established outpost at Domasi.[35] Yet the contribution that the two Chiyao speakers made to Scott and Hetherwick's work on Chimang'anja is merely one example of the multilingual situation in which the dictionary emerged. Nor was it unusual for early missionary linguistics in Africa to be based on work among refugees and resettled people.[36] What was less usual was the way in which Scott was receptive to the complex linguistic-political condition around him. Where many missionaries saw ethno-linguistic diversity, he saw common humanity.

In July 1889, Scott entered into the unpublished Blantyre Mission journal these laconic remarks: 'Dictionary finished, after seven years work at it...May it be useful by God's blessing. This along with Church work, church plans, and the work of the whole station has been a considerable strain.'[37] The words with which he signed off the dictionary's preface were rather more high-sounding.

[32] LWBCA, December 1892.
[33] Ross, *Blantyre Mission*, 80; Harry Kambwiri Matecheta, *Blantyre Mission: Nkhani za ciyambi cace*, Blantyre: Hetherwick Press, 1951, 6; translated as Harry. K. Matecheta, *Blantyre Mission: Stories of Its Beginning*, trans. Thokozani Chilembwe, Berlin: Wichern-Verlag, 2016, 35.
[34] John McCracken, 'Mungo Murray Chisuse and the Early History of Photography in Malawi', *The Society of Malawi Journal*, 61 (2), 2008, 3.
[35] Scott to Robertson, 5 January 1885.   [36] Irvine, 'Subjected Words', 330.
[37] The Blantyre Mission Journal, 27 July 1889, NLS, Acc 9218.

Enough is known of the languages to get at the heart of the people. We wholly believe that language is the poetic or creative attempt of a people to incarnate will and spirit in sound and word, and that it is neither a copy of nature, nor an unconscious reproduction of it, nor spasmodic sound. The consciousness by which it is formed is poetic and prophetic, not interpretative; it remains for the spirit bevisioned of a Christian civilisation, in the faith of the Son of man and the ministry of the Spirit, to interpret these voices for the salvation of the world.[38]

No doubt it was words such as these, which Scott appears to have cultivated from his writing to his sermons to his everyday conversations, that led Hetherwick to comment decades later that Scott 'lived and moved on a plane high above his fellows – and in consequence very many failed to understand him'.[39] Yet as Hetherwick went on to remark, Scott was also a practical man who pursued the objectives of an industrial mission even when the Foreign Mission Committee in Edinburgh had ruled out such objectives in the aftermath of the first attempt in Blantyre.[40] In his language ideology, Scott was no less keen to show the practical consequences of the lofty ideals he was able to identify in the vernacular. Precisely by speaking to the whole humanity, the vernacular carried lessons for us all.

A Living Philosophy

The composition of dictionaries in missionary encounters was informed by historically variable ideas about religion and authority as well as by pragmatic concerns to rule and to discipline.[41] Scott's dictionary was his magnum opus of over 700 pages, whose scope surpassed such pragmatic concerns to convey philosophical and theological ideas in the vernacular. One example of the vernacular lessons he drew is the entries in the dictionary that sometimes went far beyond what a mere definition would look like. The influence of both what he had come to learn in central Africa and what he knew would colour the judgment of his European readers is apparent throughout those pages,

---

[38] Scott, *A Cyclopaedic*, vi.
[39] Alexander Hetherwick, *The Romance of Blantyre: How Livingstone's Dream Came True*, Edinburgh: Lassodie Press, 1931, 34.
[40] See e.g. Ross, *Blantyre Mission*, 63–5.
[41] Derek R. Peterson, 'Translating the Word: Dialogism and Debate in Two Gikuyu Dictionaries', *Journal of Religious History*, 23 (1), 1999, 31–50.

not least in the entries on spiritual matters. As was seen in the previous chapter, Scott could insert into his definitions of words, for instance in his entry on *mankhwala* for 'medicine', notes such as 'nowhere...is there found the thick darkness which one is taught to look for'.[42] A matter-of-fact tone could also challenge European prejudices on concepts such as *mzimu* for 'spirit'.[43] On the other hand, Scott remarked on *mfiti* for 'witch' that it was 'the centre of African darkness'.[44] This rare instance of negative comment hardly contradicted Chimang'anja speakers' own hostility towards witches. Nor did Scott add to his description of the witch's works any further condemnation of the practices.

As a work in vernacular philosophy and theology, the dictionary was crucial to Scott's vision for common humanity. It was in his comments on the various names for 'God' that Scott displayed particularly consistently his determination not only to bring vernacular concepts into the universal fold but also to suggest what contemporary English speakers could learn from them. In so far as concepts such as *Chiuta*, *Mpambe*, *Mlezi*, and *Mulungu* were different names for one God, Scott's first task was to convince his readers that no idolatry was at issue. God was personified, not the signs by which 'He' became known in the world, such as the natural phenomena of rain and thunder. 'Every person has at least two names, every chief three, most have more names', Scott explained the link between persons and multiple names.[45] His overview of God's names is worth quoting in full.

Chiuta is thus God in space and the rainbow sign across; *Mpambe*, God Almighty (*ku pambana*, excel), of whose active power the thunder and the rain are signs; *Mlezi*, God the Sustainer, because He takes care of and nourishes (*ku leza*) the earth and all things; and *Mulungu*, God who is Spirit, who works those things in human life which are beyond our power, in whose hands are all things. These are not fanciful but real meanings, and really so understood.[46]

Scott summoned vernacular exegesis to demonstrate that while the plural form of *Mulungu* as *Milungu* was available, it was never used: '*Sangaike mirungu chifukwa kuti Mulungu ndi mmodzi omwe*, you can't put the plural because God is one.'[47] He also had to account for

---

[42] Scott, *A Cyclopaedic*, 315–16. [43] Ibid., 415–16. [44] Ibid., 345.
[45] Ibid., 107. [46] Ibid. [47] Ibid., 403.

the presence of spirits in the plural and for the sacrifices that were made to them and to God. 'Spirits are', he submitted, 'spirits of people who have died, not gods'. Sacrifices were made to spirits, but not exclusively to them. God was not to be 'confounded with spirits in general, who as spirits are supposed to be *with* him'. Moreover, an analogy between God and other figures of authority suggested lessons to be learnt for Scott's readers. Just as *mfumu* (chief) and *mlandu* (lawsuit, debate), as seen in the previous chapter, led to comparisons to what Europeans had or did not have, so too did vernacular communication with God commend itself when compared to how Europeans worshipped.

> This is quite the genius of the language, and the free talk about the Europeans they really respect, their free intercourse with their own chiefs whom they really fear, their free shouting in the world in a way we hardly dare to or think of, show that the native standpoint is very much freer in their talk of God than ours.[48]

For some missionaries, monotheism was a near-forgotten tradition in Africa waiting to be revived.[49] Scott, by contrast, proposed no temporal gap between the various African practices and ideas he described and those aspects of Christianity that defined for him common humanity. That the dictionary engaged vernacular thought as a living philosophy is also evident in Scott's admission of conceptual change. In a characteristically high-minded expression, he ended the guide to the dictionary with insisting that the vernacular 'changes from time to time as it has a right to do, it throws out branches, it can create fresh forms, it is living in every atom, and yet it never loses the dignity of its spirit birth'.[50] Rather than being frozen in time, the vernacular had a 'right' to change as a living language and philosophy. Just as Scott was not unduly concerned to delineate 'a people' as its proper owner, so too had he none of the fear for 'impure' forms that would exercise both Europeans and Africans in years to come.

---

[48] Ibid., 373.
[49] Dmitri van den Bersselaar, 'Missionary Ethnographers and the History of Anthropology: The Case of G. T. Basden', in Patrick Harries and David Maxwell, eds, *The Spiritual in the Secular: Missionaries and Knowledge about Africa*, Grand Rapids, MI: William B. Eerdmans, 2012, 149; Honoré Vinck, 'Ideology in Missionary Scholarly Knowledge in Belgian Congo: *Aequatoria, Centre de recherches africanistes;* The Mission Station of Bamanya (RDC), 1937–2007', in ibid., 238.
[50] Scott, *A Cyclopaedic*, xxii.

Contemporary Critics

Although the era of inter-mission collaboration in translation and linguistics was yet to commence, Scott's lexicographical work, and its far-reaching inferences, by no means passed without notice among his missionary colleagues in central Africa. Alluding to the Universities' Mission to Central Africa (UMCA), the Anglican mission based on Lake Malawi's Likoma island, Scott noted in his Mission magazine in 1893 that 'our gentle rivals at the Lake' had issued criticisms of the dictionary.[51] While he accepted the criticisms as 'good and very fair', he went on to remark that 'it need not be thought that we accept the corrections because we approve the spirit, but these will be the subject of criticism at the proper time'. No such criticism of criticisms seems to have ensued, but *The Nyasa News*, the magazine published from Likoma by Chauncy Maples between 1893 and 1895,[52] continued what it called its 'ungracious task of fault finding' after the Blantyre magazine's comment.[53] A central criticism concerned the meaning and evidential basis of some of Scott's grandest ideas.

One aspect of Scott's description of the language was his notion that different letters signified different moods. The letter 'p', for example, had as its 'general idea' 'incisiveness; also openness'.[54] Maples, who was to become the Bishop of Likoma in 1895,[55] took it as an example of a statement for which 'other students of the language who have the same data for a process of induction, would be likely to come to a very different conclusion'.[56] After recommending 'a little more diffidence in statements on a subject of so much difficulty', Maples proceeded to question the conceptual edifice on which Scott's ideas were erected. Pursuing his interest in single letters, Scott had written in his guide that 'in being made a noun the idea accepts an initial impress. The first letters of the noun show the character and meaning of that impress; and the impress is repeated as a detached particle to claim the attributes belonging to the noun, and the verb which speaks for it'.[57] From these thoughts Scott drew the conclusion that the verb may not be a

---

[51] LWBCA, June 1893.
[52] Beryl Brough, 'The Role of the U.M.C.A. in 19th-Century Malawi', *The Society of Malawi Journal* 52 (1), 1999, 18.
[53] *The Nyasa News*, August 1893.   [54] Scott, *A Cyclopaedic*, 497.
[55] Brough, 'The Role', 16.   [56] *The Nyasa News*, August 1893.
[57] Scott, *A Cyclopaedic*, x.

verb as conventionally understood but 'an attribute joined to the noun by its representative particle'.[58]

To the empirically minded critic in *The Nyasa News*, these statements called for a great deal more clarification than was available in the dictionary. The verb, for example, had in Chimang'anja, as in other Bantu languages, pronominal and temporal prefixes and infixes, but they did not make them any less 'true' as verbs.[59] 'We cannot help asking "what *does* it all mean?"', Maples wrote in some despair after referring to Scott's reflections on verbal suffixes or 'terminations': 'These terminations are characterised by certain letters which bear characteristic meanings, and may be called *verbal letters*. The moods above mentioned take meaning not from grammatical division, but from the root idea or force of these verbal letters. It is evident, therefore, that there are really as many moods as there are characteristic consonantal sounds used in verb-making.'[60] Maples admitted that 'it would be unfair to criticize what we confess we do not understand', but he urged Scott to provide comparative observations on Bantu languages to elucidate 'the root idea or force of these verbal letters'.[61] As for the comparison to the biblical languages, discussed below, Maples raised no reservations in principle. The above conjecture on reduplication, however, baffled the critic one more time: 'As to the *signification* of the reduplicated words, if there be any analogy therein between Greek and Mang'anja, interested indeed shall we be, if Mr Scott will point it out to us.'

In the end, the critic went to some lengths to acknowledge Scott's dictionary 'as an outstanding witness, full of superlative merit, to his linguistic ability, his learning, his industry, and his research'. Yet the conciliatory ending could not conceal irreconcilable differences in approach. Scott's speculations on individual letters and other linguistic features, for which he did not – and could not – furnish empirical support, present rather less reason to be recovered from oblivion than many other aspects of his visionary practice. At the same time, those speculations were consistent with a language ideology that saw in the vernacular the properties that called for a serious consideration of their consequences for understanding language – *any* language. Philosophical and spiritual inspiration soared above the confines of

---

[58] Ibid., xi.   [59] *The Nyasa News*, August 1893.
[60] Scott, *A Cyclopaedic*, xviii.   [61] *The Nyasa News*, August 1893.

empirical scholarship that had produced the bulk of the dictionary to critical acclaim.

Another 'gentle rival' at the lake also came to express reservations about Scott's dictionary. William Percival Johnson served the UMCA there from 1876 until 1928.[62] A former student of Sanskrit at Oxford, Johnson embarked on Chinyanja scholarship with enthusiasm that resulted in, despite his partial eyesight, published translations of the Scriptures and vernacular proverbs, among other studies.[63] Nothing that he published surpassed the scope of Scott's dictionary, but Johnson too found reason to advise caution when consulting it. The issue was the association of *mfiti* or 'witch' with cannibalism. Writing long after Scott's death, Johnson quoted him as glossing a central tenet in the concept as 'the wizard does not kill for spite but in order to obtain the flesh to eat'.[64] Johnson commented that 'much devilry seems practised in which the cannibal horror falls into the background, and I should hesitate to speak as definitely as Dr. Scott does'.

Johnson omitted to quote from the lengthy paragraph that accompanied Scott's definition. Among other things, Scott wrote that 'what makes the power so dreaded is not that the *mfiti* exercises this power for reasons of spite, but (as it is supposed) to eat the body; he therefore belongs entirely to the region of the horrible'.[65] Cannibalism was the apotheosis of evil in vernacular thought rather than a constant feature of witchcraft, let alone an actual custom.[66] A few years after his dictionary was published, Scott was compelled to correct the sensationalist account of cannibalism by Harry Johnston, the new protectorate's first Commissioner. He had stated that 'while cannibalism in the main disappeared as an avowed custom, it has lingered as a horrible practice amongst depraved people'.[67] Scott pointed out that any serious student of vernacular thought would also get the response that 'of course there is

---

[62] Adrian Hastings, *The Church in Africa, 1450–1950*, Oxford: Clarendon Press, 1994, 265.
[63] Brough, 'The Role', 20–1.
[64] William Percival Johnson, *Nyasa the Great Water: Being a Description of the Lake and the Life of the People*, London: Oxford University Press, 1922, 120.
[65] Scott, *A Cyclopaedic*, 345.
[66] Francis B. Nyamnjoh, 'Introduction: Cannibalism as Food for Thought', in Francis B. Nyamnjoh, ed., *Eating and Being Eaten*, Bamenda: Langaa, 2018.
[67] Harry H. Johnston, *British Central Africa: An Attempt to Give Some Account of a Portion of the Territories under British Influence North of the Zambezi*, London: Methuen & Co, 1897, 447.

no proof'.[68] Just as his dictionary did not reduce the vernacular thought on evil to cannibalism, neither would Scott overlook the possibility of scepticism and doubt in the vernacular ideas of evil.

Despite their rivalry over Chinyanja / Chimang'anja scholarship, Johnson and Maples were, at least *prima facie*, Scott's kindred spirits in their approach to the missionary vocation. Maples was known to call his African followers 'his brothers for Christ's sake'.[69] Johnson also pursued the Church in Africa as 'a true native development and not a foreign intrusion'.[70] 'This must be insisted on', he stated, 'by keeping its thought, its agents, its appointments as entirely native as possible'. Yet it was this insistence on keeping the Church 'as entirely native as possible' that betrayed the difference between the visions Johnson and Scott pursued. An interracial African Church, based on the African–European communion carried in the African vernacular, presupposed mutual recognition and status reversal rather than an urge to keep it 'native'. Indeed, Johnson may have had Blantyre under Scott in mind when he declared, in 1894, that he and his compatriots at the UMCA lived among Africans 'in no sense as chiefs'.[71] 'We never hear any case of law at all', he continued, 'never arbitrate, have no *bwalo* (court) at which native disputes can be brought out'. Although these statements were consistent with the UMCA policy in this period to assume little or no temporal authority,[72] they also expressed an increasingly prevalent missionary position at the turn of the century. Its drift was to separate congregations along racial lines. In so far as Africans were recognized as knowers in the encounter at all, their vernacular thought became folklore rather than philosophy.

A Division of Translation Labour

Beyond the comments in the Mission magazines, Scott, Johnson, and Maples appear to have found few occasions to explore the similarities

---

[68] LWBCA, August–December 1897.   [69] Cited in Brough, 'The Role', 16.
[70] Cited in Bertram Herbert Barnes, *Johnson of Nyasaland: A Study of the Life and Work of William Percival Johnson, D.D., Archdeacon of Nyasa, Missionary Pioneer, 1876–1928*, London: Universities' Mission to Central Africa, 1933, 140.
[71] Cited in Brough, 'The Role', 16.
[72] Roland Oliver, *The Missionary Factor in East Africa*, London: Longmans Green, 1952, 51.

and differences between their visions. Scott's exchanges with other missionaries in matters of vernacular thought were confined to fellow Presbyterians in Malawi, particularly when he pursued 'the unity of the Church European and African' in his work of translation. From his early correspondence it becomes apparent that he had attempted to translate the Old Testament. Writing to Robert Laws of Livingstonia Mission, he indicated that 'I have translated the first 8 pages of Genesis carefully according to the Hebrew, and use it in school'.[73] Laws, who was himself somewhat ahead of Scott in translating, was the recipient of letters describing the tedium and joy of translation, with a hint of rivalry between the translators. Deploying a common vernacular idiom, Scott reported in 1882 that 'I am beginning Genesis, slowly slowly or pang'ono pang'ono – a first experience in Africa'.[74] A division of translation labour had appeared between the two missionaries without either of them specifically proposing such an arrangement. If anything, Scott felt pushed to devote himself to the Old Testament against his own preferences: 'The more I think of it the less can I deny myself the pleasure of New Testament translation.'[75] Yet Laws's initiative demanded praise and the humble acceptance of one's task in 'God's giving'.

I am anxiously awaiting for the N.T. Most gladly would I have translated it. You do not know the joy that such a work is to me and how it fits with my mental and spiritual attitude – and so you may know how I rejoice that God has thus honoured you. As to the O.T., I do not want to do it from any other motive than that it falls to me in God's giving.[76]

In the same letter, Scott went further and asserted the importance of co-operation between the two Scottish missions: 'I do think successful work in Africa depends a great deal upon the union of the various missions. It would simply be disgraceful if we could not unite for God's work.' Although Laws and Scott appear to have worked on their translations with little systematic attempt to co-ordinate them, Laws's proposal to that effect did receive Scott's response that 'I very much like the idea of a combined work at the Bible', adding his usual compliment: 'I note you are getting on well with the New Testament.

---

[73] David Clement Scott to Robert Laws, 3 May 1882, NLS, MS 7903.
[74] Scott to Laws, 14 November 1882.   [75] Scott to Laws, 3 May 1882.
[76] Ibid.

The Old Testament will be most joyful work.' Systematic, collective efforts at translating the entire Bible would have to wait until after Scott's departure when Hetherwick took the initiative to convene an inter-mission committee for the purpose.

In the end, Laws completed his translation well before Scott, who wrote to him to say that 'I am very glad to hear the N.T. is done. I do congratulate you on having been given to do it; and rejoice in your felicity. I can't tell you how great the privilege is and no man can take this honour unto himself.'[77] For his own part, the tedium continued: 'I am going on with the O.T. a little bit.' The need to accommodate Laws had disappeared, however, and Scott felt able to try translating anything he pleased in the Scriptures. Still in 1889, increasingly mired in time-consuming controversies over his leadership and theology, he was pursuing the translation of the whole Bible, writing to James Robertson in Edinburgh that 'I am trying hard to get the Bible translated with an hour a day, but it is slow work'.[78]

In Scott's mission, the Scriptures thus entered the vernacular in pieces rather than as a whole. He used parts of the translated Genesis in the classroom in a manuscript form, while the published Gospels and hymns by no means added up to one coherent story of peoplehood that would galvanize so much of the colonial world in the decades to come. Scott had noted the peculiar sequence by which the Scriptures were being introduced in the unforeseen division of labour between himself and Laws: 'Strange how things are reversed. The new is first now – then comes the old in full understanding.'[79]

Translation Is a World in Itself

Just as the English language had receded into a secondary status in preaching, so too was it to be avoided in Bible translation. Scott announced the publication of more translated Gospels in 1894 by stating that 'it goes without saying, [the Gospels] are translated out of the original tongues, with former translations diligently disregarded'.[80] The pun was on the phrases used in several early-modern English Bibles, such as the words 'the former translations diligently

---

[77] Scott to Laws, n.d.   [78] Scott to Robertson, 10 May 1889.
[79] Scott to Laws, 14 November 1882.   [80] LWBCA, June 1894.

compared and revised' in the title of the King James Version of 1611.[81] While the earlier translations were not without merit, Scott insisted on an 'ineradicable presbyterianism' in which 'every interpretation must be absolutely original'. 'What we claim for this', he added, 'is that the translation has been made under the inspiration of *rhythm* and in the case of each Gospel under the sway of a uniform line of thought and feeling'. Almost a decade earlier, he had already in a private letter anticipated that the Chimang'anja translations would be 'more level to the comprehension of all than the English Bible has ever yet been'.[82] The reason was not an attempt at simplifying the Scriptures, nor the translator's blind obedience to the original. Rather, from the encounter between the biblical languages and Chimang'anja would another 'absolutely original interpretation' arise, one that Scott was inclined to see as superior to the English Bible.

The powers of the African vernacular were, in other words, on a par with the biblical languages. Nothing could be further from Scott's vision than the claim, made with reference to Christian missionaries elsewhere in nineteenth-century southern Africa, that at issue was 'the process of making difference into similarity, or reducing the lower order diversities of the non-European world to the universalistic categories of the West'.[83] 'Translation is a world in itself', Scott wrote in a private letter to describe the daunting, and yet inspiring, task he had set himself to pursue an original interpretation.[84] Far from 'reducing' the vernacular to 'the universalistic categories of the West', Scott promised 'new light thrown upon the interpretation of Scripture'.[85] The study of African languages, he argued, 'promises to add an important quota to the revolution of translation and interpretation, grammar and mode of thought'.[86] Reform rather than reduction was on his mind as he asserted an equivalence between the African vernacular and the biblical languages: 'Hebrew shines in a new light, and even Greek the

---

[81] Naomi Tadmor, *The Social Universe of the English Bible: Scripture, Society, and Culture in Early Modern England*, Cambridge: Cambridge University Press, 2010, 173.
[82] Scott to Robertson, 5 January 1885.
[83] Jean Comaroff and John Comaroff, *Of Revelation and Revolution: Christianity, Colonialism, and Consciousness in South Africa. Volume One*, Chicago, IL: University of Chicago Press. 1991, 221.
[84] Scott to Robertson, 5 January 1885.   [85] LWBCA, June 1894.
[86] Ibid., November 1892.

civilization of the past has closer affinities with Mang'anja than the modern language of today.'[87]

In the 'general guide' to his dictionary, Scott used the biblical languages as his touchstones for comparative linguistics. The different moods of the Chimang'anja verb were 'very like those of the Hebrew verb', while a 'striking' analogy could be observed 'between reduplication in the Greek verb and Mang'anja reduplication'.[88] These and other grammatical features 'point[ed] towards the establishment of a grammatical unity of speech and natural thought in all languages hitherto not recognised'. In other words, rather than being confined to 'a people', Chimang'anja provided insights into human language in general and promised similar revelations about other 'languages hitherto not recognised'.

What Scott and Laws held in common was their ability to see in the African vernacular grammatical elements of the biblical languages from which they translated. Laws admitted that he had to reach beyond the European languages he knew to find anything familiar in Chinyanja syntax and grammar. 'The Hebrew causative', he later wrote, 'was the only thing that threw any light on African languages'.[89] While Laws sought in Hebrew practical guidance for language learning, Scott grew up in an environment where the appreciation of Greek went beyond both practical and biblical associations. It is said of Affleck Scott, his younger brother who joined the Blantyre Mission as a physician, that 'of Latin he was very fond, but he never quite forgave it for being the language of the Romans, whom he detested, as a people who, he thought, subordinated poetry and art to the idea of law and order'.[90] Greek, by contrast, was the language of a people with 'pre-eminence in art and poetry'. His older brother's partiality to poetic expression, along with his propensity to see something universal in the vernacular, would seem to make the comparison to Greek very high praise indeed for Chimang'anja.

As for Hebrew, Scott offered intriguing, if somewhat eccentric, comparisons with the African vernacular.[91] In what was basically an elevation of the noun-class system in Bantu languages into a

---

[87] Scott to Robertson, 5 January 1885.   [88] Scott, *A Cyclopaedic*, xx.
[89] Laws, *Reminiscences*, 129.
[90] W. Henry Rankine, *A Hero of the Dark Continent: Memoir of Rev. Wm. Affleck Scott*, Edinburgh: William Blackwood and Sons, 1896, 19.
[91] LWBCA, April 1897.

phenomenology, Scott observed that 'there are no such things as phenomena pure and simple, each phenomenon is qualified or modified by the good offices of some other phenomenon, or of several'. After giving examples of attributes and demonstratives in the vernacular, Scott wrote, 'This is the main idea of the language and it throws wondrous light upon the essentials and the unity of grammatical idea in the human race'. Hebrew also joined 'one phenomenon to another somewhat similarly', but 'it feels that the important phenomenon, the one qualified, *modifies itself* to serve the qualifying phenomena, that it may be served by them – it serves with girded loins because it is "lord and master"'. Scott emphasized 'a hierarchy of speech in Hebrew under only one Lord' and affirmed that the vernacular gave this hierarchy 'its willing obedience…while at the same time it has room for our Western emphasis and extra emphasis of time, so foreign to Eastern ideas'. Far from being buried in its own narrow sphere, the vernacular linked disparate philosophies into a unity of 'the human race'.

The Social World of the Chimang'anja Bible

The close association, in Scott's thought, between the biblical languages and the African vernacular suggested a relatively uncomplicated process of translation. For late-twentieth-century Bible translators, the versions that the nineteenth-century pioneers in central Africa produced, Hetherwick's committee included, were often all too literal.[92] Yet as Scott's language ideology has already indicated, at issue was not simply word-for-word faithfulness to the original but profound trust in the capacity of the vernacular to express the Word. At the same time, for the interpretation to be new, the Word had to transform language as much as it did lives. Here Scott's approach to translation prefigured a critical insight in early-twentieth-century translation theory – that good translation reforms rather than reproduces language.[93] By seeing the universal in the vernacular, he may

---

[92] Ernst R. Wendland, *Buku Loyera: An Introduction to the New Chichewa Bible Translation*, Blantyre: Christian Literature Association in Malawi, 1998, 24.
[93] Walter Benjamin, 'The Task of the Translator', trans. Harry Zohn, in Rainer Schulte and John Biguenet, eds, *Theories of Translation: An Anthology of Essays from Dryden to Derrida*, Chicago, IL: University of Chicago Press, 1992 [1923], 71–82.

even have prefigured a much more recent insight – that the early-twentieth-century injunction 'to leave our language and go to the other'[94] maintained, in its us–them opposition, the illusion of discrete languages.[95]

In point of fact, it was the New Testament published in 2002 in 'present-day Chichewa' (*Chichewa cha lero*) that used an idiom from the English rather than the Hebrew Bible.[96] The idiom was 'love thy neighbour', which the 2002 version rendered literally as *ukonde mnansi wako monga iwe mwini* (Matt. 19:19). The most comprehensive recent dictionary has defined *mnansi* as an acquaintance, neighbour, relative, or family member,[97] while the monolingual Chinyanja dictionary of 2000 emphasized the connotation of kinship: 'Relative from the same clan' (*munthu wachibale chifukwa chochokera fuko limodzi*).[98] Scott had himself defined *mnansi* in his dictionary as 'a neighbour; an acquaintance; one who is known, or comes from the same "part", not necessarily a friend'.[99] Both Scott's translation of St Matthew's Gospel and the Bible translated by Hetherwick's committee, by contrast, used the Hebrew idiom of friendship instead of neighbour. The verse was *konda mnzako ngati iwe mwini* in Scott's translation and *uzikonda mnzako monga udzikonda iwe mwini* in the committee Bible, both based on *mnzako* as 'your friend'.[100] While the monolingual dictionary does not list it, the recent Chichewa–English dictionary mentions no connotations of neighbourliness or kinship for *mnzako*: your colleague, your friend, your partner, your mate, your contemporary, and your namesake.[101] Scott's dictionary has no

---

[94] José Ortega Y Gasset, 'The Misery and Splendor of Translation', trans. Elizabeth Gamble Müller, in ibid. [1937], 93–112.
[95] Susan Gal, 'The Politics of Translation', *Annual Review of Anthropology*, 44, 2015, 230.
[96] International Bible Society, *Chipangano chatsopano: Mu Chichewa cha lero*, Nairobi: International Bible Society, 2002.
[97] Steven Paas, *Oxford Chichewa–English, English–Chichewa Dictionary*, Oxford: Oxford University Press, 2016, 325.
[98] Centre of Language Studies (University of Malawi), *Mtanthauzira mawu wa Chinyanja*, Blantyre: Dzuka, 2000, 221.
[99] Scott, *A Cyclopaedic*, 365.
[100] National Bible Society of Scotland, *Utenga wa bwino wa St Matthaio*, Edinburgh: National Bible Society of Scotland, 1892; Bible Society of Malawi, *Buku lopatulika ndilo mau a Mulungu*, Blantyre: Bible Society of Malawi, 1992 [1922].
[101] Paas, *Oxford Chichewa*, 328.

mnzako but uses its third-person equivalent *mnzake* to indicate not only friendship and neighbourliness but also enmity: 'One's neighbour and friend or neighbour and enemy, one's fellow man.'[102]

Although Scott thus acknowledged a degree of semantic overlap between neighbours and friends, his translation, continued in the committee Bible, had two important features. The first was its foundation in the Hebrew rather than the English Bible. The idea that the friend, as a 'fellow man', was also one's co-resident in a local community was absent from the Hebrew Bible.[103] When friendship became neighbourliness, so the historian Naomi Tadmor has argued, a semantic shift occurred 'away from universalism and towards parochialism'.[104] Instead of rendering 'the biblical language of interpersonal relations...in the language of manorial and parochial life' in the English Bible,[105] with which Scott was entirely familiar, he exploited the semantic resources of the vernacular to express an idea of universal significance. Here he delivered on his early expectation, shared with his friend in Scotland, that his translation would 'be more level to the comprehension of all than the English Bible has ever yet been'.[106]

The second important feature of Scott's use of *mnzako* rather than *mnansi* was that the universal could also become locally plausible in its historical specificity. Just as the English idiom suited the early-modern English life in local communities, so too did *mnzako* apply to a social world in which slaves, refugees, long-distance traders, and new political constellations made the prospect of a stable neighbourhood life somewhat remote. Moreover, true to his commitment to translation as a creative process aimed at reforming language, Scott extended the Hebrew original by deploying an idiom that had not only amity but also enmity within its semantic range. It corresponded well to a historical situation in which transforming one's enemy into one's friend – whether through shared Christian faith or other forms of alliance – was often an urgent task.

Slaves and Servants

In the same social world, however, the apparently egalitarian connotations of friendship had various kinds of hierarchical relationships as

---

[102] Scott, *A Cyclopaedic*, 367. [103] Tadmor, *The Social Universe*, 26.
[104] Ibid. [105] Ibid., 29. [106] Scott to Robertson, 5 January 1885.

their ever-present counterparts. Matt 19:19 also urges respect for one's father and mother – *lemekeza atate ndi amako* in Scott's translation, *lemekeza atate wako ndi amako* in the committee Bible. Of particular interest is the parable of the labourers' wages in Matt 20:1–16. Here Scott's translation entered a social world in which the questions of land and labour were becoming acutely controversial. By 1892, the year of its publication, he and his colleagues at the Blantyre Mission were embroiled in challenging some of the methods by which White farmers were acquiring agricultural land and labour (see Chapter 6).

In the broader Protestant context of the nineteenth century, the parable's tale of a landowner hiring casual labour had become an allegory less for obedience to God than for the equality of grace in God's giving.[107] It is the parable in which the words 'the last shall be the first' describe how the poor who were hired last and worked a shorter day than their richer colleagues received the same pay as everyone else. In a reading of the parable that may shed light on its uses in nineteenth-century central Africa, the rich are not to assume that they have rights over and above the poor.[108] They need to be capable of rejoicing when God allows the poor to take precedence over those who have wealth.

'The last shall be the first' was, as seen in the previous chapter, what Scott wrote in his reflections on the curse of Ham and on status reversals between Black and White. In St Matthew's Gospel, he translated the words as *omalizira adzakala oyamba, ndipo oyamba adzakala omarizira*, translated in a virtually identical way in the committee Bible. Curiously, however, Scott added to this sixteenth verse of Matt 20 the words 'for many are called, but few are chosen' (*pakuti ali ambiri oitanidwa koma ang'ono osankidwa*). Both the committee Bible and the new translation in 2002 had those words where they normally are in the Bible, the fourteenth verse of Matt 22. There they appear in the parable about a wedding feast in which the rejection of the wedding invitation serves as an allegory for rejecting the gospel. Scott left no explanation as to why he took the liberty of moving the words in this way. Although he did also repeat them in Matt 22:14, his decision

---

[107] Jacques Ellul, *On Freedom, Love, and Power*, trans. Willem H. Vanderburg, Toronto: University of Toronto Press, 2010, 180.
[108] Ibid., 185.

added a remarkable degree of poetic licence to the creativity of translation.

Scott's poetic licence was governed by both the Hebrew Bible and the social world in which he worked. Another example is the mention of slavery in the Scriptures. The Hebrew word for slave recurs 799 times in the Bible, but the early-modern English translations, the King James Version of 1611 at their apex, had deployed the word for servant rather than slave.[109] These translations were consistent with a social world in which 'slave' had become a term of contempt. As Tadmor has argued, 'sweeping, long-term, and potentially life-long relationships of submission were translated in terms of interpersonal contract'. No doubt the Hebrew concept allowed for enough semantic range to make the shift from 'slave' to 'servant' unremarkable in certain respects.[110] Yet the semantic shift did coincide with historical transformations specific to early modern England, where life-cycle transitions from service to mastership were becoming harder to attain and were being replaced by class differences.[111] In late-nineteenth-century central Africa, by contrast, slavery continued to be a potent possibility despite efforts to eradicate it. It also provided a compelling idiom when Scott raised the spectre of a 'new slavery' in the alienation of land by White interests (see Chapter 6).

Into that social world Scott introduced the biblical concept of slave, 'duly disregarding' the authoritative English translations. Where the King James Version had translated Matt 20:26–27, for example, as 'whosoever will be chief among you, let him be your servant', Scott's translation deployed *kapolo*, the most common Chimang'anja word for slave: *Maka iye amene ali ense angafune kukala wamkulu wakupambana mwa inu adzakala kapolo wakutumika wanu*. In a literal English rendition, this passage stated that 'whoever wanted to be the greatest among you will be your slave sent out for tasks'. Scott used the verb *kutumika*, which his dictionary defined as 'to be able to be sent, to be one who is sent'.[112] Children were the typical subjects of such commands, but by deploying *kapolo*, Scott detached the reversal depicted in the passage from a phase in the life cycle to emphasize its permanence. In the seventeenth and eighteenth centuries, on the other hand, those who had grown accustomed to a biblical language of

---

[109] Tadmor, *The Social Universe*, 87–9.   [110] Ibid., 100–1.   [111] Ibid., 107.
[112] Scott, *A Cyclopaedic*, 638.

service needed other idioms for the slavery they instituted in the New World.[113] The curse of Ham provided the idea of permanent inferiority, oblivious to the reversals that Scott, inspired by the Hebrew Bible and the African vernacular, found so apposite in nineteenth-century central Africa.

The Struggle Begins

Peoplehood was, patently, only one of the interpretative possibilities the Bible presented in Africa, however important it would eventually be to ethno-nationalist projects. The inspiration it provided at the turn of the century varied and was inseparable from the controversies that specific historical circumstances produced. While Scott's translations of the Hebrew idioms of friendship and slavery attended to a political and economic world beset by dislocation and unfreedom, other preoccupations could prove more salient elsewhere. Striving towards a new economic and political order with their elders, young Kikuyu men in Kenya in the early twentieth century, for example, found in the New Testament 'a vernacular phrasebook of generational debate'.[114]

What the African recipients of Scott's translations derived from them was not, of course, determined by the translations alone. A whole host of issues could be debated as they circulated in text and through sermons. Little is known about African debates that may have drawn on these specific translations, but the interest here is the influence of the African vernacular on Scott's own thought. As seen in the previous chapter, he came to develop his vision for the African Church only after personal experiences of life in central Africa. Friendship, chiefly authority, and the proceedings of the *mlandu* deliberations all paved the way for an appreciation of the vernacular in turbulent political circumstances. Grammatical commonalities between the biblical languages and the African vernacular were merely an aspect of their philosophical and theological equivalence. At once universal and vernacular, Chimang'anja brought the Gospels to life by expressing them in the idioms of late-nineteenth-century central Africa.

---

[113] Tadmor, *The Social Universe*, 114.
[114] Derek R. Peterson, *Creative Writing: Translation, Bookkeeping, and the Work of Imagination in Colonial Kenya*, Portsmouth, NH: Heinemann, 2004, 66.

Unbeknown to Scott, Jacques-François Roger, the French governor of the Senegal colony in the early nineteenth century, had pursued linguistic work on Wolof as a contribution to 'an argument against the slave trade, on grounds of a fundamental human equality revealed in language'.[115] Yet a shift from 'egalitarian universalism' to an emphasis on 'race' occurred already by the mid-century in Parisian theological and linguistic circles.[116] Views influenced by German and Danish philologists came to emphasize a link between language and the spirit of a people, while Parisian scholars had seen language as the product of analytical intelligence common to all human beings. The ripples of a similar process reached Blantyre in the aftermath of Scott's departure as Hetherwick identified the vernacular with peoplehood (see Chapter 9).

Both Roger and Scott may have been heirs to an Enlightenment tradition in Europe, but the missionary and colonial situation in which Scott operated offered little philosophical impetus beyond the Protestant imperative to learn vernacular languages for proselytization. Scott's prime impetus came from the social world of the African vernacular itself. It was an impetus that would grow into a struggle for justice when it became apparent that his fellow Europeans were not prepared to live and learn in accordance with his vision. Scott's struggle, as the following chapters show, took place on several other planes than the philosophical or the theological, but it never lost sight of what he had learned from the African vernacular.

[115] Irvine, 'Mastering', 30.   [116] Ibid., 36.

5 | *Frightful Libel upon Humanity*

On his first journey to Africa in 1883, Alexander Hetherwick found himself in stimulating company. On board the steamer that had left the Egyptian port of Aden were fellow missionary reinforcements for the Livingstonia Mission as well as Henry Henderson, the so-called founder of the Blantyre Mission returning from furlough.[1] While Henderson's tales of searching for the mission site would summon some of the physical and political features of the territory that the young missionary was about to enter, another passenger proved more influential. He impressed upon Hetherwick an idea about the fundamental divide between Black and White. This passenger was Henry Drummond, a novice in Africa like Hetherwick but uninhibited in his observations and opinions.

Drummond was on board courtesy of a few wealthy Glaswegian Christians who wanted to know more of the prospects for the African Lakes Company beyond the Scottish missionary influence.[2] A lecturer since 1878 and, from 1884, professor in Natural Science at the Free Church College in Glasgow,[3] Drummond was on a scientific as much as commercial expedition. He and Hetherwick continued their journey together after landing on the continent, and it was then, in the company of African porters, that the idea of a high cognitive wall between White and Black people came upon the two Scotsmen. 'A burly native porter' caught their attention for the apparent ease with which he

---

[1] William P. Livingstone, *A Prince of Missionaries: The Rev. Alexander Hetherwick of Blantyre, Central Africa*, London: James Clarke, 1931, 15–16.
[2] Thomas E. Corts, 'Introduction: Who Was Henry Drummond?', in Thomas E. Corts, ed., *Henry Drummond: A Perpetual Benediction*, Edinburgh: T. & T. Clark, 1999, xxviii.
[3] Andrew L. Drummond and James Bulloch, *The Church in Late Victorian Scotland 1874–1900*, Edinburgh: The Saint Andrew Press, 1978, 27.

103

carried his load under the sweltering African sun.[4] Hetherwick described the moment in these words:

> Sinewy and lithe in his every movement and gesture, he gaily moved ahead of us while the perspiration poured from head and shoulders in trickling beads over chest and arms. Happy and carefree he appeared to us as he tramped along singing his chant in a sustained monotone for mile after mile through that hot August noonday. Stopping for a moment in his march, Drummond turned to me and said: 'I would give all I possess to get inside that fellow for just half an hour.'[5]

The Scotsmen may have made it inside Africa, but getting inside the African mind was the final frontier that would elude Hetherwick for all of his missionary life (Chapter 9). Drummond's sojourn in Africa, on the other hand, lasted for only ten months, but it resulted in *Tropical Africa*, a volume of travel writing and observation on people, plants, and animals.[6] Although he had not been invited by the Blantyre and Livingstonia missionaries, he enjoyed their hospitality and returned the favours with some well-chosen words in his book. 'Towards the sunset the following evening our caravan filed into Blantyre', he eulogized.[7] 'On the beauty and interest of this ideal mission I shall not dwell. But if anyone wishes to find out what can be done with the virgin African, what can be done by broad and practical missionary methods, let him visit the Rev. D. Clement Scott and his friends at Blantyre.' Bearing in mind that the Blantyre atrocities were still fresh in the memory of Scotland's reading public, Drummond had this to add:

> Travellers have been pleased to say unkind things of missionaries. That they are sometimes right, I will not question. But I will say of the Livingstonia missionaries, and of the Blantyre missionaries, and count it an honour to say it, that they are brave, efficient, single-hearted men, who need our sympathy more than we know, and are equally above our criticism and our praise.[8]

David Clement Scott read *Tropical Africa* upon its publication but reserved his comments on it to a private letter to his friend in Edinburgh. 'I have never read such nonsense as Drummond's book',

---

[4] Alexander Hetherwick, *The Gospel and The African*, Edinburgh: T. & T. Clark, 1932, 2.
[5] Ibid.
[6] Henry Drummond, *Tropical Africa*, London: Hodder and Stoughton, 1888.
[7] Ibid., 24.   [8] Ibid., 42.

he confided in James Robertson.[9] 'It is frightful libel upon humanity. I would write but he praises the mission so much that one's mouth is shut, and one's time is so limited.' Pragmatism trumped principle on this rare occasion of self-censorship in Scott's thought. The 'frightful libel upon humanity' stood to be corrected in the practice of Scott's vision, in the conviction that the mission was founded on common humanity between the missionaries and their African interlocutors. Scott's language ideology, as described in the previous chapter, contained a vigorous assertion of that common humanity. While late-twentieth-century social scientists would come to question 'humanity' as a notion of any consequence in progressive politics, Scott lived in an era when its true scope was open to debate – and to openly racist efforts to restrict the scope. It is, therefore, instructive to consider what the 'frightful libel' in *Tropical Africa* may have been so as to bring into starker relief the intellectual, spiritual, and political stakes in Scott's visionary practice.

Half-Humanity

The early pages of *Tropical Africa* were particularly brazen, perhaps in part to entice its public back home to read further. 'It is a wonderful thing to look at this weird world of human beings', Drummond stated early on, 'half animal half children, wholly savage and wholly heathen'.[10] So 'weird' was the world that Drummond entered with his reader that even the human element in its creatures was more child than adult. No joyful curiosity appeared possible, however, in the first introduction to Black Africa at Zanzibar, the hub for preparing expeditions into the interior. 'Oriental in its appearance, Mohameddan in its religion, Arabian in its morals, this cesspool of wickedness is a fit capital for the Dark Continent.'[11] Drummond reported that consensus prevailed among European travellers in Africa that 'for laziness, ugliness, stupidness, and wickedness, these men are not to be matched on any continent in the world'. He conveyed despair at 'seeing them transgress every commandment in turn before your eyes – and you yourself being powerless to check them except by a wholesale breach of the sixth'.[12]

---

[9] David Clement Scott to James Robertson, 19 October 1888, EUL, Gen. 717-10.
[10] Drummond, *Tropical Africa*, 4.   [11] Ibid., 5.   [12] Ibid., 6.

Once he reached the interior and began his proper expedition, Drummond's tone became that of a Christian scientist interested in evolution. 'To the ignorant these men are animals; but the eye of evolution looks on them with kindlier and more instructed sense', he assured the reader.[13] 'They are what we were once; possibly they may become what we are now.' This possibility – the achievement of civilization and thus full humanity – was present in Africans' existing institutions. In the drum they had their 'national musical instrument'; in the 'fear of evil spirits', their religion; and in the 'council of headmen', their 'chamber of justice'. Yet evolution, if not accelerated by Christianity and commerce, would be slow. For one thing, they appeared to have no history: 'No one knows exactly who these people are…even their names are unknown, and their languages – for there are many – are unintelligible.'[14] For another, their way of life – marked by idleness punctuated only by agricultural work of the simplest kind – made a decidedly unfavourable impression on the observer. 'I have tried to think of something else that these people habitually do, but their vacuous life leaves nothing more to tell.'[15]

If the African way of life was 'weird' and 'vacuous' to Drummond, he was moved to wonder why Africans allowed him to wander amongst them with no apparent risk of murder or robbery. The explanation lay in what the White man possessed: 'It is his moral power, his education, his civilisation.'[16] 'To the African the white man is a supreme being. His commonest acts are miracles; his clothes, his guns, his cooking utensils are supernatural…Everywhere his word is law.' Zanzibar, where breaching the sixth commandment had crossed his mind, seemed rather far away at this point in Drummond's expedition. The obverse of the White man's moral power was, of course, 'an unprincipled man', who exploited this awe and admiration so as to 'drain a country of its ivory – the only native wealth'.[17] Evolution could always give way to degeneration if not checked by high Christian morals and character-building activities.[18]

---

[13] Ibid., 60. [14] Ibid., 58. [15] Ibid., 59. [16] Ibid., 105. [17] Ibid., 106.
[18] Markku Hokkanen and J. A. Mangan, 'Further Variations on a Theme: The Games Ethic Further Adapted – Scottish Moral Missionaries and Muscular Christians in Malawi', *The International Journal of the History of Sport*, 23 (8), 2006, 1261–2.

While *Tropical Africa* appears to hold some interest to the twenty-first-century student of insect life,[19] such is its depiction of African people that Scott's comment on its libellous content seems warranted. Yet it occasioned less public interest and response than Drummond's other writings did, not least *Natural Law in the Spiritual World*, which had been published shortly before his journey to Africa[20] and which catapulted him into a 'subject of newspaper reviews, cartoon drawings, and controversy' during his absence from Scotland.[21] At the end of the twentieth century, an imagery uncannily similar to what Drummond himself may have used suggested that upon his return from Africa, 'he stepped from darkness into the brilliant light of sudden fame'.[22] No doubt this fame ensured a broad readership for *Tropical Africa*, but it was Drummond's ability to reconcile science and religion that struck a chord with the reading public's anxiety over the new theories of evolution.[23] Drummond's view on evolution offered optimism where a godless scheme was feared to be taking hold. It is ironic that the same author who wrote libellous prose about Africans was also able to posit altruism as the key principle of evolution. In *The Ascent of Man*, based on the Lowell Lectures he delivered in the United States in 1893, he named the principle as The Struggle for the Life of Others, declaring that 'the direct, personal, gratuitous, unrewarded help of another creature is a condition of existence'.[24] The principle extended to virtually all living things: 'Even in the lowliest world of plants the labours of Maternity begin.'

Such reassuring sentiments do little to nuance the convictions Drummond held during his African expedition. On the contrary, this expedition, along with an even shorter visit to Australia and South-East Asia in 1890, allowed him to lecture on evolution with particular

---

[19] Brian Morris, *An Environmental History of Southern Malawi*, New York: Palgrave Macmillan, 2016, 13–46.
[20] Henry Drummond, *Natural Law in the Spiritual World*, London: Hodder and Stoughton, 1883.
[21] Thomas E. Corts and Marla Haas Corts, 'Henry Drummond: From Scotland to America with Love', in Thomas E. Corts, ed., *Henry Drummond: A Perpetual Benediction*, Edinburgh: T. & T. Clark, 1999, 76.
[22] Ibid.
[23] Markku Hokkanen, *Medicine and Scottish Missionaries in the Northern Malawi Region 1875–1830: Quests for Health in a Colonial Society*, New York: Edwin Mellen Press, 2007, 115–18.
[24] Henry Drummond, *The Lowell Lectures on the Ascent of Man*, London: Hodder and Stoughton, 1894, 23.

authority. 'No one should pronounce upon the Evolution of Mind till he has seen a savage', he challenged.[25] Not any 'savage' would do – Drummond was dismissive about 'the show savage of an Australian town-...the quay Kaffir of a South African port...the Reservation Indian of a Western State'.[26] Drummond insisted, with the gravitas of first-hand experience, on 'the savage as his is in reality, and as he may be seen to-day by any who care to look upon so weird a spectacle'. The topic of the mind presented an opportunity to elaborate on what had vexed him upon his arrival in Africa. While Drummond beheld 'the half-finished product from which humanity [had] been evolved', he drew attention to 'the ceaseless mystery of his thoughts'.[27] Examples from Southern Pacific inspired the author in much the same way as Africans did to 'realize the gulf between himself and them' and 'the utter impossibility of framing to himself an image of the mental world of men and women whose only world is this'.[28]

One reason why the problem of accessing other minds exercised Drummond may have been his early renown for mesmerism. He is known to have practised hypnotism during his student days.[29] Indeed, he entertained at least once his fellow Scotsmen in this vein during his central African expedition, only to fail in his efforts to read the mind of Robert Laws of Livingstonia.[30] Where the likes of Laws simply possessed 'a willpower stronger than [Drummond's] own', the impenetrable minds of Africans marked a major divide in the concept of humanity.

Drummond's thoughts appeared to meet a demand. Already a bestselling author, he saw *The Ascension of Man* selling 10,000 copies within a year.[31] The commercial success followed the enormous interest in his Lowell Lectures in Boston, where 'for every person who attended, ten people were turned away', forcing him 'to give each lecture a second time to a second audience'.[32] At the same time, the book was severely criticized by scientists and theologians alike.[33] The late-twentieth-century verdict that he was 'an amateur and a dilettante,

---

[25] Ibid., 180. [26] Ibid., 180–1. [27] Ibid. [28] Ibid., 182.
[29] James R. Moore, 'Evangelicals and Evolution: Henry Drummond, Herbert Spencer, and the Naturalisation of the Spiritual World', *Scottish Journal of Theology*, 38 (3), 1985, 393.
[30] Livingstone, *A Prince of Missionaries*, 32.
[31] Moore, 'Evangelicals and Evolution', 386.
[32] Corts and Corts, 'Henry Drummond', 83.
[33] David W. Bebbington, 'Henry Drummond, Evangelicalism and Science', in Thomas E. Corts, ed., *Henry Drummond: A Perpetual Benediction*, Edinburgh: T. & T. Clark, 1999, 37–8.

of no importance as scientist or theologian'[34] echoed these criticisms a hundred years earlier, but at issue was the principle of altruism in evolution rather than the fundamental divide in humanity that Drummond's theory entailed. The chapter on the evolution of the mind did become the focus of a critique published in the magazine of the Universities' Mission to Central Africa, an Anglican mission at Lake Malawi.[35] Instead of unsettling the hierarchy in civilization and cognitive capacities that Drummond had asserted, the critique merely emphasized the need for a conducive environment: 'It is this environment in its highest and best sense which, as missionaries, we are creating for central Africa, by setting up there the Kingdom of God and His Christ.'

Histories of Humanity

It is remarkable that no critical intent informed Hetherwick's evocation of Drummond's thought at the dawn of the 1930s when the scope of humanity was freshly in question in Europe. Equally remarkable is how, in a more recent evaluation of Drummond's thought, his African expedition is remembered for his 'passionate commitment to the antislavery cause'.[36] Rarely has the postcolonial indictment, quoted at the beginning of this book, that 'the attack on slavery represented hatred of a concept rather than love of its victims' been more appropriate than in Drummond's case.[37]

David Clement Scott, as has already been seen in his reflections on the curse of Ham, was inclined to assert status reversals where public figures such as Drummond emphasized White superiority. In Scott's thought on slavery, the 'love of its victims' grew into what Andrew Ross has called 'a daring theological concept'.[38] The enslaved African demanded recognition not as a measure of the moral progress that the British pursued in the world but as the figure of the risen Christ. Far

---

[34] Drummond and Bulloch, *The Church*, 26.
[35] *Central Africa*, Volume 12, 1894, retrieved from British Online Archives, https://microform.digital/boa/
[36] Bebbington, 'Henry Drummond', 23.
[37] H. Alan C. Cairns: *Prelude to Imperialism: British Reactions to Central African Society 1840–1890*, London: Routledge & Kegan Paul, 1965, 140.
[38] Andrew C. Ross, *Blantyre Mission and the Making of Modern Malawi*, Blantyre: Christian Literature Association of Malawi, 1996, 129.

from being morally superior, the powers of Europe had to make their sacrifices to atone for what Scott came to call in 1897 their 'selfishness, meanness, falsehoods, lusts, and the whole burden of sins'.[39] In the 1889 call to arms to combat slave trade, Scott's concept of humanity played as central a role as in his later insistence on 'a proper doctrine of humanity'. Calling on different European powers, he was prepared to de-emphasize his own particular vantage point: 'The basis is wider than Protestantism, it is humanity, it is the Church of Christ.'[40]

Scott's doctrine of humanity was ineluctably Christian, even if it declined to have Protestantism as its sole paradigm. It reveals a late-nineteenth-century alternative to the concept of humanity that Drummond popularized. It was a concept of humanity in which those assuming the authority to define it did not place themselves at the apotheosis of the construct of their own creation. On the contrary, the figure of the risen Christ inspired an altogether more searching look at one's own complicity in hindering the humanity of others. In Scott's appreciation of language and the many aspects of life it carried lay another contrast to Drummond's condescending remarks on the African ways of life. Humanity in Africa had no 'half animal, half child' nature to impede it; nor did its flourishing simply await the introduction of European and Christian civilization. Just as Africans had moral, spiritual, and political resources, so too did Europe's exploitative manoeuvres cast a shadow of doubt over its own form of civilization.

Both Scott and Drummond came to describe their time in Africa in the idiom of education, but their pedagogies were worlds apart. A spectator in 'the weird world of human beings', Drummond felt that 'it is an education to see this sight – an education in the meaning and history of Man'.[41] Scott, as mentioned, was in the habit of insisting to every newcomer from Europe that 'Africa is an education; here you come to school again'.[42] In another comment, he maintained that 'it is a liberal education to get to understand the African, and European blunders and failures in Africa chiefly arise from want of this'.[43] Just as

---

[39] *Life and Work in British Central Africa* (LWBCA), August–December 1897.
[40] Ibid., June 1889. [41] Drummond, *Tropical Africa*, 4.
[42] Alexander Hetherwick, *The Romance of Blantyre; How Livingstone's Dream Came True*, Edinburgh: Lassodie Press, 1931, 155.
[43] LWBCA, November 1892.

Africa demanded sacrifices from the European powers, so too did it urge each European who wished to spend time there to embrace humility and the will to learn.

Drummond and Scott were bound to be influenced by both the universalism and the persistent division of humanity into 'us' and 'others' in relation to progress in the Scottish Enlightenment.[44] Yet their differences reveal some of the contrasting directions to which this influence could develop. The imagery in David Livingstone's, and subsequently in Drummond's,[45] description of the slave trade as 'the open sore of the world' would become a clichéd rallying cry for combating Africa's ills, but the twentieth century taught critics to be wary of appeals to abstract humanity. As Hannah Arendt saw particularly clearly, the issue was not simply the need to be a citizen to have the rights available to everyone by virtue of their being human.[46] In the midst of the horrors of the twentieth-century world wars, the catastrophic consequences of being 'merely' human would become evident when some people did not qualify for membership in a political community. 'When you are only human and nothing else', as a more recent comment puts it, 'then, and only then, can you be expelled from humanity itself'.[47]

For critics, a distinction had been drawn between two types of life, *bio* and *zoe*, a life with history and a bare life.[48] It is a distinction that has haunted the growing field of humanitarian assistance – the inequality of lives that appeals to abstract humanity can do little to ameliorate.[49] Drummond may have been scandalized by the evil trade in humans, but so abstract – and so self-serving – was his indignation that it never allowed him to regard Africans as fully human with

---

[44] Silvia Sebastiani, *The Scottish Enlightenment: Race, Gender, and the Limits of Progress*, New York: Palgrave Macmillan, 2013, 133.
[45] Drummond, *Tropical Africa*, preface.
[46] Hannah Arendt, *The Origins of Totalitarianism*, New York: Harcourt Brace, 1973 [1951].
[47] Ilana Feldman and Miriam Ticktin, 'Introduction: Government and Humanity', in Ilana Feldman and Miriam Ticktin, eds, *In the Name of Humanity: The Government of Care and Threat*, Durham NC: Duke University Press, 2010, 7.
[48] Giorgio Agamben, *Homo Sacer: Sovereign Power and Bare Life*, trans. D. Heller-Roazen, Stanford, CA: Stanford University Press, 1998.
[49] Didier Fassin, 'Inequality of Lives, Hierarchies of Humanity: Moral Constraints and Ethical Dilemmas of Humanitarianism', in Ilana Feldman and Miriam Ticktin, eds, *In the Name of Humanity: The Government of Care and Threat*, Durham, NC: Duke University Press, 2010, 239.

histories of their own. Scott, on the other hand, had in his idea of Christianity a means by which common humanity – including the burdens it placed on those in power – could be envisaged.

The Unity of Race and Spirit

It was a Christianity with as much African as European complexion. Scott's practice of interracial services advanced this conviction, as did his startling admission, already cited, that 'the native may be saved without us, but we doubt if we here can be saved without the native'.[50] While his 'Africa is an education' maxim expected Europeans to prepare themselves for personal transformation, Scott nevertheless was a missionary seeking to increase the number of Africans in his church. The Church of Scotland eventually came to doubt his liturgical as well as practical orientations, but Scott never expressed doubt about the theological roots of his vocation in Africa. Local customs at odds with his idea of Christianity had to be modified or eradicated altogether. Yet he differed from his missionary contemporaries and successors in Malawi in important respects.

Scott did not evoke African history in order to invent traditions that would either provide pretexts to govern distinct 'peoples' or serve as charters for tribal pride and cohesion.[51] Instead, not only did the Africans at and around the Mission have histories that pre-dated the arrival of Europeans, those histories would be, once written, entirely on a par with the heroic histories that Europeans told themselves. 'The history of the Yao conquest', Scott offered as an example, 'the conquering chiefs, the divisions of the conquered land, are as clearly written in the memories of the old men round about us, as was the Hiad upon the heart of the Homeric bard'.[52] Epic rather than tribal history would be the result of rendering those memories in writing: 'Kaffir history would, if it were written out, be a Kaffir epic as truly as

---

[50] LWBCA, December 1891.
[51] Terence Ranger, 'The Invention of Tradition in Colonial Africa', in Eric J. Hobsbawm and Terence O. Ranger, eds, *The Invention of Tradition*, Cambridge: Cambridge University Press, 1983; Terence Ranger, 'The Invention of Tradition Revisited: The Case of Africa', in Terence Ranger and O. Vaughan, eds, *Legitimacy and the State in Twentieth Century Africa*, London: Macmillan, 1993; Thomas Spear, 'Neo-traditionalism and the Limits of Invention in British Colonial Africa', *Journal of African History*, 44 (1), 2003, 3–27.
[52] LWBCA, January 1893.

the Sagas of the north or the poem of Camoens were the pride of birth to German or Portuguese.'

Scott made these remarks to preface his defence of Africans' land rights. Yet while history thus evoked could justify taking African interests seriously, Africans had themselves seen enough to start commenting on the differences between Black and White ways of life. By 1890, Scott had become accustomed to being told in some court cases that the culprit may have been a witch (*mfiti*), their murderous crime enshrouded in secrecy. 'We deny such secret medicine power and call the accuser of the so-called *mfiti* murderer.'[53] Intrinsic to Scott's denial was not simply a contrast between science and superstition – or even between Christianity and paganism. 'The native appeal to tradition is met by our appeal to tradition antecedent and the unity of race.' Aware of the racism among some of those who might read his words, he added: 'Even if unity of descent should by some be denied we appeal to unity of spirit.' Far from proving the ultimate separation of Black from White, witchcraft accusations called for a tradition in which the unity of race and spirit could be affirmed.

In more innocuous examples of local custom, such as beer drinking or late-night dancing, Scott distinguished himself from other Protestant missionaries by warning against confronting them with such vigour that it would only antagonize Black and White.[54] He could see beauty in the offering of beer on ritual occasions before a single-minded condemnation of all uses of alcohol became the hallmark of Presbyterianism in Malawi.[55] As for the *unyago* dances that marked Yao girls' initiation ceremonies, Scott's entry in the Mission journal in 1889 carried a brief note on 'dance going on at Kapeni's. Propose going early tomorrow – if God will – to stop it'.[56] The Mission magazine gave the following month a fuller account of the approach taken. Once Chief Kapeni had been located, the 'opportunity was afforded of speaking peaceably to the crowds that gathered close round'.[57] Scott made two immediate observations to support his request for bringing the dances to a halt. On one hand, they were taking place on a Sunday. On the other, 'the taking of Mission boys

---

[53] Ibid., July 1890.   [54] Ibid., August 1889.
[55] Todd Statham, 'Teetotalism in Malawian Protestantism: Missionary Origins, African Appropriation', *Studies in World Christianity*, 21 (2), 2015, 165.
[56] The Blantyre Mission Journal, 27 July 1889, NLS, Acc 9218.
[57] LWBCA, August 1889.

was made a special ground for interference'. As such, he claimed some of the participants – likely to include girls as well as boys – as citizens of the Mission and made the dances impossible to reconcile with the rights and duties of that particular membership. Yet unlike many other Christian missionaries somewhat later in the region, such as a White Father of the Catholic Church in central Malawi who stormed into dances to slash the drums in 1918,[58] Scott did adopt a conciliatory tone to persuade participants to accept transformation. 'No good whatever', he pointed out, 'is done by rudely rushing in and overthrowing conscientious things (however dark the conscience that does them) which have held ground for centuries'. Instead, participants 'are compelled by gentleness rather than silenced by fear'.[59]

Music Lessons

Scott's objections to certain dances did not prevent him from seeing (or hearing) in music another instance of common humanity. Scott was, Hetherwick recalled, 'a skilled musician, both as vocalist and organist'.[60] This training in music enabled him to analyze African music for its similarities and differences vis-à-vis European music. The first observation he made in his 1893 article entitled 'Stray Notes from African Music', however, was on the importance of adopting the stance of a learner.[61] 'Count the African a revelation from heaven; believe there are volumes he can teach you', Scott urged on the pages of another Universities' Mission magazine published in central Africa. Reversal was again on his mind: 'You will be much nearer the truth than if you enter Africa with the idea that you are a revelation to them' – to which he added wryly, 'So you are probably – of a kind'. Addressing his readers as an 'audience of savants', he was anxious to establish the African as an authority on knowledge about Africa.

He has peered into every dark stream bed, searched every rock, cranny, and tree hole, and is better fitted than any one [sic] else to teach a booted and beleathered civilization what this land is, and what is its name, than any expeditioner from Kaiser or from Kew.

---

[58] Ian Linden with Jane Linden, *Catholics, Peasants, and Chewa Resistance in Nyasaland, 1889–1939*, London: Heinemann, 1974, 122.
[59] LWBCA, August 1889.   [60] Hetherwick, *The Romance of Blantyre*, 36.
[61] *The Nyasa News*, August 1893.

The contrast could not be starker to Drummond's expeditioner, who claimed that Africans had neither history nor known names. The contrast grew starker still when Scott found in aspects of music the grounds for asserting common humanity. Rhythm, for example, called forth unity: 'It is strange that 3 + 1 = 4 should be a fundamental rhythm in the three great races of the earth.' Aware that his 'audience of savants' could be reluctant to admit Africans among the great races, Scott assured them with added emphasis that 'Africa will bear its part, and prove its unity with us, as *one of the three*'. After all, 'an African dances as other human beings do, to music; not as lambs which dance to sunlight alone'. The very first sentence used striking imagery to convey the relationship between rhythm and revelation: 'The African is a prophet of God for our civilization down to the tips of his toes.'

As with rhythm, so with gamut – the African 'has a gamut very like our own'. Yet unity was no recipe for obliterating differences. The topic of semitones inspired Scott to offer one of his comparisons in which the European civilization by no means had the monopoly of the good and the beautiful. European semitones were artificial, adjusted to musical devices such as piano and harmonium.

The African gamut is *natural*, and ours is *artificial*: so is African language, so are its customs; and we, with our leather shoes, our stiff cut breeches, our gaiters, and tall hats, come with our miserable devices, of which we are so proud, to bind the beauty of divine naturalness, and make the people and their song, a huddled holocaust for scientific barbarity.

The 'savants' able to read such lines hardly expected to find them in a mission magazine, but Scott had even more to say about the relationship between music and science. 'I do not know, it seems horrible to say it', he prefaced his next provocation, 'whether the beauties of Beethoven and of Bach are not simply scientific beauty, a very high type (before the angels) of vulgar self-love after all'. It was not simply the naturalness of African music that Scott proceeded to demonstrate through examples of song and dance in various contexts. It was the idea of freedom that he ended with, freedom both in African music and among those who came to Africa to learn: 'It is freedom which is the subtle charm which recalls all men to Africa who have "once drunk of its water": and the liberty comes to those best who by the "enthusiasm of humanity" have found therein the Christ of God.'

The monotone of African chanting that Hetherwick evoked in his reflections on the divide between European and African minds had all the colour and complexity in Scott's appreciation of freedom. In song, 'the varieties of expression are infinite', just as 'every song is an epos, a fugue, a progress, in its interlacing and beat, as in its theme'. If it took the 'enthusiasm of humanity' to recognize such features in African life, Scott had more of it than most Europeans writing about central Africa at the end of the nineteenth century. To see in the African 'a prophet of God for our civilization' required enthusiasm and the recognition of freedom. At the same time, precisely because the African was knowable through his or her actual practices and not as an object of theological wonder, it was also necessary to identify practices inimical to that prophetic pledge.

Poisonous Custom

The *mwavi* poison ordeal presented one of the most uncompromising instances in which the missionary could only reject local practice. As Scott described it in his dictionary, *mwavi* (*mwabvi* in his spelling) was concocted from tree bark and water and given as a drink to those who stood suspected of some crime, typically witchcraft.[62] According to Scott, 'the poison is drunk amid a great concourse of people, and as some time lapses between the drinking and the effects, the one who has drunk it sits waiting till he vomit or die. If he vomit he is clear; if he die he is supposed to be guilty, and his body is mutilated and cast out'. Despite the gendered pronoun in Scott's description, *mwavi* was administered on women as well as men. Just as suspicions and accusations of witchcraft appeared to increase during the colonial period, rather than being a timeless superstition,[63] so too did Scott encounter *mwavi* during a time of crisis. While the ordeal had been frequently used in the 1830s before the Ngoni invasions and the expansion of long-distance trade, recourse to it was taken even more widely in the region, including by the Ngoni themselves, in the late nineteenth

---

[62] D. C. Scott: *A Cyclopaedic Dictionary of the Mang'anja Language Spoken in British Central Africa*, Edinburgh: Foreign Mission Committee of the Church of Scotland, 1892, 407–8.
[63] Audrey I. Richards, 'A Modern Movement of Witch-Finders', *Africa*, 8 (4), 1935, 448–61.

century.[64] One of Scott's most dramatic interventions into the *mwavi* issue occurred at the interface between local custom and international relations.

Chief Katunga's headquarters by the Shire River, thirty miles from the Mission, served as the port for Blantyre. It had become the final frontier in the Portuguese expansion towards Lake Malawi after a new generation of Portuguese imperialists had redoubled the efforts to occupy areas by making treaties with Yao chiefs.[65] These developments alarmed the Scottish missionaries of both churches, but Lord Salisbury rejected their calls in 1888 to provide British protection. However, such were the Portuguese advances, widely reported in the British press, that he came to present the Portuguese government with an ultimatum in January 1890 to withdraw its forces from the Shire. The Portuguese government complied the following month by ordering the commander at Katunga to withdraw his troops, soldiers of mostly Zulu origins. As late as in May a Portuguese official with the title of Governor of Shire was still felt by the Scottish missionaries to pose a threat to peace.[66] In June, Katunga died, and Scott travelled to this tense situation to reason against the use of *mwavi* to determine the cause of death. The impact of the uncertainties caused by the wider geopolitics was not lost on Scott. Commenting in a letter to James Robertson how Katunga and his neighbour Chief Masea had become 'devout worshippers' in the Mission, he noted an irony amid the political turbulence: 'The Portuguese war with its so many seeming evils and real goods may have done this inestimable service to Katunga and Masea.'[67]

In the same letter, Scott gave a detailed account of his approach to *mwavi*. Recalling his success at stopping the ordeal at Chief Kasisi's death, another neighbour of Katunga's, and 'when like a bush fire smouldering it broke out again and ever so many died, we were able to put a stop to it again', Scott felt buoyed to pursue his policy at Katunga's. He arrived in 'the lull between the burial and the *mwabvi*

---

[64] John McCracken, *Politics and Christianity in Malawi 1875–1940: The Impact of the Livingstonia Mission in the Northern Province*, Cambridge: Cambridge University Press, 1977, 14.
[65] A. J. Hanna, *The Beginnings of Nyasaland and North-Eastern Rhodesia 1859–95*, Oxford: Clarendon Press, 1956, 132–49; John McCracken, *A History of Malawi 1859–1966*, Oxford: James Currey, 2012, 50–7.
[66] Ross, *Blantyre Mission*, 109.   [67] Scott to Robertson, 16 June 1890.

drinking' to learn that 'the wives, sons, chiefs, and people were all to drink it'. He called a large meeting of Mang'anja elders and had 'never seen a larger assemblage of old headmen'. This gave Scott the confidence that he had achieved 'a most influential gathering'. The crowd 'listened with all their ears' to the 'splendid arguments' that Scott had 'on our side', and he 'spared no time nor pains to enforce them'. Although the letter contains little evidence on how, and to what effect, he enforced his 'splendid arguments', Scott's observation that 'Katunga's head wife and others bent their heads down to the ground' may have indicated popular compliance. At any rate, the gathering also became another showcase for the Mission's success in attracting people: 'A great number of the boys, the chiefs' sons, our married teachers sat on the mat near us.' Spatially separated from the rest, the people associated with the Mission alluded by their very presence to a form of existence in which *mwavi* had no role.

From Ostracism to Diplomacy

What the battle against *mwavi* shows is that a sense of crisis both accentuated controversial local customs and presented opportunities to spread the gospel. People fleeing slavery, in both its domestic and international dimensions, were another constituency of potential new Christians. They would gain their freedom from their masters by becoming subjects of Mission control and teaching. At no point would these domestic slaves be 'mere' human beings abstracted from their ties to others, however abusive. Scott and his colleagues grappled with the same dilemmas that the pioneering party in Blantyre had faced – how to negotiate local politics and how to prevent an unmanageable flood of people into the Mission? The negotiations were bound to be fraught. For example, in 1888 a man due to appear before Chief Matope in a *mlandu* case fled, and the local headman 'caught this man's wife, mother, and relations to the number of eight, and gave them to Matope'.[68] Scott sent a messenger 'to tell Matope that to enslave free Yaos was the ruin of their tribe, that Matope should know this; that the man had really no right to give these people, and that the case should be conducted with the man himself'. Scott 'took the liberty of friendship' to ask if Matope could free them against work that Scott

---

[68] LWBCA, February 1888.

would give them. 'The reply was that Matope would not enslave them but could not let them work for liberty, as he would require trusses of cloth.'

Matope may have been aware that Scott had paid chiefs compensation in cloth for some of the fugitives who had made the Mission villages their homes in the era of the pioneering party.[69] The Mission magazine published in 1889 the letter in Chimang'anja that marked 'the first case of liberty gained by working for it'.[70] It deployed the verb for 'buying' (*kugula*) to define the transaction in which 32 yards of cloth had been paid for the man. While persons like him would work for their liberty at the Mission, Scott was not inclined to repeat his predecessors' mistake by accepting more fugitives. As such, he had to rely on the 'friendship' he mentioned to Matope and to apply his powers of persuasion where fresh instances of enslavement came to his notice.

Two cases in 1890 show how provisional the agreements to end captivity could be when they were backed by little else than expressions of friendship. In a group that had previously fled the Ngoni to the Mission, a slave owner had died.[71] Of the slaves he left behind, 'an oldish man, thin and afflicted...was not considered valuable enough to keep'. Added to his predicament was the negation of his conjugal and parental rights: 'His wife had been taken from him, and his two children; one of which, a young girl, had been taken as a slave wife by one of the free masters.' Scott stated that 'we cannot receive slaves, nor can we help the slaves against the masters'. However, he told the free masters in no uncertain terms what the 'European' attitude to slavery was. 'The mere statement of that attitude was sufficient to make the men promise to give the man his human rights, upon which the man returned with his two children, who had run away to their father, and the case concluded.'

This unusual mention of 'human rights' in Scott's thought referred to conjugal and parental rights – to the ties that made a man fully adult rather than to an abstract principle of individual humanity. A similar predicament of violated parental rights occurred in another case in which a 'mere statement' proved to have little effect. A woman and one of her children had been paid by a man called Mitoche as

[69] Ross, *Blantyre Mission*, 69, 81. [70] LWBCA, March 1889.
[71] Ibid., March 1890.

compensation to another called Majombe for capturing some of Majombe's people and goods.[72] Chiefs in the Ndirande area near the Mission had pressed Mitoche 'for his good name's sake with them all to give in so far as to make payment'. Majombe had, however, left the young son behind, which alarmed the captured mother who fled to plead at the Mission. 'She did not ask for liberty for herself or child, only that those to whom she had been paid "would buy her son also".' Scott appears to have summoned both men who were presiding over her and her son's future and elicited from them a promise to honour the woman's wish. Although 'the woman believing our word went back with them', the oral agreement with no threat of sanctions resulted in further torment for the woman. The men 'failed to keep their word, and the boy was sold for a goat by Mitoche. The woman ran away again, but has apparently gone back without her son, whom she will of course never see again'.

Scott took part in *milandu* court cases to deploy his powers of persuasion, not to mete out punishments as his missionary predecessors had done to their own cost. At the same time, the Mission station was the sphere where he and his colleagues could exercise jurisdiction to the point of ostracizing wrongdoers. Although this course of action was uncommon for a mission seeking to increase its numbers, Scott did resort to it when trade in ivory threatened to become a distraction among the Africans at the Mission. European hunters had begun to appear in the Shire Highlands in increasing numbers in the 1880s following the African Lakes Company's offer to buy all the ivory they acquired.[73] They soon overshadowed Yao and Swahili traders in what Scott came to liken to a 'gold digging fever'.[74] While European hunters recruited African assistants in their expeditions, Scott complained that 'very many of the best workers have been spoilt by indiscriminate loans of guns and powder for elephant shooting'. Indeed, African workers at the Mission had 'the prospect of tripling or quadrupling their meagre salaries' by joining these expeditions.[75]

Among others thus enticed was a man named Mlomba, who had shot an elephant and had concealed the tusks from the Mission.[76]

---

[72] Ibid.
[73] John McCracken, '"Marginal Men": The Colonial Experience in Malawi', *Journal of Southern African Studies*, 15 (4), 1989, 546.
[74] LWBCA, January 1889.   [75] McCracken, 'Marginal Men', 547.
[76] LWBCA, March 1889.

In accordance with custom, Chief Kapeni had claimed one of the tusks for the shooting had taken place in his territory, but Mlomba was close to selling the other when the Mission came to know about the incident. Scott stated the Mission's position as 'unless Mlomba gave up the tusk (the question as to whom it really belonged to be settled by all the chiefs concerned), he must be considered as involving the Mission in quarrels with which they have nothing to do'. At issue was as much the Mission's imperative to maintain healthy diplomatic relations with its neighbouring chiefs as the need to guard against new commercial interests that would undermine the Mission's primary objectives. A judicious cultivation of diplomacy was necessary against the looming geopolitical threats in the late 1880s: 'The strength of the community will be felt soon, in face of Arab and Portuguese problems, to depend upon the consistent, disinterested, solid, righteous hold which we as a community have upon the native constituency around us.'

Mlomba's fate was to sustain that hold on the diplomatic relations by leaving the Mission. A White planter prepared to receive him had been identified, and Scott furnished Mlomba with a letter stating that 'I have sent him away from Blantyre for ivory shooting but have no fault to find with him in any other respect. I have given him liberty to go where he pleases, and he has desired of me this letter of introduction to you.' Warning the White planter that the case may not have been closed, Scott added that 'it would of course be best to look into this ivory case, for probably Kapeni will come to you about it'. Scott's approach to Mission subjects engaged in ivory hunting quickly hardened into the position that 'the natives on Mission ground, who, under Mission protection, hunt elephants, practically enrich themselves in the Mission's name by what is considered robbery by the chiefs'.[77] Inevitably, Scott had to declare that everyone living on the Mission lands, whether they were employed by the Mission or not, were prohibited from hunting for ivory.[78]

Building the African Church

The occupation that most strikingly drew African labour to the Mission was, of course, the building of the church. Paid in cloth, it

[77] Ibid., May 1889.   [78] Ibid., June 1889.

Figure 5.1 The foundations ceremony, 1888. David Clement Scott is seated on the ground on the right, next to John Bowie. Reproduced with the permission of the National Library of Scotland and the Church of Scotland World Mission Board

provided one of the rare opportunities for people associated with different sides of local politics to work together. As mentioned in Chapter 3, Hetherwick noted that the building work was the first time that large numbers of Ngoni had appeared in the Shire Highlands after their raids there.[79] Scott had embarked on his vision for the church soon after his return from furlough in 1888 and reported in October that year the composition of labour on the site (Figure 5.1). 'Skilled labour', among whom he included sawyers, brickmakers, and bricklayers, amounted to one hundred men, chiefly of Yao background, while sixty Chipetas, inherited from the Blantyre pioneers, were 'working for their freedom'.[80] Ngoni men numbered fifty at that stage, while the 'others', Scott estimated, were 810 people 'engaged on common work' and coming 'from different parts'. Four months earlier he had already described the scale and pace of the work that had recently started. 10,000 bricks were turned out weekly, and about

---

[79] Hetherwick, *The Romance of Blantyre*, 52.   [80] LWBCA, October 1888.

59,000 bricks had already been put into the foundations.[81] While 20,000 bricks were waiting to be burned, ten men were 'constantly in the bush cutting firewood for the furnaces and one cart [was] employed to bring it in'.

Scott's published accounts of the building work were largely confined to these two early entries in the Mission magazine. He had embarked on the ambitious project without seeking permission from the Foreign Mission Committee, which, upon learning about it in 1888, had expressed 'shock' at Scott's audacity.[82] It was not until 1891when the building was completed and dedicated that Scott sent a photograph of it to the Committee and received praise for his achievement. No doubt the praise was forthcoming also because of the admiring publicity the building earned in the United Kingdom, with the *Illustrated London News*, for example, hailing it as 'an edifice that would be creditable to any town or city in Great Britain' and as 'the handsomest church in Africa, including such cities as Cape Town, Port Elizabeth, and Durban'.[83] As the 1890s wore on, the Foreign Mission Committee would become rather less laudatory in its communications with Scott. The effects of his vision from liturgical matters to expenditure resulted in 1893 in the firm words that 'the Committee have laid down the rule that no building is to be proceeded with which has not been sanctioned by them'.[84]

At its dedication in 1891, the building was still 'thatched just enough to protect the brickwork from the weather',[85] and it fell on Hetherwick over several years to oversee the interior decorations and furnishings.[86] Nevertheless, Scott's architectural vision had come to fruition in the Byzantine domes and turrets and the many designs adorning the walls, based on eighty-one different brick patterns carved by Scott himself and his brother Affleck Scott (Figures 5.2 and 5.3).[87] As Hetherwick remarked, 'Scott had no previous knowledge of architecture or

---

[81] Ibid., June 1888.   [82] Ross, *Blantyre Mission*, 144–5.
[83] Cited in William Robertson, *The Martyrs of Blantyre: Henry Henderson, Dr John Bowie, Robert Cleland*, London: James Nisbet & Co., 1892, 50.
[84] Archibald Scott to David Clement Scott, 18 September 1893, NLS, Ms 7553.
[85] Thomas Price, *History of the Blantyre Mission, 1876–1956*, manuscript, 57, NLS, Acc 9069.
[86] Livingstone, *A Prince*, 69; Alexander Hetherwick, *The Building of the Blantyre Church, Nyasaland, 1888–1891: Being the Story of a Great Achievement*, Blantyre: Hetherwick Press, 1926.
[87] Ross, *Blantyre Mission*, 84.

Figure 5.2 St Michael's and All Angels Church, 1926. Reproduced with the permission of the National Library of Scotland and the Church of Scotland World Mission Board

Figure 5.3 St Michael's and All Angels Church, 2018

building construction', nor had he ever seen a brick made or laid.[88] He had no plan on paper beyond a few geometrical figures representing the theme of the church. In its sumptuous appropriation of a range of influences, the St Michael's and All Angels Church gave a concrete form to Scott's vision for a catholic African Church which, he came to state provocatively, 'has not been troubled by Greek and Roman schism, which knows nothing of Protestants and Papists'.[89]

Scott's vision may have soared above his highest domes, but the building work kept his feet firmly on the ground. Even his hands became occupied when he determined in 1890 that John McIlwain, the Mission's carpenter who had done much to train African workers, needed a holiday. Writing to Robertson in Edinburgh, Scott observed that McIlwain had become 'hypochondriac' and that he had taken on McIlwain's carpentry at the building site.[90] Despite adding to his already 'ridiculous' amount of work, the carpentry, Scott wrote, 'gives me the opportunity of splendid contact with the workers, and lets me just exactly know the whole work experimentally'. As in worship so too in manual work – Scott's vision was to build, quite literally, the African Church as a joint enterprise between White and Black. The African workers, few of whom were devout Christians, were expected to attend weekday meetings at the Mission.[91] Each day they would be assembled for prayers before and after work.[92] Scott's 'splendid contact' with the workers could not, however, govern entirely how they understood the project. Building for years a structure of unprecedented scale was bound to stir rumour and speculation among those to whom the very concept of the church was shrouded in mystery.

The rumours ranged from the innocuous to the potentially disruptive. Some workers thought that the building was to house Scott himself, others speculated that a still greater White man was to arrive to occupy it.[93] Human sacrifices were commonly feared to mark its completion, possibly presided over by Scott and other White people. Had serious accidents occurred while the works were in progress, such rumours may well have resulted in behaviour that would have contested Scott's vision of togetherness from the African point of view. After all, his brother-in-law John Bowie had as the Mission's physician

---

[88] Hetherwick, *The Romance of Blantyre*, 77.   [89] LWBCA, May 1894.
[90] Scott to Robertson, 16 June 1890.   [91] LWBCA, October 1888.
[92] Price, *History*, 57.   [93] Livingstone, *A Prince*, 68.

a little earlier failed in his attempt to establish a separate hospital building.[94] The grass-and-clay construction, which Bowie boldly named 'St Bartholomew's', saw its first patient die, after which no African would venture inside. Bowie continued to see patients in his own house, but no such drawback appears to have hindered the building of the church. Instead, Scott's vision had a widely felt triumph when, after a solemn dedication, hundreds of Africans – men, women, children – gathered with the Mission's White population for a feast of rice and roast beef.[95]

Race Relations Recast

For all his vision for an African Church, and for all his admiration for the vernacular language, Scott never presented himself as an African. The European–African distinction recurs in his writings, but so too, as has been seen, does the emphasis on their mutual dependence. The next chapter describes the collision course on which Scott embarked with White settler and imperialist interests by insisting on Africans as the true owners of the land. At the level of ideas, the European–African distinction was the basis for asserting common humanity as fellow Christians, not the high wall between cognitive and moral capacities that Drummond felt unable to scale. Nor was the White superiority propagated by Drummond the only form of racialized thought that Scott took exception to. Segregation for Black people's alleged own good was equally remote from his own vision for race relations. Reflecting on the African Church in 1890, he stated that 'it is not like the African church in America left to itself'.[96] Black and White would come together in a common search for the Word: 'The free teaching and preaching is as freely received without forcing and without terrorism or tyranny as any congregation of free-thinkers could desire.' No one could claim to be free from blemish: 'The Mission Station is growing up as a communion amid heathenism without and a heathenism within.'

Scott's notion of an interracial communion was not challenged only by Drummond and White settlers. An initiative to repatriate people of African descent to their 'Fatherland' also sought endorsement from

[94] Hetherwick, *The Romance of Blantyre*, 72. [95] Ross, *Blantyre Mission*, 143.
[96] LWBCA, October 1890.

Scott. Its mastermind was J. Albert Thorne, who had been born in the West Indies and had graduated from medicine at the University of Edinburgh. In 1896, he self-published a pamphlet entitled *An Appeal Addressed to the Friends of the African Race* to galvanize interest in what he called the African Colonial Enterprise.[97] Families of African descent from the West Indies and the United States would be relocated to the area that closely corresponded to the Scottish missionary influence in Malawi. Thorne required 10,000 acres of land in the first instance, divided into ten blocks of one hundred acres to provide the families with land to cultivate. Funds were being solicited to ensure a 'liberal supply of food and clothing' for the first three years, after which the families would continue to receive an annual payment for another ten years.[98] Overall, Thorne envisaged the 'process of transportation' to be repeated over a period of 'fifty years or so'. The intent was to find 'the most effectual way of opening up the Dark Continent' as well as 'a true, complete, and perfectly feasible solution of the race problem as it is now understood in European Countries'.[99]

Thorne's scheme, which he tried to revive while based in Harlem in the 1920s, 'never even approached realization'.[100] Frustrated, he came to accuse Marcus Garvey of plagiarizing the scheme he had conceived decades before Garvey.[101] While Garvey would cement his stature as a charismatic champion of Black emancipation, Thorne died in 'total obscurity'.[102] Yet both men – Thorne born in Barbados, Garvey a Jamaican – were a part of a triangle in which the West Indies, United States, and Africa combined in the imagination of several nineteenth- and early-twentieth-century figures to inspire nationalism in Africa itself.[103] The 'Fatherland' that Thorne evoked was resolutely racialized, even if a major motivation for his scheme was 'the opening up of the Dark Continent' for Christianity and commerce much in the vein of David Livingstone's legacy, to whom, along with the abolitionist

---

[97] J. Albert Thorne, *An Appeal Addressed to the Friends of the African Race*, 1896, NLS, Ms 7873.
[98] Ibid., 11.   [99] Ibid., 10.
[100] Robert G. Weisbord, 'J. Albert Thorne, Back-to-Africanist', *Negro History Bulletin*, 32 (3), 1969, 16.
[101] Ibid., 15.   [102] Ibid., 16.
[103] George Shepperson, 'Notes on Negro American Influences on the Emergence of African Nationalism', *Journal of African History*, 1 (2), 1960, 299–312.

William Wilberforce, the pamphlet was dedicated. Funding for the African Colonial Enterprise would begin to compensate for the horrors of transnational slave trade, but Thorne was aware of the argument that had people of his kind not been taken to slavery in far-away lands, they may have been enslaved by Africans themselves. He countered the argument by pointing out the 'extenuating circumstances' in which it was 'a savage people' who committed the crime of slavery.[104] No such circumstances could be identified for the 'highly-civilized and Christian communities' that had included slave owners.

Nationalism, Christianity, and capitalism, rather than a defence of indigenous African culture, drove Thorne's vision. It had its inconsistencies, such as the unremarked manner in which the pamphlet's repeated stress on 'the intrinsic worth of the race'[105] – that is, 'the African race'[106] – could, at one point, give way to a comment on 'the mere accident of complexion'.[107] Yet once conceived, the idea of a Black fatherland could give rise to demands for equal recognition anywhere where there were sizeable numbers of people of African descent. Among the 'Public Men in Great Britain'[108] from whom Thorne elicited endorsements for his scheme, was Captain Lugard, later Lord Lugard, the principal architect of indirect rule in British colonialism.[109] Thorne begged to differ with 'the gallant Captain' over European representation in the local executive committee.[110] If Lugard felt it was a mistake to exclude Europeans from such a committee, Thorne queried, 'is it not also a mistake not to include Africans in the executive affairs of a European colony in Africa or in other lands where they form either an overwhelming majority or a very large proportion of the population?'

Although superior to the 'savages' they would encounter in Africa, the families in Thorne's scheme would nevertheless be defined as racially belonging to the African continent. Why fight racial prejudices, went another of his challenges, in the far-away lands where they had been taken against their will? The answer was clear: 'Instead of wasting time and energy in endeavouring to overcome prejudices that are so

---

[104] Thorne, *An Appeal*, 19. [105] Ibid. [106] Ibid., 21. [107] Ibid., 22.
[108] Ibid., 34–5.
[109] Lord Lugard, *The Dual Mandate in British Tropical Africa*, London: Frank Cass and Co, 1922.
[110] Thorne, *An Appeal*, 21–2.

hard to die, our enterprising young men and women will be better employed in directing their steps to the Fatherland.' After 'conversing' with 'eminent physiologists', Thorne had come to the view that people of African descent were also for physiological reasons much better-placed to colonize the continent than White people.[111] He italicized both conclusions that 'we are immuned from the more virulent forms of fever' and that 'Europeans never acclimatise at all'. It was a view that Harry Johnston, the first Commissioner in the British Central Africa protectorate, disputed in his correspondence with Thorne in 1896. 'Men of this type do not stand the climate much better than Europeans or Indians', Johnston submitted.[112] More devastating to Thorne's scheme was his retort that 'we are not particularly anxious to have American or West Indian negroes'.

Whatever Thorne's success in eliciting endorsements for his pamphlet from 'Public Men in Great Britain', it was this sort of response in correspondence with officials that spelled a death knell on his scheme. In the Church of Scotland, John McMurtrie wrote back to him in 1895 on behalf of the Foreign Mission Committee to regret that no support would be forthcoming for his scheme.[113] In a brief statement, McMurtrie advised that the committee would focus on 'our own plan – now and for many years in full operation – of training natives of the country for missionary and industrial work'. 'Your desire', he signed off the letter, 'to elevate the African race has our full sympathy, though we think that your proposed method requires very careful reconsideration'. McMurtrie's response, negative as it was, shows the hold that the idea of an 'African race' needing elevation could have even on the people who questioned Thorne's method. Undeterred, Thorne sent him the pamphlet the following year with a letter explaining that 'the advancement of the African race' was, in the words that Thorne had underlined, 'a subject of vital importance to us'.[114]

Apart from Captain Lugard, Scottish clergymen predominated Thorne's list of 'Public Men in Great Britain', recruited, it seems, to vouch as much for Thorne's character as for his scheme. No one except

---

[111] Ibid., 23.   [112] Cited in Weisbord, 'J. Albert Thorne', 15.
[113] John McMurtrie to J. Albert Thorne, 17 July 1895, NLS, Ms 7535.
[114] J. Albert Thorne to John McMurtrie, 16 June 1896, NLS, Ms 7873.

Captain Lugard and David Clement Scott questioned the scheme's racialized nature, albeit for incompatible reasons. Where Lugard wished for European representation on the local executive committee, Scott's praise subverted the scheme's basic rationale. His endorsement published in the pamphlet read as follows:

Dear Dr. Thorne, I think your scheme a very good one, and believe that it will do real service and valuable work. All will depend, however, upon the character of the men and the wives who form your colony. The fact that they belong to the same great race, as that to which the Bantu people belong, will not, I think, help very much; but I quite understand the desire for home: in the heart of these races in America, and certainly the kindredness will be no hindrance to their reception of the Kaffir. The African takes men and things upon their merit, and I have no doubt that the liberty and space given to those from Barbados will prove them to be men of the right stamp and powerful for good.[115]

Character was what Scott sought to propose as an alternative to Thorne's overriding emphasis on race. Although sympathetic to 'the desire for home' among the descendants of the slave trade in America, Scott inserted in his praise a warning against taking the African for granted. Merit was the principle by which he thought the African would evaluate 'men and things' – a principle by which character eclipsed complexion. Here Scott was consistent with his idea of common humanity that informed his own practice in Blantyre. When compared with this idea, Drummond's fantasy of White superiority and Thorne's Africanism had uncanny similarities in their racialized concepts of humanity. One of Drummond and Thorne's many differences, on the other hand, derived from their high regard for Christian civilization. Where humanity was divided into the irreconcilable realms of White and Black for Drummond, Thorne recognized morally and spiritually infused hierarchy in the Black condition itself.

Scott, by contrast, was committed to establishing an interracial African Church, enchanted as he was by aspects of vernacular language and custom. By the same token, failure to live as a Christian did not ask for complexion – there was, as mentioned, a 'heathenism without and a heathenism within'. Yet an attempt to deracialize all

---

[115] Thorne, *An Appeal*, 34.

differences would have been premature. 'European' and 'African' were necessary categories to express power differentials and the reversals that Scott's vision imagined. It was when the moral and theological imagination met with political intrigues that Scott's vision faced its greatest test. No issue was more testing than the arrival of the British rule. No figure was more threatening than that of Cecil Rhodes.

6 | *Rhodes Must Not Rise*

'I don't think you have ever realised the bitter hatred borne you by these Scotch missionaries in Blantyre. They hate you because you are an Englishman, because you threaten to overshadow their own petty meddling and muddling with grander schemes that will outshine mission work in popular favour.'[1] These words were written by Harry Johnston, British Central Africa's newly minted Commissioner, to Cecil Rhodes in June 1893. They were in a private letter left out from Johnston's dispatches to the Foreign Office in London. He warned Rhodes that the Scottish missionaries in Blantyre were 'the most serious enemies you possess', singling out both David Clement Scott and Alexander Hetherwick. Indeed, only two months before this letter, Scott had issued a warning of his own in the Mission magazine. Left to pursue his expanding mining and agricultural interests, Rhodes would commit a betrayal on several fronts: 'Justice becomes a chimera, native interests so much loot, and Britain is asked to look the other way for a bit until Mr. Rhodes sticks his knife in.'[2]

By 1893, Scott's antipathy towards both Johnston and Rhodes was as deep as was his concern over the direction that the new protectorate's administration had taken. More than a decade of work to commence an African Church – with all the diplomatic, entrepreneurial, and linguistic dimensions of that effort – had come under threat by the very forces that the Scottish missionaries had called on for peace and protection. In the high politics of the British Empire, they undoubtedly had played a role in persuading the British government to consider this hinterland as a worthy addition to the Empire. The declaration of the protectorate in 1891 followed, however, a period of manoeuvring that left them deeply suspicious of Johnston. He proceeded with a campaign of violence against disobedient Yao chiefs,

---

[1] Harry Johnston to Cecil Rhodes, 7 June 1893, NAZ, CT/1/16/4/1.
[2] *Life and Work in British Central Africa* (*LWBCA*), April 1893.

waged in the name of suppressing the slave trade – a campaign that did nothing to sustain Scott's diplomatic successes. Darker still was the shadow cast by Rhodes, whose apparent generosity in financing the British government's early venture in Malawi was, in Scott's estimation, a recipe for tyranny and monopoly. At the heart of the controversy was the question of to whom the land truly belonged. As the 1890s wore on, Scott would face increasingly bitter confrontations with colonists of lesser stature than Rhodes but who were more directly involved in alienating African land and labour in the Shire Highlands. Scott's vision for an interracial African future, based on the mutual recognition of Africans and Europeans as co-knowers, was being overridden by colonial and capitalist capture.

The Unprotected Protectorate

Towards the end of the 1880s, the missionaries in Blantyre were appealing to their colleagues in the Church of Scotland to secure the attention of the British government. 'I can locate mental pain which is not a pleasant thing to do', Scott described to his friend in Edinburgh the personal toll the predicament had started to take in 1888.[3] John Buchanan, the gardener of the pioneering mission in Blantyre, had become the Acting Consul but, so Scott remarked, 'can do nothing'. His visit to the Yao chief Makanjira to press an end to the slave trade had resulted in the humiliation of being 'stripped and almost killed'. Makanjira may have been made aware of the Acting Consul's weakness by the impunity with which Mlozi, an Arab slaver, presided over a reign of terror at the north end of Lake Malawi in Karonga.[4] Although far from the Blantyre Mission sphere, the operations there offered Scott a glimmer of hope. Added to the African Lakes Company's military efforts to drive Mlozi out was the arrival of a British soldier. He was Captain Lugard, whom Scott described to his friend as 'really a fine man'.[5] He had arranged a meeting between Lugard and Buchanan before the expedition to the north and had himself had 'a long conversation' with this newcomer to Africa. It was characteristic of Scott's faith in African institutions that his praise for Lugard's contribution

---

[3] David Clement Scott to James Robertson, 19 October 1888, EUL, Gen. 717-10.
[4] Andrew C. Ross, *Blantyre Mission and the Making of Modern Malawi*, Blantyre: Christian Literature Association of Malawi, 1996, 98.
[5] Scott to Robertson, 19 October 1888.

took no account of his military prowess and instead commended his use of the *mlandu* process for settling disputes:

> He managed at the North End to restrain the natives from the capture of women simply by the power of the very moral influence in *mlandu*, which I think so much of, and which is so powerful for good; and this against the white men themselves who said such a thing was impossible. I call such influence heroic.

Lugard was, however, in Malawi only for a brief period and would go on to gain dubious renown for modifying, or appropriating, African institutions for the colonial method of indirect rule.[6] Yet still in 1888, in addition to the threat posed by Arab stockades, Scott wrote, 'Portugal is pressing us hard'.[7] 'It is now or never with her, I do hope it is never; but please work for us you dear people at home; we need it sorely.' This *cri du coeur* emanated from the discouraging meeting John McMurtrie of the Foreign Mission Committee had had with Prime Minister Salisbury. 'Why not do it yourselves?' had been the Prime Minister's retort when McMurtrie had requested military support.[8] Yet before he became the new Consul in November 1888, Johnston had been sent by Salisbury to Lisbon to negotiate a draft agreement about the Zambezia region.[9] It resolved to divide the region in such a way that the Shire Highlands went to Portugal. Scott's reaction to the news was one of incredulity – 'We don't believe it', he wrote in the Mission magazine.[10] His jubilation at the further news that Salisbury had rejected Johnston's draft may have been premature, because then came the moment Rhodes had been waiting for.

The Coming Tyranny

When a Portuguese expedition moved northwards up the Shire River and noticed the Union Jack flying in one of the villages in October 1889, fighting ensued between the Portuguese and the Africans that made the headlines in Britain and Portugal. The British reading public

---

[6] Lord Lugard, *The Dual Mandate in British Tropical Africa*, London: Frank Cass and Co, 1922; Michael Crowder, 'Indirect Rule – French and British Style', *Africa*, 34 (3), 1964, 187–205.
[7] Scott to Robertson, 19 October 1888.
[8] John McMurtrie to David Clement Scott, 10 May 1888, NLS, Ms 7534.
[9] Ross, *Blantyre Mission*, 106.   [10] LWBCA, June 1889.

was told that their flag had been insulted, an outrage that brought back to the fore old suspicions of the Portuguese as slavers, not to mention prejudices against the Roman Catholic Church. Thus far left on their own, the Scottish missionaries learned that Salisbury had sent a naval force to occupy the Mozambique Island as well as forces to Gibraltar to put pressure on Lisbon. Faced with an ultimatum in January 1890, the Portuguese forces began their withdrawal from the Shire and, in June, a final agreement was reached between the two countries that extended the British territory to southern Malawi.

Clearly, as Harvey Sindima has put it, 'Malawi was a child that Britain never wanted'.[11] The protectorate of British Central Africa in 1891 and Nyasaland from 1907 emerged from a complex combination of contradictory interests, all in the context of the Treasury's doctrine that it had no more money for new African ventures.[12] The Scottish missionaries demanded British protection for the viability of their own work and, as they saw it, for the welfare of Africans. For a short while in 1889, they did support Consul Johnston's early task of making treaties with chiefs by furnishing him with British flags, sewn together in the manse dining room in Blantyre.[13] With an eye on mineral-rich Zimbabwe, Rhodes had persuaded Salisbury to grant him the administration of Malawi in exchange for a Royal Charter for his newly created British South Africa Company.[14] He would take over the African Lakes Company and pay the British government the annual sum of £10,000. Even though Rhodes may have had few designs for Malawi, the British South Africa Company did retain its mineral rights in the territory after it had withdrawn from land claims there in 1895.[15] For the British government, the annual fee paid by Rhodes provided the pretext to claim the territory without burdening the British taxpayer.

The protectorate's early years offer evidence of Rhodes's direct transactions with British officials in bringing vast areas of Africa under

---

[11] Harvey J. Sindima, *Malawi's First Republic: An Economic and Political Analysis*, Lanham, MD: University Press of America, 2002, 34.
[12] Ross, *Blantyre Mission*, 111.
[13] Alexander Hetherwick, *The Romance of Blantyre; How Livingstone's Dream Came True*, Edinburgh: Lassodie Press, 1931, 69.
[14] John McCracken, *A History of Malawi 1859–1966*, Oxford: James Currey, 2012, 54–7; Landeg White, *Magomero: Portrait of an African Village*, Cambridge: Cambridge University Press, 1987, 81.
[15] Ross, *Blantyre Mission*, 133.

his company's imperial rule. Those years also offer, particularly in the articles penned by Scott for the Mission magazine, evidence of passionate opposition against his ascension even as it was happening. In August 1890, for example, he commented on the rumour that the Shire Highlands might come under the jurisdiction of the Cape Colony in South Africa.[16] Neither it nor Rhodes's Chartered Company would ensure the independence of the new British Commissioner. Scott went on to deliver one of his many statements on the desirable relationship between government and commercial interests:

A large Company *aided by Government* is welcome indeed; but the relegation of all interests, missionary, trader, settler, and especially native interests, to the sole judgment of a large monopolizing commercial concern, is not and never has been considered help at all, is certainly not protection. We want judgment and appeal to Britain herself as her own free children and loyal citizens.

Scott's tone was even more combative when he revisited the theme of government–company relations two months later.[17] His first swipe was aimed at those seeking to silence these critics in Blantyre. 'In reply we would answer', Scott asserted, 'we did not as weaklings at our last gasp ask for help willing to take whatever kind of help might be given, we are not as conquered suing for protection which is just to mean an exchange of misfortune; we are free children of Britain, legitimately here'. No less defiant was his comment that 'an old spectre' was being played out in central Africa. Just as the treasures of India had been 'plundered', so too 'this same lean spectre here must fill the pockets of its shareholders with money from the African'. The issue of taxation provided a prime example of how a country should be governed.

No one objects to taxation when that taxation is spent *for the country*, and a Government which rules the country must be supported by the country; but a Chartered Company is not a government and never can be. To be ruled by such is to be ruled for commercial ends by absentee directors and shareholders whose real interests are only served by tangible dividends.

The spectre of Company rule was nothing if not nightmarish: 'The horrors that loom in the near future of prison, flogging, deportation,

---

[16] LWBCA, August 1890.   [17] Ibid., October 1890.

and taxation, the horrors of irresponsible oppression of chiefs and people, are the advent of a new slavery.' Scott and Hetherwick's protests seemed to bear fruit in February 1891 when Salisbury approved a scheme in which the British territory north of the Zambesi was divided into two. One was the Company sphere and the other, including all mission stations, would belong to the protectorate administered by the Foreign Office.[18] Included in the scheme was a provision that did little to assuage the Scotsmen's concerns. Johnston would be the administrator for both spheres, and would be paid £10,000 a year by the Company for general administration. In April 1893 came the time for Scott to name the name publicly in response to the news that Rhodes had made a well-received speech in England.[19] 'The ignorant applause this evoked is said to have been extravagant, and to us falls the difficult task of enlightening the British public.' What Rhodes had presented as a gift had become a loan – a loan that would force 'the British government to hand over to him its crown jewels'. This striking image was a measure of Scott's love for central Africa, for the crown jewel was the protectorate itself: 'The pledge in pawn is about the fairest jewel, if a small one (jewels do not always go by size), in Her Majesty's crown.'

'Not a penny of this debt is due by us, and not a fraction of claim has Mr. Rhodes over us', went on Scott's defiant language. At no point in his reflections on the government–Company relations, however, did Scott question the benefit of expanding commercial activities in the region. Livingstone's doctrine of Christianity and commerce had already stated as much, as had the wider British desire for 'legitimate trade' as an alternative to slave trade. After all, the diatribe of October 1890 also assured the reader that 'the more commerce you have the better, the larger the Company the better, the more of them the better'.[20] At the same time, Scott's was no laissez-faire economics, because his attack was as much on monopoly as on the 'new slavery' that the lack of governmental oversight would enable. The example of India, moreover, served to remind his readers of the historical juncture at which they found themselves – the one in which British plunder threatened to overwhelm yet another corner of the world.

---

[18] McCracken, *A History of Malawi*, 57.   [19] LWBCA, April 1893.
[20] Ibid., October 1890.

The Impertinent Imperialist

Rhodes himself was acutely aware of recent precedents in imperial policies when he presented his demands to the British government. In a letter to Johnston in April 1893, he cited the example of Botswana (then Bechuanaland) as a territory where an agreement was in place between his Company and the British government.[21] 'The Colonial Office have agreed', he reminded Johnston, 'that subsequent to the granting of Her Majesty's Charter no concessions within that area shall be recognised as valid, except they be in favour of the Chartered Company'. After pointing out that even the concessions made prior to this agreement would come under review, Rhodes used two issues to press similar requirements on Johnston. One was the promise of an increased subsidy from £10,000 to £17,500 per year. The other was the observation that in Botswana the government was contributing the annual sum of £100,000, while the Chartered Company was meeting alone the administrative costs in the new protectorate of British Central Africa. With a promise of building railways and telegraph communications, Rhodes further tied Johnston into a knot of reciprocity. Johnston's obligation was to secure the Company's 'undoubted right to the vacant and undeveloped land and the minerals of the sphere'. 'From a shareholder's point of view', Rhodes reasoned, 'it is essential that our rights, in return for our subsidy, must be acknowledged'.

It was not for any lack of enthusiasm for the reciprocal arrangement that Johnston discovered the limits of Rhodes's apparent benevolence. No sooner had he confided in Rhodes about the hatred against him among the Blantyre missionaries in June 1893 than the two men were in a bitter dispute over Johnston's proposal to make the subsidy liable to taxation.[22] The fallout was fierce in both official and personal terms: 'Rhodes expressed contempt of Johnston to all and sundry, ridiculing his physique as well as vilifying his character.'[23] In a semi-official letter to his friend in the Foreign Office, Johnston puzzled over 'the riddle' of 'Rhodes's inexplicable wrath and reviling'.[24] Included in his list of

---

[21] Cecil Rhodes to Harry Johnston, 30 April 1893, NAUK, FO 2/54.
[22] A. J. Hanna, *The Beginnings of Nyasaland and North-Eastern Rhodesia 1859–95*, Oxford: Clarendon Press, 1956, 252–3.
[23] Ibid., 255.
[24] Harry Johnston to Percy Anderson, 10 October 1893, NAUK, FO 2/55.

favours to Rhodes was the revealing admission that 'I have induced chiefs to sign away their mining rights'.

Two days earlier, he had written to the imperialist himself a twenty-one-page account of his loyalty.[25] Acknowledging how 'anything approaching sentimentality grates on you', Johnston none the less wished to assure Rhodes that he had 'but one religion, and that was the extension and development of the British Empire'. So compatible were the two men's ambitions, he pointed out, that the phrase 'Cape to Cairo', though often credited to Rhodes, was Johnston's own invention. Not that he wanted to claim any of the limelight from the great imperialist. 'As a paymaster', he admitted, 'I scarcely think anyone could have been more generous than you have been'. 'For all this you have earned my sincerest gratitude.' Yet Rhodes's 'intemperate' and 'rude' remarks on him had left Johnston 'a much-injured man'. He wished to convey some of his tribulations to the imperialist who was far removed from the daily drudgery of administering the new protectorate:

Sundays and week days, mornings and evenings, I am to be found either slaving at my desk or tearing about the country on horseback, or trudging 20 miles a day on foot, or sweltering in boats, or being horribly sea sick on Lake Nyasa steamers. I have to carry on in my office, myself, a most onerous correspondence in Swahili which I have to write in the Arabic character, in Portuguese, in French, and in English.

Johnston used comparison with better-endowed colonial officials in India to drive his point home. 'The Anglo-Indian official, to begin with, is much better paid, he leads a far more comfortable life, he has not such a crushing sense of responsibility, and, above all', Johnston added meaningfully, 'he does not have to serve two masters and please them both'. With these remarks, Johnston's service for the two masters was coming to an end. Weary of his frequent requests for additional small amounts of funding, the Treasury eventually took the initiative to offer a fixed annual grant, effectively making the protectorate responsible to the British government for its expenditure and making Rhodes withdraw the Company's sphere north of the Zambesi to what came to be called Northern Rhodesia.[26]

---

[25] Harry Johnston to Cecil Rhodes, 8 October 1893, NAUK, FO 2/55.
[26] Hanna, *The Beginnings*, 263.

The War Commissioner

As an 'absentee director', Rhodes had no direct experience of Scott's outrage. Such experience was the prerogative of the protectorate's first Commissioner. Johnston, as mentioned, had aroused the Scottish missionaries' suspicions already before his arrival as the Commissioner by conceding the Shire Highlands to Portugal in his draft agreement. The news of his approach in 1891 occasioned sardonic comments on his material possessions, never mind Scott's own need for champagne in the early days of his African life. Johnston, he wrote in a private letter, 'has a huge caravan on the road'.[27] Scott's understanding was that '100 tons of stuff' contained 'the luxuries of European life'. As it turned out, Johnston did insist on 'a white table cloth, cut glass, and silver cutlery when he dined in the bush'.[28] While Johnston settled in Zomba, 'a convenient 40 miles from the disputatious Scots at Blantyre', as John McCracken put it,[29] he set himself the urgent task of making the missionaries and Africans feel the presence of his administration. Aiding him was a 'police force', the term agreed with Rhodes's Company for what was a tiny army. It included seventy-one soldiers from India and some reinforcements from Zanzibar.[30] The troops were under the command of Captain Cecil Maguire, the brother of Rochfort Maguire, Rhodes's private secretary.

Johnston wasted little time in putting his armed forces to work. In one of his first dispatches to Salisbury from Zomba, he referred to 'your Lordship's earnest injunction conveyed in my formal instructions "to suppress the slave trade by every legitimate means in my power"'.[31] From 1891 until 1895, he commissioned a series of military campaigns in the name of 'the unfortunate mass of the people who are robbed, raided, and carried into captivity to satisfy the greed and lust of bloodshed prevailing among a few chieftains of the Yao race'.[32] An early success in subduing Chikumbu in Mulanje, who had harassed European planters for additional tribute, was followed by fiercer fighting as other Yao chiefs proved more difficult to bring under the British

---

[27] Scott to Robertson, 17 July 1891.   [28] Hanna, *The Beginnings*, 229.
[29] McCracken, *A History of Malawi*, 57.   [30] Hanna, *The Beginnings*, 188.
[31] Harry Johnston to the Marquis of Salisbury, 24 November and 29 December 1891, NAUK, FO 84/2114.
[32] Ibid.

rule.³³ None was more exacting than Makanjira, the chief who had humiliated Buchanan some years earlier. It took several attempts to defeat him, with heavy losses of men and artillery suffered by Maguire's troops. In December 1891, Maguire himself was killed, but it was not until 1893 that Rhodes considered, after appeals from Johnston, the situation critical enough to grant the administration an extra £10,000 to bring the war against Makanjira to an end.³⁴ A contingent of an additional two hundred Sikhs from the Indian army arrived, along with increasing numbers of African soldiers. A sense of personal honour, influenced by a deeper commitment to Islam than was common among Yao chiefs at the time, probably contributed to Makanjira's and his subjects' relentless resistance.³⁵ Crossing the British–Portuguese frontier as it suited him, Makanjira eventually found himself much impoverished, his villages in the British territory burnt to the ground and his headmen shifting their loyalties.

By releasing slaves and seizing ivory, powder, and guns during these campaigns, Johnston may well have felt that all the violence had been vindicated. Yet a perspective less persuaded by his justification has pointed out that Johnston, in his desire to establish a Crown Colony, would have subjugated disgruntled chiefs even without the pretext that their involvement in slave trade provided.³⁶ As for the missionaries at Blantyre, it has been suggested that their condemnation of Johnston's campaigns applied only to those chiefs who had become their 'clients'.³⁷ No doubt the loss of diplomatic gains irked them. During the 1889 campaign to get chiefs to sign Johnston's treaties, Scott had noted in private correspondence the disconcerting response from some of them that 'the English are the same as the Portuguese' – the latter having burnt at least one village on their expedition along the Shire River.³⁸ On the other hand, the Blantyre missionaries protested the treatment of even those chiefs who were in no way their 'clients'. For instance, Chikumbu, one of the Yao chiefs with whom the Mission had

---

³³ Hanna, *The Beginnings*, 188–9; McCracken, *A History of Malawi*, 58–9.
³⁴ Hanna, *The Beginnings*, 195–201.
³⁵ McCracken, *A History of Malawi*, 60.
³⁶ Eric Stokes, 'Malawi Political Systems and the Introduction of Colonial Rule', in Eric Stokes and Richard Brown, eds, *The Zambesian Past: Studies in Central African History*, Manchester: Manchester University Press, 1965.
³⁷ For a response to this claim, see Ross, *Blantyre Mission*, 121.
³⁸ Scott to Robertson, 18 September 1889.

not been able to establish cooperation, had been embroiled in a disagreement which, Scott argued, 'could without much difficulty have been settled by *Mlandu*'.[39] When the administration continued its wars later in the 1890s against Ngoni chiefs, executing Gomani in 1896, the Mission magazine was no less vociferous in its condemnation despite the lack of contact between these chiefs and the Mission.[40]

The Commissioner's Critics

Alongside the wars, minor skirmishes took place between the administration and Africans. The Blantyre missionaries commented on them in letters to, and meetings with, the Commissioner, not least because they were often the ones to whom disgruntled Africans would turn to report on misconduct. With Scott away on furlough in Scotland in September 1891, Hetherwick took the reins in Blantyre and embraced the distinction that some Africans had made between the Mission and the administration. Johnston felt that the administration urgently required tax revenue if it was to offer protection in British Central Africa. Already in November 1891, Hetherwick responded with an article that bemoaned the high rate of six shillings per adult male and complained that the policy had not been explained to the people.[41] Indeed, the rate was more than two months' cash wages that an African labourer could earn.[42] Most of it was, in practice, payable in produce, and after pressure from both Blantyre and the Foreign Office, Johnston reduced it to three shillings in 1893, payable on each hut instead of on each adult male. Yet because it applied, in these early years, only to the Shire Highlands and Valley – the area where the administration had some prospect of enforcing it – it also brought the popular discontent to Blantyre's doorstep.

In a series of letters in late 1891, Hetherwick sought to inform the Commissioner of these grievances and to advise him on how to conduct his administration. Within the space of five days in December, for example, he wrote twice to Johnston 'to bring to [his] notice certain actions of the agents of the Administration'.[43] The first of these letters described how a man had come to the Mission's dispensary 'bearing

---

[39] LWBCA, August 1891.   [40] Ibid., December 1896.
[41] LWBCA, November 1891.   [42] Hanna, *The Beginnings*, 241–4.
[43] Alexander Hetherwick to Harry Johnston, 13 December 1891 and 8 December 1891, NAM, 50/BMC/2/1/2.

marks of cruel treatment – his back side and arms have a large number of open gashes'. While the man explained that they had been inflicted 'by the agent of the administration by way of punishment', Hetherwick declined to comment on 'the merits of the case'. His only objective was 'to call your attention to what I consider the brutal treatment to which the man has been subjected'. The next time he wrote, Hetherwick had the administration's raids on whole villages to condemn. Naming Buchanan as one of the administration's agents indulging in such behaviour, he had received reports on two villages being burnt, one because of a woman having been stolen, the other because of a theft at the African Lakes Company. Particularly in the former case, Hetherwick did not intend to question the seriousness of the crime, but he criticized Johnston for allowing his agents wreak havoc on entire villages.

Johnston was not impressed with such criticisms. On New Year's Day in 1893, he wrote to the Secretary of State for Foreign Affairs to report that the Blantyre missionaries were still far from 'reconciling themselves to the position of ordinary citizens, cheerfully conforming to the laws in force'.[44] He recalled that upon his arrival in 1891, he had found the missionaries 'resolved to have themselves regarded as something far superior to the ordinary run of Europeans'. Since then, he had endured 'continual persecution' and had come to the conclusion that 'some term ought to be put on this reckless system of libel pursued by 4 or 5 vain and ambitious men'. At this point, because of Scott's absence in Scotland, Johnston singled out as his main opponents Hetherwick and Adam Currie, a new member of the Mission posted in Mulanje in 1891. They had written to the Foreign Office as well as to the Church of Scotland to complain about Johnston's methods and to accuse him of being a 'paid servant' of Rhodes's Company.[45] 'The sole foundation for their calumnies', Johnston responded, 'is an occasional police incident of a most ordinary kind', while he wished to put the record straight that he had 'never received at any time any emolument whatever either from Mr Rhodes or from the Company'.[46] As for his two critics, Johnston had restrained himself from bringing 'very grave charges against the Rev Adam Currie and the Rev A. Hetherwick

---

[44] Harry Johnston to the Earl of Rosebery, 1 January 1893, NAUK, FO 2/54.
[45] Alexander Hetherwick to Archibald Scott, 19 June 1892 and 28 June 1892; Adam Currie to Archibald Scott, 12 June 1892, NLS, Ms 7534
[46] Johnston to the Earl of Rosebery, 1 January 1893.

for attempting to stir up trouble between the natives and the Administration'.

Later in the same month, Johnston's antipathy towards 'this objectionable creature Hetherwick' was still so raw that Hetherwick's recent departure from Zomba to Blantyre occasioned the sarcastic comment that 'we should be far happier if he would extend his journey beyond Blantyre to Great Britain and remain there'.[47] By then, Scott had returned to resume his leadership at Blantyre, and Johnston was cautiously optimistic that, 'unless there is a further outbreak of priestly arrogance', 'a sensible reconciliation' was in prospect. To that end, 'a great deal of tea-drinking, early-dining, church-going, and other amenities' with Scott was taking up the Commissioner's time, while a 'timely subscription towards the Mission Hospital' represented another diplomatic gesture, duly recorded in the Mission magazine.[48] It was further motivated by Johnston's observation that 'in spite of their crankiness they *do* do some good'.[49]

Scott soon distinguished himself, however, as the administration's chief critic in Johnston's eyes. While listing all the British consuls and vice-consuls who before him had been 'harassed' by Scott and Hetherwick, Johnston suggested an altogether more personal reason for Scott's antagonism towards him.[50] 'People at home', he wrote to an official in the Foreign Office, had 'puffed up Mr Scott with the idea that he was going to be made Commissioner for Nyasaland and he never forgave me for receiving the appointment instead'. Johnston's mistrust of Scott also led him to believe that when the Mission magazine published a letter to the editor that was critical of the Chartered Company,[51] the signature 'D.' at its end could be attributed to Scott himself, never mind that he was the editor to whom the letter had been addressed.[52]

Chimerical Justice

The delivery of justice, rather than personal vendettas, was the area in which Hetherwick and Scott sought to take Johnston to task. In his 1891 article, Hetherwick reiterated Scott's emphasis on the *mlandu*

[47] Harry Johnston to Percy Anderson, 21 January 1893, NAUK, FO 2/54.
[48] LWBCA, August 1893.   [49] Johnston to Anderson, 21 January 1893.
[50] Harry Johnston to Villiers Lister, 4 June 1893, NAUK, FO 2/54.
[51] LWBCA, April 1893.   [52] Johnston to Lister, 4 June 1893.

process as the locally appropriate way of solving disputes.[53] The same month he wrote a letter to Johnston in which he regretted the administration's reliance on the English law and warned that it would cause confusion among Africans.[54] As 'British-protected persons', rather than British subjects at that stage, Africans accused of some offence could appear before a chief's court or a British magistrate.[55]

A sense of exasperation among the missionaries can be detected, for example, in their comments in October 1894. The Matope road in the Shire Highlands had acquired notoriety for attacks on caravans transporting goods to the African Lakes Company. Once when government soldiers had claimed to have tracked the footsteps of the perpetrators to the village of Chief Malunga, the chief had himself been arrested along with his headmen and put on trial. In his letter to Archibald Scott of St George's Parish, Edinburgh, who was also the Convenor of the Foreign Mission Committee, Scott described how Malunga had been 'knocked down by the soldiers twice and beaten with the lash'.[56] 'Old, deaf, and blind with cataract', Malunga had been brought before a British magistrate. As also recorded in the Mission journal entry of 17 October 1894, Hetherwick, Scott, and the latter's brother Affleck Scott had gone to hear the case.[57] To their dismay, none of the soldiers had been identified or charged.

In his letter, Scott explained that the missionaries' suspicion of the soldiers had made his brother investigate the tracking of the footsteps.[58] 'This he did most thoroughly', Scott reported, 'and must have walked about 100 miles in the doing of it'. It transpired that 'the so-called tracking was absolute nonsense', but the missionaries' prime concern was how evidence was treated in the court. 'The case was wholly prosecution', Scott wrote in the journal.[59] 'Leading questions were asked of witnesses', he continued, 'and no notice taken of conflicting evidence or discrepancies in accounts of witnesses *before* and *during* trial'. While Malunga was given no time to reply to the charges,

---

[53] LWBCA, November 1891.   [54] Hetherwick to Johnston, 27 November 1891.
[55] Harry H. Johnston, *British Central Africa: An Attempt to Give Some Account of a Portion of the Territories under British Influence North of the Zambezi*, London: Methuen & Co, 1897, 114.
[56] David Clement Scott to Archibald Scott, 18 October 1894, NLS, Ms 7535.
[57] The Blantyre Mission Journal, 17 October 1894, NLS, Acc. 9218.
[58] Scott to Scott, 18 October 1894.
[59] The Blantyre Mission Journal, 17 October 1894.

the missionaries also had to observe the proceedings in silence: 'None of us was allowed to say anything to help Malunga.' In his letter to Archibald Scott dated a day later than Scott's, Hetherwick drew conclusions beyond the case itself: 'The system of administering justice is most unjust. The head of the police is both prosecutor and judge.'[60] The system needed to change, and the influential Edinburgh clergyman was the recipient of Hetherwick's call for 'agitation at home'. On behalf of the Foreign Mission Committee, John McMurtrie, in turn, forwarded to the Secretary of State for Foreign Affairs the letters from Scott and Hetherwick. Inserting a diplomatic tone to the correspondence, McMurtrie begged that 'your Lordship must excuse the heat with which the letters have been written'.[61]

If justice would become a chimera under Rhodes's Company rule, as Scott had warned in 1893,[62] it was not faring perceptibly better under Johnston's administration. In 1892, Hetherwick told the tale of a headman's daughter on the pages of the Mission magazine.[63] She had been abducted by a 'coast man from Mozambique', who had been working for a European traveller. 'The same coast man has returned', Hetherwick reported, 'this time in the employment of the British Central Africa Administration'. The woman had accompanied him, and upon hearing of his daughter's return, the headman had appealed to the administration for her to be brought back to him. The headman had been informed that 'the case could not be entered into till he had paid taxes'. Hetherwick drew a cutting conclusion.

Here then is a British Administration, acting in the name of the English people, entering into a country, and attempting to levy a tax, arbitrary in its imposition and exorbitant in its amount, while it refuses a demand for a simple justice in a case in which one of its own employees is concerned, because this tax of 16 per cent of a man's income has not been paid.

The moral conduct of the administration's European agents was also a concern. Insisting that what he had reported to Johnston on another occasion was 'no idle tittle tattle or gossip', Hetherwick elicited in 1891 from him the pledge that 'no person shall continue to serve the administration who is dishonourable, unjust, or whose immorality is a

---

[60] Alexander Hetherwick to Archibald Scott, 19 October 1894, NLS, Ms 7535.
[61] John McMurtrie to the Secretary of State for Foreign Affairs, 29 December 1894, NLS, Ms 7535.
[62] LWBCA, April 1893.   [63] Ibid., September 1892.

cause of public scandal'.[64] Immorality was, in fact, a concern beyond the missives from the missionaries. In his correspondence with the Foreign Office, Johnston associated immoral behaviour with other Europeans than those working for the administration. An air of self-satisfied righteousness sweeps through this correspondence. Just as the 'vain and ambitious men' in the Blantyre Mission had made him seem Her Majesty's humble servant, so too did his tales of misbehaving Europeans convey the high moral standards with which he wished the Foreign Office to credit his administration.

There was, for example, Daniel Rankin, the agent of a German company. Before Johnston had arrived in Zomba as the Commissioner, he had been reported by another British agent of this company for 'purchasing a slave girl for immoral purposes'.[65] He had bought the girl, 'about thirteen or fourteen years of age', at Sena in Mozambique but was forced to surrender her to the girl's mother who had followed them to Tete. Johnston returned to this transgression in 1893 when he dismissed the legitimacy of the German company's land transfers prior to the protectorate.[66] Rankin was now remembered for 'the buying of little girls for immoral purposes from a Portuguese mulatto woman' and for bringing into the territory his Arab accomplices whom he had permitted to take slaves.

Then there was 'a wild Irishman named Bradshaw', a coffee planter and an example of more ordinary inconvenience in the Commissioner's life.[67] According to Johnston, 'Bradshaw had cast his eyes on one of the Chief's wives, and had "ordered" the said Chief to send the woman to his house'. The chief's refusal to do so had resulted in threats from Bradshaw who, when inquiries by Johnston's agent showed him liable to imprisonment should such threats be carried out, had 'fancied himself to be a very injured person'. 'When I leave this country for pleasanter scenes', Johnston predicted, 'I think the general impression of my memory will be that I never had a more disagreeable lot of people to deal with in my life than these Missionaries, planters, and traders of Nyasaland'. The disagreeable state of affairs, he stressed to the Foreign Office, was by no means of his own making. 'As a matter

---

[64] Hetherwick to Johnston, 27 November 1891.
[65] Louis P. Bowler to the Governor of Quilimane, 18 May 1891, NAUK, FO 84/2114.
[66] Harry Johnston to the Earl of Rosebery, 31 January 1893, NAUK, FO 2/54.
[67] Johnston to Anderson, 21 January 1893.

of fact', Johnston observed, 'a more peace-loving being than myself never entered Africa'.

Divide and Rule

Whatever the high moral ground that Johnston attempted to claim for himself, a degree of double-dealing characterized his relationship with the Blantyre Mission. At the end of 1892, Scott's entry into the Mission journal described in detail how the issue of personal morality had figured for much of the 'interview' between him and Johnston.[68] In attendance were also Affleck Scott and Vice-Consul Alfred Sharpe, who would succeed Johnston as the protectorate's Commissioner in 1896.[69] Scott recorded in the journal that 'Buchanan's case' had been the subject of a 'very hot argument'. The reference must have been to John Buchanan, because his younger brothers had by then relieved him of the day-to-day management of his business interests.[70] What is not clear from this journal entry or other extant sources is the nature of Buchanan's transgression; the question of morality would seem to suggest something else than the violence of burning down villages that Hetherwick had complained about in 1891.

According to Scott, Johnston said that he had been instructed by the Foreign Office to pursue action against defamation, but that 'he himself, if the Mission would not push [the charge against Buchanan] but would let bygones be bygones, would not raise the question'. Scott replied by noting that Buchanan had promised to resign from the government but had not done so. Yet Scott also stressed that he had 'kept from making a public scandal of Buchanan's case for the sake of the man himself, that for the same reason [he] had no wish further to prosecute, nor any further demand to make'. Striking a conciliatory note, Johnston had then assured Scott that 'he himself made a point of morality whatever his private opinions were and that he had said as much to Buchanan'. The two sides in the 'very hot argument' appeared thus to reach some common ground, but, Scott continued his entry, 'Mr. Johnston then made a strong tirade against the Mission's spirit and attitude, accusing it of jealousy and wanting power'. Apart from resulting from pent-up irritation, such tirade may have been provoked

[68] The Blantyre Mission Journal, 23 December 1892.
[69] Hanna, *The Beginnings*, 204.   [70] Ibid.

by Scott's remark earlier in their conversation that the administration's approach to chiefs was a 'policy of *divide et impera*' and 'a totally wrong one'.

A historian familiar with government sources, rather than the missionary ones, came to regard 'gossip' as an aspect of the 'constant vendetta' that the Mission waged against the administration.[71] He cited Johnston as ridiculing the missionaries for assuming that when a member of his administration built a hunting lodge in the bush, it was to keep a harem. When the same official passed through Blantyre with two wives of the headman he had arrested in Mulanje, the missionaries had inferred, Johnston claimed, that the official was in the habit of travelling with women other than his wife. Another historian, steeped in the Mission sources, conceded that 'inaccuracies' had 'crept into' the missionaries' concerns about morality in the administration.[72] None the less, the journal entry in 1892 indicates that the question of morality was as much the subject of face-to-face debate between Scott and Johnston as it was gossip on the pages of the Mission magazine.[73] Moreover, despite his conciliatory tone in the matter of morality, Johnston was harbouring sentiments of divide and rule vis-à-vis the missionaries themselves.

It was the Blantyre missionaries' 'meddling and muddling', as he described it to Rhodes in 1893, that made Johnston contemplate countermeasures that came close to the principle of divide and rule. In the same letter to Rhodes, he outlined those countermeasures to include a government newspaper and 'a religious cleavage'.[74] After noting with evident delight – but incorrectly – the Blantyre Mission's quarrel with the Free Church Mission at Livingstonia, Johnston informed Rhodes that he had forwarded a cheque in the latter's name to the Universities' Mission to Central Africa in recognition of its friendly attitude towards the Company and the administration. The donation in Rhodes's name was desirable lest money directly from the government 'would look rather too much like a bribe'. Even more insidious was Johnston's plan to fund the building of an Anglican church in Blantyre.

While much of this letter undoubtedly sought to appease Rhodes, Johnston's exasperation with Scott and his colleagues was palpable.

---

[71] Ibid., 205–6.   [72] Ross, *Blantyre Mission*, 122–3.
[73] LWBCA, May 1893.   [74] Johnston to Rhodes, 7 June 1893.

He was at pains to convince the Foreign Office that his dealings with the half-a-dozen other Christian missions in the territory 'have at all times been amicable and characterised by complete accord on all native questions'.[75] 'The plain fact is', he wrote to the Foreign Office on another occasion, 'that this trouble arises from the presence of two men in the country – the Rev D. C. Scott and the Rev Alexander Hetherwick'.[76] Deportation, though never implemented, was also evoked in 1894 when Sharpe wrote to the Secretary of State for Foreign Affairs as the Acting Commissioner:

Mr Commissioner Johnston in his Despatches advised that there would be no permanent and satisfactory state of things with regard to this Mission until two Missionaries, the Rev. D. C. Scott and the Rev. Alexander Hetherwick were removed from the country...The Mission are taking a course which makes them appear in the eyes of the natives of this Protectorate as an Opposition Party to H.M. Administration. Natives accused of any crime in Blantyre at once run to the Mission and ask for protection against the law.[77]

The relationship between the Mission and the administration would continue to be tense both on the pages of the Mission magazine and in personal meetings, as attested by Scott's account to his friend in Edinburgh of another 'heavy day's fighting' with Johnston in 1893.[78] It was premature for Scott to celebrate in this letter 'the bloodless victory we have had over the Administration policy', although his journal entry the previous year had recorded the reduction of tax to three shillings as Scott's own idea.[79] Yet little may be understood of Scott's vision if he is assumed to have conducted the Mission as an opposition party, or as a 'rival sovereign power',[80] not to mention the charge that his was a 'narrowly theocratic' outlook that 'could not reconcile itself to being divested of all temporal power by a purely secular authority'.[81] It would certainly have been inconsistent, if not disingenuous, for a mission to appeal for governmental oversight only

---

[75] Johnston to Rosebery, 1 January 1893.   [76] Johnston to Lister, 4 June 1893.
[77] Alfred Sharpe to the Earl of Kimberley, 31 October 1894, NAUK, FO 2/67.
[78] Scott to Robertson, 20 March 1893.
[79] The Blantyre Mission Journal, 23 December 1892.
[80] John McCracken, *Politics and Christianity in Malawi 1875–1940: The Impact of the Livingstonia Mission in the Northern Province*, Cambridge: Cambridge University Press, 1977, 167.
[81] Hanna, *The Beginnings*, 42.

to emerge as its fiercest enemy. No less inconsistent would it have been for a critic of monopoly to long for exclusive rights to rule, whether militarily or commercially. As has been seen, military might was what the Blantyre missionaries wished London to provide against threats to their and many Africans' security. Moreover, large companies were to be welcomed in Scott's scheme as long as they benefitted Africa.

The roots of his opposition have to be found in what always was his priority – the establishment of an interracial African Church. 'The bloodless victory' over the administration had to be celebrated, because 'the breaking up I dreaded of our Native Christian church has resulted in making it firmer than it was before'.[82] The African Church was to epitomize what prosperous future would look like for everyone in central Africa. In 1897, the year after Johnston had left his post, Scott pointed out that 'it was not to make a state that Sir Harry Johnston was sent out but to deliver from Portuguese occupation a state already made'.[83] Only by ignoring the central tenets of Scott's vision for an interracial African future could this statement be read to expound a 'narrowly theocratic' outlook. It was not a state of the Mission's own making that Scott thought the British government would find in central Africa but a state in which Black and White were attempting to live together. The depths of racist thought in Johnston's predisposition became particularly clear in the book he wrote as an introduction to British Central Africa.[84] It was when reviewing this book that Scott remarked on 'a state already made'.

Other Than Human

Not unlike Henry Drummond's *Tropical Africa* in the 1880s,[85] Johnston's book attempted a comprehensive account of natural history and anthropology. While Drummond wrote his as a Christian scientist on an expedition, Johnston ascribed to himself the authority of the territory's first Commissioner with several years of experience in the region. It is, as such, revealing to consider how the inaugural Commissioner chose to portray the human subjects of Britain's new dominion. The chapter on 'The Natives of British Central Africa' came

---

[82] Scott to Robertson, 20 March 1893.   [83] LWBCA, August–December 1897.
[84] Johnston, *British Central Africa*.
[85] Henry Drummond, *Tropical Africa*, London: Hodder and Stoughton, 1888.

after the chapters on 'Botany' and 'Zoology' and was the one, as discussed below, Scott considered 'degrading' in his review.[86]

For Johnston, Africans in British Central Africa fell into ten different groups, variously called 'tribes', 'races', and 'stock'.[87] Although mindful of individual variation throughout his account, Johnston's intent was to offer an analysis of all aspects of their physical and mental features with a view to general observations on human evolution. He performed, as such, forensic anthropology on living bodies. Before training his gaze on each body part in turn, Johnston devoted some thoughts to the issue of skin colour. Despite 'a considerable amount of variation', he pronounced, 'as a rule the negro of British Central Africa is decidedly black'.[88] From the colour of the skin it was convenient to move to its texture, which in turn led to the topic of perspiration. Much as wearing clothes may have been a mark of civilization, it seemed to come at the cost of undesirable odour in the central African: 'In the clothed negro it is sometimes offensive to an appalling degree, rendering it well nigh impossible to remain in a closed room with him.'[89]

No external organ or limb, male or female, could escape Johnston's notice as he enumerated and described the bodily composition. Sexual organs were mentioned among others – from facial features to body hair to finger nails – and attracted comparative reflections: 'In both sexes the development of the external sexual organs is large – larger than in the European (white) race, more considerable still than among the Mongoloid (yellow) races of Asia, America, and the Pacific.'[90] The uses of those organs loomed large as Johnston began to broach the topic of intellectual and moral faculties: 'To these people almost without arts and science and the refined pleasures of the senses, the only acute enjoyment offered them by nature is sexual intercourse.'[91] Johnston hastened to add, however, that 'in this land of nudity' he did not 'remember once having seen an indecent gesture on the part of either man or woman'. At this point in his account, Johnston was able to concede that 'the average negro of British Central Africa is not a born fool'. His stern view on evolution, and indeed retrogression, came to the fore after a look into the political and social life of his subjects.

---

[86] LWBCA, August–December 1897.
[87] Johnston, *British Central Africa*, 389–91.   [88] Ibid., 393.
[89] Ibid., 395–6.   [90] Ibid., 399.   [91] Ibid., 408.

'The life of an African is rigidly ruled by custom', Johnson informed his readers.[92] 'He is more of a slave to custom than the average European.' The issue of witchcraft, moreover, showed that 'negroes are gulled most easily and by the rudest sleight-of-hand. They believe almost any stories they are told'.[93] Not even the *mlandu* process of settling disputes, so often emphasized by Scott as one of central Africa's finest contributions to humanity, could earn Johnston's admiration. He did admit that 'some of the speaking is remarkably good – the argument being subtle, well-sustained, and copiously illustrated with analogies and references to other cases'.[94] This admission came, however, after a lengthy description of brutal punishments unleashed on wrongdoers, from the poison ordeal to plunging a hand into boiling water to a death sentence.

As if to leave no doubt about the savage nature of the central African, Johnston presented his view on evolution in the chapter's final paragraph. 'Such is the Negro of south central Africa', he began.[95] 'I have endeavoured to place before the reader an accurate summing up of his physical and mental characteristics. He is a fine animal, but in his wild state exhibits a stunted mind and a dull content with his surroundings which induced mental stagnation, cessation of all upward progress, and even of retrogression towards the brute.' So captivating was, for Johnston, the notion of retrogression that he chose to elaborate on it before closing his chapter. Had it not been for the Arab and European influence – never mind the involvement of many of them in the loathsome slave trade – Africans may have faced a transition from 'a fine animal' to something altogether more monstrous.

I can believe it possible that had Africa been more isolated from contact with the rest of the world, and cut off from the immigration of the Arab and the European, the purely negroid races, left to themselves, so far from advancing towards a higher type of humanity, might have actually reverted by degrees to a type no longer human…Fortunately for the black man, in all his varieties but two or three most retrograde, he is not too far gone for recovery and for an upward turn upon the evolutionary path – a turn which, if resolutely followed, may with steady strides bring him upon a level at some future day with the white and yellow species of man.

---

[92] Ibid., 452. [93] Ibid., 448. [94] Ibid., 469. [95] Ibid., 472.

Rarely has the case for colonialism been made in starker terms than in Johnston's call to halt the retrogression of a population into 'a type no longer human'. Yet it is not such views that his 'rare brilliance of mind' is remembered for in modern scholarship.[96] Just as twentieth-century historians have, as seen in the previous chapter, overlooked Drummond's opinions of Africans in favour of his anti-slavery sentiments, so too has Johnston's energetic service as the first Commissioner eclipsed the evolutionary views described above.[97] Not so for Scott – while he felt unable to express his criticism of Drummond's libellous account elsewhere than in a private letter, he did publish his disapproval of Johnston's slanderous chapter, albeit after Johnston had stepped down and left the protectorate.[98]

Describing Johnston's book 'as a sort of encyclopoedia [sic] of central Africa gossip', Scott's review was an exercise in sardonic wit. His disappointment at the offensive misconceptions led to comments on the author's own integrity. 'Sir Harry', he wrote, was 'a master in the art of playing to his audience'. Not only did the author seem poised to promote any prejudice his reading public might hold about Africans, his authority to write the book in the first place seemed rather tenuous. 'Out of a single short term of Administratorship', Scott remarked, Johnston had 'succeeded in reaping a *kudos*, which is an object lesson for all who wish to learn the art of "getting-on"'. These *ad hominem* remarks aside, the review made the sober observation that readers should not expect to find in the book 'serious treatment, far less any philosophy of language, race, life, or Missions'. Its view of the African was 'degrading', and by dwelling on cannibalism and witchcraft, Johnston had prevented his readers from recognizing that 'the native, as native, is pure, honest, brave, and compos mentis'. He had, in effect, cannibalized central African concepts for his own advancement.[99] To support another point of view, Scott evoked his pet example – the *mlandu* process of deliberation.

---

[96] Hanna, *The Beginnings*, 203.
[97] Roland Oliver, *Sir Harry Johnston and the Scramble for Africa*, London: Chatto and Windus, 1957.
[98] LWBCA, August–December 1897.
[99] Compare Francis B. Nyamnjoh, 'Introduction: Cannibalism as Food for Thought', in Francis B. Nyamnjoh, ed., *Eating and Being Eaten*, Bamenda: Langaa, 2018, 12–13.

A native chief in a court case in the centre of Africa throws, in a dignity and grasp of the subject, keenness of insight, and practical application of legal maxims, his interlocutor, Sir Harry himself, deep into the shade.[100]

Overall, Scott's vision for an interracial African future was in a striking contrast to Johnston's vision of a racialized division of labour in the new Africa. Africa, Johnston had stated during his tenure in the protectorate, 'must be ruled by whites, developed by Indians, and worked by blacks'.[101] Each 'race' in its place, Johnston's vision left no space for the status reversals so prominent in Scott's alternative vision, nor for the timely allocation of new responsibilities to Africans that would provoke deepening resentment among Whites against Scott during the 1890s.

The New Slavery

Johnston had initially sought funds to import Indian cultivators to introduce Africans 'to higher modes of agriculture than their present thriftless procedure'.[102] In contrast to the proposal, as discussed in the previous chapter, to allow settlers from the African diaspora, Johnston argued that 'in the case of all respectable Indians who came with some small capital to invest, that free grants of Government land should be given to enable them to settle and to cultivate'.[103] When no funds were forthcoming for such a scheme, he turned to the small community of Europeans who were in the early 1890s in the Shire Highlands as traders, transporters, and ivory hunters.[104]

The years between 1891 and 1895 saw transfers of land on a massive scale. Indeed, so prolific was the Commissioner in writing these titles that, by 1893, he was complaining that 'the action of handwriting [had] become almost unbearable to me'.[105] The transfers paved the way for coffee cultivation as the mainstay of plantation economy, complemented by tobacco and cotton cultivation in the new century. The impact in the Shire Highlands was more significant than elsewhere, with nearly half of the total area alienated to

[100] LWBCA, August–December 1897.
[101] Johnston to Anderson, 10 October 1893.
[102] Johnston, *British Central Africa*, 424.
[103] Harry Johnston to the Earl of Kimberley, 3 January 1895, NAUK, FO 2/88.
[104] McCracken, *A History of Malawi*, 77.
[105] Johnston to Kimberley, 21 January 1893.

Europeans by Johnston's scheme. It coincided with a period of return from hilltops to lower slopes by those Africans who had at least two generations earlier fled Ngoni and Arabs.[106] 'Tired of hoeing among stones', as the Mission magazine reported, they saw the relatively peaceful moment as an opportunity to start cultivating the more fertile soil.[107] A perfect storm of historical contingencies thus further undermined Scott's vision. Africans were returning to their ancestral lands just as the new administration encouraged European encroachment on an apparently unoccupied land.

While the numbers of both Africans and Europeans may have been too modest to make their divergent interests immediately volatile, the question of agricultural labour soon brought conflicts to the fore. In the 1891–2 planting season when Scott was on furlough, Hetherwick wrote in the Mission magazine scathing articles about what he regarded as the new slavery. He provided the example of a European pursuing 'a lawless and a cruel mode of asserting the owner's right to the soil'.[108] 'A number of natives', Hetherwick reported, 'have had part of their maize crops cut down by a European owner of land who is also native magistrate for the district, and on whose ground they have had their gardens for the past year or two'. In a letter, Affleck Scott was forthright about the identity of 'the European': 'Buchanan cuts down native crops to force the natives to hoe his coffee.'[109]

The attack had taken place during the busiest period in the agricultural season when the would-be workers were preoccupied in their own gardens. Hetherwick went on to report that a threat of similar action forced others to work for the European: 'Terrified lest their gardens should be treated as those mentioned above the owners turned out and obeyed the summary behest of the new lord of the soil.'[110] Hetherwick's plea echoed, at this point, Scott's search for mutual recognition: 'The prosperity of both Europeans and natives depends on a harmony between them which a few repetitions of such actions can not [sic] fail to destroy.'

---

[106] Megan Vaughan, 'Food Production and Family Labour in Southern Malawi: The Shire Highlands and Upper Shire Valley in the Early Colonial Period', *Journal of African History*, 23 (3), 1982, 357–9.
[107] LWBCA, August 1895.   [108] Ibid., February 1892.
[109] Affleck Scott to Archibald Scott, 9 June 1892, NLS, Ms 7534.
[110] LWBCA, February 1892.

A letter to the editor and Hetherwick's response to it were published in the Mission magazine the following month.[111] A reader calling himself a 'European Colonist' took exception to Hetherwick's report for having overstated the extent of damage to the Africans' crops. The European colonist also wanted to set the record straight that African workers were being paid in 'beads, calico, or coloured cloth'. He further lamented recent difficulties to recruit enough African porters to transport goods. In the European colonist's experience, Africans 'do not readily respond to any call for help unless that call is backed up by the promise of a present or a threat of something else'. He seemed sceptical about the Mission magazine's interest in his plight, because 'it is apt to give more sympathy to the African than to the European'. He nevertheless ended his contribution with these words:

No doubt the native is not as black as he is often painted, yet it is well to bear in mind that the light of civilization has only been burning in the Shire Highlands for some sixteen years, and the aborigines are still like children, and we should bear in mind that good old precept – 'Spare the rod and spoil the child.'

Hetherwick's response was nearly five times the length of the European colonist's text and issued a blow-by-blow rebuttal of its claims. While a dispute over destroyed crops would normally be considered by the *mlandu* process or an impartial magistrate, 'in this instance however the magistrate himself was one of the parties concerned'. Thanking the European colonist for putting 'clearly and frankly the position we have been endeavouring to combat', Hetherwick devoted a good deal of space to his calculations on how the small compensation that European planters paid their African workers ensured the former a handsome profit. He prefaced those calculations by asserting that 'the employer may pay the native a wage – eight yards of cloth per month valued at three shillings, but the value of the natives' work to him is far more than the amount he pays for it'. Moreover, by acquiring land through a present to the chief, Hetherwick stated with added emphasis, '*the people living or hoeing on the land get nothing*'. Both the manner of land acquisition and what Hetherwick called 'forced labour' amounted to what Scott had warned against before: 'There is but a step between this condition and slavery, and the step is not a long one.'

---

[111] Ibid., March 1892.

As for the European colonist's difficulties to recruit porters, Hetherwick recommended introducing ox carts, because as long as transportation was 'carried on in primitive fashion by native bearers', it would be 'hampered during the garden season by failure of the supply of carriers'. He also disputed the allegation that the Mission magazine harboured a bias against Europeans: 'We have always held that the interests of the native and the European are one – side by side both will prosper, but apart both will suffer.' 'We prophesy no dark saying of our own', Hetherwick stated when he evoked the spectre of South Africa. There 'native and European life have separated entirely'. This was his comment on children and the rod to punish them:

> We are surprised that our frank correspondent should quote the saying of the Wise King to clench his argument. 'Spare the rod and spoil the child.' True – when the rod is for the child's advantage. But when the application of the rod is for the advantage and profit of him who wields it, the case assumes a different aspect.

Hetherwick's willingness to use the metaphor of the rod and the child may have prefigured the paternalist impulse that would define his leadership at the Blantyre Mission after Scott's departure (Chapter 9). Yet in the early 1890s, his views on land, labour, and taxation were virtually identical to Scott's. What escaped Hetherwick was a vision in which the land question was but a component of a larger controversy over epistemic justice.

The Land Is Not Ours

In 1885, years before any assurance of formal protection by the British, Scott had in a private letter warned against the idiom that was increasingly common among would-be colonists. '"Opening up the country" is', he wrote, 'often a cloak used to cover motives purely selfish, and even blind'.[112] His reflections on what Europeans would find in the country that they thought awaited 'opening up' anticipated the remark on 'the state already made' in his review of Johnston's book: 'It seems to me less a primitive than a developed state; and all the tribes seem to have equal capacity for such development.' As ever in Scott's thought, the gaze had to be turned to the European as much as to the African in

---

[112] Scott to Robertson, 5 January 1885.

these reflections on colonization and missionary work. 'The depraved civilization as seen among colonial Portuguese and in the fearful state of our own lapsed society at home may be less won than overcome.' The equal capacity for development among Africans, along with the 'depraved' and 'lapsed' condition among Europeans, heralded an interracial future decidedly at odds with what Johnston's racialized division of labour would propose.

Developed as the African state may have been even without European intervention, in Scott's thought the prosperity of all demanded increased contact and cooperation. As mentioned, neither taxation nor the arrival of commercial ventures troubled him. The question was always how they would benefit Africa. By 1889, a sense of ambivalence had begun to haunt him: 'The future is full of the gravest anxiety, but there is ground for great hope.'[113] Scott felt it prudent to reassert the reason why Europeans found themselves in Africa: 'The country is its people and they are God's. It is for their sakes we have come, and it is absolutely nothing but missionary enthusiasm which has founded this land.' This realization called for a clear sense of duty in the Mission and at home. 'The purchase of land, the right of native appeal, the continuance of the native chiefs, are all questions with which as missionaries we are deeply concerned.' His friend in Edinburgh received this instruction: 'With you at home lies the duty of seeing that provision is made to the full for native rights and law, as well as for missionary appeal in the protection of these native rights, in the new charter proposed.' Yet Robertson also received the encouragement to find people for agricultural development. 'If you have any good man to send out', Scott urged him, £500 'would start him', while '£1,500 would establish a plantation – and make it pay. Do let us go heart and soul into the development of this land'.

Long before it became the idiom in which the postcolonial relations between Africa and Europe would be negotiated, development, rather than colonization, was what Scott urged people in Britain to put their 'heart and soul' into. Just as his interracial vision bore no resemblance to what the likes of Johnston proposed, so too did his idea of development have little in common with the neocolonial project of international development that critics attacked in the late twentieth

---

[113] Ibid., 16 August 1889.

century.[114] Scott's concern over 'native rights' focused his mind on the rights to agricultural land. While in Edinburgh for his furlough at the end of 1891, Scott wrote a letter, presumably to Johnston, to outline his view on the land question.[115] Already in its first line he made clear the principle that informed his argument: 'The land is not ours to begin with, and we cannot treat the natives as a conquered race.'[116] What Scott called the present condition of 'land-greed' and 'land-grabbing' was bound to obscure how Africans owned land.

As anthropologists would elaborate decades later, Scott observed that 'the chiefs hold the land *with* the people and rule the relationship (and thus inclusively the land) *for* the people; the chief for the tribe admits the European into relationship'.[117] Incipient in Scott's insight was the subsequent anthropological finding that land tenure in central Africa was subject to honouring obligations associated with political and social status.[118] At the heart of the present land-grabbing, as Scott saw it, was a misunderstanding among Africans about the nature of the land titles to which chiefs had been pressured to affix their mark. Scott thought that they would never have been signed if the Africans had understood the radically different sense of ownership they sought to enshrine. Besides, 'unworthy incentives were employed in many cases', while the chiefs had 'no right to sign away their people's land' in the first place. 'The yoke of a new slaver' beckoned in the Shire Highlands, resolutely at odds with Scott's insistence that 'we in the country are with the chiefs as *associated chiefs* under arrangements of associated co-occupation'.[119]

The notion that African land ownership was a matter of relationships between people would eventually solidify into what Martin

---

[114] Samir Amin, *Unequal Development: An Essay on the Social Formations of Peripheral Capitalism*, trans. Brian Pearce, Hassocks; Harvester Press, 1976; André Gunder Frank, *Dependent Accumulation and Underdevelopment*, London: Macmillan, 1978.

[115] The letter is introduced and reproduced in full in David Stuart-Mogg, 'The Rev. David Clement Scott and the Issue of Land Title in British Central Africa', *The Society of Malawi Journal*, 57 (2), 2004, 21–34.

[116] Ibid., 28. [117] Ibid., 29.

[118] Max Gluckman, *The Ideas in Barotse Jurisprudence*, New Haven, CT: Yale University Press, 1965; Elizabeth Colson, 'The Impact of the Colonial Period on the Definition of Land Rights', in Victor Turner, ed., *Colonialism in Africa, 1870–1960. Volume 3: Profiles of Change*, Cambridge: Cambridge University Press, 1971.

[119] Stuart-Mogg, 'The Rev. David Clement Scott', 30.

Chanock has called a 'frozen custom', variably deployed by colonial regimes to deprive Africans of individual titles to land and hailed by African nationalists (and socialists) as pre-capitalist egalitarianism.[120] Scott's evocation of 'associated chiefs' and 'associated co-occupation' expressed something very different. Not only did it allude to a hierarchy in which persons of certain status were entrusted with the welfare of others. It also outlined an entirely unprecedented circumstance and a future in which, as mentioned, the African chief had admitted the European co-chief into a relationship. The purpose of that relationship, as always in Scott's thought, was future prosperity for all. The argument about a radically different form of land ownership issued no appeal to leave the African land tenure untouched. It sought the grounds for a more just and more productive relationship than the one he described as land grabbing. Africans had to be recognized as co-knowers in the condition of co-occupation. Much as Europeans might become associated chiefs, their superior access to capital and their propensity to make new laws had to be monitored.

> Let us regulate individual occupation, and make good laws; let us have open hearing for the natives by fair and impartial judges, with no interest in the land; do not make men with land possessions tax-gatherers and collectors of custom; let taxes be levied, fair though substantial, on Europeans, not upon natives.[121]

The comment summed up Scott's principled recognition of inequality in the racialized encounter that was unfolding before his eyes in the central Africa of the 1890s. Much as his vision for the future was based on the idea of common humanity, the new encounter, as he saw it, did not take place between equals. The status reversals described in the previous chapter were some of his attempts to address those inequalities in an African Church to which both Black and White belonged. By the same token, his vision left room neither to infantilize Africans nor to indulge in the evolutionary fantasies peddled by Drummond and Johnston. In his allocation of responsibilities to Africans lay one important reason for his eventual downfall, not because they proved

---

[120] Martin Chanock, 'A Peculiar Sharpness: An Essay on Property in the History of Customary Law in Colonial Africa', *Journal of African History*, 32 (1), 1991, 71.
[121] Stuart-Mogg, 'The Rev. David Clement Scott', 31.

unworthy of his trust but because the colonial and settler interests were steering the country to another direction entirely. Although Rhodes never really became the absentee landlord in Malawi that Scott had feared, rise he did, and with him rose various degrees of racialized rule across the region. The end of the beginning in Scott's mission was the beginning of the end for an interracial African future.

7 A Future Foreclosed

'The Mission gets no easier', David Clement Scott began his letter to James Robertson in Edinburgh in August 1891. 'In fact the difficulties we foresaw long ago are getting round us like hunters round their game. Without my brother-in-law and without Mr Henderson, and without at present my wife's counsel, I feel very much alone and the responsibility is very heavy.'[1]

If one year had to be singled out as a watershed moment in Scott's tenure at Blantyre, 1891 would be the obvious choice. Not only did the religious and administrative landscape change with the dedication of the church and the coming of the British rule. The year also started with major personal losses to Scott when John Bowie, Isobel Scott's brother and the Mission's physician, and Henry Henderson, the Blantyre pioneer, died in January and February, respectively. The premonition expressed in the above letter proved prescient as the 1890s wore on and more clouds gathered over the Mission. Some of them were caused by more losses of the most personal kind, while others involved increasingly bitter conflicts with both White settlers in central Africa and the Church authorities in Scotland. The European staff at the Mission had gradually begun to include persons unconnected to Scott's 'clan', whether through kinship, marriage or close personal ties.[2] In 1891, George Robertson and Adam Currie were the new arrivals not chosen by Scott himself. They had been preceded by a teacher named Robert Hynde, who had been in the Shire Highlands since 1888. He would later start a local newspaper from which some of the attacks on Scott's vision were launched.

The Mission's African contingent, by contrast, caused Scott little trouble. His own transformation through the vernacular combined

---

[1] David Clement Scott to James Robertson, 5 August 1891, EUL, Gen. 717-10.
[2] Andrew C. Ross, *Blantyre Mission and the Making of Modern Malawi*, Blantyre: Christian Literature Association of Malawi, 1996, 158.

with a common Protestant emphasis that baptism should be at the person's own initiative.[3] The method of baptism, on the other hand, was a matter of some debate in Blantyre, apparently among Europeans and Africans alike. Some preferred immersion in water, others the water to be sprinkled.[4] Without quoting anyone in particular, Scott adopted a conciliatory position in this debate, seeing theological merit in both methods while pointing out their historical coincidence in the early church. Yet any dogmatic defence of immersion, in which 'one portion of scripture is taken as against others', received the warning that 'one would rather hold to sprinkling than yield one atom of the liberty which we have in Christ'. In a characteristic swipe at doctrinal schisms, he added: 'The Brethrenism bondage to symbol is as popish as Romish bondage to symbol.' Some Europeans in and around Blantyre, however, would come to evoke high-churchism in their undoing of Scott's vision.

That Scott's downfall was the making of Europeans rather than Africans is evident, among other things, in the number of baptisms at Blantyre. In the 1890s, they exceeded the number of baptisms at any other mission of the Church of Scotland put together except in the Punjab.[5] At baptism, Africans were not forced to adopt European or 'Christian' names as was the case in other missions,[6] and the baptismal lists for 1888–1898 show that thirty percent of the baptized kept their African names.[7] Baptisms were profoundly moving occasions to Scott himself. Describing them on Easter Sunday in 1895, 'the Birth day [sic] of the Risen Saviour', he noted that of the twenty-two baptized then, several were boarders at the Mission school while 'the majority however were from the outside villages'.[8] What delighted Scott in particular were those who had in the past attended the school either at the Mission or in one of its outposts but whom 'even oneself [had] sometimes forgotten'. Among the returnees were 'old women', who had

---

[3] *Life and Work in British Central Africa* (LWBCA), February 1893.
[4] LWBCA, September 1893.   [5] Ross, *Blantyre Mission*, 163.
[6] Thomas O. Beidelman, *Colonial Evangelism: A Socio-Historical Study of an East African Mission at the Grassroots*, Bloomington, IN: Indiana University Press, 1982, 139; Jean Comaroff and John Comaroff, *Of Revelation and Revolution: Christianity, Colonialism, and Consciousness in South Africa, Volume One*, Chicago, IL: University of Chicago Press, 1991, 219.
[7] Ross, *Blantyre Mission*, 156.   [8] LWBCA, May 1895.

once been members of a women's class held on Sunday afternoons at the Mission.

Conversion, to the extent that it describes the increasing influence of the Mission, was inseparable from the experience of membership in a new community. The African involvement in the Mission saw the building of churches and schools by villagers themselves – a practice consistent with meagre financial support from Scotland, but it was also a matter of principle for Scott. In this vein, Scott's vision for the African Church came to flourish in the 1890s, but it did so with certain decidedly un-Protestant aspects of his liturgy and with the establishment of an African deaconate. While both of these developments would loom large in the European onslaught on Scott's methods, the severity – and the tragedy – of that onslaught can be properly understood only if life at the Mission is examined further. It was life shaped by innovations in gender and race relations no less than in liturgy.

Mothering the Mission

Scott was left without his wife's counsel in the latter part of 1891, because Isobel Scott had relocated to Britain to give birth to their daughter. Scott followed her there after the birth in September, but not before John McMurtrie of the Foreign Mission Committee had broken the news to him with the earnest request that he rejoin his wife for the sake of his own health: 'It is just because your life is precious to us all that I think it is your duty to take a furlough, especially after what you have come through.'[9] Yet Isobel Scott's role was by no means confined to giving birth to Scott's children and to supporting him as the missionary's wife. She has already appeared as a peacemaker during Scott's visits to suspicious chiefs and as the critical editor of her husband's sermons. Her pragmatism proved essential in moving from his loftiest ideas to transforming lives. The same pragmatism produced ideas of her own, such as the introduction of female industries to complement those offered to men. No less significant were the connections she cultivated with parishioners in Britain. Here her work was supported by similar efforts among other missionary wives, including Elizabeth Hetherwick, the widow of the notorious Blantyre

---

[9] John McMurtrie to David Clement Scott, 22 September 1891, NLS, MS 7534.

Figure 7.1 David Clement Scott and female missionaries. Harriet Henderson is seated in the middle, Elizabeth Hetherwick is seated on the right. Isobel Scott is standing in the middle. Reproduced with the permission of the National Library of Scotland and the Church of Scotland World Mission Board

pioneer and trader George Fenwick and the wife of Alexander Hetherwick from 1893.[10]

The White women at the Blantyre Mission, no less than their male counterparts, represented some of the divisions in the European community. While Isobel Scott and her younger sister Harriet Bowie, who was to marry Henry Henderson, were the children of the secretary of Edinburgh's Philosophical Society, Elizabeth Hetherwick was of an entirely different pedigree (Figure 7.1). Born as Elizabeth Pithie to a seaman-father and a shopkeeper-mother in Aberdeen, she lost her father as an infant and became an orphan at the age of eleven.[11] A group of middle-class well-wishers in Aberdeen offered to pay her salary as a teacher in Blantyre in 1878. The following year she became, at the age of eighteen, one of the Blantyre pioneers and the first

---

[10] LWBCA, June 1893.
[11] John McCracken, 'Class, Violence and Gender in Early Colonial Malawi: The Curious Case of Elizabeth Pithie', *The Society of Malawi Journal*, 64 (2), 2011, 2–3.

unmarried White woman to work in the region. By 1893 when she married Alexander Hetherwick, she had endured marginalization and calamity as George Fenwick's wife, including the threat of becoming a part of the compensation payment upon his death, as described in Chapter 3. Although Scott had been dismissive of the White panic that the circumstances around Fenwick's death had caused, he and Isobel Scott showed compassion by inviting Elizabeth Fenwick to join their household. Scott's sensitivity to the class difference between them was apparent in his remarks to the Foreign Mission Committee. Wary of 'taking advantage of her' and determined to treat her 'as one of ourselves in every way', Scott had decided to pay her 'to help Mrs. Scott without quite being a servant'.[12]

When Elizabeth Fenwick, as she was still known then, went on her first furlough in 1888, it was commended by these heartfelt words of Scott's: 'Her knowledge of the language, her sympathy with the people and her gentleness of disposition have made [Africans] regard her as belonging to them, and her going seems almost the losing of one of themselves.'[13] Indeed, apart from teaching, White women at the Blantyre Mission were engaged in a variety of other activities to further its cause. After all, the Mission did not receive its funds only from the collections and legacies solicited by the Foreign Mission Committee. An important feature of fundraising was direct links to particular parishes in Scotland and London. Here women held considerable responsibility as the ones engaged in maintaining such links. Some parishes had missionary work parties whose female activists wanted their collections, however modest, to be passed directly on to Isobel Scott.[14] Others had Sunday Schools where, in a pattern reminiscent of more recent philanthropic gestures, the request was made to correspond with specific, identifiable African youths.[15] In 1894, for example, McMurtrie informed Hetherwick of a Sunday School in Glasgow where the children had showed much interest in the missions in Africa, China and, India.[16] He asked her to identify 'a scholar or two

---

[12] Extract letter from D. C. Scott, 11 October 1884, in John Maclagan to Dr Thomas Farquhar, 21 January 1885, NLS, MS 7547.
[13] LWBCA, February 1888.
[14] John Maclagan to Isobel Scott, 24 December 1886, NLS, MS 7548.
[15] Erica Bornstein, *The Spirit of Development: Protestant NGOs, Morality, and Economics in Zimbabwe*, London: Routledge, 2003, 67–95.
[16] John McMurtrie to Elizabeth Hetherwick, 20 October 1894, NLS, MS 7535.

who would like to get a letter' from these keen followers of mission work.

Harry Kambwiri Matecheta, who became the Blantyre Mission's first ordained African minister in 1911 after beginning his schooling there decades earlier, had his early education supported by one of these schemes. Isobel Scott had told him, 'Your friends are from St Columba's in London, Pont Street. You should send a letter to them, to their Sunday School.'[17] Matecheta recalled that other pupils were also told 'their friends and their churches'. David Clement Scott had described in another context St Columba's as the place of worship where 'many of our Scotch nobility in London find their presbyterian [sic] home and religious sustenance'.[18]

The long-distance affective work in cultivating interest in the Mission coincided with new opportunities for girls and women in Blantyre. Scott's predecessor Duff Macdonald had already opened a school for both male and female boarders and had advanced there not only literacy in the vernacular but also the use of English.[19] As has been seen, one of Scott's first tasks was to close the school and to re-open it on a new basis, largely to force the male boarders to come to it without their personal attendants. According to Matecheta, both girls and boys were accommodated in the Maganga building, the 'stone house' or 'manse' where the head of the Mission lived.[20] Scott soon had a separate girls' dormitory built in a nearby area called Nyambadwe, along with houses for female missionaries.

Mothercraft – preparing girls and women, whether White or Black, for motherhood – would become a preoccupation in missions in the new century.[21] In the meantime, as Matecheta recalled, African girls and women found new income-generating opportunities at the Blantyre Mission. Where printing and carpentry offered men new

---

[17] Harry K. Matecheta, *Blantyre Mission: Nkhani za ciyambi cace*, Blantyre: Hetherwick Press, 1951, 12; translated as Harry. K. Matecheta, *Blantyre Mission: Stories of Its Beginning*, trans. Thokozani Chilembwe, Berlin: Wichern-Verlag, 2016, 34.
[18] LWBCA, September 1893.   [19] Ross, *Blantyre Mission*, 72–3.
[20] Matecheta, *Blantyre Mission: Nkhani za ciyambi cace*, 8; Matecheta, *Blantyre Mission: Stories of Its Beginning*, 30.
[21] Hendrina Kachapila, 'Mothercraft in the DRCM: *Mthenga* Newspaper, Missionary Wives and African Women', in Kenneth R. Ross and Wapulumuka O. Mulwafu, eds, *Politics, Christianity, and Society in Malawi: Essays in Honour of John McCracken*, Mzuzu: Mzuni Press, 2020, 163–90.

vocational skills, women found similar opportunities in laundry.[22] Mature African women provided a service in which Europeans within and without the Mission would send their clothes to them to be washed, with young boys, such as Matecheta, drawing water for the women. The occupation was introduced by European women at the Blantyre and Domasi Missions: Isobel Scott, Harriet Henderson, Elizabeth Hetherwick – and the unmarried missionary Janet Beck. She was one of three sisters who had resolved that one of them should become a missionary while the other two would remain home to work to support her.[23] She had been a member of Greenside Church in Edinburgh with David Clement Scott and had chosen Blantyre as her missionary field. For nearly thirty years, she took a particular interest in the condition of girls and women, many of whom called her their 'mother' or 'grandmother'. Working as a teacher, she also trained women in needlework and tailoring. The products her team made were sold to support new mission stations.

Blantyre was not unique among the Church of Scotland missions to include several female missionaries – by 1900, 66 percent of all Church of Scotland missionaries were women, of whom the majority were unmarried.[24] The contrast was stark to the Universities' Mission in Malawi, which had been divided over whether women should go to Africa at all.[25] Once in Africa, their moves were closely supervised by men. However, David Clement Scott broke convention even by the standards of the Church of Scotland. He sent two unmarried female missionaries – Janet Beck and Alice Werner – to work with Matecheta in the newly established mission station of Nthumbi in Ntcheu District in 1893.[26] Convention was broken on two counts at this station. Not only were White women working for the first time in central Africa directly with a Black man, the Black man himself was entrusted with establishing a new station among the previously hostile Ngoni long

---

[22] Matecheta, *Blantyre Mission: Nkhani za ciyambi cace*, 10–11; Matecheta, *Blantyre Mission: Stories of Its Beginning*, 32–3.
[23] Alexander Hetherwick, *The Romance of Blantyre: How Livingstone's Dream Came True*, Edinburgh: Lassodie Press, 1931, 57–8.
[24] T. M. Devine, *To the Ends of the Earth: Scotland's Global Diaspora 1750–2010*, London: Allen Lane, 2011, 204–5.
[25] Owen Chadwick, *Mackenzie's Grave*, London: Hodder & Stoughton, 1959, 112.
[26] Ross, *Blantyre Mission*, 150; Matecheta, *Blantyre Mission: Nkhani za ciyambi cace*, 17–18; Matecheta, *Blantyre Mission: Stories of Its Beginning*, 39–0.

before he had been ordained as a minister. The response from Scotland was predictably disapproving, and not only from men. Gender, race, and class came together in the condemnation expressed by the Women's Committee for Foreign Mission.[27] The ladies in Scotland not only objected to White women working with a Black man but reminded everyone in Blantyre that female missionaries were to serve only ordained or medical missionaries, not artisan missionaries.

Some of the inspiration Beck and Werner sparked among girls can be gauged from Scott's comment in 1895 that the Nthumbi schools were 'flourishing, but the scholars [were] chiefly girls with a very small sprinkling of boys'.[28] Alas, problems with malaria cut the women's stay at Nthumbi to one year and made them return to Blantyre.[29] Werner had been at Nthumbi as an anthropologist and linguist as much as a teacher and would in 1917 become one of the first to be recruited to the faculty at the School of Oriental and African Studies in London.[30] For his part, Matecheta moved briefly in 1896 to the Mulanje station which had been vacated by Europeans fleeing political turmoil, as discussed below, and in the same year at Blantyre he married Jeannie Chendetsa, who had worked as a maid for Clement Hetherwick, the Hetherwicks' young son (Figure 7.2). Their return to Nthumbi showed the terrible toll that malaria could take on Africans as well as Europeans. 'Four of my children were buried there' (*ana anga anai ankwiriridwa konko*), Matecheta wrote laconically in his autobiography.

Schooling to Convert?

The deaths suffered by both Africans and Europeans dealt blows on the Mission throughout its early decades, but the deaths in the 1890s, as will be seen in the next chapter, made the sense of sacrifice very personal indeed to David Clement Scott. Mundane setbacks also continued to hamper his vision. Although the African adherents and

---

[27] John McMurtrie to David Clement Scott, 1 February 1894, NLS, MS 7535.
[28] LWBCA, May 1895.
[29] Matecheta, *Blantyre Mission: Nkhani za ciyambi cace*, 19; Matecheta, *Blantyre Mission: Stories of Its Beginning*, 40–1.
[30] John McCracken, ed., *Voices from the Chilembwe Rising: Witness Testimonies Made to the Nyasaland Rising Commission Inquiry, 1915*, Oxford: Oxford University Press for the British Academy, 2015, 155.

Figure 7.2 Harry Kambwiri Matecheta, Jeannie Chendetsa, and their child. Reproduced with the permission of the National Library of Scotland and the Church of Scotland World Mission Board

workers did not plot his downfall, they included people who were enticed by opportunities at odds with Mission policies. The monetary attractions of ivory hunting have already been seen in the case of Donald Malota. Alcoholism could also cut short an African's career at the Mission. According to Matecheta, the Mission had eight African teachers and one European teacher when he started his schooling.[31] Of the eight African teachers, five would eventually be unable to continue teaching because of drunkenness. Two other teachers – a married couple – also disturbed the Mission by having a marriage in which there was no peace (*mukwati wao munalibe mtendere*).

[31] Matecheta, *Blantyre Mission: Nkhani za ciyambi cace*, 7–8; Matecheta, *Blantyre Mission: Stories of Its Beginning*, 29–30.

Reflecting on the state of the Mission's schools in 1897, which turned out to be his final year in Blantyre, Scott was troubled by a different issue. Older girls generally left the school to be married, 'a calamity', he observed, 'that we do not seem able to prevent'.[32] Yet he also saw much reason to be proud of the schooling at the Mission and its outposts. The first school outside the Mission compound was opened at Ndirande in 1886, followed by at least nine other schools during Scott's tenure, all employing African teachers.[33] They were generally feeder schools for Blantyre, where pupils could proceed to higher classes. By 1897, the girls' school in Blantyre had been divided into eight classes, and the academic results were 'eminently satisfactory'.[34] Both girls and boys progressed from counting in English up to ten in the small children's class to counting to one thousand in the oldest class, which also was able to add sums with six lines, read Chimang'anja fluently and translate increasingly demanding English sentences. Apart from Chimang'anja, English, and arithmetic, the school subjects included Bible history and sewing. The pupils would also carry out a number of tasks outside the school according to their age and gender, including cutting trees for firewood, drawing water for the laundry, sweeping floors in Europeans' houses and guarding crops in their gardens.[35]

Scott considered Chimang'anja as 'of course the first thing a child learns at school'.[36] He further called the ability to read it the '*sine qua non* of Mission education'. Reading began with learning combinations of syllables from cards hung on the wall and proceeded to the use of slates for simple exercises in reading and writing. A Chimang'anja primer awaited more advanced classes and paved the way for reading the Gospel. The children had given the primer the name of *Kanyaminyami*, because, Scott explained, 'one of the sentences containing the word caught their fancy'. A crotalaria plant, its precise impact on their fancy was not described in this explanation. As for English, it was likewise 'desirable' that it be taught 'at a very early

---

[32] LWBCA, May, June, and July 1897.
[33] Gilbert Phiri, *A History of Education in the Blantyre Synod*, Doctoral Dissertation, Mzuzu University, 2021.
[34] LWBCA, May, June, and July 1897.
[35] Matecheta, *Blantyre Mission: Nkhani za ciyambi cace*, 9; Matecheta, *Blantyre Mission: Stories of Its Beginning*, 31.
[36] LWBCA, May, June, and July 1897.

stage', but the Mission had resolved to 'impart it conversationally'. 'No Home Primers', Scott commented, were 'of any avail'.

The catechism was another essential component of schooling in Blantyre, 'a compilation in Mang'anja of Bible history with doctrinal and practical questions arising out of it'. It followed a scheme in eight main parts, entitled God; The Works of God; The Work of Redemption; Jesus Christ Our Saviour; The Holy Spirit; The Message of Salvation; Manifestations of Redemption; and The Last Things. Along the way, the catechumens would be introduced to themes such as, among others, Creation; The Fall of Man; Cain, Abel, and Seth; Babel; Moses; The Apostles' Creed; The Ten Commandments; The Lord's Prayer; The Devil; Baptism; The Resurrection; and The New Heaven and New Earth. Because the Bible was published in Chinyanja well after Scott's departure, the catechism was based on rather fragmentary translations, some of them prepared only for the classroom and others more complete texts, notably the translated Gospels that Scott finalized in the early 1890s. The Africans selected to become so-called deacons pursued, as described below, a further programme of study in both secular and Christian subjects.

Scott's observations on schooling in 1897, published in the Mission magazine, were naturally an aspect of the public relations work that some of the White women did between specific congregations in Britain and schoolchildren in central Africa. As such, it is not surprising that his notes on the syllabus and academic results were followed by an article entitled 'Acknowledgement of Boxes'. Here Scott conveyed some of the materiality that accompanied learning at the Mission schools. From St George's Parish in Edinburgh, for example, had come 'a most useful, wisely devised, and well-made set of shirts, jackets, calicos, petticoats, dresses etc'. Suits were to be despatched to village headmen, who came 'dressed to church and [took] prominent seats amid the congregation'. Other parishes and individuals were also named by Scott for having supplied, among other things, 'white school shirts for boys and school dresses for girls', along with shawls, pink frocks, small jackets, and handkerchiefs.

Exotic as some of these items may have been to central Africans, the exposure to objects acquired from afar was by no means new, as David Livingstone's experience described in the introduction has shown. The boxes that arrived from Europe entered a social world in and around the Mission that was complex in the range of ideas and material objects to which Europeans and Africans had access. As James Pritchett has written about mission stations in the region at the turn of the century, Africans there could be:

teachers, lay preachers, schoolchildren, carpenters, bricklayers, mechanics, craftspersons, cooks, cleaners, launderers, seamstresses, farmhands, herders, buyers, clerks, accountants, stockers, or day laborers. In many instances these were occupational categories that had not long existed, whose gender assignments remained unclear, and whose relative hierarchical rankings had yet to be sorted out.[37]

No doubt new hierarchies were also in the making among Africans associated with the Blantyre Mission in the late nineteenth century. Although Matecheta noted candidly decades later that the African teachers 'did not complete [their] studies very well' because of the urgency to fill vacancies,[38] their position as the emerging African elite found here, as elsewhere in African mission stations, its expression in clothing.[39] Scott's mention of forwarding suits to village headmen indicated how European clothes could be distributed to uphold some of the old hierarchies too. Another example of Scott's quite explicit attempt to present the adherents as a distinct group was when they sat together in village gatherings. Yet his and other missionaries' efforts to build a new community were qualified not only by the hierarchies among and between its African and European constituents. Vital was also the specific vision that Scott brought to bear on such efforts. The vision was about an interracial African Church inspired by the figure of Africa as the risen Christ, unrecognized by Europe's established Christians and yet poised to educate them too. To see the European-style schooling introduced by Christian missions not only as epistemic injustice but as a weapon of outright 'epistemicide', as some twenty-first-century critics do,[40] would be to miss out on the vision that drove it in this particular instance. Just as Africans could retain their old

---

[37] James A. Pritchett, 'Christian Mission Stations in South-Central Africa: Eddies in the Flow of Global Culture', in Harri Englund, ed., *Christianity and Public Culture in Africa*, Athens, OH: Ohio University Press, 2011, 27.
[38] Matecheta, *Blantyre Mission: Nkhani za ciyambi cace*, 7–8; Matecheta, *Blantyre Mission: Stories of Its Beginning*, 31.
[39] Justin Willis, 'The Nature of a Mission Community: The Universities' Mission to Central Africa in Bonde', *Past and Present*, 140 (1), 1993, 144–5.
[40] Sabelo Ndlovu-Gatsheni, *Epistemic Freedom in Africa: Deprovincialization and Decolonization*, London: Routledge, 2018.

names at baptism, so too did they have, as Scott repeatedly insisted, their own contribution to make to Christianity.

It is here that conversion, an inevitable issue in the study of Christian missions, can appear in its central African inflection.[41] Consistent with the shift in scholarship from a focus on interiority in a cognitive sense to an emphasis on social identification, conversion at the Blantyre Mission under Scott is best seen as a matter of membership.[42] New doctrines and practices taught by missionaries and African catechists became conditions for the membership and were crucial for converts to regard themselves, and to be regarded by others, as Christians. Those doctrines and practices could entail profound changes in the ways of life – and serious disputes over what a Christian life would look like – but the Blantyre Mission under Scott was also founded on a missionary approach in which social and economic work often outweighed individual conversion. It was an approach pioneered by David Livingstone, himself influenced by St Boniface's mission to Germany in the eighth century, and one that seemed disconcertingly secular to some Protestants in the nineteenth century.[43] Yet at its core was the mission station as an interracial community of spiritual, intellectual, and pragmatic encounters.[44]

Blantyre Lads in Britain

If the traffic in ideas went both ways in Scott's approach, so did the traffic in people. While the numbers of Africans travelling to Britain were no match to how many Europeans came to Blantyre, the ramifications of the African visitors' tales told when back in central Africa cannot be discounted. As was seen in Chapter 4, Scott paid single-handedly for Nacho Ntimawanzako and Mungo Chisuse's sojourn in Edinburgh in the mid-1880s. Ten years later Chisuse made a second journey to Britain with John Gray Kamlinje, another Blantyre

---

[41] Robert W. Hefner, ed., *Conversion to Christianity: Historical and Anthropological Perspectives on a Great Transformation*, Berkeley, CA: University of California Press, 1993.
[42] J. D. Y. Peel, *Religious Encounter and the Making of the Yoruba*, Bloomington, IN: Indiana University Press, 2000, 216.
[43] Andrew C. Ross, *David Livingstone: Mission and Empire*, London: Humbledon and London, 2002, 122.
[44] Adrian Hastings, *The Church in Africa, 1450–1950*, Oxford: Clarendon Press, 1994, 274.

stalwart.[45] They had conceived the idea by themselves and were asked on the way, so they reported in a letter to the Mission magazine dated 30th October 1897, where they were going 'without a master'. The African Lakes Company sponsored their journey on the Shire River to Chinde, where they waited for five weeks for the steamer to take them to Durban. Incidentally, while waiting at Chinde, they spent some time with Joseph Booth and John Chilembwe, the two pioneers of African nationalism in Malawi a few years later.[46] Scott had made arrangements with the Rennie Line for the 'lads' to work for their passage to Durban and onwards to London.

Their stay in London and Scotland relied on a network of Mission friends.[47] Henry Grattan Guinness, the founder of the East London Institute for Home and Foreign Missions at Harley House, was their host in London. Their experiences there included a three-hour ride on the top of an omnibus to see the sights, followed by the 'wonder' of the underground. Then it was time to take the Flying Scotsman train to Edinburgh's Waverly Station, where the duo was met by Janet Beck and her sisters. Scott had arranged accommodation for Chisuse and Kamlinje at his aunt Marjorie Scott's house, and James Robertson, described by Scott as 'our oldest and staunchest Blantyre Mission friend in the Scotch Ministry', was one of the many enlisted to entertain them. Their main professional activities were work at the Nelsons' printing house for Chisuse and bookkeeping with a chartered accountant for Kamlinje. Yet the intense schedule also included visits to Aberdeen and Glasgow and exposure to a range of new skills. For example, Mr Hardie gave both lessons in violin, 'that queen of instrumental expression', as Scott put it. Mr Maclaren taught them to ride a bicycle, while Miss Blyth presented them with the gift of a typewriter. Mr Inglis, Chisuse's classmate in Stewart's College a decade earlier, had become a photographer and also showed them 'much kindness'. He was almost certainly Francis Caird Inglis, later to become a Royal Warrant photographer to King George V.[48]

Chisuse indeed became the first African photographer in Malawi a few years after their return. Kamlinje, on the other hand, was

---

[45] LWBCA, August–December 1897.
[46] John McCracken, 'Mungo Murray Chisuse and the Early History of Photography in Malawi', *The Society of Malawi Journal*, 61 (2), 2008, 6.
[47] LWBCA, August–December 1897.   [48] McCracken, 'Mungo', 4.

performing violin solos at the Mission even sooner.[49] He had also been heard to explain with enthusiasm to his African co-workers the difference between debtor and creditor books in accountancy.[50] Overall, as the duo noted in their letter to the Mission magazine, 'it will take us years to tell it all'. Yet the exposure had not made them uncritical of the White people's world. Before disembarking in Durban, they had been startled to be questioned by 'a detective', but as they put it, 'we being strangers to Durban did not quite understand their laws to the Natives'. Their observations on racial divides would sharpen rapidly – Chisuse wrote soon after the return a scathing article about White people's refusal to eat African food.[51]

Chisuse would experience more cause for resentment in the era after Scott's departure when the Mission's printing press came under a European's tutelage. Hamilton Currie wrote in 1907 patronizingly about Chisuse, by then a vastly experienced printer, that he showed 'skill and workmanship and [had] taken an intelligent grasp of anything new that I have been able teach at the Mission Press'.[52] In the aftermath of the 1915 rising led by John Chilembwe, Chisuse recalled conversing in 1897 with him and Joseph Booth, who had warned them against Europeans' treacherous ways.[53] Although Chisuse did not participate in the rising, he had had, through travel and as Scott's close associate, ample opportunity to develop critical perspectives on the European civilization. In fact, his photography – inclined to document new buildings and Africans in neat suits and dresses rather than in the robes and loincloths that had caught Europeans' eyes – can be seen as an expression of African pride and self-respect in a new world.[54]

Scott himself saw the 1897 journey as an opportunity for learning across racial divides. Reversing the perspective from the benefits Chisuse and Kamlinje reaped from their exposure to new skills, Scott observed: 'It must have been a revelation to our home folks really to see and hold intercourse with our Blantyre lads.'[55] The revelation was not simply about how well the Mission had succeeded in its work of conversion. Rather, the intercourse that Scott envisaged had brought about 'interracial communion without in any way destroying dispensational difference and respect'. Just as his pursuit of epistemic justice

[49] LWBCA, January 1898. [50] Ibid., August–December 1897.
[51] Ibid., April 1898. [52] Ibid., January–April 1907.
[53] McCracken, ed., *Voices from the Chilembwe Rising*.
[54] McCracken, 'Mungo', 10. [55] LWBCA, August–December 1897.

saw something universal in the vernacular without negating it as an *African* vernacular, so too was 'interracial communion' compatible with 'dispensational difference'. Moreover, as always in Scott's thought, his was not a happy story of cultural relativism. 'Mutual respect in dispensational difference', he added, 'is the lesson we so much need at this time – and we say nothing in the interrelation of races as to which side holds most of dispensation power'. The encounter would never be equal, but mutual respect and recognition would enable all parties to learn from it.

The African Deaconate

Chisuse and Kamlinje were two of the inaugural seven in the African deaconate in Blantyre, Scott's most direct method of achieving the African Church. He envisaged it as a step towards full ordination as a minister and set the deacons on a tight schedule of training.[56] It included instructional sessions twice a day, covering history, geography, and English as well as theological and biblical topics, complemented by their work as teachers or printers. In December 1892 came the announcement in the Mission magazine of the seven names called to one year's 'novitiate'.[57] Scott applauded them for being 'strong and consecrated enough to bear the strain of Missionary self-sacrifice'. In fact, the sense of sacrifice placed on them could be even more momentous than that faced by missionaries from Scotland: 'The promise of a lifelong surrender to God's service in a work like this is rarely asked at home, and at all times, when it is really made, is regarded as a sacrifice of a most uncommon kind.' It was one thing to be in the country as a foreign missionary for a fixed period of time. It was quite another to accept 'a lifelong surrender to God's service' among one's relatives and neighbours who may not have shared the same urgency to sacrifice.

The June 1893 issue of the Mission magazine reported that the seven deacons had been 'received publicly for trial' at the evening service on April 30.[58] In November 1894, a further seven names were announced to have entered the training, and 'behind these again are seven more for whom we are waiting a short time'.[59] The next month came with the note that 'our deacons have scattered for necessary work'.[60] Six

---

[56] Ross, *Blantyre Mission*, 151–2.   [57] LWBCA, December 1892.
[58] Ibid., June 1893.   [59] Ibid., November 1894.   [60] Ibid., December 1894.

mission stations beyond Blantyre itself, including in the previously hostile Ngoniland, had been populated by African deacons.

In his sermon delivered in Scotland in 1901, Scott returned to the early deacons with vignettes and words of praise.[61] The names he mentioned were not confined to the first seven deacons, but among the inaugural cohort were persons who would play major roles in church and society well beyond Scott's lifetime. Harry Kambwiri Matecheta was one of them, the deacon sent to Ngoniland, hailed by Scott as 'the honestest man I know, white or black'. Another was Mungo Chisuse, who had, as Scott put it, 'returned unspoiled' from Scotland. At issue was not the preservation of some putative African purity. On the contrary, Scott's praise for Chisuse described him as 'the civilised, the best fitted to meet and interpret the incoming civilisation'.

Among the inaugural seven was also John Gray Kufa, who was executed for his involvement in the rising led by John Chilembwe in 1915.[62] By all accounts, Kufa radiated rare brilliance, having proved his leadership credentials at the mission station where the Zambesi and Chinde Rivers met.[63] He lived in a little hut beside a small school. The territory crossed into the Portuguese sphere of influence, and although it was where Kufa had come from to Blantyre, his mission encountered considerable resistance. Scott recalled how Kufa 'stood unarmed...against a yelling crowd of natives with their spears and guns'.[64] Kufa would become the first African to achieve 90 per cent marks in the surgical examination administered at Blantyre.[65] Before his demise in the rising, Kufa rose to the rank of chief medical assistant at the Mission and, after he left the Mission, became an independent estate owner with 140 acres of land.[66]

Praise and affection drove Scott's vignettes of all the deacons he mentioned. One of them was a deaconess, Rosie Majonanga, whom he compared to Chisuse for being 'the most "civilised" of them all, and

---

[61] Rev, D. C. Ruffelle Scott, *'Living Stones': Sermon upon the Church of Scotland Blantyre Mission, British Central Africa*, Edinburgh: William Blackwood and Sons, 1901, 22–4.
[62] McCracken, ed., *Voices from the Chilembwe Rising*, 609.
[63] George Shepperson and Thomas Price, *Independent African: John Chilembwe and the Origins, Setting, and Significance of the Nyasaland Native Rising of 1915*, Edinburgh: Edinburgh University Press, 1958, 59.
[64] Scott, *'Living Stones'*, 23.   [65] LWBCA, 15 August 1898.
[66] McCracken, ed., *Voices from the Chilembwe Rising*, 609.

reliable and strong'.⁶⁷ She was the other half of the couple whose marriage had, according to Matecheta, no peace.⁶⁸ Specific skills and accomplishments earned mention in some of Scott's sketches. James Gray Kamlinje, for example, not only read Scott's Chimang'anja gospels 'as quickly and forcibly' as Scott read English; he was also the Mission foreman who assembled 'on Monday mornings three or four hundred workers, paying them in cloth on Saturday'.⁶⁹ Where John Macrae Chipuliko was 'the philosopher, the Marcus Aurelius of our band', Cedric Kalaliche turned out to be knowledgeable about gardening and planting coffee.⁷⁰ It was in sketching Kalaliche that Scott found an opportunity to insert his characteristic dictum: 'The African is an all-round man, entirely capable and broad-hearted.'

The difficulties described above, from the distractions of alcohol and fast money to disease and death, suggest that Scott's celebration of the African deaconate may have overstated the extent to which it cohered around the new Christian way of life. Yet it is also the case that the Blantyre-educated elite who were entrusted with increasing responsibilities during Scott's tenure were small enough in numbers to form a relatively close-knit unit.⁷¹ It did not prevent them from finding diverse paths to follow as devout Christians, as the discussion of the 1915 rising in Chapter 9 will show. Crucial to understanding Scott's own thought is the conceptual work he saw as underlying the African deaconate. It was another instance of his reflections on sacrifice and service, and on what it took to build an interracial African Church.

The Deliberative Deaconate

Scott explained in 1894 that 'no other word than DIAKONOS would suit such an office, and there is no office at home exactly like it: it is distinctly African'.⁷² Indeed, Scott had an altogether different concept of deacon in mind than the usual custodian of church property in Presbyterian traditions.⁷³ He emphasized the 'industrial mission' as the setting in which 'our deacon' would be 'almost the exact

---

⁶⁷ Scott, 'Living Stones', 24.
⁶⁸ Matecheta, *Blantyre Mission: Nkhani za ciyambi cace*, 8; Matecheta, *Blantyre Mission: Stories of Its Beginning*, 30.
⁶⁹ Scott, 'Living Stones', 22.   ⁷⁰ Ibid., 23.
⁷¹ McCracken, ed., *Voices from the Chilembwe Rising*, 105.
⁷² LWBCA, November 1894.   ⁷³ Ross, *Blantyre Mission*, 151.

counterpart of the deacon in Apostolic times'.[74] Practical and evangelical work combined in such a role. The deacon looked after gardens and workers, read the Scriptures in the vernacular in the church, taught or was a printer or a carpenter, all the while taking part in the care and management of the church. Scott's 1901 sermon elaborated on the sense of service in the deaconate. 'The deep question at issue', he stated, was 'the relation of service to liberty'.[75] While one would be a slave towards a master, one would be a deacon towards one's work. The African aspect revealed itself in dress and comportment. Scott used the vernacular word *tewera*, loincloth, to indicate how Africans had toiled for centuries in service of others. *Tewera* was 'portrayed upon the temples of Egypt, on the then Kaffir toilers, you see it building pyramids. You see it putting together today British gunboats upon Lake Nyasa, carrying bales of merchandise into the heart of the land, fishing, hunting, travelling, working'.[76]

The relation of service to liberty, however, made Scott emphasize that 'it is the servant who *possesses* the beautiful land'. In spite of centuries of service that was actually servitude or bondage, the African approached service with a 'sunny' disposition. Scott summoned the following images when Africa was routinely described by Europeans – and even by some diasporic Africans, such as Albert Thorne (Chapter 5) – as the Dark Continent: 'Africa is the freest, openest land in the world (*apricus*, open, sunny)', and the African, Scott went on to repeat his characteristic conviction, was 'the freest man, the broadest-hearted'. Aware that his inspired words might be misinterpreted by the Scottish congregation, he entered this clarification: 'It is not the land of licence, but of loving liberty of service.' This liberty of service and the sunny disposition that accompanied it did not mark Africans out as a race apart from Europeans. On the contrary, they indicated God's work before any Christian missionary or European had entered the land. It was in the work of one God that the deacon's service had its origins: 'This diaconate [sic] exercised is, in its exercise, a kingship, a priesthood to God. To power, a slave; to work, a deacon; to God, a king and priest, a priest-king!'

Just as Scott's language ideology made room for both lofty pronouncements and practical lessons, so too did his idea of the African deaconate see in service the principle of liberty no less than actual

---

[74] LWBCA, November 1894.   [75] Scott, 'Living Stones', 7.   [76] Ibid., 8.

work. Where the vernacular, moreover, offered inspiration to understanding all language, the *mlandu* process of deliberation introduced to the deaconate an African element of universal import. Scott established a deacons' court to deliberate and to hear cases in much the same way as the *mlandu* process took place in chiefs' courts. Scott himself presided over these sessions, but their conduct had at their core the expression of diverse viewpoints. Apart from deliberating on disputes, the sessions merged with Scott's tea parties to afford a forum for wide-ranging discussions with the deacons and their spouses.[77] No doubt to avoid clashes with chiefs' courts, the deacons' court restricted its jurisdiction to cases that implicated members of the Mission, rather than everyone in its vicinity, whether attending the church or not.

Scott's reflections on the deaconate in 1894 were prefaced by a brief note on the work that the deacons' court was engaged in.[78] A man who had responsibilities over a particular Mission area had been charged with 'having permitted and encouraged native ceremonies'. The note reported that 'he was called to answer, and after long and close investigation satisfactorily and completely cleared himself'. 'One could wish for no weightier justice', Scott wrote after this example, 'than that of native *mlandu* power Christianized into a Church Court'. It was here, between the note on the deacons' court and the reflections on the notion of 'diakonos', that Scott inserted one of his appreciations of *mlandu* for its rhetorical and deliberative powers: 'There are few finer experiences than a well-spoken native *mlandu*.'

Isms and Schisms

The onslaught against Scott's vision gathered momentum over several years, and it took issue with theological and financial matters as much as with his trust in African capabilities. In 1893, for example, Archibald Scott, of St George's Parish in Edinburgh and the Convenor of the Foreign Mission Committee, wrote to him to warn that 'not a few "rumours" have been in circulation here as to the "ritualistic" proclivities of the Blantyre and Domasi missionaries'.[79] Although he assured Scott that those who 'know and trust [you] have uniformly contradicted and ridiculed' such rumours, the warning was

---

[77] Ross, *Blantyre Mission*, 75.   [78] LWBCA, November 1894.
[79] Archibald Scott to David Clement Scott, 18 September 1893, NLS, Ms 7553.

unequivocal: 'I will be very sorry indeed if anything in the conduct of the Mission gives colour and support to them.' Coming in the same letter that laid down the rule that the approval of the Committee in Edinburgh was required for any new building work, the warning did little to win Scott's compliance.

He reflected on it and similar criticisms in a letter not to Archibald Scott but to his confidant in Edinburgh, James Robertson. If Scott's reference to the risen Christ in his discussion of slavery already entailed 'a daring theological concept',[80] his thoughts on the great rift within the Christian Church came close to a heresy. 'I can't feel the schism between East and West was right', he wrote to Robertson, 'and all later schisms seem to take origin from it'.[81] Scott's African formation was again evident in the way he had arrived at this conclusion: 'There is no need of sowing sectarianism in the heart of the broad-minded, broad church, practical people.' Indeed, Africa could show the path beyond isms altogether: 'The relief to get away from the necessities of *-isms* even of *introspective Augustinianism* and Westernism is very great.'

Yet it was, in the final analysis, Presbyterianism that he saw as the most promising ism for broad-minded and practical people and for historical sensibility. It was the type of Christianity where one could, he wrote with added emphasis, 'interpret, assimilate, and bring to fruit *historically* the *whole history of the church*'. Heretic as he may have sounded, Scott did not doubt his Christian foundations even when confronted by criticisms from the Church of Scotland. On the contrary, in the issue of 'high-churchism', as associated with 'ritualism' for example, it was his critics who had 'defaulted from the Church standards'. Liturgy was for Scott 'an attempt to educate rather than the imposition of a service'. In Scotland, however, 'at college there is no education in liturgies'.

The rumours that had reached Archibald Scott could not appreciate what Scott had adopted from vernacular practice to Sunday services. The prayers allowed for call and response much in the same vein as singing and chanting outside church services were antiphonal.[82] Even in his above letter to Robertson, Scott continued to be confident about the prospects of the African Church: 'The Church here seems to be growing up with great vigour. I could never have believed I would see

---

[80] Ross, *Blantyre Mission*, 129.   [81] Scott to Robertson, 16 December 1893.
[82] Ross, *Blantyre Mission*, 156.

so much life, and life so fully Christian.'[83] It was this emphasis on *living* that Scott adopted as one of the more conceptual lessons from his African formation, and its apotheosis was his vision of Africa as the risen Christ. Although the catechumens in Blantyre did learn, as mentioned, about 'the New Heaven and New Earth', eschatological themes are notably sparse in Scott's thought. His emphasis on life rather than death was consistent with the relative lack of elaboration on afterlife in Bantu cosmologies.[84] The risen Christ was a living being, alive in the Africans who may or may not have been practising Christians.

Just as he had been inspired by William Koyi to extol the virtues of friendship as a 'living thing' in his first letter to Robertson in 1881,[85] so too did his sermon twenty years later revisit the theme of living. 'God's policy is "living"', he told the Scottish congregation.[86] 'Christ's gifts are living men. His temple is of living stones.' Where there was life, there was *rhythm*, another idiom emphasized by Scott on various occasions. In response to the mounting European criticism of his liturgical proclivities, Scott had this to say in the Mission magazine in 1894:

What we have really done here is to seek to restore the liturgy of the Church as it was before schism of East and West, of Syrian North and South, yea even of Jews and Gentile. We want the *rhythm we have lost*, in Service, in Scriptures, in the order of daily life – hence our Liturgy.[87]

Members of the Foreign Mission Committee had little patience to entertain such convictions when, at the same time, the Blantyre Mission was embroiled in political and financial predicaments. After his return in 1896 from a furlough in Scotland for what turned out to be his final term in Blantyre, Scott received two letters from Archibald Scott. The first of them lamented the critical allusions to Harry Johnston, the Commissioner, in the Mission magazine and advised Scott to 'exercise a rigid censorship'.[88] Moreover, Archibald Scott admitted his incomprehension over the paragraphs about 'the future Church in Africa' in the same magazine and had 'found it difficult to

---

[83] Scott to Robertson, 16 December 1893.
[84] Richard Gray, *Black Christians and White Missionaries*, New Haven: Yale University Press, 1990, 67–9.
[85] Scott to Robertson, December 1881.   [86] Scott, *'Living Stones'*, 11.
[87] LWBCA, July 1894.
[88] Archibald Scott to David Clement Scott, 4 December 1896, NLS, Ms 7536.

explain your position to friends of the Mission here'. The grave theological stakes were evident in the observation that Scott may have been 'playing into the hands of those who allege that your aim is to form the Mission after an Episcopal and not a Presbyterian line'. Scott's pleas for reaching beyond theological schisms had fallen on deaf ears, and the letter brought to his attention two practical measures. One was to introduce to Scott an accountant who would 'relieve you and set you free to attend to your spiritual work'. The other was the suggestion for a Session, based on the model of Kirk Sessions in the Church of Scotland, to provide a body overseeing Mission affairs. Scott had called an annual Mission Council from 1889, but it was with the African deaconate that he discussed matters on a regular basis.[89] Making no mention of the African deaconate, Archibald Scott pointed out that 'you surely have among the European lay missionaries materials for a good eldership'.

Archibald Scott's second letter was written shortly after the first and reported on the meeting of the African sub-committee.[90] It had been convened to consider highly damaging newspaper articles about the Blantyre Mission and to add further weight to the Foreign Mission Committee's previous warnings against Scott's methods. Archibald Scott had learned to his dismay that such warnings had been ignored, including the practice that had often featured in the correspondence and newspapers – the alleged turning to the east by the choir when reciting the creed. It was one example of the 'ritualism' associated with worship in Blantyre, but so incensed was Archibald Scott with this apparent insubordination that he did not mince his words: 'I cannot express to you the surprise and pain which this has caused me. It is the last kind of conduct which I would have expected of you and the information comes at a time when it is most calculated to increase our trouble.' Unless Scott was to heed the instructions from Edinburgh, Archibald Scott felt moved to threaten resignation from his Convenorship and 'state publicly' his reasons. However, he was not the one to abandon his flock in time of need: 'We have a storm to face just now, and I am not the man to leave my post just at such a time.'

These words came after extensive correspondence throughout the 1890s from not only Archibald Scott but also the subcommittee's secretary John McMurtrie. Scott chose to ignore much of what they

[89] Ross, *Blantyre Mission*, 151–2.   [90] Scott to Scott, 4 December 1896.

wrote and gave his rebuttals in the Mission magazine and in his comments on the report by the Committee of Inquiry into the allegations against his Mission in 1897, as is discussed below. Even after the Committee report was published and had largely exonerated him, Scott continued to receive requests to confirm that the choir indeed now faced the congregation rather than the wall when reciting the creed.[91] Although often milder in his tone than Archibald Scott, McMurtrie also continued to doubt Scott's trust in the African deaconate. Towards the end of 1897, for example, he was still questioning Scott about liturgy.[92] 'In whose hands is it put?', he asked before noting that Hetherwick had told him while visiting Edinburgh that it had been 'put in the hands of the young men – the deacons or the catechumens, I forget which'. The mistrust Scott's trust in Africans caused in Edinburgh had found another expression a few years earlier in the request, also ignored by him, to provide full translations of the vernacular services in Blantyre.[93] There could hardly be a more poignant example of how a missionary's embrace of the vernacular aroused suspicion rather than approval among his compatriots.

The Capabilities of the Planter

It is worth recalling that all this correspondence about liturgy and finances took place at the same time as the Blantyre Mission was embroiled in controversies with the commercial and military schemes pursued by Rhodes and Johnston. The Commissioner could not resist expressing his views on the Mission's expenditure while taking exception to what the Mission magazine was saying about his administration. 'I wonder whether the philanthropic people in Scotland', Johnston wrote to the Foreign Office in 1893, 'who subscribe the money which supports the East African Mission of the Established Church of Scotland, realise the way in which their money is expended and the results which are achieved?'[94] He suspected that few such people were aware that instead of supporting 'schools and schooling and religious propaganda', much of their subscriptions went into 'the erection of unnecessarily elaborate and fancy churches, elegant and

[91] John McMurtrie to David Clement Scott, 3 December 1897, NLS, Ms 7536.
[92] McMurtrie to Scott, 26 November 1897.
[93] David Hunter to David Clement Scott, 23 March 1894, NLS, Ms 7535.
[94] Harry Johnston to Villiers Lister, 4 June 1893, NAUK, FO 2/54.

comfortable manses, dairies (the produce of which adds to the decided well-being of the missionaries and their families)'. As Scott's observations on the Commissioner's own penchant for 'the luxuries of European life' have already attested,[95] the arguments about Europeans' relative comfort went both ways. Yet Johnston's comments merely fuelled the flames already fought by the Foreign Mission Committee. While the missionaries' personal comfort was rarely an issue in the letters Scott received from Edinburgh, the anxiety over public opinion about expenditure was a recurrent theme in that correspondence from the late 1880s onwards.

One of Scott's indirect responses to such anxiety was to assert the industrial nature of the Blantyre Mission. On one hand, he rejected any expectation that the Mission's philanthropic supporters should see a material return on their investment. The meaning of the term 'industrial', he advised in the Mission magazine in 1893, entails a 'symbolic success'.[96] To those who wanted to combine trading or agriculture with mission work so as to get a return on their money, Scott had this to say: 'They may rest assured that if they get the monetary return they have nothing else – "they have their reward".' Such sharp separation of financial and spiritual interests may have served the purpose of reminding some readers in Scotland of the Mission's core objective. Yet the very insistence on an *industrial* mission went against the recommendation made by James Rankin and Alexander Pringle in their report on the Blantyre atrocities in 1881 (see Chapter 2). Precisely by including vocational training in mission work, the Blantyre Mission under Scott did combine practical and spiritual concerns. Only a few months before the above public statement, Scott had admitted in a private letter that 'in self-defence I have begun to plant coffee'.[97] The aim was to reduce the reliance on funds from Scotland: 'In three years this will more than pay the working expenses of the Mission.' At the same time, the initiative was ambivalent. 'I must say', Scott added, 'I do not like entering into the labour field with the other colonists to whom we have to be the Church of Christ'.

It was these 'other colonists', chiefly planters, who would play a decisive role in Scott's downfall, their voices amplified by articles in newspapers. Archibald Scott noted in his letter to Scott in 1893 'the

---

[95] Scott to Robertson, 17 July 1891.   [96] LWBCA, August 1893.
[97] Scott to Robertson, 20 March 1893.

attacks made upon the Mission first by a correspondent manifestly residing in your neighbourhood, then by Dr Rankin and by other smaller critics'.[98] The 'correspondent manifestly residing in your neighbourhood' was Robert Hynde, who had joined the Mission in 1888 as a teacher at the Domasi station led by Hetherwick. The men took an immediate dislike to each other, but it was against Scott that Hynde launched his most vicious attacks, both as a close friend of Rankin and, from 1896, as the founding editor of *Central African Planter* (later *Central African Times*).[99] He resigned from the Mission in 1893 to join his brother as a planter and would, from 1903, take the lead in developing tobacco as a major cash crop.[100]

Hynde motivated his resignation by raising a number of grievances, but McMurtrie admonished him for not putting them forward through proper channels before taking the drastic action of resignation.[101] Among others, Hynde complained about the lack of representation by European teachers on the Mission Council. While McMurtrie assured him of the African subcommittee's opinion along the same lines, he was less supportive of another reason for Hynde's resignation. It was the use and ownership of the Mission's printing press for which Hetherwick had adopted responsibility despite Hynde's soliciting a part of its costs as a personal gift from friends. Seeking to establish a distinction between individual gain and common good, McMurtrie explained: 'You see, we are accustomed to our missionaries when at home raising funds among their friends for the press...or a school, or a church, or a boat, something which is to benefit the Mission.' High-churchism and Mission expenditure also featured in Hynde's reasons for resignation. When he wrote to Scott about the resignation, McMurtrie found yet another opportunity to remind him of the theological stakes in the emerging controversy: 'Remember that most of the supporters of the Mission are low church in doctrine and practice.'[102]

Hynde deployed *Central African Planter* to discredit Scott's mission for, among other things, its alleged high-churchism. An anonymous letter to the editor in 1896, for example, gave this description of church services in Blantyre:

[98] Scott to Scott, 24 October 1893. [99] Ross, *Blantyre Mission*, 157.
[100] McCracken, ed., *Voices from the Chilembwe Rising*, 345.
[101] John McMurtrie to Robert Hynde, 15 June 1893, NAM, 50/BMC/217.
[102] John McMurtrie to David Clement Scott, 15 June 1893, NAM, 50/BMC/217.

If some of those at home who do most in support of Missions could find themselves some day in Blantyre Church, they would weep at the rut of ritualism so closely observed, beginning with the formal robed procession, continued by the galloping chant, prolonged by the formally read prayers and essay sermon, interspersed by successive 'Jack-in-the-box' -like appearances and disappearances at no less than three rostrums in the course of an hour's service, and concluded by the inevitable procession.[103]

Hynde was one of the first among the 'new men' from Scotland who felt little allegiance to Scott, whether in personal or spiritual terms. The mission station in Mulanje became a hub of discontent against him, run as it was not only by Robertson and Currie but also a teacher named Henry D. Herd, who would soon contribute White supremacist views to *Central African Planter*. Scott himself courted controversy by adding his own comments to the reports from Mulanje published in the Mission magazine. He disagreed, among other things, with the Mulanje missionaries' disparaging views on African children's abilities at school.[104] When the station had no European staff after Herd had been invalided home, Robertson had become the doctor for Europeans in Blantyre and Currie had resigned, Hynde wrote in his newspaper to protest against allocating responsibility for it to an African deacon. 'The fact is', he asserted, 'no native can, or will for years to come, be able to fulfil, even in a moderate degree, the place of a European'.[105]

The same issue of *Central African Planter* carried on its frontpage Herd's extensive article under the title 'The Capabilities of the Native'.[106] To the extent that its objective was to justify not only White presence but White supremacy in the territory, its turns of phrase were hardly original. 'It will be readily granted', Herd asserted early on, 'that the average native is lazy'. Common was also the irritation, if not fear, felt among White colonists about Africans' adoption of European modes of dress and comportment. The African, Herd submitted, 'ape-like copies the white man in dress and as far as he can, in manner of life'. The blow dealt specifically on Scott's vision of an industrial mission and African responsibilities was the low opinion on Africans' capabilities to advance through

---

[103] 'The Blantyre Mission', *Central African Planter*, May 1896.
[104] LWBCA, July 1894.
[105] 'The Mlanje Mission', *Central African Planter*, April 1896.
[106] 'The Capabilities of the Native', *Central African Planter*, April 1896.

education. The article acknowledged 'rote learning' as the pedagogy most suited for the African, for 'he is capable of being trained to a very high degree of proficiency as a craftsman so far as mere ability to use tools is concerned, if the patience of the teacher be long enough'. The distance between these views and those informing Scott's vision grew larger still with this statement: 'His physical proportions are those of a giant and his moral those of a dwarf.' The African, came the fiercest verdict of all, was 'an object for contempt from a moral point of view'.

Humanity Urges Us on

The 'frightful libel upon humanity' in Henry Drummond's book and the ruminations on retrogression in Harry Johnston's were, for all their offensiveness, somewhat academic when compared with the White supremacist views expressed by the new settlers in and around Blantyre. While struggling to keep his vision alive, Scott retained a measure of ironic humour. In 1893, he inserted this note into the Mission magazine:

We have read somewhere a description of the Britons long ago by Julius Caesar or someone like him, as thievish, drunken, disobedient, worthless, brutish – what was the good of doing anything to them? Many a Caesar of very late date has said the same about the African perhaps with like truth.[107]

Three years later, and on the eve of Herd's article, a similar quip came with a greater punch:

It was good old Dion Cassius we believe who once described a certain race as 'an idle, indolent, thievish, lying lot of scoundrels'. We have heard or read almost the same words used to describe certain tribes in our Protectorate. The Latin historian's strong epithets referred however to the English.[108]

More sober in the same issue of the Mission magazine was the reflection on the increasing costs of running the Mission. With the arrival and expansion of administrative, commercial, and agricultural interests, Scott pointed out, the price of both labour and food had increased. 'There are plenty of resources in the Church of Scotland', he continued. His air of self-confidence was unlikely to endear many as he added: 'The Church of Scotland has yet to be taught to make

[107] LWBCA, May 1893. [108] Ibid., March 1896.

sacrifices – personal sacrifices – for her work and her faith. That stage of spiritual development she has not yet reached.' Where some White colonists were convinced of Africans' limited capabilities to learn, Scott had the audacity to suggest that spiritual development in the Church of Scotland was not at the required stage. This audacity and self-confidence also made him propose in 1897, when everything seemed to be conspiring against him, an ambitious new scheme of mission development.

The Mission Council, despite its formal bid to assemble once a year, had been dormant for several years when Scott reconvened it in 1897 to pass the new scheme. He was the chair, and the document was signed by only three other members of the Mission.[109] Neil Macvicar, who had joined the Mission the previous year to replace Affleck Scott, was the secretary, while the other two signatories, Henry Scott (no relation to Affleck and David Clement Scott) and James Reid, had been in Blantyre since the early 1890s and were notable chiefly for their loyalty to Scott.[110] The scheme proposed fundamental changes to how the Mission would be organized and what tasks it would take on in the future. 'Humanity urges us on', it stated as it described how the 'four outer spheres' beyond Blantyre would receive the status of Main Stations while Blantyre would be called the Central Station. 'The best boys' in each sphere would be sent away to 'pioneer' work in new areas. To increase the number of women in the Mission, the scheme proposed that 'the Ladies Committee be invited to send one, or even two ladies to each main station'. The proposal was in line with the pledge that 'we think it very important that at each main station girls' industries should be encouraged'.

The scheme further proposed vernacular literature to be prepared in science, history, and other subjects, noting that 'hardly any of the primers in use at home are in the least degree adapted to the native modes of thought either as they are or translated'. This work 'would bequeath a literature to the native Church in Africa'. Scott's emphasis on the vernacular was also evident in the pledge that 'language work and services' would be 'made available for use in the new spheres'. As to the costs of what effectively was a major expansion in mission work,

---

[109] British Central Africa Missionary Council, *Scheme of Mission Development*, NAM, 50/BMC/1/1/1.
[110] Ross, *Blantyre Mission*, 159, 169–70.

the proposal had little to say. It merely noted that the proposed scheme would be 'too large for the present constitution of the Foreign Mission Committee' and suggested that a separate Africa committee should be formed.

At a time when profound questions remained unanswered in the Blantyre Mission's theological and financial matters, the scheme's forward-looking approach was audacious to the point of being cavalier. While it may have indicated Scott's intent to stay as the Head of Mission for years to come, the Foreign Mission Committee gave the scheme short shrift. Scott's Council noted in its minutes from October 1897 that they had been informed that 'the Committee were not now in a position financially to carry out' the scheme.[111] To add insult to injury, it had also dawned on the Council that the Committee had not supplied the General Assembly with copies of the scheme despite receiving a sufficient number of them in good time. Such was the Council's urge to advance the cause of humanity that it had prepared the scheme as 'an appeal to the whole Church through the Assembly'. The proposal to separate the Africa Committee from the Foreign Mission Committee may well have been unpopular among the latter, but the Council felt that 'they were within the limit of their prescribed duty in making such recommendations'. Wounded and overlooked, the Council could only record its regret 'that a matter which is so important, and to which they gave so much time and thought, should be laid aside by the Committee with hardly a comment'.

Rather than the scheme for its development, it was a formally constituted Committee of Inquiry that once again brought the Blantyre Mission to the attention of not only the Church of Scotland but the wider reading public in Scotland and beyond. Where the 1881 inquiry had atrocities to consider, the complaints investigated by the 1897 committee were rather less dramatic, though deeply felt by those who had made them: Hynde, Rankin, and Robertson. The General Assembly appointed four 'laymen accustomed to deal with evidence' to hold hearings in Edinburgh and to peruse any books, correspondence, and other documents they thought were pertinent to the investigation.[112] Hetherwick was in Edinburgh during the hearings

[111] British Central Africa Missionary Council Minutes, 7 October 1897, NAM, 50/BMC/1/1/1.
[112] Report of the Committee of Inquiry into Complaints against the Mission, 1897, NAM, 50/BMC/1/1/1.

and, although 'he acted without special authority, took charge to some extent of the interests of Rev. Dr D. C. Scott', who had remained in Africa. Seventeen witnesses were heard in total, all of them Scotsmen apart from one Scotswoman, Janet Beck. Members of the Mission were only one constituent interviewed, others including representatives of planters, the African Lakes Company, and the Church of Scotland. Herd, the above-mentioned author of the White supremacist piece in *Central African Planter*, was one of them.

Among the allegations, the Mission's poor management of finances, high-churchism, and Scott's autocratic leadership stood out. The Committee noted that the Foreign Mission Committee had been aware of the rapidly increasing costs in Blantyre but had done little about them. An 80 per cent rise in expenditure had taken place in 1891 as compared with 1890, largely on account of the unauthorized 'extravagance' in building the Blantyre church. The Committee of Inquiry also commented on allegations against the Mission's boarding school, both that the system 'led to a good deal of petting and pampering' and that new boarders had been admitted with little regard to how to sustain them. The Committee responded to the first part of the allegation by stating that 'we would not dream of suggesting that the system should be abandoned, for its advantages from a missionary point of view are apparent to outsiders, and the results, so far as we can judge, are on the whole good'. The Committee did recommend that the number of boarders should be fixed by the Foreign Mission Committee and that Sunday Schools and individuals in Scotland should be encouraged to contribute more generally to Mission purposes beyond the current sponsorship of particular boys or girls. Overall, the Committee expressed its astonishment that there had been 'absolutely no audit' of the accounts in Blantyre. It found the situation 'clearly wrong and unbusinesslike'.

As for high-churchism, the Committee observed that any doctrinal issues would be beyond its competence, but restricted itself to the 'legality and propriety' of the practices described in the allegations. The Committee had satisfied itself as to the following facts:

At both [Chimang'anja and English] services the choir enter in procession from the vestry, followed by the minister, and wearing over their clothes white Arab shirts, which, we think, the complainers are justified in speaking of as surplices, see that they hang in the vestry, are in form and appearance practically identical with the Anglican surplice, are not worn by the other missionary boys, and are undoubtedly, so far as their use by the choir is concerned, ecclesiastical vestments. The officiating minister wears a surplice and stole. Till recently both minister and choir turned to the east when saying the Creed (which we gathered was said only at the native service), but this coming to the knowledge of the [Foreign Mission] Committee a peremptory order was sent out that the practice was to be discontinued.

The Committee of Inquiry concurred with the Foreign Mission Committee's earlier decision not to interfere with the procession and the wearing of the surplices. It bypassed the sensitivities over the alleged Anglican elements by elaborating on the differences between the needs of the African and European congregations. The early part of its reasoning seemed compatible with Scott's vision. Recommending that missionaries ought to be given 'a certain amount of discretion as to the type of the Church which they are to found', the Committee stated that 'it would be unreasonable to demand or expect that that Church should conform exactly to the type of the Church at home'. However, the Committee's subsequent comments on this subject betrayed its lack of understanding of what Scott had sought to achieve in Blantyre. 'Forms of worship', the report pointed out, 'which suit the Scottish character and temperament may fail to attract or impress the African mind'. The distinction between 'the Scottish character' and 'the African mind', though made with a benevolent intent, was oblivious to Scott's teachings on learning and sacrifice. By acknowledging that some Europeans may have found the Blantyre services 'distasteful', the Committee's view also foreshadowed the apparently liberal sentiment that would lead to two racially separate congregations in Blantyre.

Scott's alleged autocracy arose in the Committee's investigations into dismissals and resignations as well as into what Rankin had called in his letter to *The Scotsman* 'a fierce and unchristian rivalry...maintained at the three stations of Blantyre, Domasi, and Mlanje'.[113] After reviewing briefly various cases of dismissal or resignation among the Mission's European staff, the Committee sided clearly with Scott and Hetherwick in its conclusion that 'any friction which occurred was due to failure on the part of the subordinates to realise their necessary subordination to the Heads of the Mission, which alone could ensure the smooth working of its business, or to an extravagant notion which they had formed of their own

---

[113] 'Letter to Editor', *The Scotsman*, 22 December 1896.

importance'. The insubordination may well have been related to the situation in which 'a missionary teacher or artisan finds himself, when he goes out to Africa, in a higher relative position than he would occupy in similar work at home'.

Affairs at the Mulanje station merited special comment as the report went through several incidents causing discord between its Scottish members and Scott in Blantyre and Hetherwick in Domasi. It was the paragraphs that Scott had published in the Mission magazine on some of these incidents that the Committee found most lacking in tact when evaluating his leadership. Indeed, those paragraphs were not the only shortcoming that the Committee identified in the magazine. 'Its character has somewhat deteriorated', the report observed and found its recent articles on liturgy 'incomprehensible to the ordinary reader, and in our opinion of doubtful utility in the pages of a Mission magazine'. The Committee came to the conclusion that the very viability of the magazine had to be questioned: 'The stoppage of the magazine would also give Dr Scott more time than he has at present for Mission work proper.'

The Last Stand

Few changes to the magazine, and indeed to the Mission, took place as a result of these investigations. 'We are far from holding an unfavourable opinion of the Mission as a whole', the Committee announced in the end. Scott and Hetherwick may well have felt exonerated by the Committee's kind words in its conclusion.

We leave the inquiry with a profound conviction that the Church of Scotland has much reason to be proud of her African Mission, and that she owes, and the African race owes, a deep debt of gratitude to the missionaries for the great and beneficent work which, under enormous difficulties and heavy discouragements, they have carried on for the last twenty-two years in the Shire Highlands.

Exonerated or not, Scott was becoming a broken man when the Committee concluded its report. The premonition in his 1891 letter about difficulties gathering 'like hunters round their game'[114] had in 1895 begun to turn into disquiet over his legacy. Scott promised his

---

[114] Scott to Robertson, 5 August 1891.

friend in Edinburgh to write 'a sort of history of the Mission for there is no one now who knows it but myself. Letters give *so* much but not the balance of retrospection, proportion, and the future lies in the vision which guided the past – for God indeed has been with us'.[115] The pledge came in a letter whose tone was exceptionally pensive, reflecting as it did on losing the nearest and dearest to death. Yet Scott was nothing if not robust when faced with difficulties. As has been seen, he was masterminding an ambitious plan for Mission development in 1897, and shortly before the year of tragedies in 1895, he had cherished the prospect of Blantyre growing as the region's capital and had projected no fewer than three different railways to serve it.[116] In a rare reference to what he had been reading, Scott described his current interest in articles about Constantinople and the 'cosmopolitan relations' there between 300 and 1200. The future Blantyre had a formidable model for its own racial and religious diversity.

The history of the Mission came to be written by others than Scott, save for the reflections he included in scattered writings and sermons, such as the one delivered in Scotland in 1901.[117] During the final year of his tenure in Blantyre, his energies were spent on other kinds of writing, notably the Mission's scheme for development and his response to the Committee of Inquiry's report. While his response was not formally published, Scott found the opportunity in the Mission magazine to settle some scores with Rankin, whose letters in *The Scotsman* had done so much to misinform the reading public in Scotland. Scott's words conveyed exasperation.

A book had been kept by the Minister of Muthil for about ten years we believe, in which every scrap of gossip...that could be gleaned by interviewing, in the interests of this attack, every individual that came home, was entered...Our sorrow is that so many years of a minister's best work and most mature years have been lost and wasted in work so futile, for nothing saps a man's strength like prejudice, and nothing confounds work like getting up a case for prejudice confounded.[118]

As if to underscore the source of his own vision, Scott once more evoked what he had learned from the *mlandu* process.

---

[115] Scott to Robertson, 27 May 1895.
[116] Scott to Robertson, September 1894.   [117] Scott, *'Living Stones'*.
[118] LWBCA, May, June, and July 1897.

Truly Mission work in Blantyre is a fire, and as in a famous *mlandu* long ago a conclusive answer was given to an accuser of even greater weight than the minister of Muthil, it might be said, is not this Missionary 'a brand plucked out of the fire'.

As mentioned, Scott had not been interviewed by the Committee, and Hetherwick had to some extent represented his interests at the hearings. Despite the exoneration, Scott felt the need to have his own account on record. A hand-written document as opposed to the printed and published Committee report, it did not circulate anywhere as widely as the report did. It was sent with a minute from the Mission Council requesting the Foreign Mission Committee to make the report and Scott's response 'as public as the original charges were made public, in order that justice may be done to the individuals attacked, and that confidence may be restored in the Mission as a whole'.[119] After the scheme for development had been virtually ignored, the silence on his response may have added to Scott's sense that his time in Blantyre was indeed coming to an end.

Scott offered a detailed, virtually a blow-by-blow response to the allegations and their investigations by the Committee.[120] On Hynde he noted that 'his attacks have been utterly unprovoked by anything whatsoever on my part'. Scott had attempted to meet Hynde after his resignation by inviting him to spend Christmas at Scott's house, but Hynde had replied that it was too late to talk. Indeed, Scott admitted that problems with communication with his other critics in the Shire Highlands had affected the information he felt inclined to share with them: 'When it became, *through conspiracy*, impossible to talk and impossible to confide, conversation with those thus afflicted became much more confined to regular business.' Scott emphasized that he had taken counsel on important matters and that, in any case, 'such counsel-taking acted as validly for the early times and for more truly than any Council gathering could have done'. Here he defended a practice he had learned while observing chiefs taking counsel from their subordinates. It is worth recalling that Scott's dictionary had stated that 'for all his seeming power, the chief is hedged in as much

---

[119] British Central Africa Missionary Council Minutes, 19 May 1897, NAM, 50/BMC/1/1/1.

[120] Copy of Dr Ruffelle Scott's Notes on the Report Referred to in the Minute of Meeting of 19 May 1897, NAM, 50/BMC/1/1/1.

as, perhaps more than, the most constitutional minister in the most civilised states'.[121] With such lessons in mind, Scott could enter this defiant claim: 'Autocratic is as pure a misnomer as you could have found. I was the reverse.'

Scott did not seek reconciliation with his critics elsewhere in his response either. On the controversies at the Mulanje station, he first cited reports from the station staff and his own paragraphs about a theft case from 1893 before declaring that he felt no remorse over his words. The Mulanje missionaries had stated that 'the native is not yet at the point of view where he can see that kindness does not necessarily imply weakness'.[122] 'The native', in their view, had to understand that 'however soft the glove, the hand within it, when it has to touch wrongdoing, is a hand of steel'. In his comment published with this account, Scott had lamented what amounted to extra-judicial measures. 'The course pursued in this case does not seem to us a missionary use of the courts of justice towards those whom we have taken from the village and set ourselves to train.' His response to the Inquiry in 1897 defended this paragraph in no uncertain terms: 'I had no choice but put it in, and never was I more thankful for any paragraph I ever wrote. It was not I but Mlanje which broke the Mission front, and I had to save the Mission as best I could.'

Scott's response to the allegation of high-churchism played down the meanings attributed to the services by his critics and emphasized adaptation to African conditions without repeating the Committee's distinction between 'Scottish character' and the 'African mind'. He pointed out that he had on a different occasion explained to authorities in Edinburgh why he did not wear black. Apart from being much better cover against the heat, 'white suits Africa; it suits the dress of the natives'. It signified nothing 'except *order and cleanliness*'. Besides, Scott added, Hynde himself had worn the 'Arab shirt' while teaching in Domasi and had asked other teachers to do the same.

Scott ended his response with a passionate defence of the Mission magazine. 'It is the *only weapon* we could get with which to work deliverance for the natives.' The results were there for all to see: 'Taxation has become payable, tyranny hides its head, dark deeds are

---

[121] David Clement Scott: *A Cyclopaedic Dictionary of the Mang'anja Language Spoken in British Central Africa*, Edinburgh: Foreign Mission Committee of the Church of Scotland, 1892, 347.

[122] LWBCA, October 1893.

afraid.' Just as Scott took counsel as the Head of the Mission, so too were the magazine's contents discussed before printing. Scott's closing salvo asserted the magazine as 'unique, a Mission history, a Mission pulpit, a philosophy, a policy, and a salvation for the people'.

Rather than taking notice of Scott's writings, whether in this response or in the magazine as the 'weapon' of deliverance for Africans, the reading public in Scotland became acquainted with the Committee's report largely through a critique that differed dramatically from Scott's. *The Scotsman* had, not least because of Rankin's contributions, taken an interest in the Mission and provided its readership with an extensive account of the Committee's report.[123] While the newspaper summarized the verdict on Scott and Hetherwick as 'not guilty; but don't do it again', it went further than the Committee in its criticism of both the Foreign Mission Committee and Scott and Hetherwick themselves.

The broad facts remain that the Foreign Mission Committee have allowed this important Mission to get sadly out of hand, so that its heads were permitted to do practically what was right in their own eyes, in the matter of expenditure, of organisation, of ritual, and of local policy and management, and that this loose handling has had, among other manifestations, persistently 'strained relations' between Blantyre and the branch stations of Molange and Domasi, and occasional friction also with the Administration and with the planting and other sections of the European community.

Using the Committee's own turns of phrase to push its conclusions further, *The Scotsman* declared that 'the heads of the Mission have also "failed to realise their own necessary subordination" to the authorities at home, and have had "extravagant notions of their own importance"'. Such rhetoric was a measure of how little had percolated through the Scottish church and society of Scott's years of learning in central Africa. His evolving thoughts on authority and service, of responsibility and sacrifice, had made him decidedly less subservient to the Church of Scotland than to his vision for an interracial African Church.

How to manage his compatriots in Blantyre had vexed him all along and not only when Hynde and Herd began their campaign to discredit him. In 1889, for example, he had described to his friend in Edinburgh

---

[123] Editorial, *The Scotsman*, 25 March 1897.

his tribulations with Jonathan Duncan the gardener and James Hamilton the teacher.[124] Rankin's involvement in what appears to have been a minor conflict prefigured his role in the much more profound one with Hynde and Herd, but Rankin's words had already been hurtful enough. 'That Rankin can use the word oppression is very bad', Scott wrote, 'it is simply a lie'. What the rebels had not realized was that 'loyalty to authority which is not that of the king (supreme) but only a governor (delegated, sent) is in reality a test of goodness'. 'It is not the men that have been oppressed but myself', Scott added and described with some feeling how 'you have in fact to study moods, stand their temper, win them round, never find fault, never tell them to do anything, to keep unity at all, thankful if they show any generosity of spirit'. Scott announced where his priorities lay: 'The chief tyranny one has to watch against is that over the natives.'

The 'delegated' rather than 'supreme' authority that he desired to exercise was a disposition learnt in central Africa. It presupposed studying vernacular concepts and expressions, countless hours spent on observing and participating in the *milandu* cases, determination to allocate spiritual and practical responsibilities to Africans. The African Church, as Scott saw it, was about to blossom when European interests gained the upper hand. The legacies of Scott's vision would live on in the African deacons and in the increasing importance of schooling. Yet as one future was foreclosed another future took shape. For Scott himself, his vision got extinguished along with tragedies of the most personal kind.

---

[124] Scott to Robertson, 10 May 1889.

8 Grief Never Wears Out

When he delivered a sermon in Scotland in 1901 about the Blantyre Mission, David Clement Scott had a curious confession to make.[1] Once during his eventful years in central Africa, he had kissed a man. The object of his affection had been John Bowie, Isobel Scott's brother and the Blantyre Mission's physician. 'I am not ashamed to own', Scott told the congregation, 'that when he and I crossed the threshold of the manse on our journey up from Katunga's (we walked then), I kissed him for very gratitude at having won him for Blantyre'. Unusual circumstances had driven him to this behaviour: 'Britishers do not often kiss one another, but we were in action at the front, and men's hearts are strangely open then.'

References to same-sex intimacies come in the idioms of friendship and kinship in Scott's correspondence and reminiscences. Homosexuality among the British men of the Victorian age may have been less exceptional than the mores of the era would have suggested, as Cecil Rhodes's case appears to show for those involved in Africa's imperial conquest.[2] Yet to sexualize intimacies at the Blantyre Mission would have little basis in the available evidence and would distract from exploring how personal intimacies contributed to the sense of sacrifice. Unlike in the early nineteenth-century Cape Colony, sexual scandal – whether interracial marriage or adultery, venereal diseases, or illegitimate children – did not supply ammunition for White settlers to discredit the missionaries.[3]

---

[1] D. C. Ruffelle Scott, *'Living-Stones': Sermon upon the Church of Scotland Blantyre Mission, British Central Africa*, Edinburgh: William Blackwood and Sons, 1901, 20.

[2] Robert I. Rotberg with Miles F. Shore, *The Founder: Cecil Rhodes and the Pursuit of Power*, Oxford: Oxford University Press, 1988, 406–8.

[3] Elizabeth Elbourne, *Blood Ground: Colonialism, Missions, and the Contest for Christianity in the Cape Colony and Britain, 1799–1853*, Montreal: McGill-Queen's University Press, 2002, 226.

By 1891, Scott's leadership in Blantyre had been buttressed by the presence of individuals – men and women, European and African – whom Scott had personally 'won for Blantyre'. There were the close ties of kinship and marriage: his younger brother William Affleck Scott, brother-in-law John Bowie, and sister-in-law Harriet Henderson, who married in 1888 the Blantyre pioneer Henry Henderson. Then there were missionaries who had been inspired by Scott in Scotland, such as Janet Beck and Robert Cleland. Scott's affection for the African deaconate has already been described. His vignettes of the deacons, included in the 1901 sermon, outlined not only a missionary vision but also his appreciation of the range of personalities within the group.

An early experience of Africa, as seen in Chapter 3, had moved Scott to reflect on friendship. William Koyi had in 1881 brought to his mind James Robertson, who would correspond with Scott from Edinburgh throughout the Blantyre years. Friendship acquired further spiritual and sociological meaning when he embarked on translating the Scriptures (Chapter 4). It found another expression in the children that chiefs and headmen sent to Blantyre's first schools (Chapter 3). In everyday lives, both joy and grief inhabited the intimacy of friendship. 'I congratulate you very heartily upon the birth of your son', Scott wrote to Robertson in 1888.[4] Scott described the event a 'revolution', but already in 1891 he had to express his sympathies to Robertson for 'the death of your dear child'.[5] A month later, it was time to send condolences to Robertson on his brother's death.[6] It was in this letter that Scott told his friend that he knew 'a little of the depth of death's *bitterness*'. Earlier that year, John Bowie, Harriet Henderson, and her young child as well as Henry Henderson had all died. 'One dies absolutely in those one has lost, and life now has changed utterly', Scott wrote with the gravitas of someone who had mourned the deaths of loved ones. Isobel Scott, then in Britain for the joyous occasion of their daughter's birth, had shown Scott 'how grief never wears out'. In the earlier letter, Scott had identified with his grieving friend in these words: 'I need not say how sorrow and bereavement have taught me

---

[4] David Clement Scott to James Robertson, 19 October 1888, EUL, Gen. 717-10.
[5] Scott to Robertson, 17 July 1891.   [6] Scott to Robertson, 5 August 1891.

the very same lessons and made me feel, as no one can feel who has not passed through it, what it means.'[7]

More sorrow and bereavement were to befall Scott, who would have cut a broken figure at his departure from central Africa in 1898 even without losing his wife and brother in 1895. The assaults on his vision for the African Church took their toll, but disease and death precipitated his departure, with more tragedy to come in his final years in Kenya. Conquering death was the great promise Christian missionaries propagated across Africa, and tranquil deathbed scenes may have featured in the stories they told audiences in Africa and at home.[8] Yet death and bereavement experienced in the intimacy of actual relationships all too often had nothing serene about them. The accounts of the deaths in 1891 and 1895 speak of profound anguish – and sheer terror – that Europeans and Africans at the Blantyre Mission felt. While the sense of sacrifice may have attributed meaning to them, the deaths were senseless enough to make the sacrifice a matter of profound existential trauma.

Consistent with Scott's vision for the African Church was his appreciation of the African methods of mourning the dead. The entry for *maliro* in his dictionary, glossed as 'mourning' but commonly also used for 'funeral', was another instance of emphasizing the unity of the human race.[9] Describing the wailing that accompanied the announcement of death, Scott remarked that 'it is about the most hopeless picture that one can see, and the excitement, if not the sorrow, seems most genuine'. Rather than attempting to replace the excitement with serene deathbed scenes, Scott saw in the sorrow a basis for common humanity: 'One need hardly say that sorrow is just as real among these so-called savage nations as among civilised.' Across such a putative divide between the 'nations', Scott could detect 'the increased bitterness of the sufferings of Christ'. Indeed, the capacity to mourn brought about equality as well as unity: 'There is a ministry of suffering and sorrow, but this postulates the innate human equality of the heathen with the nations of civilisation.'

---

[7] Scott to Robertson, 17 July 1891.
[8] Rebekah Lee and Megan Vaughan, 'Death and Dying in the History of Africa since 1800', *Journal of African History*, 49 (3), 2008, 352–3.
[9] David Clement Scott, *A Cyclopaedic Dictionary of the Mang'anja Language Spoken in British Central Africa*, Edinburgh: Foreign Mission Committee of the Church of Scotland, 1892, 309–10.

Theological compatibility inhered not only in the unity and equality of death and mourning but also in the regeneration emphasized by central African and Christian dispositions. The carefully followed stages of funerary rituals prepared the bereaved for new life after death, not unlike how 'the sufferings of Christ' gave way to the renewal promised by the resurrection. Afterlife, as mentioned, received little elaboration from Scott and his African advisers – the emphasis was on *living*. It is no wonder, therefore, that Scott was receptive to requests by the Africans around the Mission to bury the best-loved Europeans in their own way. An African funeral, as is seen below, awaited Bowie in particular, but remarkable about the African reactions to deaths among the Europeans was the deep sorrow they expressed about losing the physicians Bowie and Affleck Scott and the female missionaries Isobel Scott and Harriet Henderson. They were the individuals who had done the most for African welfare, whether by healing them or by providing them with opportunities for women's employment and for connecting them with far-flung well-wishers. As for Scott himself, the departure in 1898 not only extinguished his vision for the African Church, it also marked his social death in central Africa, a condition that made many Africans reluctant to mourn the eventual sad news from Kenya.

Giving Lives to Africa

While death would mark the ultimate sacrifice, the Europeans closest to Scott had also made other kinds of sacrifices to join him in central Africa. Bowie, the son of the secretary of the Philosophical Institution in Edinburgh, had been destined to an affluent urban life.[10] After substituting a career in business for studies in medicine, with gold medals and other honours paving his way, Bowie had joined a 'large and lucrative' practice in London. Well-liked by his patients, he and Sara Hankey – his wife and the daughter of a retired colonial officer in India – none the less felt compelled by his sister's and brother-in-law's tales of Blantyre. Forsaking a comfortable income and an impressive London home, they were undeterred by the modest remuneration offered by the Foreign Mission Committee. 'Oh', exclaimed Bowie's

---

[10] William Robertson, *The Martyrs of Blantyre: Henry Henderson, Dr. John Bowie, Robert Cleland*, London: John Nisbet and Co, 1892, 77–80.

nineteenth-century biographer, 'how small one feels in the presence of such noble self-sacrifice as that!'[11]

Affleck Scott's life gave rise to similar acclaim among Europeans and Africans alike. In his case, the medical and theological qualifications had been preceded by excellence as a student, athlete, and flautist.[12] Added to it was the kind of service to the poor that tested the conventions of even the most ardent Christian philanthropists. Scott's biographer recalled the bewilderment of Scott's friend, who had witnessed a band of flute-playing 'ragamuffins' parading in central Edinburgh.[13] Amongst them was Scott, 'playing one of the instruments with all his might, as if he had no greater satisfaction in the world'. It was one of the many activities he engaged in as a student bent on mingling with the city's 'motley crew' of 'labourers, scavengers, performers at "penny gaffs", rag-pickers, street-loafers of every description, fallen women'.[14] He rented a small room away from his fellow students in a particularly deprived area of the city and opened it to young lads whom even the Church of Scotland had largely ignored. 'Dissatisfied with Church life as it showed itself throughout the city',[15] Scott was quick to follow his brother's footsteps to central Africa. The Foreign Mission Committee felt as unable to support him financially as it did Bowie. Scott agreed on a salary of £150 instead of the usual £300.[16] 'Half-pay for him meant', his brother recalled in 1901, 'with his wife and child sent home, that he lived on rice, rice, and the gravy of a skinny fowl'.[17]

The deaths in 1891 left vacancies that new men not chosen by David Clement Scott came to fill. It was a measure of the cleavage between the old and the new that in one of his first letters to Adam Currie, John McMurtrie of the Foreign Mission Committee had to respond to Currie's complaint about salary (Figure 8.1).[18] McMurtrie pointed out that 'two young ministers who preceded you and who are also doctors, went out on £150'. Currie had queried why only £250 had been proposed as his salary when the committee's chair Archibald

---

[11] Ibid., 81.
[12] W. Henry Rankine, *A Hero of the Dark Continent: Memoir of Rev. Wm. Affleck Scott*, Edinburgh: William Blackwood and Sons, 1896.
[13] Ibid., 71–2.   [14] Ibid., 70.   [15] Ibid., 79.
[16] Andrew C. Ross, *Blantyre Mission and the Making of Modern Malawi*, Blantyre: Christian Literature Association of Malawi, 1996, 30.
[17] Scott, *'Living-Stones'*, 20.
[18] John McMurtrie to Adam Currie, 26 March 1891, NLS, Ms 7534.

Figure 8.1 Adam Currie and pupils. Reproduced with the permission of the National Library of Scotland and the Church of Scotland World Mission Board

Scott had indicated £300 to him. While Scott had, upon McMurtrie's investigation, offered to cover the £50 shortfall, McMurtrie felt obliged to let the committee know that in his opinion, £250 would be enough 'for the health and comfort of a young bachelor'. In 1893, now posted at Mulanje and accompanied by his young wife, Currie received a pointed reminder from McMurtrie that his report on the mission activities was overdue.[19] At a time when fresh scepticism about the mission in central Africa had begun to be expressed in *The Scotsman*, McMurtrie told Currie that 'we don't know exactly how all your time is filled up at Milanje on Sundays and weekdays'. On

---

[19] McMurtrie to Currie, 9 November 1893, NLS, Ms 7534.

Currie's request for funds to build a new house, McMurtrie advised him to cut costs by building it himself with local assistance. 'An African missionary has to put his hand to many things that ministers at home never think of.'

Sacrifice, whether financial or physical, hardly described Currie's missionary vocation or that of his compatriots in Mulanje where, as seen in the previous chapter, the European discontent with Scott's vision first came to be roused. The lack of sacrifice coincided with gender and race relations decidedly at odds with what was the practice in Blantyre. Currie caused Scott some irritation, for instance, when he failed to attend meetings in Blantyre on the pretext that his wife could not be left without a White man in Mulanje.[20] Isobel Scott, among other European women, had faced far greater dangers without special provisions for her safety. The Mulanje staff also abandoned their station twice in late 1893 upon hearing rumours about imminent attacks by the Yao chief Mkanda. Ever the attentive husband, Currie had resolved to abandon the station, because 'a woman had to be protected'.[21] Jessie Monteath Currie recalled her husband giving her a loaded revolver 'to put a bullet in [her] own head' if the 'wild chief's' men captured her. When the rumour appeared for the second time, Mkanda did lead his men against Europeans in the Mulanje area, and the missionaries fled leaving guns and ammunition behind. They were later used by Mkanda's men against the British Commissioner's tiny army. Scott's scathing remark on the Mulanje staff's cowardice carried the authority of someone who had learnt the arts of diplomacy from African chiefs themselves.[22]

The Breath of Death

'I don't think there could be a nicer place to work in than here.'[23] Where Jessie Monteath Currie's reminiscences of central Africa conveyed fear and idleness, Harriet Henderson's words in a letter to home brimmed with enthusiasm. She became, among other things, one

---

[20] Ross, *Blantyre Mission*, 159–61.
[21] Jessie Monteath Currie, *The Hill of Good-bye: The Story of a Solitary White Woman's Life in Central Africa*, London: George Routledge and Sons, 1920, 133.
[22] *Life and Work in British Central Africa* (LWBCA), December 1893.
[23] Robertson, *The Martyrs*, 71.

of the founders of the Blantyre laundry that would offer women an industry where men had the printing press. A dozen girls who had completed schooling had joined the laundry, while some sixty girls were attending school when Henderson wrote one of her last letters before tragedy struck.[24] She reported with some pride that Chief Masea had recently sent his five daughters to the school, accompanied by five other daughters of his various headmen. Henderson's own recent motherhood appeared to enhance her affection for the schoolgirls: 'The children are what one might call "jolly" – full of fun and brightness.'

Henry Henderson, the father of her toddler-son, on the other hand, cut a decidedly less fun and bright figure when ill health struck him. The young wife felt that her fever-stricken, 'altogether miserable' husband looked 'about 150 years old just now' and could be mistaken for their son's grandfather.[25] Yet it was the mother and the child who would precede him to the grave. Within ten days, the Blantyre Mission was to lose the Hendersons' son, Harriet Henderson, and her brother John Bowie. The tragedy came in the aftermath of an influenza epidemic that had killed more than twenty people within a five-mile radius from Blantyre.[26] It had its impact on Bowie's vigour as the only medical doctor in the area, but the actual cause of the three deaths was diphtheria. Affleck Scott, who had missed Harriet Henderson's demise while visiting Mulanje, reflected subsequently on the mysterious origins of the disease.[27] He could not be certain whether African children had suffered from it, but the only known cases in the Shire Highlands had afflicted European children. The causation felt 'inexplicable' because water and milk were generally boiled before consumption. 'There was nothing epidemic about the disease' that took the three lives in Blantyre, he wrote in his medical report for the year. The mother had been infected by her child before the symptoms were recognized, while Bowie got it after sucking the tracheotomy tube to relieve the child. The disease appeared to spread no further from its three victims.

The uncertainty over causation could only add to the shock felt by the Mission's European and African members. The suffering, indeed the terror, that had captured the patients must have been unbearable to behold. So unbearable it was that the doctor himself, aware of 'the

[24] Ibid., 70–1. [25] Ibid., 72. [26] Ibid., 95. [27] Rankine, *A Hero*, 207–8.

breathing of death' he took, decided to relieve the child by sucking for several times the membrane from his throat.[28] It brought the child temporary respite, but he was the first to die. Bowie later performed the same procedure on his sister despite becoming increasingly bedridden himself. The deathbed scenes here gave rise to memories of both love and terror. Harriet Henderson died as her soon-to-die brother whispered words of comfort into her ear.[29] Affleck Scott, too late to be by her bedside, witnessed Bowie's final moments. Scott's medical knowledge made him describe the disease as 'giving symptoms similar to those of hydrophobia and much of its terror'.[30] He and Henry Scott, no relation, and the medical missionary called to attend from Domasi, decided against tracheotomy as the patient seemed to breathe almost normally. Yet the end came with the terror they both had dreaded – 'a noisy, utterly incoherent delirium, ceaseless restlessness, and fearful distress'.

Before the diphtheria attacks, Henry Henderson had been ordered by Bowie to take furlough for health reasons. The journey to Scotland had to wait until he had buried his wife and child in Blantyre. The fragile Blantyre pioneer made it to Quilimane in Mozambique, where he was buried in the Protestant section of a Catholic cemetery.[31] David Clement Scott described the two men who had lost a wife and a sister in these words: 'I do not think I ever heard a more heartrending sound than the voice of these two strong men, Henry Henderson and Jack Bowie, in loud and bitter weeping upon each other's shoulders.' The deaths were an 'awful prelude of the breaking up which followed', Scott remarked with hindsight. In the immediate aftermath of the tragedies, however, he resolved to 'pull [himself] together to save what of the Mission we could'.

Angels of Mercy

When Affleck Scott hurried from Mulanje to Blantyre with his African associates, covering a four days' journey in forty-eight hours, they encountered keen interest in Bowie's condition in each of the villages they passed through.[32] Scott and his men did not bring the news to these villagers – on the contrary, some villagers claimed to know more

[28] Robertson, *The Martyrs*, 96. [29] Ibid., 99. [30] Rankine, *A Hero*, 203–4.
[31] Scott, *'Living-Stones'*, 17–18. [32] Rankine, *A Hero*, 202.

than they did, such as the word that Bowie's condition was improving. The interest and the anguish felt far and wide led to the demand by the Africans in and around the Mission that they were given the task of digging his grave.[33] Here they positioned themselves as Bowie's *adzukulu*, the term for grandchildren but also used for those who performed funeral labour, regardless of the actual genealogical connection. David Clement Scott would have understood the request's meaning, having glossed the singular form *mdzukulu* in his dictionary, before listing the genealogical connotation, as 'one who buries another, even a stranger who performs that office'.[34] He explained that the office-holders 'lay out the body, wash and swathe it, and put it outside the house'. These duties came with the privilege to 'eat the sacrifices' – the food that had been arranged for the departed. Eating this food was another instance of the intimacy that the funeral labour forged between the deceased and the *adzukulu*.

The request was granted, and Bowie became the first European in Blantyre to be buried in this fashion.[35] Scott and his deacons' court had not prescribed in any detail how funerals should be conducted in the Christian key. They did rule out certain already obsolete practices – notably the slaying of people to accompany a chief to the grave – while replacing others – such as dances and songs – with Christian hymns and readings. Much remained familiar to central Africans, however, including the corpse being placed outside the house before the final journey to the graveyard. There awaited the grave dug into an L-shape, where two of the *adzukulu* placed it into the side compartment. Scott was able to detect in African funerals, as in so many other aspects of central African life, Christian elements to warrant his vision for the African Church. The offering of beer at the anniversary of a chief's death, for example, reminded him of the blood of Christ pouring out.[36] It led to one of his characteristic reflections on the lessons for the missionary to learn: 'Missionaries lose much by failing to understand the frequent beauty and even naturalness of heathen custom.'

The request to bury Bowie in the African way was, of course, a mark of respect to the deceased rather than to Scott's vision for the African Church. Bowie had earned this accolade by attending to the sick regardless of their race or status. For example, when many in

---

[33] Robertson, *The Martyrs*, 100–1.
[34] Scott, *A Cyclopaedic Dictionary*, 342.
[35] Ross, *Blantyre Mission*, 153–4.
[36] LWBCA, January 1895.

Europe's ruling and educated elites were still bewildered by the tracheotomy performed on the German Emperor in 1888,[37] Bowie was carrying out a similar operation on an illiterate old woman in central Africa.[38] A cancerous growth in her throat had all but devastated the woman, but Bowie offered, with her and her relations' consent, to perform the tracheotomy operation on her. It was a measure of their trust that the operation could take place, and for some twelve months, the woman lived by breathing through the tube, the quality of her life greatly improved. The amount of care that her condition required cannot be overestimated. The tube had to be cleaned daily by Bowie or his assistant Nacho Ntimawanzako, one of the Africans who had accompanied David Clement Scott to Scotland. It is not clear to whom the woman was related, but the extent of care she required made it likely that she lived at or near the Mission. For Bowie, her deformed figure could not conceal a human being worthy of care, respect, and affection. He wrote thus in a letter:

To a casual observer our old patient would appear a most wretched, dirty, ugly creature. She is old, shrivelled, and wrinkled, her faced deformed by the once ornamental scars, her upper lip huge and pendulous, and more disfigured by the hole in which, before her operation, she carried a large *pelele* ring. In addition, she has a cataract in her left eye, and when she looks up to you the greyish-green colour of the pupil gives her almost an uncanny look. And beneath all this there is a fine human being, and even her face becomes noble to those who have watched her in her long illness.

The intimacy and affection forged in the acts of care could not distract Bowie from his ethical commitments as a medical doctor. Later in the same letter, he described how the woman had, after the twelve additional months to her life had passed, whispered to him, 'I am very tired; will you give me some medicine to make me die?' Such a request did not merit in Bowie's account other than an acknowledgement of how 'very sad' it was to see her suffer. Nor did Affleck Scott administer more than 'a whiff of chloroform' when Bowie himself was lying on his deathbed delirious and distressed.[39] He did so in the knowledge that it would 'relieve him and not hasten the end'. The two doctors remained

---

[37] John C. G. Röhl, *Young Wilhelm: The Kaiser's Early Life, 1859–1888*, trans. Jeremy Gaines and Rebecca Wallach, Cambridge: Cambridge University Press, 1998, 778–82.
[38] Robertson, *The Martyrs*, 92–4.   [39] Rankine, *A Hero*, 204.

loyal to the passage in the Hippocratic oath that states, 'I will not give any man a fatal poison, even if he asks me for it'.[40] Yet unlike the medical humanitarians working in twentieth-century catastrophes, they did not face human suffering on such a massive scale as to make the saving of anonymous, abstract 'bare life' their mission. They were physicians driven by the kind of Christian humanism that David Clement Scott pursued in his vision for the African Church. It involved discerning 'a fine human being' even in a person shattered by disease – an intimacy of care in which lives were always lived in specific relationships, brought together in common worship as much as in common humanity.

Affleck Scott's service in central Africa also included acts of care and compassion that would make his death in 1895 another momentous occasion. Alexander Hetherwick recalled telling him to take a portable hammock (*machila*) for his own comfort on a journey when he was not feeling well.[41] To Hetherwick's query after the journey if he had taken it, Scott replied, 'Yes, but the *machila* did not take me'. It had brought back a sick African patient. Other journeys to administer medicine showed a similar tendency to put his patients' comfort before his own, such as walking routinely from Blantyre to Mulanje for this purpose. His habit of walking long distances astonished Africans who had grown accustomed to seeing Europeans being carried on their journeys. Scott had called his legs 'my donkey' (*bulu wanga*).[42] Where Scott's compassion won him admiration among Africans, it befuddled European planters. After his death, one of them described witnessing Scott saving a drowning African: 'I saw him once swim the Shire to help a damned n*****.'[43]

The acts of care and compassion should not be taken as acts of heroism. 'A hero of the Dark Continent' was what Scott's biographer called him in a doubly mistaken portrayal.[44] Scott neither presented himself as a hero nor would he have called Africa the Dark Continent.

---

[40] Giorgio Agamben, *Homo Sacer: Sovereign Power and Bare Life*, trans. Daniel Heller-Roazen, Stanford, CA: Stanford University Press, 1998, 143.

[41] Alexander Hetherwick, *The Romance of Blantyre: How Livingstone's Dream Came True*, Edinburgh: Lassodie Press, 1931, 100.

[42] Harry K. Matecheta, *Blantyre Mission: Nkhani za ciyambi cace*, Blantyre: Hetherwick Press, 1951, 15; *bulu* is translated as 'horse' in Harry. K. Matecheta, *Blantyre Mission: Stories of Its Beginning*, trans. Thokozani Chilembwe, Berlin: Wichern-Verlag, 2016, 37.

[43] Hetherwick, *The Romance*, 100.   [44] Rankine, *A Hero*.

Angel Michael slaying the dragon did appear in the Blantyre church window dedicated to his memory and designed by David Clement Scott as 'a most appropriate tribute to the memory of one who was young, vigorous, and devoted and whose work was the slaying of the dragon in his attack upon the bodies and souls of men'.[45] None the less, responding to a request for information for a possible biography about his brother in 1895, Scott was sober in his assessment: 'My brother's life was in actual service a short one and one lived to do unostentatious work. Material for a volume will scarcely be found I fear, but there is at least enough for a good-sized pamphlet.'[46] The Africans who crowded into the Mission on hearing the news of his death came to mourn not so much a hero as a healer. 'We have no doctor now!', was the cry heard among the people at Ndirande whose missionary Affleck Scott had been.[47]

Heart-rending was also the letter that Scott's domestic servant wrote to his widow in Scotland.[48] It conveyed the fear of destitution when not only the doctor but his wife was thought to have disappeared from the lives of her African dependants. Addressing her as 'my *donna*', Abrey Ndendermere told the widow that 'I have kept in mind that my *donna* said she would come back, and I have remembered it every day. But now I know she will not come back to me, and that my eyes will never see her again.' Her words 'now I am a poor girl – for my master is dead' were typical of the predicament, as seen in Chapter 2, in which freedom lay in the capacity to associate oneself with those who had the wherewithal to enable the flourishing of others. Ndendermere may, of course, have written her poignant words to remind the widow of her African obligations beyond her husband's death. What the letter and the mourning confirmed, in any case, was the extent to which the lives of some Blantyre missionaries became so entwined with African lives that their deaths shattered Africans and Europeans alike.

They Buried Her While I Was Unconscious

It may come as a surprise to learn that, for all his care and compassion, Affleck Scott's death had been precipitated by participation in a military campaign. In early 1895, he joined the small army convened by

---

[45] LWBCA, August 1896. [46] Scott to Robertson, 15 August 1895.
[47] Rankine, *A Hero*, 302–3. [48] Ibid., 305–6.

Acting Commissioner Alfred Sharpe not as a combatant but as a medic to neutralize the threat posed by Yao chief Kawinga. Scott's participation may appear all the more surprising, if his irate letters about Commissioner Harry Johnston's military campaigns only three years earlier are recalled. In 1892, for example, he wrote to Archibald Scott in Edinburgh that 'we shall soon be like the Portuguese, unable to advance because the people know that our coming means injustice and oppression'.[49] Having accused Johnston earlier in the letter for being Rhodes's 'paid servant', Scott stated in no uncertain terms that 'we want no colonials here'.

It was not for any sudden desire to defend colonial occupation that Scott offered his medical support in 1895. Kawinga posed an existential threat to the Domasi mission station, the settlement with Europeans nearest to the prominent slaver's stronghold in the Chikala hill some twenty miles away.[50] Matters came to a head when he attacked Chief Malemia, his rival and the Mission's old ally, in January 1895.[51] Unlike the European staff at Mulanje who had in 1893 abandoned the station after hearing rumours, everyone at Domasi refused to move to the administrative capital Zomba despite Sharpe's orders. Sikh and Tonga soldiers then came to erect a stockade at Malemia's three miles from the mission station and were promptly attacked by Kawinga's men. It was on the subsequent punitive expedition up the strenuous, rain-soaked hill path that Scott, who had already contracted fever, found himself along with the soldiers and a few other civilian volunteers.[52] Kawinga's standing among his headmen was rapidly waning, and the superior firepower soon annihilated the threat he had posed.

During these troubles, the Domasi station was run by David Clement Scott.[53] Alexander and Elizabeth Hetherwick had returned from furlough with their young son Clement in late 1894 and had agreed with Scott to stay in Blantyre while he and Isobel Scott would

---

[49] William Affleck Scott to Archibald Scott, 9 June 1892, NLS, Ms 7534.
[50] Hetherwick, *The Romance*, 97–101; William P. Livingstone, *A Prince of Missionaries: The Rev. Alexander Hetherwick of Blantyre, Central Africa*, London: James Clarke and Co, 1931, 88–90.
[51] John McCracken, ed., *Voices from the Chilembwe Rising: Witness Testimonies Made to the Nyasaland Rising Commission Inquiry, 1915*, Oxford: Oxford University Press for the British Academy, 2015, 366.
[52] Rankine, *A Hero*, 289–96.
[53] Hetherwick, *The Romance*, 100–1; Livingstone, *A Prince*, 88.

seek some peace and quiet in Domasi. His intent was to complete translation work; her words in a letter to a friend, on the other hand, assume bitter poignancy when the subsequent tragedy is recalled: 'It is the first time my husband and I have been alone together since we were married.'[54] Scott may have wanted to counter with bravery and diplomacy the cowardice he had seen among the Mulanje staff. So strained was the uncertainty when the punitive expedition disappeared for several days that his wife's health began to deteriorate rapidly. By March, Scott had decided to take her to Scotland. When they arrived in Blantyre, they found Affleck Scott bed-ridden and weak, delivering orders on his treatment to George Robertson, the former Mulanje missionary and now Europeans' physician in Blantyre.[55] David Clement Scott took to monitoring his brother's pulse, but he could only watch him perish. 'That last Sunday evening', Hetherwick later wrote, 'we shall never forget. The shadow hung over his brother and his wife, but he came forth from it to preach at the evening service as we have never heard him preach before or since'.[56] After the brother's death, he left his colleagues in Blantyre to bury him and proceeded with his wife to Mozambique to board a steamer.

No sooner had they taken to the sea than Isobel Scott died.[57] They turned back, and she was buried in Mozambique. Some two months later, Scott had recovered enough to tell his friend in Edinburgh about the tragedy.[58] James Robertson had already sent him his condolences, but Scott felt compelled to share some of the turmoil that had engulfed him for over two months. He had had little or no sleep for those two months, and little to eat, and when he prepared his wife for the funeral, he collapsed. 'I had dressed my darling and bound her dear face when there swept over me the meaning of it all and then I was done for. They buried her while I was unconscious.' Isobel Scott – his companion on diplomatic expeditions to suspicious chiefs, the connection between African pupils and their British well-wishers, the champion of women's industries – had played a very full part in Scott's vision for the African Church. 'There was not the smallest portion of work which I did not do with and in a way *to* my wife, and in every one of life's interests I found I had died in the shock which came upon me at Mozambique.'

[54] LWBCA, September–October 1907.
[55] Rankine, *A Hero*, 301–2.
[56] LWBCA, September–October 1907.
[57] Ibid.
[58] Scott to Robertson, 27 May 1895.

After the deaths of John Bowie, Harriet Henderson, and Affleck Scott, Isobel Scott's failing health alarmed Africans associated with the Mission. 'Let us go and die with her', was the cry Henry Tilowa at Blantyre's printing press used to galvanize his colleagues to join him on a journey to Domasi.[59] A dozen young men set off, armed with rifles from the Acting Commissioner, but the punitive expedition had departed before they arrived. Instead, they were the ones who would soon help Scott carry her to Blantyre.

After the burial in Mozambique, Scott continued the journey to Scotland as 'a broken man', as Hetherwick put it, adding, 'He was never the same again.'[60] In his letter to Robertson, however, Scott described his road to recovery.[61] Janet Beck, the unmarried missionary who had attended the same parish as Scott in Edinburgh, had accompanied him and his wife on the ill-fated journey. Beck, who stayed with him until Zanzibar, began to read for Scott to distract him from dark thoughts. He summoned his inner strength in response: 'Every atom of interest I could get I took hold of to build up life again.' Alone at sea, he found inspiration in his late mother: 'Sea air acted as a marvellous restoration and a sort of elasticity of nature which I inherit from my mother helped with determination to bring me round – but I need not attempt to tell with what desolation and misery.' Scott would return to Blantyre in July 1896 after an absence that had included a visit to Australia, marriage to Edith Ruffelle and an honorary doctorate in Divinity bestowed on him by the University of Edinburgh.[62] By then, however, the end of his vision for the African Church was imminent.

Homebound

Scott suffered the personal tragedies of 1891 and 1895 precisely when he and his closest associates were embroiled, among other things, in protests against the administration's military campaigns, in the mounting criticisms of liturgy and expenditure, and in the new missionaries' reluctance to support his vision for the African Church. Between the premonition of his letter in 1891 (see previous chapter) and the hindsight of his 1901 sermon, life and work went on despite

---

[59] Hetherwick, *The Romance*, 101.   [60] Ibid.
[61] Scott to Robertson, 27 May 1895.
[62] Ross, *Blantyre Mission*, 164; *The Edinburgh University Calendar 1896–97*, Edinburgh: James Thin, 1896.

tragedy and disappointment. Edith Ruffelle Scott took on what Isobel Scott had begun in Blantyre and appears to have gained the trust of both Africans and the Foreign Mission Committee. She worked in the dairy and the laundry as well as in the sewing and Bible schools.[63] She also became the head of the Blantyre school.[64] Just as Isobel Scott and Elizabeth Hetherwick had taken the responsibility of connecting African schoolchildren with well-wishers in Britain, her correspondence with the Foreign Mission Committee included exchanges about schoolchildren supported in this way.[65]

David Clement Ruffelle Scott, as he had begun to call himself after the second marriage,[66] was the recipient of correspondence from the Foreign Mission Committee that combined solicitude over his health with reprimands over his conduct. In December 1896, for example, Archibald Scott wrote to him to complain that 'you had again got strained, and [were] drawing upon regions of which alas you have no "reserve"'.[67] 'I am very sorry', he continued, 'that you had to return so soon'. Far from lamenting inactivity at Blantyre, however, this was also the letter in which he, prompted by fresh allusions to Johnston, advised Scott to exercise 'a rigid censorship' in the Mission magazine. Concerns over health and policy became difficult to distinguish in the period around Scott's departure from Blantyre in January 1898. The strain on Scott's health was indeed considerable. The Commission of Inquiry may have exonerated him formally in 1897, but the toll taken on him by constant, and public, criticisms should not be underestimated. Added to these ordeals in the months preceding the departure was the death in Blantyre of Edith Ruffelle Scott's first and only child.

'Welcome home!' was the merry message that John McMurtrie sent to Scott in April 1898.[68] The 'home' on this occasion was at Edith Ruffelle Scott's parents estate in Tunbridge Wells, England, while the two daughters from Scott's first marriage, Margery and Isobel, had been sent to live with Sara Bowie, John Bowie's widow in Edinburgh.

---

[63] Foreign Mission Committee papers in John William Arthur Papers, EUL, Coll-207.
[64] Matecheta, *Blantyre Mission: Nkhani za ciyambi cace*, 9; Matecheta, *Blantyre Mission: Stories of Its Beginning*, 31.
[65] John McMurtrie to Edith Ruffelle Scott, 17 September 1897, NLS, Ms 7625.
[66] LWBCA, August 1896.
[67] Archibald Scott to David Clement Ruffelle Scott, 4 December 1896, NLS, Ms 7536.
[68] John McMurtrie to David Clement Ruffelle Scott, 4 April 1898, NLS, Ms 7536.

Continuing with his uplifting tone, McMurtrie reported seeing the daughters and finding them 'looking very well'. Margery, he added, 'is tall and straight as a willow'. No less complimentary was McMurtrie's comment on Edith Ruffelle Scott: 'She has done splendidly in Africa: everyone there says so.' As for Scott himself, 'you have borne a heavy strain in Africa since you left', and 'to rest is your duty just now'. The tone was, in effect, to dissuade Scott from contemplating further missionary work.

The correspondence after the return to Britain indicates, however, that Scott may not have considered his departure from Blantyre final at all. The Church officials in Edinburgh went to some lengths to address his impatience to resume the missionary vocation. McMurtrie welcomed Scott's self-reported improvements in health in October 1898 but avoided answering his question about return to Blantyre.[69] Instead, he praised Scott's offer of translation work for the Africa subcommittee. Now resident with Edith Ruffelle Scott and his daughters at Sara Bowie's house in Edinburgh, Scott continued to pursue a medical clearance that the subcommittee had established as one condition for his return to missionary work. By mid-1899, he had secured such a certificate, but McMurtrie had to break the news to him that the subcommittee had declined to give its approval for Scott's return.[70] It had, he quoted from the minutes, 'resolved to recommend that for the present it would be unwise for Rev Dr Clement Ruffelle Scott to return to Blantyre'. It fell on McMurtrie to suggest other ways in which Scott might occupy himself. The subcommittee thought, he explained, that 'you can do more for Africa here at home' and was willing to arrange a Scottish parish for Scott to run. Concern over another bout of ill health was the ostensible reason for the subcommittee's decision. 'You gain many hearts when you preach', McMurtrie pointed out, 'but if you came home again invalided, you might find this changed'.

Because not even a doctor's certificate had convinced the Church authorities to grant Scott his wish to return to Blantyre, more than concern over health may have been at issue. After all, Scott had left Blantyre under the dark clouds of political, financial, and theological controversy, and Hetherwick's long experience made him the obvious successor as the head of the Mission. Yet it is also important to

---

[69] McMurtrie to Scott, 11 October 1898, NLS, Ms 7536.
[70] McMurtrie to Scott, 9 June 1899, NLS, Ms 7537.

recognize that the concern over health may have expressed disquiet about other than mere physical aspects of a person's condition. When McMurtrie noted that Edith Ruffelle Scott was 'not very strong', his view may have been influenced less by the usual anxiety about 'white ladies' in Africa than by his awareness of her trials and tribulations. Mental health was not singled out as a separate concern in these exchanges, but Scott's insight into how 'grief never wears out' after Isobel Scott had lost her brother, sister, and nephew within ten days put into words the depression she suffered from. Edith Ruffelle Scott, who had lost her infant in Blantyre, was 'not very strong' either physically or mentally. When she died after only a short time in Kenya, the question was who should bear responsibility for the tragedy.

Of Prayers and Potatoes

Scott's persistence won in the end. Yet it was not to the Shire Highlands but to the Kikuyu highlands that he took his wife and daughters. The East African Scottish Mission had begun in the early 1890s as a private, non-denominational initiative among pioneering White settlers in Kenya to buttress their economic interests with the assumed civilizing effects of a Christian mission.[71] Less than a decade would pass before its custodians realized that qualified missionaries were few and far between. They decided to approach the Church of Scotland, where McMurtrie responded with some enthusiasm to their offer to hand the Mission over to the Foreign Mission Committee.[72] In a warning that would have been all too familiar to Scott, he added that the committee had no capacity to increase its 'pecuniary burden'.

The 'considerable embarrassment' that Scott's enforced idleness in Edinburgh was beginning to cause to the Foreign Mission Committee had found a solution.[73] Much was different, however, from the way the Blantyre Mission had been established among its African neighbours. Before Scott's arrival, the Mission had been built on possessing as much Kikuyu land as possible to encompass its people within the Mission's boundaries. In an apparent contradiction to his conviction in

---

[71] Brian G. McIntosh, *The Scottish Mission in Kenya, 1891–1923*, Doctoral Dissertation, University of Edinburgh, 1969, 35, 50.
[72] John McMurtrie to Donald Macleod, 19 December 1900, NLS, Ms 7538.
[73] McIntosh, *The Scottish Mission*, 156.

Malawi that the African land belonged to the Africans, Scott actually extended the Kikuyu Mission's land holdings and, after eighteen months of hard bargaining with the Commissioner and the Land Officer, acquired an estate of over three thousand acres.[74] Here he not only accepted the prevailing notion that Africans could not have titles to land, but he also actively promoted European settlement and commerce. For as Arthur Ruffelle Barlow, Edith Ruffelle's nephew who joined the Mission in 1903 as a seventeen-year-old, came to reminisce, he found Scott dedicating himself 'unsparingly' to an ambitious scheme of agricultural development to increase the 'extremely limited' Mission funds.[75]

While Andrew Ross's verdict that 'Scott was unable to repeat his Blantyre miracle' in Kenya is sound,[76] the apparent shift in his methods may not be as puzzling or 'strange' as it seems.[77] On one hand, Scott had recently emerged from years of arguments about expenditure with the Church of Scotland that was unable or unwilling to increase its funding. As has been seen, he had in 1893 started to plant coffee in Blantyre in 'self-defence' against such parsimony despite misgivings about 'entering into the labour field with the other colonists'.[78] The move to Kenya saw this approach becoming the Mission's main method of raising revenue. Yet just as he had pursued the model of an industrial mission in Blantyre, so too in Kenya was the agricultural scheme a means of both revenue and revelation. The Africans already on the land would provide a supply of workers and converts.[79] Europeans would provide connections for marketing the produce. Scott was as convinced as everyone else in Kenya's White population that their numbers would only increase in the future. Christianity and commerce would, in his vision, keep Black and White together for the prosperity of all. In another of the bitter ironies of Scott's legacy, the Africans living on the Mission land came to be treated as 'squatters' after his demise.[80]

---

[74] Ibid., 175–7.
[75] Arthur Ruffelle Barlow, 'Some Early Memories', n. d., EUL, Gen. 1786-1.
[76] Andrew C. Ross, 'Scott, David Clement Ruffelle', in Gerald H. Anderson, ed., *Biographical Dictionary of Christian Missions*, New York: Simon & Schuster, 1998, 608.
[77] Adrian Hastings, *The Church in Africa*, Oxford: Clarendon Press, 1996, 427.
[78] Scott to Robertson, 20 March 1893.
[79] McIntosh, *The Scottish Mission*, 177.   [80] Hastings, *The Church*, 427.

Of Prayers and Potatoes 221

Although Scott was driven by a similar enthusiasm to that which he had possessed in Blantyre, the scheme of agricultural development was both a financial failure and a source of missionary discord. Rather than start with cultivating coffee, whose first produce would take years to appear, Scott focused his efforts on cultivating beans and, above all, potatoes.[81] 'Not a few prayers [went] unanswered with regard to consignments of potatoes', Scott is said to have confessed years later.[82] The pressure was great to get the produce to foreign markets before it perished, and major setbacks occurred when, for example, a consignment of potatoes was left to rot on the Mombasa dockside and another was stolen at Delagoa Bay.[83] Such losses were grave, because Scott had invested all his capital in this single venture. All financial and administrative responsibility rested on Scott himself and a small number of friends in Edinburgh, including his brother Andrew Scott, who had formed an industrial committee to support him.[84] James Robertson, with whom he had corresponded during the Blantyre years, was also instrumental in convincing the Church authorities to permit the scheme. Such was the ignominy that Scott eventually suffered, however, that he came under threat of court proceedings for his large overdraft at a Mombasa bank.[85] A. H. Charteris, his long-time mentor in Edinburgh, came to his rescue during the final months of his life. By soliciting a substantial donation, he prevented bankruptcy.[86] Its deposit in Scott's private bank account would, after his death, cause controversy with the Foreign Mission Committee, as described below.

The Church of Scotland Mission's subsequent impact on Kenyan political and social life would make it comparable to what the Blantyre Mission achieved in Malawi, not least when Jomo Kenyatta, the Mission-schooled future president of Kenya, became the general secretary of the Kikuyu Central Association in the 1920s.[87] Such developments followed a change of course that the young missionaries Barlow and John William Arthur charted away from Scott's emphasis on

---

[81] McIntosh, *The Scottish Mission*, 179–80.
[82] John William Arthur to his mother, 4 June 1907, EUL, Coll-207.
[83] McIntosh, *The Scottish Mission*, 179–80.   [84] Ibid., 174–5.   [85] Ibid., 188.
[86] A. H. Charteris, *In Memoriam: David Ruffelle Scott*, Edinburgh: R & R Clark, 1907, 17, *Nyasaland and Kikuyu Vol. V: 1906–8*, Centre for the Study of World Christianity, University of Edinburgh.
[87] John Lonsdale, 'Kikuyu Christianities: A History of Intimate Diversity', in David Maxwell and Ingrid Lawrie, eds, *Christianity and the African Imagination: Essays in Honour of Adrian Hastings*, Leiden: Brill, 2002, 172–3.

agriculture to education. One of Scott's methods of introducing the Gospel to the Kikuyu workers was to hold a service of twenty minutes every morning before they scattered into the fields.[88] A dozen men had become a dedicated class working towards baptism by Christmas 1907 – too late, as it turned out, for Scott.[89] Indeed, he saw adults rather than children as the Mission's primary constituency and conveyed his impatience to the recently arrived Arthur in 1907: 'Why wait for a dozen years for your children to grow up?'[90] He added, 'Blantyre is all very well, but why wait for the ten years of Blantyre before you have your converts?' These rhetorical questions did not stop the shift of emphasis from the industrial mission to teaching and preaching.

Theologically and politically, the evidence on Scott's sustained commitment to the vision for the African Church is thin. He never reached the linguistic and philosophical heights of his formative years at Blantyre. Still in 1907, his Gikuyu language remained so rudimentary that he gave his sermons with an interpreter. He was able to use Swahili in the sermons, but a mixture of Hebrew and Greek was also their feature.[91] It would fall on Barlow to achieve for Gikuyu something comparable to Scott's work on Chimang'anja, although his early vocabularies hardly suggested a philosophical interest. In language examinations, for example, Barlow made missionaries translate orders such as 'I want six trees felled, barked, and brought here'.[92]

A Queer Kind of Love

The first letters that the young John William Arthur wrote to his mother from Kenya illustrate both the esteem and the anxiety that Scott inspired in the new generation of missionaries. Arthur arrived in the Mission when Scott was absent, but his reputation was much on Arthur's mind. 'In Blantyre the natives one day came to him to pray for rain', he wrote to his mother, 'and within an hour it had come in sheets'.[93] The power of Christian prayers to supplant non-Christian methods in attracting rain was as serious a prospect to many

---

[88] Arthur to his mother, 4 June 1907. [89] Charteris, *In Memoriam*, 21.
[90] Arthur to his mother, 4 June 1907. [91] Arthur to his mother, 19 July 1907.
[92] Derek R. Peterson, *Creative Writing: Translation, Bookkeeping, and the Work of Imagination in Colonial Kenya*, Portsmouth, NH: Heinemann, 2004, 42.
[93] Arthur to his mother, 10 March 1907.

nineteenth-century European missionaries as it was to Africans.⁹⁴ Scott was a man of 'a tremendous faith' who could, however, be 'a little difficult to work with at first'.⁹⁵ Arthur anticipated a 'difficult time' when his 'faith may be very strongly tested', and he asked his mother to pray for him. If it was a formidable personality that gave Arthur cause for concern, mission policy would from the outset create tension between them. Scott was lukewarm about Arthur's ambition to expand the boys' boarding school but 'tremendously keen on the agricultural policy'. 'I saw', Arthur noted, 'that our boys and girls work will be almost entirely dependent on ourselves, as he appears to me to lay far too much stress on the adult work'.

Once he had the opportunity to spend an hour and a half with Scott one morning, Arthur discovered greatness that their differences over policy expressed at committee meetings had not revealed. Scott was, Arthur concluded, 'one of the greatest men of the world in every respect. No matter what profession he had taken up, he would have made his mark. He has tremendous brain; no matter what the subject, he seems to know all about it. He knows all about the stars and is very musical. He has a splendid deep base [*sic*] voice'. Even the agricultural scheme had to be understood as a sign of his greatness: 'He simply couldn't do things on a small scale.' Clearly flattered by the sense of becoming Scott's 'confidant', Arthur listened keenly to his account of his own conversion and missionary work in the Shetlands before the departure to Africa. Evidently aware of his reputation, Scott 'admits he has the prophetic vision but he thinks there are too few of them nowadays'. Despite the tensions over policy, Arthur left the conversation feeling 'no fear of our getting on together'.

Whatever the awe, and perhaps affection, that Scott inspired in his young colleagues, his final years in Kenya were marred by a sense of isolation. Edith Ruffelle Scott, who never recovered her physical and mental strength from the loss of her child in Blantyre, died in December 1902. As if to atone for the unconscious state in which he had lain during Isobel Scott's funeral, he made all the funerary arrangements himself and conducted the funeral service.⁹⁶ Only a few others

---

⁹⁴ Paul Stuart Landau, *In the Realm of the Word: Language, Gender, and Christianity in a Southern African Kingdom*, Portsmouth, NH: Heinemann, 1995, 26.
⁹⁵ Arthur to his mother, 10 March 1907.
⁹⁶ Arthur to his mother, 19 July 1907.

attended it – six Europeans from the Mission and a small number of Africans working there.[97] On the white stone over her grave Scott had inscriptions engraved – in a different language on each face of it: Hebrew, Greek, Latin, and English.

As early as in 1901, Scott yearned the company of his African collaborators in the Shire Highlands, but Hetherwick declined to send any of them to Kikuyu.[98] While his stature among colonial officers, White planters, and Christian missionaries would grow over the years in Kenya, he appears to have enjoyed little of the camaraderie, whether European or African, that had enlivened his Blantyre heyday. Barlow, of 'a reserved and hypersensitive nature',[99] was no John Bowie or Affleck Scott. The Kikuyu men in his class, no doubt at least partly because of Scott's own linguistic limitations, proved no match to the affection and intellectual stimulus he had enjoyed with the African deacons in Blantyre.

His daughters back with Sara Bowie in Edinburgh, Scott again sought solace in male friendship. It came in the figure of George Abercromby, an agnostic and a civil servant in Britain, who had come to Kenya on Scott's invitation to assist him with accounts. Much of Abercromby's time in Kenya was spent in a Nairobi hospital after he had contracted malaria. Despite his own difficulties to walk, Scott would pay him frequent visits and wrote these words to his sister: 'O, Rene, how I have come to love Abercromby. I never felt the same way for a man before. It is a queer kind of love, almost as if he were my son, and I could sacrifice anything for him.'[100] Intimacy in the idiom of kinship and friendship had as little to do with sexuality as did kissing John Bowie in Blantyre. Sacrifice is the key notion here – the lengths one would go for the sake of faith, friendship, and love.

Debts of Honour

Edith Ruffelle Scott's death confronted the bereaved with the question of whether Scott had gone too far in his mission to give lives to Africa. John McMurtrie had the thoroughly unpleasant task of addressing her father's bitterness at her untimely death. He sought to absolve himself

---

[97] Arthur in a circular, 14 October 1907.
[98] McIntosh, *The Scottish Mission*, 182.
[99] Ibid., 190.
[100] Charteris, *In Memoriam*, 19.

and his committee in Edinburgh of any blame.[101] Against the committee's advice, 'both Dr and Mrs Scott were bent on going together'. Scott had issued an ultimatum. 'They were deeply attached, and Dr Scott claimed his right to take his wife with him, and his daughters, and intimated that he would resign if his request was refused.' Her determination, with a touch of premonition, had made her tell a friend, 'If I go, I shall die, I know; but if he goes without me, he will die.'[102]

In February 1902, McMurtrie had written his first letter to Scott after the move to Kenya.[103] He was concerned about the delay in constructing a house to accommodate the ailing Mrs Scott – 'that was why', McMurtrie wrote pointedly, 'I pressed you to go out alone for 6 months'. He was similarly concerned about the well-being of Scott's daughters: 'I fear the girls would have a rough experience among the uncivilised and heathen people at Kikuyu.' So lacking in building materials for a house suitable for 'a lady in delicate health' was Kikuyu deemed to be that a large house was ordered to be built in Glasgow.[104] Scott, whose previous architectural designs included the St Michael's and All Angels in Blantyre, sent the plan to Glasgow and learned only after the house had been built how expensive it was. He had tried to cancel the order, reporting to the committee that suitable clay had been found locally for making bricks, but the house had already left for Africa on a steamer. To make a fiasco out of a miscalculation, the steamer had got stranded on the coast of Africa and was estimated by McMurtrie to be a wreck when he wrote to Scott's father-in-law.

There was, in other words, plenty to weigh on Scott's body and mind during the final years of his life. The bitterness of death he had described in his letter to Robertson in 1891 continued to haunt him in ways he could not have foreseen then.[105] The question of responsibility for Edith Ruffelle Scott's death only compounded what losing their child and Isobel Scott, and other deaths around him, must have done to his own condition. Along with a receding vision for the African

---

[101] John McMurtrie to W. Ruffelle, 10 February 1903, NLS, Ms 7539.
[102] James Robertson, *In Memoriam: David Ruffelle Scott D.D.*, Edinburgh: William Blackwood and Sons, 1907, 12, *Nyasaland and Kikuyu Vol. V: 1906–8*, Centre for the Study of World Christianity, University of Edinburgh.
[103] McMurtrie to Scott, 28 February 1902, NLS, Ms 7539.
[104] McMurtrie to Ruffelle, 10 February 1903.
[105] Scott to Robertson, 5 August 1891.

Church, and the personal isolation at Kikuyu, Scott had changed from a broken man at his departure from Blantyre to a crippled man by 1907. Rising up to lay the foundation stone of a new hospital had required major effort.[106] When the end came on 13 October that year, Scott had been barely able to walk any longer, having suffered from thrombosis of the veins in his legs.[107]

The financial difficulties in Kenya posed other questions of responsibility after Scott's death. Charteris courted controversy when he mentioned in his extensive obituary that the Foreign Mission Committee had 'made the strange condition that they would have no monetary responsibility for his agricultural work'.[108] During his visit home in 1906, Scott 'had to run a gauntlet of severe criticism which it makes one sad to remember'. Charteris claimed that the Committee had acknowledged its debt to Scott but that no compensation had been forthcoming. An extract letter from McMurtrie appended to the obituary, dated 19 December 1907, protested against these allegations and expressed regret at not having seen a draft of the obituary. McMurtrie considered it 'unfair' to present the issue in this manner to the public and cited a minute from the Committee's meeting in 1903. 'They acted on the understanding', he told Charteris, 'that a small Industrial Committee, of which you were a member, "took entire financial responsibility for and charge of the industrial scheme"'.

It may be pathetic that a dispute over financial accounting should have tarnished the immediate aftermath of the visionary's death. Yet it brought to the fore, somewhat in the vein of Edith Ruffelle Scott's death, questions of obligation and debt that needed answers. Whether prompted by Charteris's allegations or not, McMurtrie swiftly convened a Special Committee to oversee a Memorial Fund in Scott's name. Composed of McMurtrie, James Robertson, Archibald Scott, and the future Lord Polwarth, Walter G. Scott, it announced in January 1908 that it would welcome donations in view of Scott having 'risked and lost a large part of his narrow private means in an attempt to develop agriculture for missionary purposes at Kikuyu'.[109] While the donors could indicate their wish for their money to be used for

---

[106] Charteris, *In Memoriam*, 20.   [107] McIntosh, *The Scottish Mission*, 190.
[108] Charteris, *In Memoriam*, 16.
[109] John McMurtrie et al., *In Memoriam: David Clement Ruffelle Scott, D.D.*, 1908, Nyasaland and Kikuyu Vol. V: 1906–8, Centre for the Study of World Christianity, University of Edinburgh.

memorial plaques in Blantyre and Kikuyu, the Special Committee expressed as their own wish to forward much of the funds to Scott's children. 'We regard it as a debt of honour.'

A former treasurer for the Foreign Mission Committee had other ideas. James Paterson pointed out that a donor, Jane Houldsworth, had pledged in 1907 to support the Kikuyu Mission with an initial £600, followed by £400 per year for four years.[110] Paterson had never seen the £600 and had later learned that it had been transferred directly into Scott's private bank account – the transaction that Charteris had alluded to in his obituary. Paterson wished, already in January 1908, to insert some sober accounting into the sentiment after Scott's death: 'Kindly feeling and generous sentiment towards Dr Ruffelle Scott and his family must be put on one side, and this matter dealt with as a business transaction.'[111] A single woman and a frequent benefactor 'living on own means' in a sixty-room property in Ayrshire,[112] Houldsworth had not specified what her sponsorship should be used for at Kikuyu; nor was it, Paterson submitted, in her power to change its purpose without the Foreign Mission Committee's explicit approval. His notion was to use the donations to the Memorial Fund to cover what should have been in the Committee's account. It evoked yet another sense of obligation in the controversy. If Paterson's proposal was not followed, 'the Foreign Mission Committee will fail in its duty to the Church', with adverse consequences for future donors' willingness to co-operate.

The treasurer's words appear to have fallen on deaf ears, because McMurtrie was able to report in May 1908 that a total of £675 had been received for the Memorial Fund.[113] Of the total, £20 had been forwarded to Blantyre and Kikuyu for the memorial plaques, while the rest had been sent to Scott's two daughters through their uncle, Andrew Scott, a chartered accountant. A receipt for £655 had been signed by all three of them, with the assurance that they would follow

---

[110] James Paterson, 'Re Miss Jane Houldsworth's Contribution of £600 to the Kikuyu Mission', 28 February 1908, Nyasaland and Kikuyu Vol. V: 1906–8, Centre for the Study of World Christianity, University of Edinburgh.

[111] James Paterson to the Members of the Finance SubCommittee, the Kikuyu Special Committee, and the Acting Committee, 17 January 1908, Nyasaland and Kikuyu Vol. V: 1906–8, Centre for the Study of World Christianity, University of Edinburgh.

[112] Jane Houldsworth, 1901 Census, retrieved from scotlandspeople.gov.uk.

[113] McMurtrie et al., In Memoriam.

the Special Committee's recommendation that the money 'be securely invested and only the interest used'. It added to the legacy expressed in Scott's will of April 1907 in which he had specified his sister-in-law, a resident of Birmingham, England, as an inheritor along with the daughters.[114] Over eighty individuals appeared on McMurtrie's list of donors, including the confidant James Robertson (a donation of £11) and the mentor A. H. Charteris (£5), while an anonymous 'Old Friend' was the source of the biggest single donation (£60). No one Scott had encountered during his Blantyre years appeared on the list, but Alexander Hetherwick had been informed by McMurtrie of the money for the commemorative plaque. It was duly produced and placed on an inside wall of the St Michael's and All Angels, the only mention of the visionary, as the final chapter will discuss, a twenty-first-century visitor will find in what became the Blantyre Synod.

The Two Deaths of David Clement Scott

It is in Arthur's letters that detailed, first-hand accounts of Scott's deathbed scene and his funeral can be found. Aware of his unique access to these final scenes, Arthur made a circular of his lengthy letter and no doubt had an eye for what a noble missionary death should look like.[115] On the other hand, his understanding of African concepts and practices of mourning was confined to the notion that, he told his readers, 'the Kikuyu custom is to take their dying out into the jungle, where wild animals may do the last rites for their dead'.[116] Yet Arthur could not fail to notice that adults had begun to cry like children upon hearing the news about the death of a man they had called Watenga, a name Scott had been given by local Kikuyu for his frequent use of the Chimang'anja verb *kutenga* (to take).[117] Bedridden and in great discomfort, Scott had had bouts of breathlessness for some days, and when he recovered enough to recognize that death was imminent, he asked Arthur and Barlow to bring Karanja, the Mission's first convert, for baptism.[118] If Scott's African life had sought reversals in race

---

[114] Wills and Testaments, Edinburgh Sheriffs Court, 'Scott, David Clement Ruffelle', retrieved from scotlandspeople.gov.uk
[115] Arthur to his mother, 22 October 1907.
[116] Arthur in a circular, 14 October 1907.
[117] McIntosh, *The Scottish Mission*, 190.
[118] Arthur in a circular, 14 October 1907.

relations, he achieved one of them on his deathbed. Instead of baptizing a dying African, the missionary himself was dying as he performed the baptism. The scene recalls one of Scott's most startling maxims, already cited in this book, that 'the native may be saved without us, but we doubt if we here can be saved without the native'.[119]

At the funeral, so Arthur wrote in his circular, fourteen settlers were present, along with representatives from the government and other Christian missions, 'the mission complement of boys, girls, and young men, all dressed in white, while in and around the building were large numbers of workers and natives belonging to the Estate'. The building was the church which Scott, despite some six years at Kikuyu, had not been able to see to its completion. 'Open to the four winds', as Arthur put it, the church bore little resemblance to the monumental St Michael's and All Angels in Blantyre. More pertinent to marking Scott's vision was the topic Charles Hurlburt, the director of the Africa Inland Mission, had chosen for the service before the burial. Speaking in Gikuyu, he expounded on friendship as a theme in Scott's thought, at its centre 'the friendship of Jesus Christ, the Friend of *all* men'. Arthur did not provide more detail on Hurlburt's address, but he specified the Scriptures read at the service as 'selections from the sixty-first of Isaiah, the fourth of the first Thessalonians, and the last chapter of Ephesians'. After the benediction, Harry Leakey of the Church Missionary Society led the procession to the graveyard. The coffin, in Arthur's words, was 'borne by the loving hands of the settlers'.

After the preceding chapters, it can only be richly ironic, if not tragic, that Scott's earthly remains should have been carried by 'the loving hands of the settlers'. Arthur, still a newcomer to Africa, left few traces of how Africans participated in mourning Scott. It is not clear, for example, whether the funeral labour of digging the grave had any similarities to the way Africans wanted to be the *adzukulu* at John Bowie's funeral. What is clear is that Africans did come in large numbers to the funeral and cried profusely. Instructive was Arthur's comparison between this funeral and those of the two other Europeans who had predeceased Scott on the Mission's estate. David Watson, who had founded the Mission in the Kikuyu highlands, had had no Africans attending his funeral. Edith Ruffelle Scott, as has been seen, had had a handful of Africans associated with the Mission at hers. The

[119] LWBCA, December 1891.

crowd of Africans of every description at Scott's funeral indicated to Arthur that 'the Kikuyu heart [was] changing', but it also marked Scott as different from other Europeans. Sociological observations were not, however, Arthur's concern in his circular. He devoted the final four paragraphs to a rousing call for more missionaries to come forward in Scotland for Africa.

Karanja himself penned two letters that Charteris's obituary saved for posterity.[120] Just as Scott would evoke friendship and kinship when expressing intimacy, such as in his comment on Abercromby, so too did Karanja see himself as a child to a father. Addressing Scott on his sickbed, Karanja began by asserting that 'I am your child in very deed. Always do I remember you as I remember my father who begat me, or my wife and child.' Swearing his commitment to 'know Church work', he added, 'and now when I see you are sick it makes me very, very sorry. I cannot make words about it'. After Scott's death, he deployed his halting English to convey compassion and kinship with Scott's daughters. He described to Isobel how her father had baptized him by putting water on his head and retaining Karanja as his name. 'I sorry because my father died', he wrote to his European sister. 'No other man could keep me like he and to help me.'

Meanwhile in Blantyre, the news about Scott's death had also been received with reverence and sorrow. It reached Hetherwick while he was at Nthumbi, the mission station overseen by Harry Kambwiri Matecheta among the Ngoni of Ntcheu District.[121] Hetherwick was quick to note that Scott would have cherished the scene there: 'A crowd of baptisms, a large communion, the first Christian marriages.' His obituary recalled the early years of Scott's life at Blantyre – the sons of Kololo chiefs as the school's first boarders, Scott's diplomatic efforts at easing hostilities, and above all his two major achievements: the dictionary and the church building. As in all his public remarks on Scott, Hetherwick lauded the uniqueness of his long-time chief.

> We could only think of him as in the early days when he was in the full vigour of his strength – brave, energetic, full of thoughts and inspirations that struggled to find utterance. He stood even then alone – apart from all other men in his thoughts of truth and God – seeing visions of men and things that few could see save himself, for he was ahead of us – far, far above us all.

[120] Charteris, *In Memoriam*, 23.   [121] LWBCA, September–October 1907.

The same issue of the Mission magazine had an article entitled 'A Native Appreciation' to follow the obituary and the words delivered at the English service by Hetherwick. Its author, Mungo Chisuse, had known Scott since his arrival in 1881 and asserted intimacy with him by claiming to know him 'better than others'. Translated from Chiyao, Chisuse's text recalled the many journeys they had made together in the Shire Highlands and beyond to advance peace, including the success at putting an end to Ngoni raids into what Chisuse called 'the Yao Country'. He did not mention a journey they had made together even further afield – to Scotland, where Chisuse had furthered his education (see Chapters 4 and 7). Instead, Chisuse proceeded to describe Scott's standing as an arbiter of disputes. People would come with their grievances and disputes to the Mission, which they called *Pa Scott*, 'at Scott's'. It was how Chisuse ended his tribute, however, that revealed the distance that Scott's prolonged absence had created between him and the people in the Shire Highlands.

When Dr. Scott went to Scotland, all were amazed, wondering if he were gone for good – till they saw he did not come back. Then they had mourned for him beforehand. Now that we have heard he is really dead, we cannot mourn – we can only stand amazed because sorrow has gone on before with mourning for Dr. Scott. And it was sorrow indeed, for all that Dr. Scott wished to see – the Church of this place – he will not himself see. Now I must stop for all that Dr. Scott did is too much to tell. Among the people here his name was widely known.

As far as the Africans in and around Blantyre were concerned, Scott had died well before he was 'really dead' in Kenya. The relationships of intimacy, of learning and working together, had not survived the departure from Blantyre. The kind of anguish that Abrey Ndendermere had conveyed in her letter to Affleck Scott's widow must have gripped an even larger number of people when they realized that the chief of *Pa Scott* would never return. It is not clear whether any of them knew that Scott had asked Hetherwick to release some of his trusted friends at the Blantyre Mission for the Mission at Kikuyu. Instead, what Chisuse's final remarks make clear is that Scott had not sustained a connection to the Africans in the Shire Highlands and had, as such, suffered a social death there. For all the fine words delivered at the English service of the St Michael's and All Angels on the first Sunday after the news of his death, no *maliro* mourning honoured Scott's memory at the very place where he had done the most for his vision for the African Church.

While delivering his words at the church service, Hetherwick pointed out that Scott had died in the year when 'the beginning of a new era in the history of the Protectorate' had dawned. An article entitled 'Nyasaland' followed Chisuse's tribute in the Mission magazine, applauding the shift from the 'clumsy and cumberous designation' British Central Africa to 'the poetical name' of Nyasaland. As the article also noted, the Commissioner had been made a Governor, while executive and legislative councils would be formed imminently. Change was palpable, but Hetherwick could have identified two other years in the recent past for uncanny coincidences. As has been seen, 1891 was the year of both the protectorate's formal inception and the premonition Scott felt as the assaults on his vision intensified. On the other hand, 1901 was not only the year when Scott's move to Kenya was confirmed, it was also the year when two separate congregations – one White, the other Black – were instituted in Blantyre.

9 | Liberal Translations

David Clement Scott and Alexander Hetherwick were classically educated theologians, whose skills included the ability to read, and to translate from, the Bible in Hebrew and Greek. Both came to compare the African vernacular to these ancient languages. Four years after his arrival in Blantyre, Scott wrote to his friend in Scotland that 'Hebrew shines in a new light, and even Greek the civilization of the past has closer affinities with Mang'anja than the modern language of today'.[1] Fifteen years later, Hetherwick used the pages of the Mission magazine, *Life and Work in British Central Africa*, to pronounce precisely the opposite: 'Greek thought flows in a wholly different groove from Mang'anja or Nyanja thought.'[2] These comments illustrate more than differences over the extent to which the vernacular could accommodate the Hebrew and Greek expressions of the Scriptures. Taken together with their other views on the vernacular and on race relations, they reveal how far apart the two colleagues travelled in the many years they spent in Africa.

Hetherwick's approach to the vernacular reflects the widening White–Black divide he oversaw as the Mission's head after Scott's departure in 1898. Described as 'paternalist' where Scott was a visionary, Hetherwick never ceased to use his moderate voice when African interests came under threat by White settlers or the colonial administration (Figure 9.1).[3] In fact, as was seen in Chapter 6, his voice was anything but moderate in 1892 when, in Scott's absence, he criticized the approaches taken by the administration and settlers. Hetherwick's

---

[1] David Clement Scott to James Robertson, 5 January 1885, EUL, Gen. 717-10.
[2] *Life and Work in British Central Africa* (LWBCA), February 1900.
[3] Andrew C. Ross, *Blantyre Mission and the Making of Modern Malawi*, Blantyre: Christian Literature Association of Malawi, 1996, 126–7; John McCracken, *Politics and Christianity in Malawi 1875–1940: The Impact of the Livingstonia Mission in the Northern Province*, Cambridge: Cambridge University Press, 1977, 173–4.

Figure 9.1 Alexander Hetherwick at his desk in Blantyre. Reproduced with the permission of the National Library of Scotland and the Church of Scotland World Mission Board

tributes to Scott were invariably heart-felt and laudatory.[4] Yet the vernacular was for Hetherwick the property of the people whose 'native' tongue it was, and if it proved limited in its capacity to express concepts and ideas in the Bible, it needed conversion as much as its speakers did. When seen as aspects of their respective convictions about race relations, the two men's language ideologies begin to seem less like differences in individual preferences than historical junctures at which African futures were being imagined in incompatible ways. Scott's insistence on sacrifice as an epistemic as well as a personal commitment to Africa as the risen Christ faded into a dispassionate and paternalistic guidance towards African self-rule in the unspecified future.

The guidance presumed a fundamental difference between Black and White even as it advanced liberal sentiments. Writing from retirement in Scotland over four decades after his first arrival in Africa,

---

[4] LWBCA, September–October 1907; Alexander Hetherwick, *The Romance of Blantyre: How Livingstone's Dream Came True*, Edinburgh: Lassodie Press, 1931, 34–6.

Hetherwick reflected on the existential gap between himself and 'the African' that his decades in Malawi had not been able to bridge.[5] Hetherwick's reflections contributed to new, apparently liberal writing on Africa, exemplified by books such as Daniel Crawford's *Thinking Black* in 1913.[6] 'To understand "the African"', as Joanna Lewis has commented on this genre, 'one had to think in a different way'.[7] 'To think as an African thinks', went Hetherwick's own reasoning, 'is an achievement impossible to me as a white man. The black man's whole upbringing, environment, and outlook, have raised a high wall between his mind and mine, that I have never got over'.[8] As was seen in Chapter 5, his very first arrival in Africa, in the company of Henry Drummond, may have left an indelible mark on his thinking along these lines. Paradoxically, it was a mode of thought that appeared compatible with the emerging rallying cry 'Africa for the Africans' – but not before unprecedented formality had been instituted at the Blantyre Mission, from Bible translation to the intimacies of Christian marriage. The so-called native rising of 1915, led by the Mission-schooled John Chilembwe, provides an apt, if tragic, finale for the transformation in which Hetherwick was an influential participant. The liberal and piecemeal work towards an 'Africa for the Africans' began to face an altogether more urgent assault on race relations.

Christian Language

In two instalments of an article entitled 'Some Translation Difficulties', and before he had convened a committee for the purpose, Hetherwick published in 1900 his thoughts on the issues confronting the translator of the Bible into Chimang'anja / Chinyanja.[9] Among others was the above-mentioned conviction that 'Greek thought flows in a wholly different groove from Mang'anja or Nyanja thought', the former characterized by 'its passive voice and its oblique constructions' and

---

[5] Alexander Hetherwick, *The Gospel and The African*, Edinburgh: T. & T. Clark, 1932.
[6] D. Crawford, *Thinking Black: 22 Years without a Break in the Long Grass of Central Africa*, London: London, Morgan, and Scott, 1913.
[7] Joanna Lewis, *Empire of Sentiment: The Death of Livingstone and the Myth of Victorian Imperialism*, Cambridge: Cambridge University Press, 2018, 113.
[8] Hetherwick, *The Gospel*, 3.   [9] LWBCA, February 1900 and March 1900.

the latter by 'vividness, action, present perception'.[10] In a marked contrast to Scott's expectation that the Chimang'anja Bible would become superior to the English one, Hetherwick hailed the King James Authorized Version of 1611 as 'the best type of a translation from the original of the New Testament tongue. It is expressed in the very purest English, and it is faithful in the highest degree to the then Received text of the sacred volume. Nowhere do we find our tongue modified or influenced by the classical idioms of the original. It preserves for us and as long as our language is spoken will continue to preserve the "well of English undefiled"'.

Hetherwick was considerably less sanguine about the prospects of Chimang'anja / Chinyanja to offer appropriate concepts and idioms in the manner of English some centuries earlier. Because Chimang'anja / Chinyanja was 'a vehicle almost entirely void of religious or theological phraseology', recourse had to be taken to more 'civilised tongues'. While long contact warranted Arabic influence on Swahili, a position some missionaries would contest in the early twentieth century,[11] translators into Chimang'anja / Chinyanja had to look elsewhere: 'As regards Mang'anja or Nyanja we have no such past association with any civilised tongue. If any foreign language is to bear to Mang'anja the relationship that Arabic has borne to Swahili that language must be English.' English words – or their Africanized versions such as *angelo* for 'angel' and *chalichi* for 'church' – were to be used where the vernacular lacked its own concepts.

Baptism, the key event in a convert's life, also had to be translated through a foreign term as it had 'no native equivalent in a religious sense'.[12] Hetherwick noted that the words *kusamba* and *kusambitsa* for 'washing' carried some of 'the original significance of the term', but he preferred a neologism derived from the Greek *baptizo* – *batiza*, already in use by Swahili translators. As for the idea of God, Hetherwick was confident that a vernacular term was 'to hand at once'.[13] *Mulungu* shared with *mzimu* the connotations of spirit or soul, but in its broadest meaning it evoked the 'great spirit or aggregate of spirits which is the source of life and all created things'. Both in its

---

[10] Ibid., February 1900.
[11] Emma Hunter, 'Language, Empire, and the World: Karl Roehl and the History of the Swahili Bible in East Africa', *Journal of Imperial and Commonwealth History*, 41 (4), 2013, 600–16.
[12] LWBCA, March 1900. [13] Ibid., February 1900.

association with the concept for spirit and in its insistence that *Mulungu* 'lacks the idea of personality', however, Hetherwick's rendition considered it an imperfect translation and differed from what Scott had proposed in his dictionary (see Chapter 4). Where Scott presented *Mulungu* as a complete conceptual expression for the idea of God, Hetherwick regarded it as 'a true and solid foundation on which to build up the structure of revealed truth regarding God'. Rather than proving the unity of the vernacular and the biblical, or Black and White, *Mulungu* gave the missionary work to do.

Although Hetherwick identified parallels to the development of biblical English in its own borrowing of foreign terms, he saw linguistic translation and religious conversion as two sides of the same coin. 'Language being the vehicle of thought must submit to conversion as well as people.' Unremarked in this statement was a relation of power in which one language appeared more advanced or 'civilized' than the other. Even if English had no actual claim to be a holy language, the relationship between it and Chimang'anja / Chinyanja was asymmetrical, with the latter rather than the former having to change in the translation process.[14]

Hetherwick's reflections on 'grace' and 'faith', for example, mentioned a few candidates for both concepts in the vernacular but lamented the difficulties of finding the 'exact equivalent' and the 'full meaning' of those concepts in it.[15] While *chisomo* has subsequently become the most common translation for 'grace',[16] its association with powerful medicine made Hetherwick reluctant to accept the connotations of agreeable or attractive disposition as 'grace'.[17] Scott, who offered no translation for 'grace' in his dictionary, had included in the definition of *chisomo* both the disposition and the medicine that made others regard oneself as having the disposition.[18] Whether received concepts could be reformed through contact with vernacular

---

[14] Compare William F. Hanks, 'The Space of Translation', in Carlo Severi and William F. Hanks, eds, *Translating Worlds: The Epistemological Space of Translation*, Chicago: HAU Books, 2015, 21–49.
[15] LWBCA, March 1900.
[16] Steven Paas, *Oxford Chichewa–English, English–Chichewa Dictionary*, Oxford: Oxford University Press, 2016, 826.
[17] LWBCA, March 1900.
[18] D. C. Scott, *A Cyclopaedic Dictionary of the Mang'anja Language Spoken in British Central Africa*, Edinburgh: Foreign Mission Committee of the Church of Scotland, 1892, 99.

concepts, as Scott had done for 'friendship' in Hebrew with a concept that had both amity and enmity within its compass, was not addressed by Hetherwick. It was the 'original native meaning' that had to be 'somewhat modified' in any such imperfect encounter.[19] Absent from his thought was also the possibility that the Greek *pistis* could lend itself to historical and theological work on the limits of concepts such as 'belief' and 'faith' to convey its meaning.[20] The recognition of vernacular alternatives to 'belief' as translations of *pistis* would, as such, have to wait until much more recent advances in comparative religion and anthropology.[21]

Impure Language

Where Scott discovered in the vernacular resources to enrich the Gospel, so 'void of religious or theological phraseology' was it for Hetherwick that a separation between Christian language and the vernacular seemed natural to him. Linguistic change induced by the Bible translation committee contrasted, however, with change that threatened the purity of the vernacular. In 1900, Hetherwick regretted that 'so few Europeans learn the native language'.[22] His complaint alluded to the failure of Scott's dream of interracial services conducted in Chimang'anja, but the main purpose of Hetherwick's piece – entitled 'Wanted – Linguists' – was to admonish Europeans and 'native speakers' alike about the spread of the language's 'pidjin' forms at the expense of its purity. Uninterested to learn the grammar and idioms in the vernacular, Europeans were guilty of 'infecting' it with expressions that should not 'pass as the native language nor any language under the sun'. The pathological state of affairs would be handed over from one European to another as 'the newcomer learns from the old hand and the evil spreads'. 'Native speakers' would likewise think that speaking the corrupt lingo was the right thing to do. 'Forms of speech thus creep into the language of the country, and the pure well of native idiom is defiled.'

---

[19] LWBCA, March 1900.
[20] W. C. Smith, *Belief and History*, Charlottesville, VA: University of Virginia Press, 1977.
[21] Malcolm Ruel, *Belief, Ritual, and the Securing of Life: Essays on a Bantu Religion*, Leiden: Brill, 1997.
[22] LWBCA, April 1900.

The remedy to the 'infection' was readily available. 'As a foreign language', Hetherwick observed, 'Mang'anja is easy of acquirement compared with a European tongue or any of the "dead languages"'. A further incentive to learn it could be found in the Europeans' self-interest. In a recommendation that would be hard to imagine stemming from Scott's pen, Hetherwick assured his readers that 'nothing gives a European more influence with the natives than the ability to harangue them in their own tongue'. Another image Hetherwick conjured enticed his readers to collect information on customs and folklore with their newly acquired linguistic prowess: 'How many a dreary evening could a planter on a lonely plantation thus fill in with profit to himself and interest to others.' While pidgin 'defiled' the purity of the vernacular, its proper domain, when it was not deployed to 'harangue' the colonized subjects, was custom and folklore.

Rather than a repository of unchanging folklore, language as a matter of repertoires and styles subject to historical change, a perspective akin to Scott's language ideology, was emphasized by one of the Blantyre Mission's first African deacons, Harry Kambwiri Matecheta.[23] What Hetherwick might have taken as examples of corrupting influences on the language, Matecheta cheerfully saw in the context of their uses. For instance, *chimbudzi*, subsequently the most common word for 'toilet', was used by the African students for the dormitories where they lived even if they had no toilet inside. The word had acquired this meaning after they had observed Scott building a toilet of bricks and entering it as if it was a house. Words such as *mbingwani* and *ngalande*, on the other hand, had their origins in English. Early missionaries had told locals to cut 'big ones' when supplying them with timber, but the phrase entered the vernacular as *mbingwani*. 'Just like England' (*cimodzi-modzi England*) was how Europeans described their practice of building water channels from the river to their village. As a consequence, *Ngalande* as 'England' originally meant these water channels. Matecheta also made humorous observations on the kind of linguistic mixing that troubled Hetherwick. A White farmer trying to control the horse he had mounted shouted, '*Leka, leka,* my man, I am not yet sit *icenene*'

---

[23] Harry K. Matecheta, *Blantyre Mission: Nkhani za ciyambi cace*, Blantyre: Hetherwick Press, 1951, 8; translated as Harry. K. Matecheta, *Blantyre Mission: Stories of Its Beginning*, trans. Thokozani Chilembwe, Berlin: Wichern-Verlag, 2016, 30–1.

('Stop, stop, my man, I am not yet sitting ready').[24] Matecheta identified the three languages in this exclamation as 'Cinyanja, Yao, CiScottish'.

While Matecheta – and Scott in his insistence that the vernacular 'changes from time to time as it has a right to do'[25] – appreciated linguistic features in their actual use, Hetherwick was apprehensive of linguistic change. Observing generational differences in the uses of certain words, Hetherwick lamented the apparent reluctance among youth to preserve their elders' language: 'When these men pass away they carry with them a certain proportion of the extant vocabulary, which cannot be recalled.'[26] Hetherwick's description of a moment of linguistic consultation illustrates the stilted approach he took to detach language from the everyday contexts of its use.

Within his tiny study he sits, a solitary white man, at a rough table on which lie piles of small slips of paper to which he refers again and again. Round him are squatted half a dozen natives in garments of varied hue and odour with whom he is talking, asking them questions in turn, now referring to his slips, now to the human figures before him, sometimes getting an answer, sometimes meeting with silence, for the head of the questioned one has sunk lower till chin rests on chest – the owner overpowered by the noontide heat.[27]

The moment described in this passage, no doubt with some humorous intent, sees a 'solitary white man' as the producer of knowledge, the one with questions for the 'human figures' wearing 'garments of varied hue and odour' to answer. While Hetherwick, no less than Scott, evidently acquired the vernacular proficiency that various supervisory, pedagogical, and recreational activities required, language as an object of knowledge could be isolated from its natural contexts for the kind of inquiry that only the White man was competent to carry out.

Towards Peoplehood

Europeans' corrupting influence on the vernacular aside, Hetherwick did anticipate a different kind of linguistic change with some optimism.

---

[24] Matecheta, *Blantyre Mission: Nkhani za ciyambi cace*, 4; Matecheta, *Blantyre Mission: Stories of Its Beginning*, 27.
[25] Scott, *A Cyclopaedic*, xxii.   [26] LWBCA, April–June 1901.
[27] William P. Livingstone, *A Prince of Missionaries: The Rev. Alexander Hetherwick of Blantyre, Central Africa*, London: James Clarke, 1931, 191.

Its positive aspects would herald the rise of one people, united in one language. 'There is taking place', he observed in 1901, 'an amount of intermingling of the tribes, such as has never occurred before'.[28] 'The inevitable consequence', he continued, 'must be an accentuation of those points in which they resemble each other, and a softening down of the dissimilarities'. Linguistic change indicated what was to follow: 'Already there is a comparatively free interchange of words noticeable in daily conversation. One finds Yaos occasionally using Mang'anja words, and Mang'anja-speaking people having recourse to Yao words: and this habit will steadily increase till use and wont efface the distinctions.'

For Hetherwick, multilingualism was an 'unstable condition' to be corrected by the emergence of one common language. Scotland offered a ready comparison. The differences between the variants of the vernacular often were 'not greater than between Aberdeenshire and Ayrshire Scotch'.[29] In central Africa, 'tribal intermingling' would be greatly assisted in achieving its 'inevitable consequence' by having the Bible in one common language.

> We know how much the Authorized Version of our English Bible has accomplished in welding together the language. So long as that version holds its place in the affections of our English speaking [sic] nationalities, so long will there be a bond of sympathy and support that no considerations of self interest [sic] will ever be able to sever. What a strength to native Christianity to find Mang'anja, Angoni, Maravi, Chipeta, Anyanja, Ambo, Ambewe, Asena, all with the same version of the Holy Scripture in their hands.

The Bible translation committee was composed of missionaries from Presbyterian and Reformed churches, including, at its first meeting in May 1900, representatives from the Blantyre, Livingstonia, Zambesi Industrial, and Mvera Missions.[30] So painstaking was the committee's approach that the Bible in so-called Union Nyanja only came out in 1922. The committee considered its responsibility grave, because the language not only belonged to a people – it helped to create a people. 'Round the Holy Scriptures the language of every race and nation fashions itself', Hetherwick had written before the first meeting.[31]

---

[28] LWBCA, April–June 1901.   [29] Ibid., 15 October 1898.
[30] Ibid., June–July 1900; Hetherwick, *The Romance*, 120–1.
[31] LWBCA, March 1900.

'Around this version', the statement issued by the first meeting declared in a remarkably similar manner, 'the Nyanja language will be established, and will become, we trust, to the dialects of central Africa what our own English Bible is to us'.[32] In contrast to those missions where linguistic work was seen as a matter of scientific discovery along with the 'discoveries' of plants and animals,[33] Hetherwick and the committee were quite explicit about their creative contribution. Union Nyanja did not await its discovery by White missionaries – it had to be forged by their efforts and for the good of the people hitherto unaware of their unity.

With a nod to the pioneering work by Scott and others, the committee's first statement further clarified that 'a fresh translation of the Bible be undertaken with the assistance of such versions of certain portions as are already in use' and that 'as the basis of a language standard for the vocabulary to be used in this version, Dr. D. C. Scott's Mang'anja Dictionary be adopted'. In actual fact, the statements and minutes issued by the first and second meetings contained lengthy lists of words that the committee had agreed on as suitable translations, along with conventions on orthography and biblical names.[34] While different parts of the Bible were divided for translation by the committee members, the procedure for their work was set out in some detail.

That when a translator has produced the best possible individual translation he can make of the portion he has undertaken, the necessary number of typewritten copies be made, and a copy be sent to each member of the committee, who, after writing down his criticisms and suggested changes on a wide margin left for the purpose, shall return it to the translator. With these various suggestions before him, the translator will then make a fresh study of each criticised passage and work out a second version on the basis of the polyglot of individual opinions. Of this second version the requisite number of copies be again made and sent to the various members of the Committee. After sufficient time has elapsed to allow each man to go over his copy carefully and write down criticisms and preferred readings, the Committee be called together for a final revision, three members of the committee, including the translator, to form a quorum.[35]

---

[32] Ibid., June–July 1900.
[33] Patrick Harries, *Butterflies and Barbarians: Swiss Missionaries and Systems of Knowledge in South-East Africa*, Oxford: James Currey, 2007, 167.
[34] LWBCA. June–July, and December 1900.   [35] Ibid., June–July 1900.

No such collective scrutiny had awaited Scott in his work of translation, however much he may have consulted the Europeans and Africans around him. Yet the apparent rigour and professionalism of the committee could not conceal translation as the prerogative of a few White men. No formalized role was available to Africans or to women when decisions were made. After the above procedure, a 'tentative edition' of a passage was to be 'circulated' for about three years, followed by further revisions before the final version was published. The circulation undoubtedly involved Africans as the audience, but little indication can be found that they were entrusted as partners in translation.

While the Bible did a good deal to establish certain uses of Chinyanja in the decades after its publication in 1922,[36] the committee's claim to have launched Union Nyanja was somewhat undermined by the unease over what speakers in central and southern Malawi saw as the use of one another's dialects in the text.[37] By then, enough had happened to entrench 'race', 'nation', and 'tribe', as Hetherwick had named them, as the parameters within which differences between languages and dialects were debated.[38] Decreasing linguistic and ethnic diversity was by no means the 'inevitable consequence' of new circumstances. The committee, as so many of its counterparts during the same period in Africa, had embarked on the standardization of orthography and vocabulary, thus heralding the era of discontent over discrimination and exclusion on ethno-linguistic grounds.[39] Union Nyanja was one example among many others in which standardization was not based on research into some putative proto-language but came as a result of negotiation among missionaries keen to establish one

---

[36] Ernst R. Wendland, *Buku Loyera: An Introduction to the New Chichewa Bible Translation*, Blantyre: Christian Literature Association in Malawi, 1998, 24–5; Hilary B. P. Mijoga, 'The Bible in Malawi: A Brief Survey of Its Impact on Society', in Gerald O. West and Musa W. Dube Shomanah, eds, *The Bible in Africa: Transactions, Trajectories, and Trends*, Leiden: Brill, 2000, 375.

[37] T. Price, 'Nyanja Linguistic Problems', *Africa*, 13 (2), 1940, 132.

[38] Leroy Vail and Landeg White, 'Tribalism in the Political History of Malawi', in Leroy Vail, ed., *The Creation of Tribalism in Southern Africa*, Berkeley: University of California Press, 1989, 151–92.

[39] Derek R. Peterson, 'Vernacular', in Gaurav Desai and Adeline Masquelier, eds, *Critical Terms for the Study of Africa*, Chicago, IL: University of Chicago Press, 2018, 331–45.

'national' language.[40] The language forms left out of the new standard were relegated to the status of dialects.

For every race and nation a language of its own – this maxim was as insidious as it seemed liberal. After all, its influence came to extend into some of the twentieth century's most exclusionary policies in Africa, at their apotheosis South Africa's regime of separate development.[41] Hetherwick would have been appalled by apartheid, but the contrast to Scott's sense of epistemic justice is clear. Where Scott wanted everyone, White as well as Black, to *learn from* the vernacular, Hetherwick urged his European compatriots merely to *learn it* for practical and recreational purposes. As the property of a people distinct from oneself, the vernacular had little of philosophical or indeed theological import to offer those who were not its natural inheritors.

The difference between the dictionaries compiled by Scott and subsequently edited by Hetherwick illustrates further the contrast. Scott's dictionary, as has been seen, did more than list and define words – it sought to convey ideas in vernacular thought. Hetherwick, on the other hand, explained in his 1929 preface to the 'enlarged' edition that 'several of the Author's anthropological notes, as well as his descriptions of certain native customs, have also been curtailed. Such notes belong more to the pages of a work on Nyanja anthropology than to the limits of a dictionary'.[42] Anthropology, as a study of customs and folklore, rather than philosophy was the discipline best suited to record vernacular achievements.

The idea of peoplehood had, as such, consequences that went beyond language ideology. In 1892, when Scott was on furlough, Hetherwick hosted a visitor from Jamaica.[43] Rev. Dr Johnston had travelled across the African continent to visit several mission fields with a view to sending Black Jamaicans to work there. His intent was 'to test by actual experiment how far Jamaican negroes were fitted for returning to Africa as mechanics and artisans in the interests of the

---

[40] Patrick Harries, 'The Roots of Ethnicity: Discourse and the Politics of Language Construction in South-East Africa', *African Affairs* 87 (346), 1988, 25–52.
[41] Saul Dubow, *Racial Segregation and the Origins of Apartheid in South Africa, 1919–36*, Basingstoke: Macmillan, 1989.
[42] Alexander Hetherwick, 'Preface', in D. C. Scott, *Dictionary of the Nyanja Language*, edited and enlarged by Alexander Hetherwick, London: Lutterworth Press, 1929, vii.
[43] LWBCA, September 1892.

various Missionary operations already at work'. Of the six men with Johnston, four returned to Jamaica prematurely. Hetherwick's conclusion on the experiment was straightforward: 'The conditions of life in Jamaica are so different from those in Africa as to preclude in the first instance the natives of that island from engaging in pioneer Mission work in Africa.' Whatever the contentious demands he was making at the time on the colonial administration and White settlers, Hetherwick was able to pronounce these words: 'The strain of African life – physical and moral – which tells so hard even on Europeans, is too much for the civilized negro with perhaps a single generation of Christian history behind him.'

Paternalism combined here with a predilection to place racialized peoplehood before common humanity. Hetherwick's response may have arisen from a similar proprietorial attitude to the Church of Scotland's mission sphere that John McMurtrie expressed three years later in his reaction to a proposal to repatriate people of African descent to the continent, as seen in Chapter 5. On the other hand, Hetherwick's response also reflected his evolving understanding of the differences between White and Black. Europeans as the White race seemed preordained to spread the Gospel for reasons both moral and physical: 'Africa will be won in the first instance only by the European Mission, planted where Europeans can live and work.' Where Scott's notion of the African Church consistently stressed its interracial composition, Hetherwick already in 1892 added an exclusionary qualification to it – it was to become 'the native African Church'. Moreover, the African Church had little of the urgency to it that so energized Scott. It 'in its time', Hetherwick wrote, 'will take its share in the work given to it. We cannot "rush" Africa'. After Scott's final departure in 1898, such thoughts paved the way for a considerable slowing down of the pace with which Africans were entrusted with major responsibilities at the Blantyre Mission.

The Presbytery Begins

Hetherwick's ascension to head the Blantyre Mission heralded a period of reform and increasing formalization in its operations. Just as the process of translating the Scriptures became ostensibly more professionalized than what Scott had practised, so too did the structures of mission work change into a more complex bureaucratic framework.

The constitution of a presbytery in 1903 was one significant change in this regard. European and African representatives from the churches at Blantyre, Domasi, Zomba, and Mulanje gathered to elect unanimously Hetherwick as its moderator and to lay down its constitution.[44] It also agreed on the designation of the presbytery as 'the Presbytery of Blantyre of the Church of Central Africa, Presbyterian'. The acronym for the latter part of the designation – CCAP – became the Church's popular name which survives until the present day in Malawi and has come to encompass not only Blantyre but also the Synods of Nkhoma in central Malawi and Livingstonia in the north. The inaugural meeting also pronounced the composition of the presbytery as '(1) All European ordained missionaries; (2) all European elders; (3) all native ordained ministers; (4) one representative native elder from each session chosen annually.'

The deepening racialization of mission work is evident in this division of membership. When it is recognized that only two – Harry Kambwiri Matecheta and Stephen Kundecha – had been selected to become ministers of the fourteen deacons trained by Scott,[45] the imbalance between White and Black is clear. It was not until 1916 that three more African ministers were ordained: Harry Mtuwa, Joseph Kaunde, and Thomas Maseya.[46] Imbalance was also evident in the presbytery's remit to serve as a court of appeal in Church matters.[47] While it had this mandate 'in all matters relative to the native church', European ministers and elders had the prerogative to appeal to the General Assembly of the Church of Scotland against any decision made by the presbytery. Its African members were, as subjects of the local Church, deprived of their European brethren's access to the geographically distant centre. Little seemed to survive in these reforms from Scott's deaconate or from the practice by which the head of the Mission managed Church and other matters in the *mlandu* fashion. Indeed, it was licentiates rather than deacons that the presbytery called the Africans who were now to be selected for eventual ordination as ministers.

In practice, it was the Mission Council that grew in importance under Hetherwick's leadership, tasked as it was with control over the

---

[44] The Presbytery of Blantyre Minutes, 13 January 1903, NAM, 50/BMC/1/2/1.
[45] Ross, *Blantyre Mission*, 177–8.   [46] Ibid., 186.
[47] The Presbytery of Blantyre Minutes, 13 January 1903.

financial resources in the field and the decisions on whom were posted in the parishes that came into being after the presbytery was established.[48] The Mission Council was, in Andrew Ross's estimation, a 'white oligarchy', but the quest for an African Church did not come to an end with the demise of Scott's deaconate. The mushrooming parishes were run by African teacher-evangelists and elders, and more villages than ever were building houses to serve as a church and school. The Blantyre Mission Jubilee celebrations of September 1901, moreover, would have pleased Scott for the prominent role that Africans played in them.[49] A group of African elders, Mungo Chisuse among them, planted trees on the site of Scott's first church building. At the conference that was organized to mark the celebrations, all papers were delivered by African Christians.

These gestures of inclusion by the Blantyre Mission's White oligarchy could not stem the changing tide in race relations. The quest was for a Church in which the 'native' portion would increase, but it would do so without Scott's vision for a racially unified African Church. 1901 was also the year, as has been mentioned, when two, racially defined congregations came into being in Blantyre. An Educational Code, first agreed in 1904 between several missions in Malawi, ranked schools teaching in the vernacular below schools where English was the medium of instruction.[50] Moreover, Scott's practice of bringing Africans to Scotland had begun to face obstacles, and in 1914 Hetherwick was warned by a friend against placing Africans in Scottish cities for the fear of inflicting on them 'a hurtful and not a helpful experience'.[51] As has also been seen, the Blantyre Mission had become the destination for missionaries who had little or no allegiance to Scott's vision. They generally had no inclination to immerse themselves in village life. One of them, E. D. Bowman, even supported the Afrikaner doctrine of separate development.[52] His view on African education may have been unusual among the new contingent of Blantyre missionaries, but his lack of intimacy with vernacular dispositions was becoming the rule rather than the exception.

---

[48] Ross, *Blantyre Mission*, 172–3.   [49] LWBCA, October–December 1901.
[50] Gilbert Phiri, *A History of Education in the Blantyre Synod*, Doctoral Dissertation, Mzuzu University, 2021.
[51] Ross, *Blantyre Mission*, 118.   [52] Ibid., 178.

From Servant to Law-Giver

A corollary of the deepening Black–White divide, and of the epistemic disparity between folklore and philosophy, was Hetherwick's determination to root out unacceptable customs. Where Scott had been able to see beauty in certain uses of alcohol, for example, Hetherwick adopted an approach that would evolve into the outright prohibition that continues to inform popular understandings of Presbyterianism in Malawi. He had made it clear that beer was not to be brewed on Mission land or given to its subjects. The Mission's hostility to alcohol became apparent to Africans far and wide when Hetherwick embarked on punitive expeditions to find the locations outside the Mission land where it was brewed. Upon discovering that 'a perfect orgy was in progress',[53] he would, accompanied by the Mission's newly arrived Scottish gardener, proceed to destroy all the pots containing the odious substance.

The Blantyre Mission was becoming more consistent than during Scott's tenure with the generalizing observations made in the academic literature on Christian missions' urge to purify 'religion' from 'culture'.[54] At the core of Hetherwick's drive to formalize the rules and principles by which Christian lives should be lived was the regulation of membership. It marked another departure from Scott's ethos of reversals in which the missionary was the one who went 'to school again'.[55] His reflections on service and leadership would recede into the White oligarchy's prerogative to pronounce on the laws of Christian life.

Baptism was naturally the area in which membership was most directly regulated. Scott's attitude had been a permissive one, so much so that many Africans had acquired important responsibilities at the Mission long before their baptism. An example, as mentioned in Chapter 7, was Mungo Chisuse himself, who printed, five years after joining the Mission, the very issue in which his baptism was announced.[56] Although the creed was to be repeated in the baptisms administered during Scott's tenure, the Presbytery of Blantyre came to

---

[53] Livingstone, *A Prince*, 103.
[54] Webb Keane, *Christian Moderns: Freedom and Fetish in the Mission Encounter*, Berkeley, CA: University of California Press, 2007.
[55] Hetherwick, *The Romance of Blantyre*, 46.   [56] LWBCA, December 1889.

codify a whole series of baptismal vows.[57] For children over three years of age, the new rules stipulated that baptism was to be delayed until they could take the vows by themselves. 'Sponsors' were required to take the vows for younger children, including answers to questions about their belief 'in God the father' and whether 'all available means' would be used to introduce the child to 'the doctrines and duties of our holy religion'.

A contrast to custom was written into the vows taken by both infants' sponsors and adults receiving the rite of baptism. They were asked to 'renounce all the practices of this land which are contrary to the Word of God'. The question specified a number of practices in Chinyanja and Chiyao, ranging from polygamy (*mitala*) to poison ordeal (*mwavi*) to initiation (*unyago*), and urged the baptized to take the vow that 'you will not follow them nor be led by them'. In another vow, he or she was asked 'by example and influence endeavour to lead the heathen around you into the Kingdom of God'. As if to distinguish the person further from those who had not been baptized, he or she was not only required to read the Word and attend the worship but also 'to observe the ordinances' of Christian marriage and to give 'alms for the care of the poor and sick'. Overall, the person had to attend religious instruction for no fewer than two years before baptism so as to give the missionary an opportunity to ascertain his or her life and character. The aspirants to the catechumens' class also had to be 'accompanied by a member of the church who [could] testify to their character'. As a minimum, the instruction before baptism was supposed to include the teaching of the Lord's Prayer, the Ten Commandments, the Sacraments, and passages from the Apostles' creed.

The increasing numbers of Africans presenting themselves for baptism no doubt warranted such detailed enumeration of rules and doctrines. Nor was, as already noted, the sharp divide between custom and Christianity peculiar to the Blantyre Mission in the history of both Protestant and Catholic missions. The specific interest here is the shift that took place from a vision for racial equality to paternalist liberalism. At the turn of the century, the reversals that had informed Scott's allocation of responsibilities to Africans were transformed into a

---

[57] The Presbytery of Blantyre Minutes, 8 July 1903, NAM, 50/BMC/1/2/1.

racialized hierarchy. A small number of White men pursued the betterment of Black people within the terms set by their White oligarchy.

'The Native Christian'

The aim of such betterment was not only to facilitate the making of a new people. It was also to advance a new kind of person. To this end, the Blantyre Presbytery resolved to discourage Christian parents 'from allowing their children to live with their heathen relations'.[58] Such resolutions were, of course, hard to enforce in practice, and much of their efficacy depended on the extent to which moral pressure would build up among Africans themselves. Yet the missionaries were not without means to regulate the new person's intimate relations. Marriage was to become a major battleground for competing values and practices, not only between Christian and 'heathen' Africans, but also between missions and the government.[59] By the beginning of the twentieth century, missions and the administration had both shifted from concern for the plight of fugitive women in the context of political turbulence to a preoccupation with marital stability. The period saw the rise of so-called customary law to regulate African marriages in the magistrates' courts. At the same time, many Christian denominations insisted on their own prerogative to act as courts of justice in marital matters. Their views could be sharply different, from the Catholic and Anglican opposition to divorce to the Presbyterians' tolerance of divorce but greater qualms about local practices around marriage.

Divorce and polygamy were, along with schooling and worship, the principal arenas in which Hetherwick oversaw the increasing regulation of new Christian lives. Divorce had historically been common in southern and central Malawi and was as readily accessible to women as to men.[60] The matrilineal pattern of land inheritance had contributed to this sense of equality, but the apparent lack of commitment among men to their own rather than to their sisters' children was a recurrent concern among missionaries and government officials alike.

---

[58] Ibid.
[59] Martin Chanock, *Law, Custom, and Social Order: The Colonial Experience in Malawi and Zambia*, Cambridge: Cambridge University Press, 1985, 150–5.
[60] Elias C. Mandala, *Work and Control in a Peasant Economy: A History of the Lower Tchiri Valley in Malawi, 1859–1960*, Madison, WI: University of Wisconsin Press, 1990, 50.

Marriages were less stable than Europeans at the turn of the century thought appropriate, but as they became regulated by new forms of law, and when men found paid employment further afield, women readily seized the opportunity to sue them for divorce on the grounds of negligence.[61] Unforeseen demands could also be presented to the new presbyteries by Christian women. In 1903, for example, the Livingstonia Presbytery sought its Blantyre counterpart's advice on the request by two women to marry their deceased sisters' husbands.[62] Perplexed by the request, the Blantyre Presbytery passed it on upwards in the Church hierarchy to the Kirk Session. At the same time, the request indicated the desirability of marriage among women, albeit not necessarily in the manner that missionaries preferred.

As in other aspects of the unequal conversation between missionaries and Africans, it should not be assumed that the question of marriage was settled in missionaries' own lives. Scott chaired the Mission Council meeting in 1893 when divergent views were mooted on the question of whether the male missionary ought to be married.[63] Adam Currie, the attentive husband mentioned in the previous chapter, regretted that the current regulations made no provision for missionary wives. The unmarried male missionary's work was hampered by his need to attend to the household chores, while married women were to be preferred to unmarried ones. Having experienced missionary life both with and without a wife, Currie stated that 'a missionary should be encouraged to marry rather than discouraged'. Hetherwick, himself notably advanced in years when he married Elizabeth Fenwick, seconded the view of Henry Scott who argued precisely for discouraging marriage until the missionary had spent a few years in the field. David Clement Scott and his brother Affleck Scott put forward the view that 'legislation limiting the missionary's free choice in the matter was unwise'. As the chair, however, Scott decided not to put the views to vote and found unanimous approval for his suggestion to send them on to the committee in Edinburgh.

While marriage was thus a matter of some discussion in their own lives, the Blantyre missionaries led by Hetherwick became increasingly

---

[61] Megan Vaughan, *The Story of an African Famine: Gender and Famine in Twentieth-Century Malawi*, Cambridge: Cambridge University Press, 1987, 137–41.
[62] The Presbytery of Blantyre Minutes, 13 October 1903, NAM, 50/BMC/1/2/1.
[63] The Blantyre Mission Council Minutes, 21 June 1893, NAM, 50/BMC/1/1/1.

determined to deploy Christian marriage as a central means to regulate African lives. Such marriages were expected to be monogamous and indissoluble, but the practice on the ground proved hard to be pinned down to the precepts of stability. The all-male Presbytery displayed remarkable confidence in stipulating on the various permutations that practice presented. For example, it debated whether a polygamist who wished to be a Christian should be given the opportunity to choose the woman he considered to be the 'real wife'.[64] The motion for the first wife to be recognized as such was carried by six votes as against two votes for the man's free choice.

The Presbytery also placed a considerable moral and material burden on Christian women whose husbands were or became polygamists. For a start, 'no woman living as the wife of a polygamist be admitted as a catechumen'.[65] The sense in which the woman would be punished for her husband's polygamy was apparent in the further rule that 'it is the duty of a Christian woman to separate herself from her husband who has become a polygamist: failing this her name must be removed from the Communion Bill'. In the era of hut tax and men's virtually exclusive access to the cash economy, such rules were likely to bring considerable hardship to Christian women. The Presbytery seemed aware of it in its ruling that 'a polygamist who puts away a wife or wives must make adequate arrangements for the maintenance of his children'.

So prominent was polygamy in the contests over Christian membership that it was a leading cause for removing individuals from the Church. In 1904, for example, the statistics compiled from the Blantyre, Domasi, Mulanje, and Zomba congregations of the Blantyre Presbytery showed that polygamy and death had been the reasons for the same number of removals.[66] For both, 35 removals had taken place – as opposed to reasons such as 'adultery' (8 individuals), 'heathenism' (17), and 'Mohamidanism' (7). The statistics did not give the gender of the individuals concerned, nor did the missionaries leave a record of reflections on the possible economic consequences of letting polygamy limit Christian membership. The issue was propriety, and elsewhere in the region marital instability and polygamy presented a

---

[64] The Presbytery of Blantyre Minutes, 13 October 1903, NAM, 50/BMC/1/2/1.
[65] The Presbytery of Blantyre Minutes, 8 July 1903, NAM, 50/BMC/1/2/1.
[66] The Presbytery of Blantyre Minutes, 25 January 1905, NAM, 50/BMC/1/2/1.

balancing act for missionaries who tended to see it as an ethnically defined contrast. Anthropologist J. A. Barnes wrote of eastern Zambia in the 1940s that 'in chastity the missionaries were allied with the Ngoni against the Chewa; in monogamy the missionaries fought against the Ngoni allied to the Chewa'.[67]

Polygamy was by no means the dominant form of marriage in the areas within the Presbytery's influence. It had been associated with chiefly authority, although as Scott noted in his dictionary, 'ordinary hereditary chiefs have several but not enormous numbers of wives'.[68] In those areas where crops were beginning to be cultivated for the market, polygamy could enhance the supply of agricultural labour in a way that monogamy did not.[69] When cotton markets were established throughout the Lower Shire Valley after 1910, for example, this economic aspect would increase the desirability of polygamy among men beyond chiefly families.[70] The process was also making certain marketable crops the prerogatives of male enterprise. The economic consequences of insisting on monogamy – and of putting pressure on women to renounce polygamy – hardly appeared in the missionaries' preoccupation with propriety.

The insistence on the monogamous and indissoluble marriage as a key characteristic of Christian life reverberated in various other efforts to shape comportment, from dress to hygiene. Yet the self-fashioning could never displace the designation of Africans as 'native Christians' in Hetherwick's imagination. They were first 'natives' and then Christians. In his questioning of the principles by which a magistrate would choose between a 'Christian' and 'heathen' point of view in marriage disputes, for example, Hetherwick advocated a third way.[71] It would recognize 'native Christianity' as a distinct legal realm in which a marriage blessed by a Christian minister would be monogamous but governed by African law in matters such as inheritance. The predicament, in its various forms beyond the question of Christian marriage, would much later be theorized by scholars as marking the

---

[67] J. A. Barnes, *Marriage in a Changing Society: A Study in Structural Change among the Fort Jameson Ngoni*, London: Oxford University Press, 1951, 19.
[68] Scott, *A Cyclopaedic Dictionary*, 347.
[69] Elizabeth Colson, *The Plateau Tonga of Northern Rhodesia: Social and Religious Studies*, Manchester: Manchester University Press, 1962, 122.
[70] Mandala, *Work and Control*, 147.
[71] Hetherwick, *The Romance of Blantyre*, 126.

not-quite status of colonial subjects.[72] The split identity afforded little more than a second-class status, but it is important to note that no authoritarian urge to rule over Africans compelled Hetherwick to hold such a view. The liberalism that made him a vocal critic of the British administration in the 1890s would continue to set him apart from much settler and official thinking. What Hetherwick's imagination lacked was Scott's vision for a racially unified African Church.

Africa for the African

Despite its superior provision of schooling, the Blantyre Mission had no monopoly over Christian teachings in southern Malawi at the beginning of the twentieth century. The imposition of the colonial rule had improved transport links which missionaries of various hues were eager to utilize. On the eve of the First World War, there was a motley mixture of missionaries across the territory, from French and Dutch priests to Afrikaans-speakers to American evangelists, with some 200 missionaries outnumbering both planters and government officials.[73] The Montfort Order of the Roman Catholic Church had sent two priests from France in 1901 and established a mission at Nguludi, close to Blantyre. Closer still was the interdenominational Zambesi Industrial Mission, established in 1892 by the Englishman Joseph Booth at Mitsidi, five miles from Blantyre. Although he would change the location and the name of his mission several times, Booth left a legacy of Christian teaching that drew radical conclusions from the protectorate's racialized order.[74] His rallying cry 'Africa for the African' expressed a sentiment that was to inform the preaching by his early African protégé John Chilembwe.

In his 1897 pamphlet that first sounded the rallying cry, Booth was scathing of missionaries and colonists alike.[75] He accused the missionary of being 'the forerunner of another set of men, sent to appropriate,

---

[72] Homi K. Bhabha, *The Location of Culture*, New York: Routledge, 1994.
[73] John McCracken, *A History of Malawi 1859–1966*, Oxford: James Currey, 2012, 107–8.
[74] Harry Langworthy, *'Africa for the African': The Life of Joseph Booth*, Blantyre: Christian Literature Association in Malawi, 1996.
[75] Joseph Booth, *Africa for the African*, Blantyre: Christian Literature Association in Malawi, 1996 [1897].

to kill, to tax, and subjugate'.[76] The pamphlet went on to describe Africa's richness, both natural and human. It was published a year after J. Albert Thorne's pamphlet which, as seen in Chapter 5, had made an appeal in Scotland for an ambitious scheme of repatriating people of African descent to Africa.[77] Apparently unaware of Thorne's appeal, and without his condescending tone about Africans in Africa, Booth put forward his own 'Christian settlement proposal'.[78] His scheme arose from the recognition that 'the labour of over two centuries of slave-toil and abuse [had] not been requited and that it [was] an hereditary debt lying upon this generation'.[79] No less radical was his insistence that the colonial administration had to be pursued 'in trust' and had to obey a clear time limit to its presence.[80]

While both settlement schemes were consigned to oblivion, Booth had introduced a link between African and African American Christians by the time of his final departure from Malawi in 1903.[81] He made his journey to the United States in 1897 with his first Malawian convert Chilembwe, who received there a theological education and became the ordained minister of an African American church.[82] The irony was clear – the Englishman who was deported from the protectorate for his radical views on race relations had done much for the confidence between White and Black by travelling together with an African and by cooperating with an African American church.

The rebellion led by Chilembwe in 1915 has been the subject of extensive scholarship by researchers as well as of mythologizing by Malawian politicians.[83] Its short-lived and spatially confined character – lasting barely a fortnight in the Shire Highlands, with three

---

[76] Ibid., 14.
[77] J. Albert Thorne, *An Appeal Addressed to the Friends of the African Race*, 1896, NLS, Ms 7873.
[78] Booth, *Africa*, 31–5.   [79] Ibid., 27.   [80] Ibid., 20.
[81] Langworthy, 'Africa', 121–31.
[82] George Shepperson and Thomas Price, *Independent African: John Chilembwe and the Origins, Setting and Significance of the Nyasaland Native Rising of 1915*, Edinburgh: Edinburgh University Press, 1958, 88.
[83] Ibid.; Jane Linden and Ian Linden, 'John Chilembwe and the New Jerusalem', *Journal of African History*, 12 (4), 1971, 629–51; Landeg White, *Magomero: Portrait of an African Village*, Cambridge: Cambridge University Press, 1987, 130–45; McCracken, *A History*, 132–7; John McCracken, ed., *Voices from the Chilembwe Rising: Witness Testimonies Made to the Nyasaland Rising Commission of Inquiry, 1915*, Oxford: Oxford University Press for the British

Europeans killed – did not prevent it from causing major disruption, resulting in a Commission of Inquiry later in the same year. While Chilembwe was tracked down and shot dead, government reprisals destroyed his church, executed dozens of his followers and flogged and imprisoned many more. When anti-colonial agitation reached its peak in the 1950s, nationalists asserted Malawi's future president Kamuzu Banda as the saviour that Chilembwe had preached about. The dawn of the democratic era in the 1990s saw, in turn, further effort to enshrine Chilembwe in the nation's memory by having his image on banknotes and by re-naming a public holiday in his honour. What is of interest here, however, is the extent to which the rebellion took to one extreme the racialized thought that had begun to inform the Blantyre Mission under Hetherwick.

Chilembwe attended one of the Blantyre Mission's schools before he became acquainted with Booth in 1893.[84] Although not in regular contact with the missionaries in Blantyre after his return from the United States, Chilembwe and his followers did use their medical services.[85] He even sought Hetherwick's advice in 1909 on polygamists desiring baptism and addressed him as 'Dear Father in Christ'. As is seen below, Hetherwick was at pains to convince the Commission of Inquiry that the contact with Chilembwe and his followers had been minimal. Yet so small was the educated African Christian elite in the Shire Highlands that their members were bound to interact independently of missionary guidance. Some of the Blantyre Mission's earliest African stalwarts knew Chilembwe well. Mungo Chisuse, for example, took the famous portraits of Chilembwe and his family dressed in smart, European clothes.[86] John Gray Kufa, by then a commercial farmer, took part in the rebellion but disobeyed the orders to attack the African Lakes Company store in Blantyre.[87] When questioned by the Commission, Harry Kambwiri Matecheta described his conversation with Chilembwe two years earlier.[88] Chilembwe had urged him to leave the Church of Scotland and to begin an independent ministry.

Academy, 2015; Joey Power, *Political Culture and Nationalism in Malawi: Building Kwacha*, Rochester, NY: University of Rochester Press, 2010, 26–8.

[84] McCracken, *A History*, 132.   [85] Ross, *Blantyre Mission*, 181.

[86] John McCracken, 'Mungo Murray Chisuse and the Early History of Photography in Malawi', *The Society of Malawi Journal*, 61 (2), 2008, 1–18.

[87] McCracken, *A History*, 141; White, *Magomero*, 124–5.

[88] McCracken, *Voices*, 150–1.

Chilembwe had further rebuked him for his preaching at a ceremony in Zomba to celebrate the coronation of George V. 'The King is not our King', Chilembwe had told Matecheta.

Chilembwe was well aware of the world beyond the Shire Highlands. One immediate influence on his decision to resort to violence was the First World War. In September 1914, the British and German troops fought in Karonga in northern Malawi, resulting in sixty casualties on the British side, of whom forty-nine were Africans, and a hundred and twenty-two on the German side, of whom over a hundred were Africans.[89] In his last public document, a letter he sent to *Nyasaland Times*, Chilembwe used this conflict to issue a fierce indictment on race relations. It attracted censorship for inflammatory phrases such as 'in time of peace, everything for Europeans only...But in time of war it has been found that we are needed to share hardships and shed our blood in equality...Let the rich men, bankers, titled men, storekeepers, farmers, and landlords go to war and get shot'.[90]

Apart from the War, many other matters troubled Chilembwe and contributed to his rebellion. He may have been influenced, for example, by the prophesy of the Watch Tower movement that the world would come to an end in October 1914, and his own health and financial problems added to the gloom he felt.[91] The final trigger, however, was something that the Blantyre missionaries had long been concerned about – the dispossession of land by White planters.

It was the Magomero estate that gave focus to the wrath among Chilembwe's congregation. A shift from tobacco to cotton cultivation among some planters in the Shire Highlands created an unprecedented demand for agricultural labour, met in part by immigrants fleeing exploitative plantations in Mozambique.[92] On the Magomero estate, managed by William Jervis Livingstone, David Livingstone's grandson, the African workers found themselves tenants with few prospects of another escape. Their obligations to pay rent and hut tax hardly adhered to formal rules, and Livingstone is said to have presided over

---

[89] Shepperson and Price, *Independent African*, 233–5; Melvin E. Page, *The Chiwaya War: Malawians and the First World War*, Boulder, CO: Westview Press, 2000.
[90] Shepperson and Price, *Independent African*, 234–5.
[91] White, *Magomero*, 132.   [92] McCracken, *A History*, 130–2.

a regime of 'gratuitous violence and occasional sexual abuse'.[93] He also banned all schools from the Magomero land and personally refused the request by Chilembwe's followers to build a church there.

Livingstone's decapitation provided the rebellion's most dramatic scene. His head was cut off in his own house and before his own family at Magomero. Chilembwe, ensconced in his church throughout the attacks, is said to have received the news 'in a mood of sad resignation'.[94] He had ordered the decapitation, apparently on the instigation of his followers, and duly exhibited the head on a pole to his congregation the following day, which was a Sunday.

The gruesome turn that African discontent, inspired by Christian teachings, could take was not anticipated by either David Clement Scott or Alexander Hetherwick. Chilembwe's eschatological vision contrasted with Scott's emphasis on living rather than the end times in his appreciation of the risen Christ, much as millenarian movements in Africa may have drawn inspiration from the narrative of resurrection.[95] Yet the Blantyre missionaries' warnings about land alienation and a new slavery from at least the early 1890s onwards had alluded to some of the dangers ahead. Recall, for example, Hetherwick's exchange with the 'European colonist' in the Mission magazine in 1892.[96] He had raised the question of 'how far any British subject is entitled to have natives – now also British subjects – living on his land whom he can force to come and work for him when he wishes with threats of eviction or something worse should they refuse to comply?' Over a decade later, the Chilembwe rebellion gave its answer to how far such entitlement could be taken.

When Joseph Booth and the South African author Olive Schreiner are remembered as the early critics of Cecil Rhodes's imperial designs,[97] it is important to note Scott's attacks in a similar vein years before them (Chapter 6). Striking, moreover, is Scott's use of the very phrase for which Booth is famous two years before the pamphlet was

---

[93] White, *Magomero*, 120.
[94] Shepperson and Price, *Independent African*, 262, 285.
[95] Karen E. Fields, *Revival and Rebellion in Colonial Central Africa*, Princeton, NJ: Princeton University Press, 1985; J. B. Peires, *The Dead Will Arise: Nongqawuse and the Great Xhosa Cattle-Killing Movement of 1856–7*, London: James Currey, 1989; Robert R. Edgar and Hilary Sapire, *African Apocalypse: The Story of Nontetha Nkwenkwe, A Twentieth-Century South African Prophet*, Athens, OH: Ohio University Press, 2000.
[96] LWBCA, March 1892. [97] Shepperson and Price, *Independent African*, 110.

published. In 1895, Scott wrote: 'Africa for the Africans has been our policy from the first.'[98] Consistent with his practice of an industrial mission, he continued: 'We believe that God has given this country into our hands that we may train its peoples how to develop its marvellous resources for themselves.' Along with his insistence that Black and White should prosper together, this policy was relentless in its recognition of inequality in the racialized encounter. The recognition of unequal power relations would be replaced by an emphasis on irreconcilable cultural and cognitive difference at the dawn of the twentieth century.

A principled critic of land alienation by Europeans, Hetherwick none the less became the key catalyst of this epochal change in Blantyre. His ruminations in retirement, revolving around the existential gap between himself and 'the black man', had been anticipated, only a few years after Scott's departure, by his conviction that Africa was 'the home of the black man and the black man alone. He alone can develop its resources under the rule and guidance of the European'.[99] Earlier still, in 1895, when Scott was on furlough, he had stated that it would be wrong to 'expect that native church life will move in the grooves cut out for it elsewhere'.[100] Nowhere in Hetherwick's thought were Europeans expected to learn as well as to teach, as in Scott's vision. Nor did the 'rule and guidance' have a time limit, unlike in Booth's idea of colonial occupation, even as the divide between White and Black would remain as wide as ever. Once Scott's vision had been extinguished, the choice for Europeans in race relations appeared to be between liberal, piecemeal paternalism, and White supremacy.

Hetherwick's Paradox

Hetherwick's ruminations in retirement also touched on the Chilembwe rebellion. He had come to regard it as a 'revenge for some private grudge [against] a neighbouring planter'.[101] To the extent that this comment appeared to trivialize the rebellion, Hetherwick merely expressed the view of the protectorate's liberal White establishment. It had both grown and become increasingly interconnected through new administrative and commercial initiatives. By 1908, Hetherwick had

[98] LWBCA, January 1895.   [99] Ibid., August 1902.
[100] Ibid., September 1895.   [101] Hetherwick, *The Romance of Blantyre*, 213.

'mellowed into a respected ecclesiastical statesman', who had been nominated by the Governor to the newly formed Legislative Council as one of the three non-governmental representatives.[102] While the two other members were White planters, Hetherwick's remit was to represent African interests. His emergence as an establishment figure was also enhanced by his foundational role in the Blantyre Chamber of Commerce, an organization for White planters and traders.[103] Yet much as he may have wanted to forget the rebellion, its immediate aftermath demanded a considered response from the head of the Blantyre Mission. Hetherwick found himself questioned for four and a half hours by the Commission of Inquiry in June 1915.[104] He was one of the sixty-five witnesses, European and African, who gave evidence to the all-male, all-White Commission chaired by a High Court judge.[105] Hetherwick's responses provide an insight into the paradoxes of his liberal thought.

The Commissioners were anxious to ascertain whether the responsibilities allocated to Africans to teach and preach virtually unsupervised by European missionaries, not least within the Blantyre Mission sphere, could result in Africans' exalted sense of their own worth. At the heart of this quandary was whether schooling was desirable among Africans in the first place. Hetherwick's liberalism can be readily contrasted with certain other views during the Commission's hearings. Robert Hynde, the planter and editor whose newspaper had launched attacks on David Clement Scott in the 1890s, emphasized in his responses the futility of schooling among the vast majority when no employment was available to educated Africans.[106] Although his opposition to African education became clear, Hynde's White supremacist views were relatively tempered at the hearings. In 1900, on the other hand, his editorial had stated that 'it is utterly wrong to teach any native he is as good as the white man because he is not. If he were, he would be on a level with the white man, but it is because he is inferior that he is under the white man'.[107]

---

[102] A. J. Hanna, *The Story of the Rhodesias and Nyasaland*, London: Faber and Faber, 1960, 217.
[103] Ross, *Blantyre Mission*, 129–30.
[104] Shepperson and Price, *Independent African*, 369; McCracken, *Voices*, 361–83.
[105] Ibid., xvi–xix.   [106] Ibid., 347.
[107] *The Central African Times*, 1 September 1900.

When contrasted with such views, Hetherwick's defence of African education was as fearless as it was principled. He pointed out that the court interpreter on whom the Commissioners depended was himself the product of schooling at the Blantyre Mission.[108] More importantly, he insisted that much of the trouble at Magomero could have been avoided had it been possible for Africans to send their children to school there – the schools would have had 'a pacifying effect'.[109]

At the same time, his concern for 'pacifying' Africans betrayed a racialized order whose foundations Hetherwick was not prepared to question. The existential gap between Black and White, he felt, did not prevent Africans from keenly observing what their European masters did. Hetherwick was known to remind his fellow Europeans that 'there was always the Native at hand watching, judging, and often imitating'.[110] This awareness of being watched by Africans gave Hetherwick reason to tell the Commission how much he had disapproved the policy to evacuate Europeans from their homes during the rebellion.[111] It had left Blantyre unguarded and could have led to 'a general destruction over the country'. Perceptions mattered, Hetherwick pointed out. 'Do you put property before the value of life?', a commissioner asked him. 'No', answered Hetherwick, 'but I put much value on prestige'. Asked then whether he was speaking as 'a layman or a military expert', Hetherwick's reply was laconic: 'I only speak from 32 years' experience of the country.'

The boundaries of prestige and privilege, along with the question of African education, were key to the way in which the rebellion exposed liberal and supremacist orientations among the protectorate's European population. A striking feature of Chilembwe's movement was his and his followers' attention to clothes. In his testimony, Matecheta told the Commission that Chilembwe had criticized Christian teachers for allowing their wives to dress in regular village clothes.[112] Chilembwe himself rarely appeared in public without wearing a three-piece suit and a bow tie, with his wife Ida in a formal dress and silk stockings. Quite apart from what he preached, the dress code among his followers unsettled the protectorate's Europeans. Photographs of his imposing new church showed 'several hundred African men and women suited and gowned for the occasion in

---

[108] McCracken, *Voices*, 378. [109] Ibid., 367. [110] Livingstone, *A Prince*, 94.
[111] McCracken, *Voices*, 365–6. [112] Ibid., 149.

disturbing mimicry of their rulers'.[113] The not-quite condition of the 'native Christian' was challenged by the appropriation of Europeans' symbols of prestige and privilege.

Hetherwick had a ready response to such acts of apparent mimicry. The issue extended well beyond Chilembwe's movement to the general European expectation that Africans would not only dress modestly but would also salute the Europeans they encountered. For African men, the expectation had acquired the name *chotsa chipewa*, 'remove the hat', and could involve corporal punishment if it was not honoured.[114] When the Commission put to Hetherwick the question of some Africans not taking off their hats, he gave this response:

> I think the native should take off his hat, and I think that if a ruling should be made, that, wherever a native salutes the European, the European should make some acknowledgement of the salute. I have seen many Europeans absolutely ignore a boy's salutation. You know that the smallest drummer boy in the British Army, if he salutes Lord Kitchener, receives a salute in return. If a native salutes a European there will be no difficulty if the European makes acknowledgement. It indicates that there are two gentlemen and not only one.[115]

Historians have been effusive about these remarks that came towards the end of Hetherwick's hearing. They have hailed them as 'a startling insistence on the oneness of humanity transcending racial difference'[116] and as Hetherwick's '*coup de grâce*', 'climax', and 'personal triumph'.[117] No doubt his remarks suggested uncommon sensibility in race relations. Yet their insistence on the 'oneness of humanity' came in a particular liberal key that posed little challenge to the racialized order itself. Not only was it the 'boy' who was still expected to make the first move in saluting the master, the 'acknowledgement' that Hetherwick called for also had a similar 'pacifying effect' as schooling – a feeling

---

[113] White, *Magomero*, 131.
[114] George Simeon Mwase, *Strike a Blow and Die: A Narrative of Race Relations in Colonial Language by George Simeon Mwase*, edited and introduced by Robert I. Rotberg, Cambridge, MA: Harvard University Press, 1967, 32.
[115] McCracken, *Voices*, 381.
[116] Andrew C. Ross, 'Hetherwick, Alexander', in Gerald H. Anderson, ed., *Biographical Dictionary of Christian Missions*, New York: Simon & Schuster, 1998, 291.
[117] Shepperson and Price, *Independent African*, 369.

among Africans that they were members of the same society as Europeans, albeit their junior partners.

Hetherwick's exchanges with the Commission also included views that anti-colonial historians may find unpalatable. To be sure, he did not miss the opportunity to take a swipe at his old foe, the former Commissioner Harry Johnston, for granting Joseph Booth land to establish his presence in the territory – 'for the beginning of this trouble you can put a certain share of blame on Commissioner Johnston'.[118] Yet Hetherwick's views also illustrate the general finding that liberal thought has long developed through exclusion and discrimination as well as through the expansion of liberties.[119] His defence of African involvement in both the Church and society stroked the common European fears of Islam.[120] Hetherwick told the Commission that the unfolding Great War was 'a war between Christianity and Islam' and that 'the future danger' in the protectorate lay in Islam.[121] The racialized order would come under threat, because Islam 'will unite natives as natives'. Asked whether 'Mohamedanism' was not rather a 'safety valve' among Africans, Hetherwick was unequivocal: 'By no means, Mohamedanism always has been aggressive.'

Hetherwick's paradox was a paradox common to liberal thought. Just as those calling for self-government and freedom in eighteenth-century America could be slave-owners,[122] so too did this enlightened advocate of civility in race relations regard some people more civilized than others. Despite the praise he has deservedly received for championing African interests, it is difficult to avoid the conclusion that Hetherwick's 'strength of purpose and practical effectiveness were accompanied by narrowness of mind'.[123] The conclusion would hardly be so starkly drawn, of course, had he not succeeded David Clement Scott as the head of the Blantyre Mission. No sense of reversals informed Hetherwick's knowledge about the condition in which he pursued his vocation. No learning with and from Africans animated his liberal views, whatever the veneration he gave to his predecessor. Whether it was their unstable languages or their no less unstable marriages, Africans stood to be corrected in the interest of a racialized

---

[118] McCracken, *Voices*, 362.
[119] Domenico Losurdo, *Liberalism: A Counter-History*, trans. Gregory Elliott, London: Verso, 2011.
[120] McCracken, *A History*, 142.   [121] McCracken, *Voices*, 370–1.
[122] Losurdo, *Liberalism*, 38.   [123] Hanna, *The Story*, 60.

order in which Europeans were in no rush to relinquish their privileges. As the Chilembwe rebellion demonstrated, the schooling offered by the Blantyre Mission had little control over the course that African discontent would take. By succumbing to a version of the prevailing racial thought, however, the Blantyre Mission under Hetherwick's leadership erased any alternatives that Scott's vision may have suggested.

10 | *The Rest Is History*

'Glory, glory, Man United!'

The song of the Manchester United Football Club provided an unexpected, though not unwelcome, soundtrack for my entry into the Maganga House in 2018. A group of young men loitered on its veranda, marvelling at the smart phone that was playing the uplifting tune. They had ample reason to spend their days at the Blantyre Synod. Apart from schools, including the Henry Henderson Institute, it had recently added a radio station and a university to its establishments. Located in the Hetherwick House, formerly the Hetherwick Press, the University of Blantyre Synod offered courses in two faculties: Theology and Commerce.

Redolent as they were of David Livingstone's combination of Christianity and commerce, the two faculties asserted no historical connection to nineteenth-century missionaries. Beyond the names of Henderson and Hetherwick, in fact, little else at the Synod recalled the Blantyre pioneers, whether European or African. When I entered the Maganga House, twenty-first-century aspiration and connectivity all around me, I was looking for nineteenth-century archives. A Synod custodian had located with some difficulty the keys to this building bearing the name of the early missionaries' residence. A sorry sight awaited us when he opened the door: a room in disrepair, housing documents at varying stages of decay (Figure 10.1). Tossed in an apparently random fashion on the floor and the shelves, they were too recent to hold much interest for my research.

The Maganga House had been the Synod officials' best guess at any archival repositories on site. Their efforts to quench my thirst for history led to a meeting with Che Chamba, a repository of oral history (Figure 10.2). A musician, he came virtually every day to the Synod's music building to give lessons and to pass time. Born in 1936 to Yao parents in Salisbury (Harare), he was sent to school in Domasi in the

Figure 10.1 Maganga House, 2018

Figure 10.2 Che Chamba, 2018

1940s. Too young to have personal memories of Alexander Hetherwick, he did recall a story about Hetherwick officiating at his grandmother's wedding. His account of Blantyre's early history was fluent and came with an agreeably Afrocentric angle. He talked of Africans – he was able to name Tom Bokwito – leading Henry Henderson to the present site. As a musician, he was familiar with Mungo Chisuse's status as Blantyre's first African organist. By failing to honour Chisuse posthumously, Malawi, he felt, had not showed Chisuse 'enough respect' (*ulemu wokwanira*).

David Clement Scott was not a name Che Chamba or anyone else I met at the Blantyre Synod would recognize. Scott himself may have been pleased to find his close African associate's name more readily remembered, even if Malawians in general know little of the man who took the photograph of John Chilembwe that appears on banknotes.[1] While the names of Henderson and Hetherwick are etched on the Synod's institutions, David Clement Scott's only appears to the discerning eye on a memorial plaque inside the St Michael's and All Angels Church he designed. His vision for the African Church long since undone, Scott receded into oblivion even as the Church of Central Africa, Presbyterian (CCAP) became Africanized in its governance. Although the rest most certainly is history, what does the recovery of his vision entail in the midst of twenty-first-century aspiration and connectivity?

An African Scotland?

The memory of the missionaries in Blantyre and Livingstonia, and of the traders in the African Lakes Company, is actively cultivated by some in Scotland to provide a narrative of almost continuous engagement between Scotland and Malawi since David Livingstone's expeditions.[2] While the narrative may have gained fresh appeal in the context of devolved governance in the United Kingdom, not to mention Scottish nationalism, the inspiration it draws for the present is welcome in so far as it recognizes the variety of ways in which the European encounter with Africa has unfolded across history. Scott and

---

[1] John McCracken, 'Mungo Murray Chisuse and the Early History of Photography in Malawi', *The Society of Malawi Journal*, 61 (2), 2008, 1–18.

[2] Kenneth R. Ross, *Malawi and Scotland: Together in the Talking Place since 1859*, Mzuzu: Mzuni Press, 2013.

Hetherwick were heirs to 'a long tradition of tension and conflict between white settlers and Scottish missionaries sympathetic to the rights of native peoples'.[3] This tradition, though, had its origins in the early-nineteenth century dissenting Presbyterianism rather than in the established Church of Scotland.[4] In the grand sweep of history, the Church of Scotland has resembled the Church of England in its promotion of imperial loyalty among settler populations.[5]

When looked at more closely, the Scotland–Malawi 'partnership' has had its contradictions, embodied, among others, in the figure of Malawi's first president, Kamuzu Banda. He obtained his medical qualifications in Edinburgh and embraced puritanism there to a degree that outstripped many Scottish churchgoers' inclinations.[6] Banda's claim to elderhood in the Church of Scotland remained a part of his paradoxical character throughout his life. It intersected with his Anglophilia in matters of dress and language use, curiously compatible with certain accoutrements of African elderhood.

John McCracken has put the historical significance of Malawi's Scottish connection in perspective.[7] Dismissing the view that Malawi was 'an African Scotland writ large' as 'seriously misleading', he pointed out how the influence of the African mission elite had declined by the 1940s when the Nyasaland African Congress was founded and civil servants, traders, and farmers proved more central to the nationalist cause than those employed by the missions, such as pastors and teachers. Many of the pioneering nationalists were indeed schooled in the Scottish missions, but already by 1940 Blantyre and Livingstonia had between them only 29 percent of all government-assisted schools. The number of Roman Catholic converts was likely to be larger than the African membership of the Scottish churches.

While not always as pivotal to Malawi's political developments as their leaders might think, the CCAP and the Church of Scotland have

---

[3] T. M. Devine, *To the Ends of the Earth: Scotland's Global Diaspora 1750–2010*, London: Allen Lane, 2011, 208.
[4] Valerie Wallace, *Scottish Presbyterianism and Settler Colonial Politics: Empire of Dissent*, New York: Palgrave Macmillan, 2018.
[5] Hilary M. Carey, *God's Empire: Religion and Colonialism in the British World, c. 1801–1908*, Cambridge: Cambridge University Press, 2011.
[6] Philip Short, *Banda*, London: Routledge and Kegan Paul, 1974, 35.
[7] John McCracken, *Politics and Christianity in Malawi 1875–1940: The Impact of the Livingstonia Mission in the Northern Province*, Cambridge: Cambridge University Press, 1977, 291–2.

certainly felt the reverberations of nationalist and democratic agitation. A major fillip in nationalist politics was the Federation of Rhodesia and Nyasaland, and the opposition against it culminated in a state of emergency in Malawi in 1959.[8] Both the Scottish missions and the home Church had entered the decade with a cautious, if not conservative, attitude to decolonization. It had not passed unnoticed among the CCAP's African officials, such as Allan Thipa and F. S. Chintali, who wrote a memorandum in 1957 to the visiting chair of the Foreign Mission Committee, James Dougall, complaining that 'some missionaries have no spirit of Fellowship within them. Some show the evil influence of the ugly head of conservatism, anti-Africanism, all tempered by anti-Semitism and the unchristian doctrine of Apartheid'.[9] Yet by the early 1950s in Scotland, the Iona Community, established by George Macleod in 1938, had begun to shift its focus from the poor in Scotland to injustices in Africa, particularly to the coming apartheid in South Africa and the Federation in central Africa.[10] After Macleod had become the Moderator of the Church in 1957, several old missionaries in Blantyre were forced to retire and more radical young clergy from Scotland took their place, including Tom Colvin.

In 1959, violent clashes between the police and pupils at the Blantyre Synod took place in the vicinity of the St Michael's and All Angels Church.[11] When Banda and other nationalists were imprisoned soon thereafter, the criticism of the colonial government came to be expressed by officials in the Church of Scotland. 'For the time being someone has to speak for the Africans', Macleod declared, 'and that someone will be the General Assembly of the Church of Scotland'.[12] Colvin, in turn, had his resolution passed by the General Assembly to demand that the detainees were either put on trial or released

---

[8] Robert I. Rotberg, *The Rise of Nationalism in Central Africa: The Making of Malawi and Zambia*, Cambridge, Mass.: Harvard University Press, 1966; Andrew C. Ross, *Colonialism to Cabinet Crisis: A Political History of Malawi*, Blantyre: Christian Literature Association of Malawi, 2009; Kings M. Phiri, John McCracken, and Wapulumuka O. Mulwafu, eds, *Malawi in Crisis: The 1959/60 Nyasaland State of Emergency and Its Legacy*, Blantyre: Christian Literature Association of Malawi, 2013; John Darwin, 'The Central African Emergency, 1959', *Journal of Imperial and Commonwealth History*, 21 (3), 1993, 217–34.
[9] Cited in John McCracken, 'Missionaries and Nationalists: Scotland and the 1959 Emergency in Malawi', in Afe Adogame and Andrew Lawrence, eds, *Africa in Scotland, Scotland in Africa: Historical Legacies and Contemporary Hybridities*, Leiden: Brill, 2014, 50.
[10] Ibid., 51, 53. [11] Ibid., 57–8. [12] Cited in ibid., 62.

immediately. The pendulum of political sympathies did not, however, take long to swing again in both Scotland and Malawi. Radical missionaries were silenced by new committee members in Edinburgh, while the support they had given to Banda during the state of emergency did not prevent him from turning his autocratic impulses against the CCAP.[13] Although Jonathan Sangaya, the first Malawian General Secretary of the Blantyre Synod, appointed in 1962, had his moments of courage,[14] a dismal verdict has befallen the CCAP and its Scottish supporters. 'Not until 1992', McCracken stated, 'would the Church of Scotland, in association with the CCAP, seek to comment on social injustice in Malawi'.[15] Lupenga Mphande's conclusion was even more forbidding: 'During the more than thirty years of [Banda's] atrocious reign of terror, never once did the Scottish-orientated Church in Malawi raise a voice of protest.'[16]

The protest, once it commenced, had much to criticize Banda's regime for. Apart from the suppression of dissent in a one-party state, Malawi remained desperately poor for its majority, some 80 percent of whom lived in rural areas as smallholder farmers.[17] Signs of relative affluence could appear in villages when Malawians exported their male labour to the mines and agricultural estates elsewhere in southern Africa. However, the demand for cheap labour on Malawian estates, along with changing attitudes to foreign labour in the other countries, had begun to undermine this option by the 1980s.[18] Economic grievances, along with the assaults on civil liberties, loomed large in the first high-profile expression of protest in Malawi since independence. It came not from the Protestant churches but as a Pastoral letter by the country's Catholic bishops, read out in all Catholic churches on the same Sunday in 1992.[19] Although a bombshell in Malawi, it followed

---

[13] Ibid., 67–8.   [14] Silas S. Ncozana, *Sangaya*, Mzuzu: Luviri Press, 2018.
[15] McCracken, 'Missionaries', 68.
[16] Lupenga Mphande, 'Dr. Hastings Kamuzu Banda and the Malawi Writers Group: The (Un)making of a Cultural Tradition', *Research in African Literatures*, 27 (1), 1996, 86.
[17] Ephraim Chirwa and Andrew Dorward, *Agricultural Input Subsidies: The Recent Malawi Experience*, Oxford: Oxford University Press, 2013.
[18] Wiseman Chijere Chirwa, 'The Malawi Government and South African Labour Recruiters, 1974–92', *Journal of Modern African Studies*, 34 (4), 1996, 623–42.
[19] Joseph C. Chakanza, 'The Pro-Democracy Movement in Malawi: The Catholic Church's Contribution, 1960–1992', in Matembo S. Nzunda and Kenneth R. Ross, eds, *Church, Law, and Political Transition in Malawi 1992–94*, Gweru: Mambo Press, 1995, 68–74; Matthew Schoffeleers, *In Search of Truth and*

similar expressions of political witness by the Catholic hierarchy in other African countries. The Blantyre and Livingstonia Synods soon took the initiative to convene an independent commission to discuss how the political system should be reformed.[20] The Public Affairs Committee included representatives from the religious, political, commercial, and legal spheres. Its attempt at inclusiveness did not spare the clergy from abuse and even death threats, voiced by zealots in the Malawi Congress Party (MCP).

Division within the Presbyterian Church also became visible in this heady period. Nkhoma, the third Synod in Malawi, withdrew its support for the process led by the other two and supplied clergy to officiate at MCP and state functions when other religious bodies were reluctant to do so.[21] Nkhoma had its origins in the Dutch Reformed Church mission from South Africa rather than in the Church of Scotland. This historical difference served to associate Blantyre and Livingstonia with more progressive politics among their Scottish supporters. Yet in better times, Nkhoma's own Scottish connection, in the form of its founding missionary, Andrew Murray, would be readily recalled.[22]

Soon after the transition to multiparty democracy, the wave of political activism at the Blantyre Synod subsided into matters of more immediate concern among its rank and file. They included financial difficulties, on one hand, and the rise of a Born-Again faction, on the other.[23] Already by the 1980s, Pentecostal-style preachers, independent and youthful, had begun to appear in the streets of Blantyre.[24]

Justice: Confrontations between Church and State in Malawi, 1960–1994, Blantyre: Christian Literature Association of Malawi, 2000.

[20] Kenneth R. Ross, 'Not Catalyst but Ferment: The Distinctive Contribution of the Churches to Political Reform in Malawi 1992–3', in Matembo S. Nzunda and Kenneth R. Ross, eds, *Church, Law, and Political Transition in Malawi 1992–94*, Gweru: Mambo Press, 1995, 32–3.

[21] Ibid., 38, 41.

[22] Ross, *Malawi and Scotland*, 46–7; Janet Wagner Parsons, 'Scots and Afrikaners in Central Africa: Andrew Charles Murray and the Dutch Reformed Church Mission in Malawi', *The Society of Malawi Journal*, 51 (1), 1998, 21–40.

[23] Peter VonDoepp, 'The Kingdom beyond *Zasintha*: Churches and Political Life in Malawi's Post-authoritarian Era', in Kings M. Phiri and Kenneth R. Ross, eds, *Democratization in Malawi: A Stocktaking*, Blantyre: Christian Literature Association of Malawi, 1998, 117–18.

[24] Rijk A. van Dijk, 'Young Puritan Preachers in Post-Independence Malawi', *Africa*, 62 (2), 1992, 159–81.

Established Pentecostal churches, such as the Apostolic Faith Mission and the Assemblies of God, have had a longer presence in Malawi, from at least the 1940s onwards.[25] Although alarmed by the new developments in Protestantism in Malawi, leaders at the Blantyre Synod could continue to draw on resources that its long association with the Church of Scotland afforded. Notable was its active role in campaigns to create awareness of the HIV pandemic, while the top clergy would intermittently enter the political sphere as fresh controversies arose. An example is the leadership they and other clergy provided when Bakili Muluzi, the democratically elected president, was mooted by his supporters for an unconstitutional third term in office in the early 2000s.[26] The CCAP again proved its capacity to mobilize resources for activism far beyond what some secular non-governmental organizations in Malawi could summon.

Fundamental as they have been, the major political events in Malawi's twentieth-century history should not obscure the legacies that have lasted. The racialized order that spelled the demise of Scott's vision continued to take various forms. The intensified nationalist agitation in the 1950s had a seemingly more conciliatory counterpart in the evocation of multiracial partnership by the outgoing colonial government. Subsequent historiography has not been kind to it, viewing it as a delaying tactic in decolonization and expressing dismay, as Scott might have done, at the relegation of Africans to the status of junior partners.[27] In the early twentieth century, Malawian migrants in South Africa experimented with other ideas, such as imperial citizenship as the basis for internationalism.[28] They drew inspiration from trade unionism and Christianity for imagining liberation beyond the confines of tribe, race, and nation.[29]

---

[25] Ulf Strohbehn, *Pentecostalism in Malawi: A History of the Apostolic Faith Mission 1931–1994*, Blantyre: Christian Literature Association of Malawi, 2005.

[26] Kenneth R. Ross, '"Worrisome Trends": The Voice of the Churches in Malawi's Third-Term Debate', *African Affairs*, 103 (410), 2004, 91–107.

[27] Robert I. Rotberg, 'The "Partnership" Hoax: How the British Government Deprived Central Africans of Their Rights', *Journal of Southern African Studies*, 45 (1), 2019, 89–110.

[28] Henry Dee, 'Central African Immigrants, Imperial Citizenship and the Politics of Free Movement in Interwar South Africa', *Journal of Southern African Studies*, 46 (2), 2020, 319–37.

[29] Henry Dee, 'Nyasa Leaders, Christianity, and African Internationalism in 1920s Johannesburg', *South African Historical Journal*, 70 (2), 2018, 383–406.

In Malawi, however, the racialized order has proven resilient in imagining political possibilities. The association of White skin with privilege informed, among others, the demands by the offspring of Anglo-African unions in the 1930s to be recognized for their European bloodline.[30] The degree of reverence afforded by Black Malawians to European ways of life is nowhere more apparent than in the status of the English language, the official language throughout the colonial and postcolonial periods and known as *Chizungu*, the language of the White people.[31] Its command remains an arbiter of sophistication and education, akin, though not reducible, to Banda's Anglophilia.

Where Scott may have countered such a mindset with appeals to common humanity as revealed in the African vernacular, Malawian intellectuals have not commonly had recourse to similar ideas. Instead, they have typically followed either of two paths to asserting African identity. One, largely confined to the university, has been to call for cultural expression, whether in English or Malawian languages, that draws on Malawian traditions.[32] The other has been more consequential, increasingly popular since the return to political pluralism from the 1990s onwards. It has asserted the primacy of peoplehood in ethnic terms, buttressed by new forms of associational life in which ethnic compatriots congregate around a set of symbols and practices that serve to distinguish their group from others.[33] Although the odd word from a minority language may be deployed, the ethnic associations

---

[30] Christopher J. Lee, *Unreasonable Histories: Nativism, Multiracial Lives, and the Genealogical Imagination in British Africa*, Durham, NC: Duke University Press, 2015, 171–2.

[31] Alfred Mtenje, 'English Imperialism and Shifting Attitudes towards African Languages: The Case of Malawi', in K. Legère and S. Fitchat., eds, *Talking Freedom: Language and Democratisation in the SADC Region*, Windhoek: Gamsberg Macmillan, 2002.

[32] Mphande, 'Dr. Hastings Kamuzu Banda', 95–6.

[33] Gregory H. Kamwendo, 'Ethnic Revival and Language Associations in the New Malawi: The Case of Chitumbuka', in Harri Englund, ed., *A Democracy of Chameleons: Politics and Culture in the New Malawi*, Uppsala: The Nordic Africa Institute, 2002; Gift Wasambo Kayira, Paul Chiudza Banda, and Amanda Lea Robinson, 'Ethnic Associations and Politics in Contemporary Malawi', *Journal of Eastern African Studies*, 13 (4), 2019, 718–38; Mwayi Lusaka, 'Dividing the Nation or Promoting Unity Ethnic Based Associations and Production of Heritage in Malawi', in Kenneth R. Ross and Wapulumuka O. Mulwafu, eds, *Politics, Christianity, and Society in Malawi: Essays in Honour of John McCracken*, Mzuzu: Mzuni Press, 2020, 372–95.

have been notably silent on language, whether in a philosophical or a practical sense. The emphasis has been on what makes one's group a people distinct from other peoples, not on how humanity might regenerate itself in every one of its vernaculars.

Recognizing the Risen Christ

Humanity rather than peoplehood was a key idea in Scott's vision for racial equality. Not only was the emphasis on ethnic or 'tribal' allegiances alien to it. It also diverged from attempts to reconcile one's belonging to a distinct nation or ethnic group with membership in the universal partnership of humanity. One example of such attempts is the way in which Johan Gottfried Herder's inspiration for nineteenth-century nationalism in eastern and central Europe has come to be rethought as 'cosmopolitan nationalism' or 'rooted cosmopolitanism'.[34] Although it is unlikely that Herder's cosmopolitan vision of *Volk* or 'Folk' left much room for non-Europeans or for women,[35] it has been recovered as one answer to the dilemma of living together in a world of difference. Each nation or people has its *Volksgeist* – its own genius or soul – but this property is also a claim to humanity. Kwame Anthony Appiah finds an illustration for what he calls 'Herder's axiom' in W. E. B. Du Bois's desire in the early twentieth century to place 'the Negro as a Folk among Folks' – that 'they *have* a place' is the axiom.[36]

The dilemma of living together in a world of difference may well be shared by Scott and more recent cosmopolitans. Appiah's call for paying attention to pragmatic accommodation rather than to apparently insurmountable value conflicts may also have appealed to Scott.[37] Yet the plurality as envisaged in the Herderian tradition – whether of nations, peoples, or cultures[38] – leaves a crucial aspect of

---

[34] Kwame Anthony Appiah, *Lines of Descent: W. E. B. Dubois and the Emergence of Identity*, Cambridge, MA: Harvard University Press, 2014, 45–51; Chris Hann, 'Towards a Rooted Anthropology: Malinowski, Gellner, and Herderian Cosmopolitanism', in Pnina Werbner, ed., *Anthropology and the New Cosmopolitanism*, Oxford: Berg, 2008, 70.

[35] John H. Zammito, *Kant, Herder, and the Birth of Anthropology*, Chicago, IL: University of Chicago Press, 2002, 18.

[36] Appiah, *Lines*, 61.

[37] Kwame Anthony Appiah, *Cosmopolitanism: Ethics in a World of Strangers*, New York: W. W. Norton, 2006, 72–8.

[38] Hann, 'Towards', 81; Raymond Williams, *Keywords: A Vocabulary of Culture and Society*, Oxford: Oxford University Press, 1985, 89.

Scott's vision unaddressed. It is the imperative of reversals. To be sure, Scott's insistence on common humanity called for unity as much as it recognized difference. As has been seen, for Scott, 'the prosperity of the European and of the native are one. We mutually depend on each other'.[39] Likewise in the Church, 'the all-important communion of Native and European in one worship before God' drove his vision.[40] Such unity could, however, be achieved only if it was informed by a theology of reversals. The encounter between Europe and Africa had inequality inscribed into it. The difference that there was reflected inequality supported by prejudice and exploitation, not *Volksgeist*. 'Dispensational difference', it will be recalled from Chapter 7, was one of Scott's descriptions of it.[41] He insisted on 'mutual respect' when confronted by such difference, mindful of 'which side holds most of dispensation power'.

The insistence on mutual recognition in an unequal encounter sought more than a reversal of roles. It ventured a permanent transformation in the relationship. Moreover, the dispensation power wielded by Europeans could not ensure them as the sole knowers in the encounter. Epistemic justice inhered in the figure of the risen Christ. Strangeness and otherness certainly confronted the European in Africa, but they did so not as an alien culture but as an injunction to examine prejudices. As mentioned at the beginning of this book, the Archbishop of Canterbury Rowan Williams captured some of this injunction in his reflections on the risen Christ a century after Scott's tenure in Blantyre. For some disciples, Williams submitted, 'the encounter with the risen Jesus began as an encounter with a stranger'.[42] They had to learn Jesus afresh rather than assume continuity from what they had known him to be. 'Just as Christ took upon Him the form of a slave long ago, so He takes upon Him the form of Africa today', went Scott's declaration of the strangeness of the risen Christ.[43] It was this strangeness that also precluded any identification of Christ with a particular community. 'Free from local limitation', Williams wrote, 'he is capable of interpreting an unlimited range of human situations'.[44] Any exclusive claim to know Christ, any attempt to domesticate him for a particular

---

[39] *Life and Work in British Central Africa* (LWBCA), December 1891.
[40] Ibid., May 1890.   [41] Ibid., August–December 1897.
[42] Rowan Williams, *Resurrection: Interpreting the Easter Gospel*, London: Darton, Longman, and Todd, 2002 [1982], 75.
[43] LWBCA, August–December 1897.   [44] Williams, *Resurrection*, 82.

community, place, or time, is thus profoundly at variance with the figure of the risen Christ. Scott's ultimately doomed impulse was to make this recognition the centrepiece of his missionary vocation.

Language – particularly translation – has appeared in this book as a major domain in which Scott pursued his vision for interracial worship in the African Church. Earlier translations of the Scriptures were to be 'diligently disregarded'[45] in the quest to make Chimang'anja assume its place with Greek and Hebrew among the languages of the sacred. Translation here was not the 'facile computation of cultural equivalence' that Emily Apter has attributed to a cosmopolitan moment in comparative literature.[46] Her advocacy of untranslatability as an antidote to shallow, seamless cultural equivalence draws on injunctions *not* to translate in traditions such as Islam. As such, it does not convey the challenge in Scott's vision for translation. Rather than denying the possibility of translation across linguistic and epistemic divides, Scott pursued it as a disruptive and creative practice. The contrast offered by Alexander Hetherwick's approach to translation in Chapter 9 served to highlight how much Scott expected the English language either to change or to recede to the margins when the Scriptures found their expression in Chimang'anja. Translation was, in Scott's practice, also an epistemic encounter in so far as idioms suggested by central African conditions, such as 'friendship', revealed knowledge of the Scriptures obscured by the English version.

Disputes over land and labour were another domain in which Scott's vision unfolded. By declaring Africans as the owners of the land, and by comparing colonial labour conditions to slavery, he courted controversy while expressing the need for reversals consistent with his vision. In 1891, as seen in Chapter 6, he described how chiefs had admitted Europeans into a relationship over land.[47] The rationale of colonial conquest faced here a reversal of the dispensation power that troubled Scott. Note that the reversal neither denied Europeans all power nor represented Africans as victims. Chiefly authority intrigued Scott, among other reasons, precisely because of the model it could suggest for a just mode of rule. Europeans would become, in his vision

---

[45] LWBCA, June 1894.
[46] Emily Apter, *Against World Literature: On the Politics of Untranslatability*, New York: Verso, 2013, 253.
[47] David Stuart-Mogg, 'The Rev. David Clement Scott and the Issue of Land Title in British Central Africa', *The Society of Malawi Journal*, 57 (2), 2004, 29.

for land tenure, 'associated chiefs' under the condition of 'associated co-occupation'.[48] Moreover, reversals, though morally vital, assumed no intrinsic righteousness in the African. The risk of the dispensation power turning into outright oppression was real enough, but it did not warrant categorical faith in the victims of oppression. 'Racism is not evil because its victims are good', as Williams wrote in another period, 'it is evil because its victims are *human*'.[49] It was in this vein, as seen in Chapter 5, that Scott questioned J. Albert Thorne's scheme for repatriating families of African descent. Their claim to African ancestry, despite its origin in the atrocity of the slave trade, guaranteed no privileged standpoint for making Africa prosper.

Reversals, evoking the biblical command to put the last first, have appeared in late-twentieth-century calls for rethinking international development. From the 1980s onwards, disillusion with expert-led, large-scale development projects became widespread among development practitioners themselves, and the promise of participatory development was to make the assumed beneficiaries central to those projects.[50] As advocated by Robert Chambers and his followers, participatory development distinguished itself from earlier, top-down models of development by re-authorizing the subjects of development as competent knowers and by proposing a range of tools for a reversal of roles in development projects. Among other responses which this approach provoked in academic research was the discovery of its Protestant roots. For critics, 'the dualistic cosmos of good and evil, the importance of reversals, the significance of personal conversion and the role of the community of believers' all amounted to a Protestant agenda in the guise of a secular and radical commitment to social and economic justice.[51]

Religious influence in international development, from faith-based organizations to some aspects of development economics, comes as no

---

[48] Ibid., 30.   [49] Williams, *Resurrection*, 11.
[50] Robert Chambers, *Rural Development: Putting the Last First*, London: Routledge, 1983; Robert Chambers, *Whose Reality Counts?: Putting the First Last*, London: Intermediate Technology, 1997; Nici Nelson and Susan Wright, eds, *Power and Participatory Development: Theory and Practice*, London: Intermediate Technology, 1995.
[51] Heiko Henkel and Roderick Stirrat, 'Participation as Spiritual Duty: Empowerment as Secular Subjection', in Bill Cooke and Uma Kothari, eds, *Participation: The New Tyranny?*, London: Zed Books, 2002, 178.

surprise to many practitioners and scholars in this field.[52] Scott's theology of reversals, however, placed greater demands on epistemic justice than what participatory development has been able to achieve in practice. The knowing subjects in participatory development are recognized as such within a framework whose origins lie beyond their participation.[53] Scott's vision was at once more modest and more radical. It never claimed anything other than Christianity as its origin, but the figure of the risen Christ also made him alert to the limits of Europeans' knowledge. As such, it presented an early alternative to the racialized order in which Africa's development has persistently drawn on the imagery of White patronage and guidance ameliorating Black suffering and ignorance.[54] Scott's interracial vision never lost sight of the dispensation difference as a *racialized* difference.

What the contemporary critics of racialized development are often reluctant to acknowledge is how some of its most ardent champions are themselves Black Africans, as seen in Malawians' reverence for the European ways of life. Boundaries between the knowers and the known in development work and activism have been asserted by Malawians themselves.[55] On the other hand, the critics of the so-called colonial mentality miss out on the possibility that by adopting apparently European manners, Africans may be making claims to common humanity in which the world's resources and opportunities ought to be distributed more evenly.[56] Paradoxically, as discussed in the introduction, it is the calls for epistemic freedom that may not be free from the primordialism that has driven racial thought.

[52] Erica Bornstein, *The Spirit of Development: Protestant NGOs, Morality, and Economics in Zimbabwe*, London: Routledge, 2003; Gerard Clarke, 'Faith Matters: Faith-Based Organizations, Civil Society, and International Development', *Journal of International Development*, 18 (6), 2006, 835–48; Daromir Rudnyckyj, *Spiritual Economies: Islam, Globalization, and the Afterlife of Development*, Ithaca, NY: Cornell University Press, 2010.

[53] Giles Mohan, 'Beyond Participation: Strategies for Deeper Empowerment', in Bill Cooke and Uma Kothari, eds, *Participation: The New Tyranny?*, London: Zed Books, 2002, 153–67.

[54] Jemima Pierre, 'The Racial Vernaculars of Development: A View from West Africa', *American Anthropologist*, 122 (1), 2020, 86–98.

[55] Harri Englund, *Prisoners of Freedom: Human Rights and the African Poor*, Berkeley, CA: University of California Press, 2006, 93–5; Crystal Biruk, *Cooking Data: Culture and Politics in an African Research World*, Durham, NC: Duke University Press, 2018, 74–80.

[56] James G. Ferguson, 'Of Mimicry and Membership: Africans and the "New World Society"', *Cultural Anthropology*, 17 (4), 2002, 551–69.

No doubt some currents in twenty-first-century African philosophy and theology are more congenial to Scott's vision than the calls for epistemic freedom. The most notable of them is Ubuntu, a public philosophy par excellence in post-apartheid South Africa.[57] Its uses and connotations are many, but when Ubuntu acquires more content than sloganeering about human interdependence, it may advance the kind of racial equality that Scott's vision expressed. For instance, the parallels some of its proponents draw to Christianity represent neither colonial mentality nor African primordialism but recognition of common humanity out of Africa.[58] More broadly, the theological movement of World Christianity has, after a period of emphasis on cultural and local diversity, rediscovered the conundrum of unity.[59] In a manner evocative of Scott's vision, the injunction is to learn '"with" and "in" World Christianity'.[60]

The Sunny Continent

Scott made no effort to name the knowledge he acquired in central Africa. No *Ubuntu* emanated from his years of African apprenticeship. Reducing what he had learned to a named body of knowledge was, of course, implausible for both practical and philosophical reasons. Scott's life was cut too short to allow him the period of reflection and writing that other missionaries enjoyed. Yet it would have been inconsistent philosophically for him to represent his new knowledge as separate from other bodies of knowledge. European knowledge and African knowledge did not exist apart from one another, as scholars now understand with regard to, for example, racial thought.[61] Scott's

---

[57] Leonhard Praeg and Siphokazi Magadla, eds, *Ubuntu: Curating the Archive*, Pietermaritzburg: University of Kwazulu-Natal Press, 2014.
[58] Francis B. Nyamnjoh, 'Ubuntuism and Africa: Actualised, Misappropriated, Endangered, and Reappraised', Africa Day Memorial Lecture, University of the Free State, Bloemfontein, 2019.
[59] Emma Wild-Wood, 'Relocating Unity and Theology in the Study of World Christianity', in Joel Cabrita, David Maxwell, and Emma Wild-Wood, eds, *Relocating World Christianity: Interdisciplinary Studies in Universal and Local Expressions of the Christian Faith*, Leiden: Brill, 2017, 324–42.
[60] Ibid., 339.
[61] Joel Cabrita, 'Writing Apartheid: Ethnographic Collaborators and the Politics of Knowledge Production in Twentieth-Century South Africa', *American Historical Review*, 125 (5), 2020, 1668–97; Jonathon Glassman, 'Toward a

theology of reversals sought epistemic justice in a world in which the racialized others barely participated as co-knowers.

For Scott, the vernacular gave a vantage point on the universal. It was not so much dogma as *method* that lay at the core of his African apprenticeship. For he came to learn some of his most profound lessons by observing and participating in disputes rather than by seeking to pin down a coherent set of precepts. The reason was less his own foresight than the turbulent conditions in which Africans had lived long before his arrival. Their modes of deliberation and diplomacy had developed amid the historical processes of long-distance trade, migration, slave raiding, chiefly intrigues, local and regional cults. Scott and his fellow missionaries entered a conversation Africans were having about spiritual, moral, and political matters. Against the common European failure to listen and to learn, Scott adopted the *mlandu* deliberation as one of his Mission's key methods.

Such adoption may seem appropriation when seen through the twenty-first-century lenses. But it informed Scott's theology of reversals as much as it did his desire to secure peaceful relations with neighbouring chiefs and to attract Africans to his Mission. Conversion into Christianity, as has been seen, could wait as Scott immersed himself in linguistic, diplomatic, and practical work. Africans assumed significant roles at the Mission well before their baptism, and Scott's emphasis was all along on how their knowledge revealed a civilization that was as Christian as that which Europeans peddled in central Africa. If anything, it could put to shame Europeans' claim to civilizational supremacy.

The oblivion from which this book has attempted to recover Scott's vision is a measure of his failure to realize it. The purpose has not been to turn biography into hagiography but to explore what scholars' neglect of Scott's life may have missed out in the history and anthropology of racialized encounters. Beyond specialist studies in regional history, Scott has not enjoyed much attention in the academic literature. While the most substantial book about Malawi's history acknowledges him as a 'visionary',[62] he earns only a few caustic remarks in Adrian Hastings's monumental *The Church in Africa, 1450–1950*. It

Comparative History of Racial Thought in Africa: Historicism, Barbarism, Autochthony', *Comparative Studies in Society and History*, 63 (1), 2021, 72–98.

[62] John McCracken, *A History of Malawi 1859–1966*, Oxford: James Currey, 2012, 47.

lumps Scott together with other Scottish missionaries for having had 'a strong tendency to be insensitively autocratic'.[63] It also asserts that Scott did not detect the apparent discrepancy between his approach to land issues in Malawi and Kenya – 'strangely', Hastings comments, 'for someone who, in Nyasaland [sic], had criticized European land-grabbing'.[64]

What such comments, and the overall oblivion of which they are symptoms, require is the biographer's pursuit of epistemic justice in which a life as lived can be seen in its complexity. When situated in biographical time, Scott's conduct appears in relation to the many currents that ran through his life. Although he was accused of autocracy towards the end of his tenure in Blantyre, the reader of this book is able to evaluate the accusation and to explain who launched it. Above all, the reader is able to account for growth in Scott's thought and the accompanying conflicts. 'The chief tyranny', he wrote in 1889, 'is that over the natives'.[65] Much would happen to make commercial agriculture one of his preoccupations in Kenya in the new century. Knowing what did happen, from his opposition to Cecil Rhodes's schemes to his financial difficulties running the Blantyre Mission, attributes no spurious coherence, let alone unqualified success, to a life lived in turbulent times. The result of an intellectual biography is knowledge gained against oblivion, an understanding of how a vision for Africa's interracial future emerged and vanished.

Darkness, as Hastings insightfully describes, was the chief metaphor among Victorian missionaries and the first generation of their African converts.[66] It could express the evils of the slave trade as well as the depravity of heathen custom. In Scott's life and thought, however, the idea of the Dark Continent had its opponent among the Victorian missionaries. As has been seen, Scott's reflections on *mankhwala*, the concept for medicine, led to the conclusion that 'nowhere is there found the thick darkness which one is taught to look for'.[67] His words

---

[63] Adrian Hastings, *The Church in Africa, 1450–1950*, Oxford: Clarendon Press, 1994, 557.
[64] Ibid., 427.
[65] David Clement Scott to James Robertson, 10 May 1889, EUL, Gen. 717-10.
[66] Hastings, *The Church*, 299.
[67] David Clement Scott, *A Cyclopaedic Dictionary of the Mang'anja Language Spoken in British Central Africa*, Edinburgh: Foreign Mission Committee of the Church of Scotland, 1892, 347.

about the African continent as 'the freest, openest land in the world (*apricus*, open, sunny)' can also be readily recalled.[68] The Sunny Continent beamed its light and warmth on the apprentice from Scotland.

Tempting as it is to describe the twilight that ensued as a tragedy in both personal and political terms, doing epistemic justice to Scott's tribulations demands a different conclusion. It can draw on the figure that animated Scott's vision: the risen Christ. The resurrection repudiates the interpretation of Christ's life as a tragedy. It 'does not go back on what has gone before; it comes after and moves on'.[69] Scott's understanding of Africa as the risen Christ tried the limits of how receptive the Victorians were to the stranger. It was an historically specific alternative to an historically specific form of racial prejudice. In the twenty-first century, struggles for racial equality are bound to look different, but Scott's vision bequeaths to posterity a challenge of timeless consequence: how open to the stranger are the philosophies by which we live?

---

[68] Rev. D. C. Ruffelle Scott, *'Living Stones': Sermon upon the Church of Scotland Blantyre Mission, British Central Africa*. Edinburgh: William Blackwood and Sons, 1901, 8.

[69] Gerard Loughlin, *Telling God's Story: Bible, Church, and Narrative Theology*, Cambridge: Cambridge University Press, 1996, 162–3.

Bibliography

Archival Sources

Edinburgh University Library Special Collections (EUL)
- David Clement Scott's letters to James Robertson, Gen. 717-10.
- Frederick T. Morrison Diary, Coll-443.
- John William Arthur Papers, Coll-207.
- Arthur Ruffelle Barlow, 'Some Early Memories', Gen. 1786-1.
- *Life and Work in British Central Africa* (mission periodical).
- *Nyasaland and Kikuyu Vol. V: 1906–08* (obituaries, pamphlets, correspondence), Centre for the Study of World Christianity, University of Edinburgh.
- *The Edinburgh University Calendar*.

National Archives of Malawi, Zomba (NAM)
- Blantyre Mission Council Papers, 50/BMC/1/1/1, 50/BMC/1/2/1, 50/BMC/2/1/2, 50/BMC/217.
- Alexander Hetherwick, 'My First Day in Blantyre', AHE 1-1.

National Archives of the United Kingdom, Kew (NAUK)
- Foreign Office Correspondence, FO 2/54, FO 2/55, FO 2/67, FO 2/88, FO 84/2114.
- *The Nyasa News* (mission periodical), included in FO 2/55.

National Archives of Zimbabwe, Harare (NAZ)
- Harry Johnston's letter to Cecil Rhodes, CT/1/16/4/1.

National Library of Scotland, Edinburgh (NLS)
- Duff Macdonald Diary, Acc 7548/D79.
- The Blantyre Mission Journal, Acc 9218.
- Foreign Mission Committee Letter Books, Ms 7534, Ms 7535, Ms 7536, Ms 7537, Ms 7538, Ms 7539, Ms 7547, Ms 7548, Ms 7553, Ms 7873, Ms 7890, Ms 7891, Ms 7902, Ms 7903.
- David Clement Scott, 'Ham Shall Be His Servant', Ms 7903.

- Thomas Price, *History of the Blantyre Mission, 1876–1956*, Acc 9069.
- J. Albert Thorne, *An Appeal Addressed to the Friends of the African Race*, Ms 7873.
- *Central African Planter* (newspaper).
- *The Central African Times* (newspaper).
- *The Scotsman* (newspaper).

Books, Articles, and Dissertations

Achebe, Chinua. *Home and Exile*, New York: Anchor Books, 2000.

Agamben, Giorgio. *Homo Sacer: Sovereign Power and Bare Life*, trans. D. Heller-Roazen, Stanford, CA: Stanford University Press, 1998.

Alpers, Edward A. *Ivory and Slaves in East Central Africa: Changing Patterns of International Trade in the Late Nineteenth Century*, London: Heinemann, 1975.

Amin, Samir. *Unequal Development: An Essay on the Social Formations of Peripheral Capitalism*, trans. Brian Pearce, Hassocks: Harvester Press, 1976.

Appiah, Kwame Anthony. *In My Father's House: Africa in the Philosophy of Culture*, London: Oxford University Press, 1992.

Cosmopolitanism: Ethics in a World of Strangers, New York: W. W. Norton, 2006

Lines of Descent: W. E. B. Dubois and the Emergence of Identity, Cambridge, MA: Harvard University Press, 2014.

Apter, Emily. *Against World Literature: On the Politics of Untranslatability*, New York: Verso, 2013.

Arendt, Hannah. *The Origins of Totalitarianism*, New York: Harcourt Brace, 1973 [1951].

Asad, Talal. *Formations of the Secular: Christianity, Islam, Modernity*, Stanford, CA: Stanford University Press, 2003.

Atieno-Odhiambo, E. S. 'From African Historiographies to an African Philosophy of History', in Toyin Falola and Christian Jennings, eds. *Africanizing Knowledge: African Studies across the Disciplines*, New Brunswick, NJ: Transaction, 2002.

Bandawe, L. M. *Memoirs of a Malawian*, Blantyre: Christian Literature Association of Malawi, 1971.

Barnes, Bertram Herbert. *Johnson of Nyasaland: A Study of the Life and Work of William Percival Johnson, D.D., Archdeacon of Nyasa, Missionary Pioneer, 1876–1928*, London: Universities' Mission to Central Africa, 1933.

Barnes, J. A. *Marriage in a Changing Society: A Study in Structural Change among the Fort Jameson Ngoni*, London: Oxford University Press, 1951.

Politics in a Changing Society: A Political History of the Fort Jameson Ngoni, London: Oxford University Press, 1954.
Bebbington, David W. 'Henry Drummond, Evangelicalism and Science', in Thomas E. Corts, ed., *Henry Drummond: A Perpetual Benediction*, Edinburgh: T. & T. Clark, 1999.
Beidelman, T. O. *Colonial Evangelism: A Socio-historical Study of an East African Mission at the Grassroots*, Bloomington: Indiana University Press, 1982.
Bell, Duncan. *Reordering the World: Essays on Liberalism and Empire*, Princeton: Princeton University Press, 2016.
Benjamin, Walter. 'The Task of the Translator', trans. Harry Zohn, in Rainer Schulte and John Biguenet, eds. *Theories of Translation: An Anthology of Essays from Dryden to Derrida*, Chicago, IL: University of Chicago Press, 1992 [1923].
Bhabha, Homi K. *The Location of Culture*, New York: Routledge, 1994.
Bible Society of Malawi. *Buku lopatulika ndilo mau a Mulungu*, Blantyre: Bible Society of Malawi, 1992 [1922].
Biruk, Crystal. *Cooking Data: Culture and Politics in an African Research World*, Durham, NC: Duke University Press, 2018.
Booth, Joseph. *Africa for the African*, Blantyre: Christian Literature Association in Malawi, 1996 [1897].
Bornstein, Erica. *The Spirit of Development: Protestant NGOs, Morality, and Economics in Zimbabwe*, London: Routledge, 2003.
Bridges, Roy. 'The Christian Vision and Secular Imperialism: Missionaries, Geography, and the Approach to East Africa, c. 1844–1890', in Dana L. Robert, ed., *Converting to Colonialism: Visions and Realities in Mission History, 1706–1914*, Grand Rapids, MI: William B. Eerdmans, 2008.
Brough, Beryl. 'The Role of the U.M.C.A. in 19th-Century Malawi', *The Society of Malawi Journal*, 52 (1), 1999, 13–24.
Cabrita, Joel. *Text and Authority in the South African Nazaretha Church*, Cambridge: Cambridge University Press for the International African Institute, 2014.
The People's Zion: Southern Africa, the United States, and a Transatlantic Faith-Healing Movement, Cambridge, MA: Harvard University Press, 2018.
'Writing Apartheid: Ethnographic Collaborators and the Politics of Knowledge Production in Twentieth-Century South Africa', *American Historical Review*, 125 (5), 2020, 1668–97.
Cairns, H. Alan C. *Prelude to Imperialism: British Reactions to Central African Society, 1840–1890*, London: Routledge & Kegan Paul, 1965.
Campbell, Gwyn. 'Bondage', in Gaurav Desai and Adeline Masquelier, eds. *Critical Terms for the Study of Africa*, Chicago, IL: University of Chicago Press, 2018.

Carey, Hilary M. *God's Empire: Religion and Colonialism in the British World, c. 1801–1908*, Cambridge: Cambridge University Press, 2011.

Centre of Language Studies (University of Malawi). *Mtanthauzira mawu wa Chinyanja*, Blantyre: Dzuka, 2000.

Chadwick, Owen. *Mackenzie's Grave*, London: Hodder and Stoughton, 1959.

Chakanza, Joseph C. 'The Pro-Democracy Movement in Malawi: The Catholic Church's Contribution, 1960–1992'. in Matembo S. Nzunda and Kenneth R. Ross, eds. *Church, Law and Political Transition in Malawi 1992–94*, Gweru: Mambo Press, 1995.

Chambers, Robert. *Rural Development: Putting the Last First*, London: Routledge, 1983.

Whose Reality Counts?: Putting the First Last, London: Intermediate Technology, 1997.

Chanock, Martin. *Law, Custom and Social Order: The Colonial Experience in Malawi and Zambia*, Cambridge: Cambridge University Press, 1985.

'A Peculiar Sharpness: An Essay on Property in the History of Customary Law in Colonial Africa', *Journal of African History*, 32 (1), 1991, 65–88.

Chidester, David. *Savage Systems: Colonialism and Comparative Religion in Southern Africa*, 1996.

Chirnside, Andrew. *The Blantyre Missionaries: Discreditable Disclosures*, London: Ridgway, 1880.

Chirwa, Ephraim and Andrew Dorward. *Agricultural Input Subsidies: The Recent Malawi Experience*, Oxford: Oxford University Press, 2013.

Chirwa, Wiseman Chijere. 'The Malawi Government and South African Labour Recruiters, 1974–92', *Journal of Modern African Studies*, 34 (4), 1996, 623–42.

Clarke, Gerard. 'Faith Matters: Faith-Based Organizations, Civil Society, and International Development', *Journal of International Development*, 18 (6), 2006, 835–48.

Colson, Elizabeth. *The Plateau Tonga of Northern Rhodesia: Social and Religious Studies*, Manchester: Manchester University Press, 1962.

'The Impact of the Colonial Period on the Definition of Land Rights', in Victor Turner, ed., *Colonialism in Africa, 1870–1960. Volume 3: Profiles of Change*, Cambridge: Cambridge University Press, 1971.

Comaroff, Jean and John. *Of Revelation and Revolution: Christianity, Colonialism, and Consciousness in South Africa. Volume One*, Chicago, IL: University of Chicago Press, 1991.

Conrad, Joseph. *Heart of Darkness*, London: Penguin Random House, 2019 [1902].

Cooper, Frederick. *Colonialism in Question: Theory, Knowledge, History*. Berkeley: University of California Press, 2005.

'The Problem of Slavery in African Studies,' *Journal of African History*, 20 (1), 1979, 103–25.

Corts, Thomas E. 'Introduction: Who Was Henry Drummond?', in Thomas E. Corts, ed., *Henry Drummond: A Perpetual Benediction*, Edinburgh: T. & T. Clark, 1999.

Corts, Thomas E. and Marla Haas Corts. 'Henry Drummond: From Scotland to America with Love', in Thomas E. Corts, ed., *Henry Drummond: A Perpetual Benediction*, Edinburgh: T. & T. Clark, 1999.

Crawford, D. *Thinking Black: 22 Years without a Break in the Long Grass of Central Africa*, London: London, Morgan and Scott, 1913.

Crowder, Michael. 'Indirect Rule – French and British Style', *Africa*, 34 (3), 1964, 187–205.

Currie, Jessie Monteath. *The Hill of Good-bye: The Story of a Solitary White Woman's Life in Central Africa*, London: George Routledge and Sons, 1920.

Darwin, John. 'The Central African Emergency, 1959', *Journal of Imperial and Commonwealth History*, 21 (3), 1993, 217–234.

Dee, Henry. 'Nyasa Leaders, Christianity and African Internationalism in 1920s Johannesburg', *South African Historical Journal*, 70 (2), 2018, 383–406.

'Central African Immigrants, Imperial Citizenship and the Politics of Free Movement in Interwar South Africa', *Journal of Southern African Studies*, 46 (2), 2020, 319–37.

Devine, T. M. *To the Ends of the Earth: Scotland's Global Diaspora 1750–2010*, London: Allen Lane, 2011.

Drummond, Andrew L. and James Bulloch. *The Church in Late Victorian Scotland 1874–1900*, Edinburgh: The Saint Andrew Press, 1978.

Drummond, Henry. *Natural Law in the Spiritual World*, London: Hodder and Stoughton, 1883.

Tropical Africa, London: Hodder and Stoughton, 1888.

The Lowell Lectures on the Ascent of Man, London: Hodder and Stoughton, 1894.

Dubow, Saul. *Racial Segregation and the Origins of Apartheid in South Africa, 1919–36*, Basingstoke: Macmillan, 1989.

Dyer, Richard. *White*, 2nd Edition, New York: Routledge, 2017.

Earle, Jonathon L. 'Dreams and Political Imagination in Colonial Buganda', *Journal of African History*, 58 (1), 2017, 85–105.

Edgar, Robert R. and Hilary Sapire. *African Apocalypse: The Story of Nontetha Nkwenkwe, A Twentieth-Century South African Prophet*, Athens: Ohio University Press, 2000.

Elbourne, Elizabeth. *Blood Ground: Colonialism, Missions, and the Contest for Christianity in the Cape Colony and Britain, 1799–1853*, Montreal: McGill-Queen's University Press, 2002.

'Word Made Flesh: Christianity, Modernity, and Cultural Colonialism in the Work of Jean and John Comaroff', *American Historical Review*, 108 (2), 2003, 435–59.
Ellul, Jacques. *On Freedom, Love, and Power*, trans. Willem H. Vanderburg, Toronto: University of Toronto Press, 2010.
Elmslie, W. A. *Among the Wild Ngoni*, Edinburgh: Oliphant, Anderson & Ferrier, 1899.
Elphick, Richard. *The Equality of Believers: Protestant Missionaries and the Racial Politics of South Africa*, Charlottesville, VA: University of Virginia Press, 2012.
Englund, Harri. *From War to Peace on the Mozambique–Malawi Borderland*, Edinburgh: Edinburgh University Press for the International African Institute, 2002.
   Prisoners of Freedom: Human Rights and the African Poor, Berkeley: University of California Press, 2006.
   Human Rights and African Airwaves: Mediating Equality on the Chichewa Radio, Bloomington: Indiana University Press, 2011.
Errington, Joseph. *Linguistics in a Colonial World: A Story of Language, Meaning, and Power*, Malden, MA: Blackwell, 2008.
Etherington, Norman. 'Introduction', in Norman Etherington, ed., *Mission and Empire*, Oxford: Oxford University Press, 2005.
Evans-Pritchard, E. E. *Witchcraft, Oracles and Magic among the Azande*, Oxford: Clarendon Press, 1937.
Fabian, Johannes. *Language and Colonial Power: The Appropriation of Swahili in the Former Belgian Congo 1880–1938*, Berkeley: University of California Press, 1986.
Fanon, Franz. *Black Skin, White Masks*, trans. by Charles Lam Markmann, London: Pluto Press, 1986 [1952, 1967].
Fassin, Didier. 'Inequality of Lives, Hierarchies of Humanity: Moral Constraints and Ethical Dilemmas of Humanitarianism', in Ilana Feldman and Miriam Ticktin, eds. *In the Name of Humanity: The Government of Care and Threat*, Durham, NC: Duke University Press, 2010.
Feldman, Ilana and Miriam Ticktin. 'Introduction: Government and Humanity', in Ilana Feldman and Miriam Ticktin, eds. *In the Name of Humanity: The Government of Care and Threat*, Durham, NC: Duke University Press, 2010.
Ferguson, James G. 'Of Mimicry and Membership: Africans and the "New World Society"', *Cultural Anthropology*, 17 (4), 2002, 551–69.
Fields, Karen E. *Revival and Rebellion in Colonial Central Africa*, Princeton, NJ: Princeton University Press, 1985.
Frank, André Gunder. *Dependent Accumulation and Underdevelopment*, London: Macmillan, 1978.

Fricker, Miranda. *Epistemic Injustice: Power and the Ethics of Knowing*, Oxford: Oxford University Press, 2007.
Gal, Susan. 'The Politics of Translation', *Annual Review of Anthropology*, 44, 2015, 225–40.
Gamitto, Antonio C. P. *King Kazembe and the Marave, Cheva, Bisa, Bemba, Lunda and Other Peoples of Southern Africa*, trans. Ian Cunnison, Lisbon: Junta de Investigações do Ultamar, 1960.
Glassman, Jonathon. *War of Words, War of Stones: Racial Thought and Violence in Colonial Zanzibar*, Bloomington: Indiana University Press, 2011.
  'Toward a Comparative History of Racial Thought in Africa: Historicism, Barbarism, Autochthony', *Comparative Studies in Society and History*, 63 (1), 2021, 72–98.
Gluckman, Max. *The Judicial Process among the Barotse of Northern Rhodesia*, Manchester: Manchester University Press, 1955.
  The Ideas in Barotse Jurisprudence, Manchester: Manchester University Press, 1972 [1965].
Goldenberg, David M. *Black and Slave: The Origins and History of the Curse of Ham*, Berlin: De Gruyter, 2017.
Gopal, Priyamvada. *Insurgent Empire: Anticolonial Resistance and British Dissent*, London: Verso, 2019.
Grant, Kevin. *A Civilised Savagery: Britain and the New Slaveries in Africa, 1884–1926*, New York: Routledge, 2004.
Gray, Richard. *Black Christians and White Missionaries*, New Haven, CT: Yale University Press, 1990.
Guy, Jeff. *The Heretic: A Study of the Life of John William Colenso 1814–1883*, Johannesburg: Ravan Press, 1983.
  'Class, Imperialism and Literary Criticism: William Ngidi, John Colenso and Matthew Arnold', *Journal of Southern African Studies*, 23 (2), 1997, 219–41.
Handman, Courtney. 'Speaking to the Soul: On Native Language and Authenticity in Papua New Guinea Bible Translation', in Miki Makihara and Bambi B. Schieffelin, eds. *Consequences of Contact: Language Ideologies and Sociocultural Transformations in Pacific Societies*, Oxford: Oxford University Press, 2007.
Hanks, William F. 'The Space of Translation', in Carlo Severi and William F. Hanks, eds. *Translating Worlds: The Epistemological Space of Translation*, Chicago, IL: HAU Books, 2015.
Hann, Chris. 'Towards a Rooted Anthropology: Malinowski, Gellner and Herderian Cosmopolitanism', in Pnina Werbner, ed., *Anthropology and the New Cosmopolitanism*, Oxford: Berg, 2008.
Hanna, A. J. *The Beginnings of Nyasaland and North-Eastern Rhodesia 1859–95*, Oxford: Clarendon Press, 1956.

The Story of the Rhodesias and Nyasaland, London: Faber and Faber, 1960.

Harries, Patrick. 'The Roots of Ethnicity: Discourse and the Politics of Language Construction in South-East Africa', *African Affairs* 87 (346), 1988, 25–52.

'Anthropology', in Norman Etherington, ed., *Mission and Empire*, Oxford: Oxford University Press, 2005.

Butterflies and Barbarians: Swiss Missionaries and Systems of Knowledge in South-East Africa, Oxford: James Currey, 2007.

Hastings, Adrian. *The Church in Africa, 1450–1950*, Oxford: Clarendon Press, 1994.

The Construction of Nationhood: Ethnicity, Religion and Nationalism, Cambridge: Cambridge University Press, 1997.

Hefner, Robert W., ed. *Conversion to Christianity: Historical and Anthropological Perspectives on a Great Transformation*, Berkeley: University of California Press, 1993.

Hegel, G. W. F. *The Philosophy of History*, trans. J. Sibree, New York: The Colonial Press, 1999.

Henkel, Heiko and Roderick Stirrat. 'Participation as Spiritual Duty: Empowerment as Secular Subjection', in Bill Cooke and Uma Kothari, eds. *Participation: The New Tyranny?*, London: Zed Books, 2002.

Hetherwick, Alexander. *The Building of the Blantyre Church, Nyasaland, 1888–1891: Being the Story of a Great Achievement*, Blantyre: Hetherwick Press, 1926.

The Romance of Blantyre: How Livingstone's Dream Came True, Edinburgh: Lassodie Press, 1931.

The Gospel and The African, Edinburgh: T. & T. Clark, 1932.

'Preface', in D. C. Scott, *Dictionary of the Nyanja Language*, edited and enlarged by Alexander Hetherwick, London: Lutterworth Press, 1929.

Higham, N. J. *The Convert Kings: Power and Religious Affiliation in Early Anglo-Saxon England*, Manchester: Manchester University Press, 1997.

Hobsbawm, Eric. *The Age of Empire 1875–1914*, London: Weidenfeld & Nicolson, 1987.

Hokkanen, Markku. '"Christ and the Imperial Games Fields" in South-Central Africa – Sport and the Scottish Missionaries in Malawi, 1880–1914: Utilitarian Compromise', *International Journal of the History of Sport*, 22 (4), 2005, 745–69.

Medicine and Scottish Missionaries in the Northern Malawi Region 1875–1830: Quests for Health in a Colonial Society, New York: Edwin Mellen Press, 2007.

Hokkanen, Markku and J. A. Mangan. 'Further Variations on a Theme: The Games Ethic Further Adapted – Scottish Moral Missionaries and Muscular Christians in Malawi', *The International Journal of the History of Sport*, 23 (8), 2006, 1257–74.

Hountondji, Paulin J. *African Philosophy: Myth and Reality*, Bloomington: Indiana University Press, 1983.

Howe, Stephen. *Afrocentrism: Mythical Pasts and Imagined Homes*, London: Verso, 1998.

Hunter, Emma. 'Language, Empire and the World: Karl Roehl and the History of the Swahili Bible in East Africa', *Journal of Imperial and Commonwealth History*, 41 (4), 2013, 600–16.

Iliffe, John. *The African Poor: A History*, Cambridge: Cambridge University Press, 1987.

   Honour in African History, Cambridge: Cambridge University Press, 2005.

International Bible Society, *Chipangano chatsopano: Mu Chichewa cha lero*, Nairobi: International Bible Society, 2002.

Irvine, Judith T. 'Mastering African Languages: The Politics of Linguistics in Nineteenth-Century Senegal', *Social Analysis*, No. 33, 1993, 27–46.

   'Subjected Words: African Linguistics and the Colonial Encounter', *Language and Communication*, 23 (4), 2008, 323–43.

Johnson, William Percival. *Nyasa, the Great Water: Being a Description of the Lake and the Life of the People*, London: Oxford University Press, 1922.

Johnston, Harry H. *British Central Africa: An Attempt to Give Some Account of a Portion of the Territories under British Influence North of the Zambezi*, London: Methuen & Co, 1897.

Kachapila, Hendrina. 'Mothercraft in the DRCM: *Mthenga* Newspaper, Missionary Wives and African Women', in Kenneth R. Ross and Wapulumuka O. Mulwafu, eds. *Politics, Christianity and Society in Malawi: Essays in Honour of John McCracken*, Mzuzu: Mzuni Press, 2020.

Kamwendo, Gregory H. 'Ethnic Revival and Language Associations in the New Malawi: The Case of Chitumbuka', in Harri Englund, ed., *A Democracy of Chameleons: Politics and Culture in the New Malawi*, Uppsala: The Nordic Africa Institute, 2002.

Kayira, Gift Wasambo, Paul Chiudza Banda and Amanda Lea Robinson. 'Ethnic Associations and Politics in Contemporary Malawi', *Journal of Eastern African Studies*, 13 (4), 2019, 718–38.

Keane, Webb. *Christian Moderns: Freedom and Fetish in the Mission Encounter*, Berkeley: University of California Press, 2007.

Kidd, Colin. *The Forging of Races: Race and Scripture in the Protestant Atlantic World, 1600–2000*, Cambridge: Cambridge University Press, 2006.
Kopytoff, Igor and Suzanne Miers. 'African "Slavery" as an Institution of Marginality,' in Suzanne Miers and Igor Kopytoff, eds. *Slavery in Africa: Historical and Anthropological Perspectives*, Madison: University of Wisconsin Press, 1977.
Landau, Paul Stuart. *In the Realm of the Word: Language, Gender, and Christianity in a Southern African Kingdom*, Portsmouth, NH: Heinemann, 1995.
Langworthy, Harry W. 'Central Malawi in the 19th Century', in R. J. Macdonald, ed., *From Nyasaland to Malawi: Studies in Colonial History*, Nairobi: East African Publishing House, 1975.
 'Africa for the African': The Life of Joseph Booth, Blantyre: Christian Literature Association in Malawi, 1996.
Laws, Robert. *Reminiscences of Livingstonia*, Edinburgh: Oliver and Boyd, 1934.
Lee, Christopher J. *Unreasonable Histories: Nativism, Multiracial Lives, and the Genealogical Imagination in British Africa*, Durham, NC: Duke University Press, 2015.
Lee, Rebekah and Megan Vaughan. 'Death and Dying in the History of Africa since 1800', *Journal of African History*, 49 (3), 2008, 341–59.
Lewis, Joanna. *Empire of Sentiment: The Death of Livingstone and the Myth of Victorian Imperialism*, Cambridge: Cambridge University Press, 2018.
Linden Ian with Jane Linden. *Catholics, Peasants, and Chewa Resistance in Nyasaland, 1889–1939*, London: Heinemann, 1974.
Linden, Jane and Ian Linden. 'John Chilembwe and the New Jerusalem', *Journal of African History*, 12 (4), 1971, 629–51.
Lindsay, Lisa A. 'Biography in African History', *History in Africa*, 44, 2017, 11–26.
Livingstone, David. *Missionary Travels in South Africa*, London: John Murray, 1857.
Livingstone, David and Charles Livingstone. *Narrative of an Expedition to the Zambezi and Its Tributaries; and of the Discovery of the Lakes Shirwa and Nyassa, 1858–64*, London: Duckworth, 2001 [1865].
Livingstone, William P. *Laws of Livingstonia*, London: Hodder and Stoughton, 1921.
 A Prince of Missionaries: The Rev. Alexander Hetherwick of Blantyre, Central Africa, London: James Clarke and Co, 1931.
Lonsdale, John. 'Kikuyu Christianities: A History of Intimate Diversity', in David Maxwell and Ingrid Lawrie, eds. *Christianity and the African Imagination: Essays in Honour of Adrian Hastings*, Leiden: Brill, 2002.

Losurdo, Domenico. *Liberalism: A Counter-History*, trans. Gregory Elliott, London: Verso, 2011.
Loughlin, Gerard. *Telling God's Story: Bible, Church and Narrative Theology*, Cambridge: Cambridge University Press, 1996.
Luck, Anna. *Charles Stokes in Africa*, Nairobi: East African Publishing House, 1972.
Lugard, Lord. *The Dual Mandate in British Tropical Africa*, London: Frank Cass and Co, 1922.
Lusaka, Mwayi. 'Dividing the Nation or Promoting Unity?: Ethnic Based Associations and Production of Heritage in Malawi', in Kenneth R. Ross and Wapulumuka O. Mulwafu, eds. *Politics, Christianity and Society in Malawi: Essays in Honour of John McCracken*, Mzuzu: Mzuni Press, 2020.
Macdonald, Duff. *Africana: The Heart of Heathen Africa, Vol. II: Mission Life*, Edinburgh: John Menzies & Co, 1881.
Macmillan, Hugh W. *The Origins and Development of the African Lakes Company, 1878–1908*, Doctoral Dissertation, University of Edinburgh, 1970.
Macola, Giacomo. *The Gun in Central Africa: A History of Technology and Politics*, Athens: Ohio University Press, 2016.
Mandala, Elias C. *Work and Control in a Peasant Economy: A History of the Lower Tchiri Valley in Malawi 1859–1960*, Madison: University of Wisconsin Press, 1990.
   The End of Chidyerano: A History of Food and Everyday Life in Malawi, 1860–2004, Portsmouth, NH: Heinemann, 2005.
Marjomaa, Risto. 'The Martial Spirit: Yao Soldiers in British Service in Nyasaland (Malawi), 1895–1939', *Journal of African History*, 44 (3), 2003, 413–32.
Marwick, M. G. 'History and Tradition in East-Central Africa through the Eyes of the Northern Rhodesian Cewa', *Journal of African History*, 4 (3), 1963, 375–90.
Matecheta, Harry Kwambwiri. *Blantyre Mission: Nkhani za ciyambi cace*, Blantyre: Hetherwick Press, 1951.
   Blantyre Mission: Stories of Its Beginning, trans. Thokozani Chilembwe, Berlin: Wichern-Verlag, 2016.
Mazrui, Ali A. *The Political Sociology of English Language: An African Perspective*, The Hague: Mouton, 1975.
Mbembe, Achille. *Critique of Black Reason*, trans. by Laurent Dubois, Durham, NC: Duke University Press, 2017.
Mbiti, John S. *African Religions and Philosophy*, Second Edition, Oxford: Heinemann, 1989 [1969].
McCaskie, Tom C. 'Exiled from History: Africa in Hegel's Academic Practice', *History in Africa*, 46, 2019, 165–94.

McCracken, John. *Politics and Christianity in Malawi 1875–1940: The Impact of the Livingstonia Mission in the Northern Province*, Cambridge: Cambridge University Press, 1977.
'"Marginal Men": The Colonial Experience in Malawi,' *Journal of Southern African Studies*, 15 (4), 1989, 338–42.
'Mungo Murray Chisuse and the Early History of Photography in Malawi', *The Society of Malawi Journal*, 61 (2), 2008, 1–18.
'Class, Violence and Gender in Early Colonial Malawi: The Curious Case of Elizabeth Pithie', *The Society of Malawi Journal*, 64 (2), 2011, 1–16.
A History of Malawi 1859–1966, Oxford: James Currey, 2012.
'Missionaries and Nationalists: Scotland and the 1959 Emergency in Malawi', in Afe Adogame and Andrew Lawrence, eds. *Africa in Scotland, Scotland in Africa: Historical Legacies and Contemporary Hybridities*, Leiden: Brill, 2014.
McCracken, John, ed. *Voices from the Chilembwe Rising: Witness Testimonies Made to the Nyasaland Rising Commission Inquiry, 1915*, Oxford: Oxford University Press for the British Academy, 2015.
McIntosh, Brian G. *The Scottish Mission in Kenya, 1891–1923*, Doctoral Dissertation, University of Edinburgh, 1969.
Miers, Suzanne and Igor Kopytoff, eds. *Slavery in Africa: Historical and Anthropological Perspectives*, Madison: University of Wisconsin Press, 1977.
Mijoga, Hilary B. P. 'The Bible in Malawi: A Brief Survey of Its Impact on Society', in Gerald O. West and Musa W. Dube Shomanah, eds. *The Bible in Africa: Transactions, Trajectories, and Trends*, Leiden: Brill, 2000.
Mohan, Giles. 'Beyond Participation: Strategies for Deeper Empowerment', in Bill Cooke and Uma Kothari, eds. *Participation: The New Tyranny?*, London: Zed Books, 2002.
Moore, James R. 'Evangelicals and Evolution: Henry Drummond, Herbert Spencer, and the Naturalisation of the Spiritual World', *Scottish Journal of Theology*, 38 (3), 1985, 383–418.
Morris, Brian. *An Environmental History of Southern Malawi*, New York: Palgrave Macmillan, 2016.
Mphande, Lupenga. 'Dr. Hastings Kamuzu Banda and the Malawi Writers Group: The (Un)making of a Cultural Tradition', *Research in African Literatures*, 27 (1), 1996, 80–101.
Mtenje, Alfred. 'English Imperialism and Shifting Attitudes towards African Languages: The Case of Malawi', in K. Legère and S. Fitchat., eds. *Talking Freedom: Language and Democratisation in the SADC Region*, Windhoek: Gamsberg Macmillan, 2002.

Mudimbe, Valentin Y. *The Invention of Africa: Gnosis, Philosophy, and the Order of Knowledge*, Bloomington: Indiana University Press, 1988.
Mwase, George Simeon. *Strike a Blow and Die: A Narrative of Race Relations in Colonial Language by George Simeon Mwase*, edited and introduced by Robert I. Rotberg, Cambridge, MA.: Harvard University Press, 1967.
National Bible Society of Scotland. *Utenga wa bwino wa St Matthaio*, Edinburgh: National Bible Society of Scotland, 1892.
Ncozana, Silas S. *Sangaya*, Mzuzu: Luviri Press, 2018.
Ndlovu-Gatsheni, Sabelo. *Epistemic Freedom in Africa: Deprovincialization and Decolonization*, London: Routledge, 2018.
Nelson, Nici and Susan Wright, eds. *Power and Participatory Development: Theory and Practice*, London: Intermediate Technology, 1995.
Ngũgĩ Wa Thiong'o. *Decolonizing the Mind: The Politics of Language in African Literature*, London: James Currey, 1986.
Niehaus, Isak. *Witchcraft and a Life in the New South Africa*, Cambridge: Cambridge University Press for the International African Institute, 2013.
Nyamnjoh, Francis B. *Drinking from the Cosmic Gourd: How Amos Tutuola Can Change Our Minds*, Bamenda: Langaa, 2017.
  'Introduction: Cannibalism as Food for Thought', in Francis B. Nyamnjoh, ed., *Eating and Being Eaten*, Bamenda: Langaa, 2018.
  'Ubuntuism and Africa: Actualised, Misappropriated, Endangered and Reappraised', Africa Day Memorial Lecture, University of the Free State, Bloemfontein, 2019.
Oliver, Roland. *The Missionary Factor in East Africa*, London: Longmans Green, 1952.
  Sir Harry Johnston and the Scramble for Africa, London: Chatto and Windus, 1957.
Ortega Y Gasset, José. 'The Misery and Splendor of Translation', trans. Elizabeth Gamble Müller, in Rainer Schulte and John Biguenet, eds. *Theories of Translation: An Anthology of Essays from Dryden to Derrida*, Chicago, IL: University of Chicago Press, 1992 [1937].
Paas, Steven. *Johannes Rebmann: A Servant of God in Africa before the Rise of Western Colonialism*, Bonn: VTR/VKW, 2011.
  Oxford Chichewa–English, English–Chichewa Dictionary, Oxford: Oxford University Press, 2016.
Page, Melvin E. *The Chiwaya War: Malawians and the First World War*, Boulder, CO: Westview Press, 2000.
Parsons, Janet Wagner. 'Scots and Afrikaners in Central Africa: Andrew Charles Murray and the Dutch Reformed Church Mission in Malawi', *The Society of Malawi Journal*, 51 (1), 1998, 21–40.

p'Bitek, Okot. *African Religions in Western Scholarship*, Nairobi: Kenya Literature Bureau, n.d.

Song of Lawino & Song of Ocol, Oxford: Heinemann, 1984 [1966, 1967].

Peel, J. D. Y. *Religious Encounter and the Making of the Yoruba*, Bloomington: Indiana University Press, 2000.

Peires, J. B. *The Dead Will Arise: Nongqawuse and the Great Xhosa Cattle-Killing Movement of 1856–7*, London: James Currey, 1989.

Pels, Peter. *A Politics of Presence: Contacts between Missionaries and the Walguru in Late Colonial Tanganyika*, Amsterdam: Harwood, 1999.

Pennycook, Alastair. *English and the Discourses of Colonialism*, New York: Routledge, 1998.

Peterson, Derek R. 'Translating the Word: Dialogism and Debate in Two Gikuyu Dictionaries', *Journal of Religious History*, 23 (1), 1999, 31–50.

Creative Writing: Translation, Bookkeeping, and the Work of Imagination in Colonial Kenya, Portsmouth, NH: Heinemann, 2004.

'Vernacular', in Gaurav Desai and Adeline Masquelier, eds. *Critical Terms for the Study of Africa*, Chicago, IL: University of Chicago Press, 2018.

Phiri, Gilbert. *A History of Education in the Blantyre Synod*, Doctoral Dissertation, Mzuzu University, 2021.

Phiri, Kings M., John McCracken and Wapulumuka O. Mulwafu, eds. *Malawi in Crisis: The 1959/60 Nyasaland State of Emergency and Its Legacy*, Blantyre: Christian Literature Association of Malawi, 2013.

Pierre, Jemima. 'The Racial Vernaculars of Development: A View from West Africa', *American Anthropologist*, 122 (1), 2020, 86–98.

Power, Joey. *Political Culture and Nationalism in Malawi: Building Kwacha*, Rochester, NY: University of Rochester Press, 2010.

Praeg, Leonhard and Siphokazi Magadla, eds. *Ubuntu: Curating the Archive*, Pietermaritzburg: University of Kwazulu-Natal Press, 2014.

Price, T. 'Nyanja Linguistic Problems', *Africa*, 13 (2), 1940, 125–37.

Prins, Gwyn. *The Hidden Hippopotamus: Reappraisal in African History: The Early Colonial Experience in Western Zambia*, Cambridge: Cambridge University Press, 1980.

Pritchett, James A. 'Christian Mission Stations in South-Central Africa: Eddies in the Flow of Global Culture', in Harri Englund, ed., *Christianity and Public Culture in Africa*, Athens: Ohio University Press, 2011.

Pugach, Sara. *Africa in Translation: A History of Colonial Linguistics in Germany and Beyond, 1814–1945*, Ann Arbor: University of Michigan Press, 2012.

Rangeley, W. H. 'Early Blantyre', *The Nyasaland Journal*, 7 (1), 1954, 36–45.

Ranger, Terence. 'The Invention of Tradition in Colonial Africa', in Eric J. Hobsbawm and Terence Ranger, eds. *The Invention of Tradition*. Cambridge: Cambridge University Press, 1983.
  'The Invention of Tradition Revisited: The Case of Africa', in Terence Ranger and O. Vaughan, eds. *Legitimacy and the State in Twentieth Century Africa*. London: Macmillan, 1993.
Rankine, W. Henry. *A Hero of the Dark Continent: Memoir of Rev. Wm. Affleck Scott*, Edinburgh: William Blackwood and Sons, 1896.
Richards, Audrey I. 'A Modern Movement of Witch-Finders', *Africa*, 8 (4), 1935, 448–61.
Robertson, Claire and Martin Klein. *Women and Slavery in Africa*, Madison: University of Wisconsin Press, 1983.
Robertson, William. *The Martyrs of Blantyre: Henry Henderson, Dr. John Bowie, Robert Cleland*, London: John Nisbet and Co, 1892.
Röhl, John C. G. *Young Wilhelm: The Kaiser's Early Life, 1859–1888*, trans. Jeremy Gaines and Rebecca Wallach, Cambridge: Cambridge University Press, 1998.
Ross, Andrew C. *Blantyre Mission and the Making of Modern Malawi*, Blantyre: Christian Literature Association of Malawi, 1996.
  'Hetherwick, Alexander', in Gerald H. Anderson, ed., *Biographical Dictionary of Christian Missions*, New York: Simon & Schuster, 1998.
  'Scott, David Clement Ruffelle', in Gerald H. Anderson, ed., *Biographical Dictionary of Christian Missions*, New York: Simon & Schuster, 1998.
  David Livingstone: Mission and Empire. London: Humbledon and London, 2002.
  Colonialism to Cabinet Crisis: A Political History of Malawi, Blantyre: Christian Literature Association of Malawi, 2009.
Ross, Kenneth R. *Gospel Ferment in Malawi: Theological Essays*, Gweru: Mambo Press, 1995.
Ross, Kenneth R. 'Not Catalyst but Ferment: The Distinctive Contribution of the Churches to Political Reform in Malawi 1992–93', in Matembo S. Nzunda and Kenneth R. Ross, eds. *Church, Law and Political Transition in Malawi 1992–94*, Gweru: Mambo Press, 1995.
  '"Worrisome Trends": The Voice of the Churches in Malawi's Third-Term Debate', *African Affairs*, 103 (410), 2004, 91–107.
  Malawi and Scotland: Together in the Talking Place since 1859, Mzuzu: Mzuni Press, 2013.
Ross, Robert. *The Borders of Race in Colonial South Africa: The Kat River Settlement, 1829–1856*, Cambridge: Cambridge University Press, 2014.
Rossi, Benedetta. 'Dependence, Unfreedom, and Slavery: Towards an Integrated Analysis,' *Africa*, 86 (3), 2016, 571–90.

Rotberg, Robert I. *The Rise of Nationalism in Central Africa: The Making of Malawi and Zambia*, Cambridge, MA: Harvard University Press, 1966.
'The "Partnership" Hoax: How the British Government Deprived Central Africans of Their Rights', *Journal of Southern African Studies*, 45 (1), 2019, 89–110.
Rotberg, Robert I. with Miles F. Shore. *The Founder: Cecil Rhodes and the Pursuit of Power*, Oxford: Oxford University Press, 1988.
Rowley, Henry. *Africa Unveiled*, London: Society for Promoting Christian Knowledge, 1876.
Rudnyckyj, Daromir. *Spiritual Economies: Islam, Globalization, and the Afterlife of Development*, Ithaca, NY: Cornell University Press, 2010.
Ruel, Malcolm. *Belief, Ritual and the Securing of Life: Essays on a Bantu Religion*, Leiden: Brill, 1997.
Sanders, Edith R. 'The Hamitic Hypothesis: Its Origins and Functions in Time Perspective', *Journal of African History*, 10 (4), 1969, 521–32.
Sanneh, Lamin. *Translating the Message: The Missionary Impact on Culture*, Maryknoll, NY: Orbis Books, 1990.
Schapera, Isaac. 'Economic Changes in South African Native Life', *Africa*, 1 (2), 1928, 170–88.
Schieffelin, Bambi B. 'Christianizing Language and the Displacement of Culture in Bosavi, Papua New Guinea', *Current Anthropology*, 55 (S10), 2014, S226–37.
Schoffeleers, J. M. *River of Blood: The Genesis of a Martyr Cult in Southern Malawi, c. A.D. 1600*, Madison, WI: University of Wisconsin Press, 1992.
In Search of Truth and Justice: Confrontations between Church and State in Malawi, 1960–1994, Blantyre: Christian Literature Association of Malawi, 2000.
Scott, D. C. *A Cyclopaedic Dictionary of the Mang'anja Language Spoken in British Central Africa*, Edinburgh: Foreign Mission Committee of the Church of Scotland, 1892.
'*Living Stones*': *Sermon upon the Church of Scotland Blantyre Mission, British Central Africa*, Edinburgh: William Blackwood and Sons, 1901.
Sebastiani, Silvia. *The Scottish Enlightenment: Race, Gender, and the Limits of Progress*, New York: Palgrave Macmillan, 2013.
Shepperson, George. 'Notes on Negro American Influences on the Emergence of African Nationalism', *Journal of African History*, 1 (2), 1960, 299–312.
'Introduction', in Duff Macdonald, *Africana: The Heart of Heathen Africa*, London: Dawsons of Pall Mall, 1969.

Shepperson, George and Thomas Price. *Independent African: John Chilembwe and the Origins, Setting and Significance of the Nyasaland Native Rising of 1915*, Edinburgh: Edinburgh University Press, 1958.

Sherman, Benjamin R. 'There's No (Testimonial) Justice: Why Pursuit of a Virtue is Not the Solution to Epistemic Injustice', *Social Epistemology*, 30 (3), 2016, 229–50.

Short, Philip. *Banda*, London: Routledge and Kegan Paul, 1974.

Sindima, Harvey J. *Malawi's First Republic: An Economic and Political Analysis*, Lanham MD: University Press of America, 2002.

Smith, Edwin W. *The Golden Stool: Some Aspects of the Conflict of Cultures in Modern Africa*, London: Edinburgh House, 1927.

Knowing the African, London: Lutterworth Press, 1946.

Smith, W. C. *Belief and History*, Charlottesville: University of Virginia Press, 1977.

de Sousa Santos, Boaventura. *The End of the Cognitive Empire: The Coming of Age of Epistemologies of the South*, Durham, NC: Duke University Press, 2018.

Spear, Thomas. 'Neo-traditionalism and the Limits of Invention in British Colonial Africa', *Journal of African History,* 44 (1), 2003, 327.

Stanley, Brian. 'Conversion to Christianity: The Colonization of the Mind?', *International Review of Mission*, no. 366, 2013, 315–31.

Statham, Todd. 'Teetotalism in Malawian Protestantism: Missionary Origins, African Appropriation', *Studies in World Christianity*, 21 (2), 2015, 161–82.

Stilwell, Sean. *Slavery and Slaving in African History*, Cambridge: Cambridge University Press, 2014.

Stokes, Eric. 'Malawi Political Systems and the Introduction of Colonial Rule', in Eric Stokes and Richard Brown, eds. *The Zambesian Past: Studies in Central African History*, Manchester: Manchester University Press, 1965.

Stolcke, Verena. 'Talking Culture: New Boundaries, New Rhetorics of Exclusion in Europe', *Current Anthropology*, 36 (1), 1995, 1–24.

Strohbehn, Ulf. *Pentecostalism in Malawi: A History of the Apostolic Faith Mission 1931–1994*, Blantyre: Christian Literature Association of Malawi, 2005.

Stuart-Mogg, David. 'The Rev. David Clement Scott and the Issue of Land Title in British Central Africa', *The Society of Malawi Journal*, 57 (2), 2004, 21–34.

Tadmor, Naomi. *The Social Universe of the English Bible: Scripture, Society, and Culture in Early Modern England*, Cambridge: Cambridge University Press, 2010.

Taiwo, Olufemi. *How Colonialism Preempted Modernity in Africa*, Bloomington: Indiana University Press, 2010.

Tempels, Placide. *Bantu Philosophy*, trans. by Colin King, Paris: Présence Africaine, 1959.
Thompson, Jack T. *Touching the Heart: Xhosa Missionaries to Malawi, 1876–1888*, Pretoria: University of South Africa Press, 1999.
  Ngoni, Xhosa and Scot: Religious and Cultural Interaction in Malawi, Zomba: Kachere Series, 2007.
Turner, Victor. *The Drums of Affliction: A Study of Religious Processes among the Ndembu of Zambia*, Oxford: Clarendon Press, 1968.
Vail, Leroy. 'Religion, Language and the Tribal Myth: The Tumbuka and Chewa of Malawi', in J. M. Schoffeleers, ed., *Guardians of the Land: Essays on Central African Territorial Cults*, Gweru: Mambo Press, 1979.
Vail, Leroy and Landeg White. 'Tribalism in the Political History of Malawi', in Leroy Vail, ed., *The Creation of Tribalism in Southern Africa*, Berkeley: University of California Press, 1989.
van den Bersselaar, Dmitri. 'Missionary Ethnographers and the History of Anthropology: The Case of G. T. Basden', in Patrick Harries and David Maxwell, eds. *The Spiritual in the Secular: Missionaries and Knowledge about Africa*, Grand Rapids, MI: William B. Eerdmans, 2012.
van Dijk, Rijk A. 'Young Puritan Preachers in Post-Independence Malawi', *Africa*, 62 (2), 1992, 159–81.
van Walraven, Klaas. 'Prologue: Reflections on Historiography and Biography and the Study of Africa's Past', in Klaas van Walraven, ed., *The Individual in African History: The Importance of Biography in African Historical Studies*, Leiden: Brill, 2020.
Vansina, Jan. *Kingdoms of the Savanna: A History of Central African States Until European Occupation*, Madison: University of Wisconsin Press, 1966.
Vaughan, Megan. 'Food Production and Family Labour in Southern Malawi: The Shire Highlands and Upper Shire Valley in the Early Colonial Period', *Journal of African History*, 23 (3), 1982, 351–64.
  'Which Family?: Problems in the Reconstruction of the History of the Family as an Economic and Cultural Unit', *Journal of African History*, 24 (2), 1983, 275–83.
  The Story of an African Famine: Gender and Famine in Twentieth-Century Malawi, Cambridge: Cambridge University Press, 1987.
Vinck, Honoré. 'Ideology in Missionary Scholarly Knowledge in Belgian Congo: *Aequatoria, Centre de recherches africanistes*; The Mission Station of Bamanya (RDC), 1937–2007', in Patrick Harries and David Maxwell, eds. *The Spiritual in the Secular: Missionaries and Knowledge about Africa*, Grand Rapids, MI: William B. Eerdmans, 2012.
VonDoepp, Peter. 'The Kingdom beyond *Zasintha*: Churches and Political Life in Malawi's Post-authoritarian Era', in Kings M. Phiri and Kenneth

R. Ross, eds. *Democratization in Malawi: A Stocktaking*, Blantyre: Christian Literature Association of Malawi, 1998.
Wallace, Valerie. *Scottish Presbyterianism and Settler Colonial Politics: Empire of Dissent*, New York: Palgrave Macmillan, 2018.
Ward, Kevin. '"A Theology of Attention": The CMS Tradition at the End of the Colonial Era in Africa: Max Warren (1904–1977) and John V. Taylor (1914–2001)', in Frieder Ludwig and Afe Adogame, eds. *European Traditions in the Study of Religion in Africa*, Wiesbaden: Harrassowitz, 2004.
Weisbord, Robert G. 'J. Albert Thorne, Back-to-Africanist', *Negro History Bulletin*, 32 (3), 1969, 14–16.
Wendland, Ernst R. *Buku Loyera: An Introduction to the New Chichewa Bible Translation*, Blantyre: Christian Literature Association in Malawi, 1998.
White, Landeg. *Magomero: Portrait of an African Village*, Cambridge: Cambridge University Press, 1987.
Wild-Wood, Emma. 'Bible Translation and the Formation of Corporate Identity in Uganda and Congo 1900–40', *Journal of African History*, 58 (3), 2017, 489–507.
  'Relocating Unity and Theology in the Study of World Christianity', in Joel Cabrita, David Maxwell and Emma Wild-Wood, eds. *Relocating World Christianity: Interdisciplinary Studies in Universal and Local Expressions of the Christian Faith*, Leiden: Brill, 2017.
Williams, Raymond. *Keywords: A Vocabulary of Culture and Society*, Oxford: Oxford University Press, 1985.
Williams, Rowan. *Resurrection: Interpreting the Easter Gospel*, London: Darton, Longman and Todd, 2002 [1982].
Willis, Justin. 'The Nature of a Mission Community: The Universities' Mission to Central Africa in Bonde', *Past and Present*, 140 (1), 1993, 127–54.
Wiredu, Kwasi. *Cultural Universals and Particulars: An African Perspective*, Bloomington: Indiana University Press, 1996.
Woolard, Kathryn A. and Bambi B. Schieffelin. 'Language Ideology', *Annual Review of Anthropology*, 23, 1994, 55–82.
Young, W. John. '"They Have Laid Hold of Some Essential Truths": Edwin W. Smith (1876-1957), A Wise Listener to African Voices', in Frieder Ludwig and Afe Adogame, eds. *European Traditions in the Study of Religion in Africa*, Wiesbaden: Harrassowitz, 2004.
Zammito, John H. *Kant, Herder, and the Birth of Anthropology*, Chicago, IL: University of Chicago Press, 2002.

Index

Abercromby, George, 224, 230
Aberdeen, 71, 166, 176, 241
Africa Inland Mission, 229
African Lakes Company, 44, 47, 53, 61, 74, 103, 120, 133, 135, 143, 145, 176, 193, 256, 267
African religion, 11, 13–15
alcohol, 20, 46, 52–4, 62, 113, 171, 180, 210, 248
Amin, Idi, 15
Anglican Church Missionary Society, 12
apartheid, 10–11, 71, 244, 269
Apostolic Faith Mission, 272
Appiah, Kwame Anthony, 274
Apter, Emily, 276
Arabic, 24, 139, 236
Arabs, 30, 37–8, 121, 133–4, 147, 153, 156
Arendt, Hannah, 111
Arthur, John William, 26, 221–3, 229
Assemblies of God, 272
Aurelius, Marcus, 180
Australia, 41, 107
Ayrshire, 227, 241

Bancks, Mary Jane, 25
Banda, Kamuzu, 256, 268, 270
baptism, 163–5, 175, 222, 228, 230, 236, 248, 280
Barbados, 127
Barlow, Arthur Ruffelle, 220–2, 224, 228
Barnes, J. A., 253
Barotseland, 18, 20, 22
Beck, Janet, 169–70, 176, 193, 202, 216
Bible, 70–1, 73, 77, 92–3, 96, 98–101, 173, 233, 235–7, 241–4
biographical method, 5–6, 29, 281

Birmingham, 228
Bismarck, Joseph, 51
Blantyre, 196
Blantyre Chamber of Commerce, 260
Blantyre Mission
  and sports, 27
  as industrial mission, 58, 85, 180, 187, 259
  as sanctuary, 21, 47–9
  church building, 54, 68, 121–6, 193, 247
  Council, 185, 188, 192, 197, 246, 251
  execution at, 45
  floggings at, 33, 44–5, 49, 61
  hospital, 126, 144, 179
  magazine, 80–1, 88, 119, 123, 132, 134, 136, 142, 144, 146, 149–50, 156, 158, 173, 176–8, 184, 186–7, 189–90, 195, 198, 217, 231–2, 258
  schools, 38, 49, 69, 78, 165, 168, 170, 172–4, 193, 217, 230, 247, 256, 260–1, 268
Bokwito, Tom, 41, 59, 267
Booth, Joseph, 8, 176–7, 254–5, 258, 263
Boston, 108
Botswana, 138
Bowie, Isobel. *See* Scott, Isobel
Bowie, John, 125, 163, 201–2, 204–5, 208–12, 216, 224, 229
Bowie, Sara, 204, 217, 224
Bowman, E. D., 247
Bridges, Roy, 6
Britain, 134, 159, 165, 173, 175–8, 217, 267
British Central Africa Protectorate, 129, 132–3, 135, 137–8, 142, 232
British Empire, 139

Index   303

British South Africa Company, 135, 140, 143–4, 146
Buchanan, John, 43, 49, 51, 133, 141, 143, 148, 156
Burns, Robert, 71

Cabrita, Joel, 13
Calderwood, Henry, 26
calico, 64, 157, 173
Cambridge, 40
cannibalism, 90–1, 154
Cape Colony, 12, 136, 201
Cape Maclear, 83
catechism, 173
Catholics, 9, 15, 114, 135, 254, 268, 270
Chambers, Robert, 277
Chanock, Martin, 160
Charteris, A. H., 26–7, 221, 226–8
Che Chamba, 265
Che Ndombo, 83
Chendetsa, Jeannie, 170
Chewa, 18, 36, 253
Chichewa, 23, 78, 97
chiefs, 19, 55, 59–64, 67–9, 121, 141, 160–1, 182, 197, 253, 276, 280
  Chifisi, 21
  Chikumbu, 65, 140–1
  Chikuse, 21, 67–8
  Chipatula, 38, 54, 62
  Gomani, 142
  Kapeni, 23, 48, 53, 61, 63, 65, 113, 121
  Kasisi, 65, 117
  Katunga, 117–18, 201
  Kawinga, 214
  Makanjira, 21, 37, 133, 141
  Malemia, 214
  Malunga, 145
  Masea, 117, 208
  Mataka, 37
  Matope, 118
  Mitochi, 65
  Mkanda, 65, 207
  Mpama, 23, 61, 65
  Mponda, 21, 37
  Mtaja, 60–2
  Ramakukan, 62
Chilembwe, Ida, 261

Chilembwe, John, 6, 31, 176–7, 235, 254–9, 261, 267
Chimang'anja, 23, 30, 76, 78, 80, 83, 86, 89, 91, 94–5, 101, 119, 172, 180, 222, 228, 233, 235, 238, 276
China, 167
Chintali, F. S., 269
Chinyanja, 23, 78, 83, 90–1, 97, 173, 235, 249
Chipeta, 69, 122
Chipuliko, John Macrae, 180
Chiradzulu, 65
Chirnside, Andrew, 44, 48
Chisuse, Mungo, 67–8, 84, 179, 231–2, 247–8, 256, 267
Chitumbuka, 24
Chiyao, 24, 42, 79, 84, 231, 249
Church Missionary Society, 229
Church of Central Africa, Presbyterian (CCAP), 246, 267–72
Church of England, 268
Church of Scotland, 5, 28, 40, 48, 73, 112, 133, 143, 164, 169, 190, 193, 199, 205, 219–20, 245, 268, 272
  African Mission Committee of, 40, 50, 52, 218
  Foreign Mission Committee of, 85, 123, 129, 134, 145, 165, 167, 182, 184–5, 187, 192, 194, 197, 199, 204–5, 217, 219, 221, 226, 269
  General Assembly of, 49–51, 192, 246, 269
  Kirk Session of, 185, 251
  Women's Committee for Foreign Mission of, 170
class differences, 36, 167, 170, 195
Cleland, Robert, 202
clothes, 27, 45–6, 152, 173–4, 177, 189, 198, 256, 261
coffee, 19, 155, 180, 187, 220
Colenso, John William, 9, 73
colonialism, 15, 50, 53, 59, 77, 116, 134, 154, 214, 254–5, 259
Colvin, Tom, 269
Comaroff, Jean and John, 7
Congo, 9–10
Constantinople, 196
conversion, 61, 165, 175, 177, 237, 280
cosmopolitanism, 196, 274–5

cotton, 19, 155, 253, 257
Crawford, Daniel, 235
Crowther, Samuel Ajayi, 12
culture, 16
Currie, Adam, 143, 163, 189, 205–7, 251
Currie, Hamilton, 177
Currie, Jessie Monteath, 207
curse of Ham, 53, 69–74, 99, 101, 109
customs, 22, 69, 112–14, 121, 153, 161, 210, 239, 244, 248

Dark Continent, 2, 105, 127, 181, 212, 281
darkness, 55, 86, 281
Dedza, 67
Denmark, 102
development, 159, 277–9
diphteria, 208–9
diplomacy, 23, 25, 64–6, 121, 207, 215, 280
divorce, 250–1
Domasi, 84, 169, 182, 188, 195, 198, 209, 214, 216, 246, 252, 265
Dougall, James, 269
Drummond, Henry, 30, 103–9, 111, 115, 126, 130, 151, 154, 161, 190, 235
Du Bois, W. E. B., 274
Duncan, Jonathan, 43, 51, 200
Durban, 176–7
Dutch Reformed Church, 271

East African Scottish Mission, 219
Edinburgh, 5, 25, 40, 42, 48, 52, 55, 58, 84, 160, 173, 176, 185, 205, 268
    Greenside Church, 169
    St George's Church, 55, 173, 182
Egypt, 181
Elmslie, W. A., 57
Elphick, Richard, 12
England, 100, 137, 217, 239
English, 24, 78, 80, 86, 93, 97–8, 139, 172–3, 178, 180, 224, 236, 239, 247, 273, 276
epistemic justice, 4–5, 8–9, 15–16, 22, 28, 53, 80, 158, 174, 177, 244, 275, 278, 280–2

ethnic distinctions, 18–21, 23, 39, 80, 84, 243, 273
European planters. *See* white settlers
Evans-Pritchard, E. E., 9
evolution, 106–9, 152–4, 161

famine, 19
Federation of Rhodesia and Nyasaland, 269
Fenwick, Elizabeth. *See* Hetherwick, Elizabeth
Fenwick, George, 38, 43–4, 47, 49, 51, 54, 63, 166
firearms, 18–21, 38, 61, 63, 66, 141, 179, 207, 214
folklore, 91, 239, 244
Foreign Office, 49, 132, 137–8, 142–4, 147, 150, 186
France, 101
Fraser, Alexander Campbell, 26
Free Church of Scotland, 40, 49
French, 139
friendship, 21–2, 25, 54, 57–8, 65, 68, 97–8, 118, 184, 201–2, 224, 229–30, 238, 276
funerals, 65, 203–4, 210, 223, 228–9

Gamitto, Antonio, 39
Garvey, Marcus, 127
gender, 3–4, 170, 252–3
Germany, 8, 11, 14, 102, 147, 175, 211, 257
Gibraltar, 135
Gikuyu, 222, 229
Glasgow, 40, 103, 167, 176, 225
Gluckman, Max, 22–3
God, 86–7, 99, 181, 237
gossip, 149, 154
Gramsci, Antonio, 7
Greek, 26, 30, 89, 94–5, 222, 224, 233, 236, 276
Guinness, Henry Grattan, 176
guns. *See* firearms

Hamilton, James, 200
Hankey, Sara. *See* Bowie, Sara
Harare, 265
Harlem, 127
Hastings, Adrian, 280–1

Hebrew, 26, 30, 92, 94–8, 222, 224, 233, 238, 276
Henderson, Harriet, 166, 169, 202, 204, 207–9, 216
Henderson, Henry, 41–2, 51, 59, 62, 68, 103, 163, 166, 202, 208–9, 267
Herd, Henry D., 189–90, 199
Herder, Johan Gottfried, 274
Hetherwick, Alexander, 6, 27, 31, 51, 65–9, 71, 75, 77, 83–5, 93, 96, 102, 109, 114, 116, 122–3, 132, 137, 146–8, 150, 165, 186, 188, 192, 194–5, 199, 212, 214, 218, 224, 228, 230–1, 247, 251, 253, 267, 276
  and paternalism, 158, 233, 245
  and the vernacular, 233–40
  first journey to Africa, 103–4
  on land and labour, 156–8, 258
  on race relations, 259–64
Hetherwick, Clement, 170
Hetherwick, Elizabeth, 49, 62, 165–9, 217, 251
Hobsbawm, Eric, 6
Houldsworth, Jane, 227
human rights, 45, 119
humanitarianism, 47, 111, 212
humanity, 28, 79–80, 85, 105–6, 111, 192
Hurlburt, Charles, 229
Hynde, Robert, 163, 188–9, 192, 197, 199, 260

idolatry, 86
Iliffe, John, 35
India, 28, 40, 43, 81, 136–7, 139–40, 155, 167, 204
Indonesia, 8
influenza, 208
Inglis, Francis Caird, 176
initiation ceremonies, 17, 37, 113, 249
intimacies, 201, 211, 224, 230
Iona Community, 269
Islam, 21, 37, 39, 84, 141, 263, 276
ivory, 18, 20, 60, 106, 120–1, 141, 171

Jamaica, 127, 244
Johnson, William Percival, 90–1

Johnston, Harry, 30, 90, 129, 135, 137, 148–9, 155, 158–9, 161, 184, 186, 190, 214, 263
  and Alexander Hetherwick, 142–4
  and Cecil Rhodes, 132, 138–40, 149–50
  and military campaigns, 140–2
  on central Africans, 151–4

Kaferanjira, Rondau, 51, 62
Kalaliche, Cedric, 180
Kamlinje, John Gray, 175–8, 180
Karonga, 133, 257
Kaunde, Joseph, 246
Keane, Webb, 7
Kenya, 25–6, 101, 203–4, 219, 231, 281
Kenyatta, Jomo, 221
Kikuyu, 101
Kikuyu Mission. See Scott, David Clement, in Kenya
Kilwa, 37
King George V, 176, 257
kinship, 21, 25, 39, 97, 201, 230
Kololo, 18–22, 39, 44, 54, 59, 62, 65, 67, 69, 230
Koyi, William, 29, 56–8, 184, 202
Kufa, John Gray, 179, 256
Kundecha, Stephen, 246

Lake Malawi, 23, 40, 88, 109, 117, 133
land, 46, 60, 73, 99–100, 113, 126, 155–6, 179, 220, 250, 257, 263, 276, 281
language ideologies, 76–81, 85, 89, 96, 105, 181, 239, 244
Latin, 26, 95, 190, 224
Latour, Bruno, 7
law, 145, 161, 250, 253
Laws, Robert, 52, 56–7, 69, 92–3, 95, 108
Leakey, Harry, 229
Lewis, Joanna, 235
liberalism, 194, 234, 254, 263
Likoma island, 88
linguistics, 11, 24, 79, 84, 88, 95, 102, 242
Lisbon, 134

Livingstone, David, 1, 18–19, 22, 35–6, 39–41, 46, 62, 111, 127, 137, 173, 175, 257, 265
Livingstone, William Jervis, 257
Livingstonia Mission, 40, 42, 49–50, 52, 56–7, 65, 69, 79–80, 92, 103, 149, 241, 251
Livingstonia Synod, 246, 271
London, 168, 176
London Missionary Society, 12
Lord Lugard, 128, 130, 133
Lord Salisbury, 117, 134–5, 137, 140
Lovedale Missionary Institution, 56

Macdonald, Duff, 33, 39, 43–6, 48–51, 54, 58–9, 61–2, 64, 79, 168
Macklin, T. Thornton, 43, 47–8, 50, 52
Macleod, George, 269
Macrae, John, 40, 50
Macvicar, Neil, 191
Magomero, 40–1, 257, 261
Maguire, Cecil, 140–1
Maguire, Rochfort, 140
Majonanga, Rosie, 179
Makerere University, 14
malaria, 170, 224
Malawi Congress Party, 271
Malindi, 37
Malota, Donald, 51, 171
Mang'anja, 18–19, 22, 36, 118
Maples, Chauncy, 88, 91
marriage, 250–3
Maseya, Thomas, 246
Matecheta, Harry Kambwiri, 50, 168–70, 174, 179–80, 230, 239, 246, 256, 261
Mbembe, Achille, 16
Mbiti, John, 14–15
Mbona, 39
McCracken, John, 140, 268, 270
McIlwain, John, 125
McMurtrie, John, 129, 134, 146, 165, 167, 185, 188, 205–7, 217–19, 224–8, 245
medicine, 55–6, 86, 237, 281
mental health, 219, 223
Methodists, 10
Milne, William, 43
mimicry, 9, 62, 189, 261–2
mission stations, 174, 191

missionaries
  and anthropology, 6–13, 244
  and death, 203, 213
  and primitivism, 8
  and sacrifice, 1–3, 170, 178, 203–4, 207
  as imperialists, 11
  liberal, 8, 10–11, 16
Moir, Frederick, 44
Moir, John, 44, 56
Mombasa, 37, 221
monotheism, 87
morality, 146, 148–9, 253
Morrison, Frederick, 74–5
Mozambique, 44, 135, 146–7, 209, 215, 257
Mphande, Lupenga, 270
Mtuwa, Harry, 246
Mudimbe, Valentin, 15
Mulanje, 65, 143, 149, 170, 189, 195, 198, 206, 208–9, 212, 214–15, 246, 252
multilingualism, 79, 84, 241
Muluzi, Bakili, 272
Murray, Andrew, 271
Mvera Mission, 241

names, 164, 175, 230
nationalism, 127, 160, 176, 256, 267, 274
Nazism, 11
Ndendermere, Abrey, 213, 231
Ndirande, 120, 172, 213
newspapers, 187, 189, 194, 199, 257, 260
Ngoni, 18, 20–1, 34–5, 39, 56, 61, 66–8, 116, 119, 122, 142, 156, 169, 230, 253
Nguludi, 254
Nkhoma Synod, 246, 271
Northern Rhodesia, 139
Ntcheu, 67, 169, 230
Ntimawanzako, Nacho, 84, 175, 211
Ntintili, Mapassa, 56
Nyambadwe, 168
Nyasaland, 135, 144, 232
Nyasaland African Congress, 268

Oman, 37
Oxford, 40, 90

Paterson, James, 227
p'Bitek, Okot, 14–15
Pemba, 37
Pentecostalism, 271
peoplehood, 77, 93, 101–2, 241, 244–5, 273
philosophy, 11, 15, 85, 91, 244, 279
Pithie, Elizabeth. *See* Hetherwick, Elizabeth
poetry, 71, 95
poison ordeal, 116–18, 249
polygamy, 249–50, 252
Portuguese, 24, 30, 35–9, 117, 121, 134–5, 139, 151, 179, 214
potatoes, 221
prejudices, 10, 13, 80, 86, 128, 154, 275
primordialism, 14, 16, 278–9
Pringle, Alexander, 48–50, 58, 187
Pritchett, James, 174
Protestantism, 78, 102, 110, 113, 175, 272, 277
Public Affairs Committee, 271
Punjab, 164

racial equality, 17, 115
  and differences, 3, 70–1, 131, 161, 177, 278
racism, 113, 277
Rankin, Daniel, 147
Rankin, James, 48–50, 52, 58, 187, 192, 194, 196, 199–200
Rebmann, Johannes, 83
refugees, 20, 34, 40, 47–8, 63–5, 68, 79, 84, 98
Reid, James, 12, 191
Rhodes, Cecil, 6, 30, 73, 132, 135, 138–40, 143, 146, 162, 186, 201, 214, 258, 281
Riddel, Alexander, 83
Robertson, George, 163, 189, 192, 215
Robertson, James, 26, 52, 55, 57–8, 63, 66, 74, 93, 105, 117, 125, 159, 176, 183, 202–3, 215, 221, 225–6, 228
Roger, Jacques-François, 102
Ross, Andrew, 29, 109, 220, 247
Rowley, Henry, 36–7
Royal Anthropological Institute, 10

Royal Geographical Society, 44
Royal High School, 25
Ruffelle, Edith. *See* Scott, Edith Ruffelle

Sangaya, Jonathan, 270
Sanskrit, 90
Schapera, Isaac, 13
School of Oriental and African Studies, 170
Schreiner, Olive, 258
Scotland, 40, 73, 84, 107, 165, 170, 176, 179, 192, 202, 213, 216, 241, 247, 255, 267–8
Scott, Affleck, 95, 145, 148, 156, 191, 202, 204–5, 208–9, 211–15, 224, 231, 251
Scott, Andrew, 221, 227
Scott, Archibald, 145–6, 182–5, 187, 206, 214, 217, 226
Scott, David Clement
  and African deacons, 178–82, 202, 224, 246
  and common humanity, 4, 8, 84, 86–7, 105, 109–10, 112, 115, 126, 130, 203, 275
  and conversion, 26, 223
  and deliberations, 22–3, 63–4, 66–7, 134, 154, 182, 280
  and finances, 185, 187, 190, 192–3, 220–1, 226–8
  and high-churchism, 27, 164, 183, 188, 193, 198
  and his mother, 25, 216
  and history, 16, 112–13, 196
  and liturgy, 183–4, 186
  and sports, 27
  and the Committee of Inquiry, 186, 192–5, 197–9
  and the dictionary, 17, 22, 27, 59, 66, 78–9, 83–91, 95, 197, 203, 210, 237, 244, 253
  and the future, 159, 163, 196, 220, 234
  and the risen Christ, 2, 32, 72, 109, 174, 183–4, 258, 275–6, 282
  and the theology of reversals, 13, 17, 72–4, 275, 278
  and the University of Edinburgh, 26–7, 216

Scott, David Clement (cont.)
  and the vernacular, 17–18, 23–4, 66, 76, 85–8, 90, 94–5, 101–2, 233, 280
  as a visionary, 6, 74–5, 85
  first journey to Blantyre, 56
  in Kenya, 219–24
  on Cecil Rhodes, 133, 135–8
  on civilization, 16, 74, 110, 115, 159, 280
  on Harry Johnston's book, 154–5
  on land, 160–1
  on music, 114–16
  the daughters of, 24, 165, 202, 217, 219, 224–5, 227, 230
  the death of, 228–32
Scott, Edith Ruffelle, 24, 217–19, 223–6, 229
Scott, Henry, 191, 209, 251
Scott, Isobel, 24–5, 52, 65, 67, 75, 163, 165–8, 201–2, 204, 207, 214–16, 219, 223, 225
Scott, Marjorie, 176
Scott, Walter G., 226
Scottish Enlightenment, 28, 71, 102, 111
security, 18, 21–2, 45, 64
segregation, 10, 82, 91, 126, 158, 232, 247
Senegal, 102
Sharpe, Alfred, 148, 150, 214
Shire Highlands, 20–1, 67–8, 120, 122, 134, 136, 140, 142, 145, 155, 160, 163, 208, 219, 231, 255, 257
Shire river, 62, 117, 134, 141, 176, 212
Shire Valley, 20, 253
Sikhs, 141, 214
Sindima, Harvey, 135
slave trade, 1, 34, 37–8, 46, 49, 61, 63, 102, 110–11, 128, 130, 133, 137, 140–1
slavery, 2, 18–19, 21, 34–7, 46, 48, 53, 63, 69–72, 100–1, 109, 118–19, 128, 157, 276
Smith, Edwin, 10–11
Soche Mountain, 61
South Africa, 10, 12, 18, 21, 56, 71, 136, 158, 258, 269, 271–2, 279
Stewart, James, 42–3, 49
Stokes, Charles, 8

Sunday Schools, 167–8, 193
Swahili, 24, 37, 80, 120, 139, 222, 236
Swaziland, 18

Tadmor, Naomi, 98, 100
Taiwo, Olufemi, 12
Tanzania, 21
taxation, 136, 138, 142, 146, 150, 158–9, 198, 257
Tempels, Placide, 9–11
Tete, 147
theology, 86, 108–9, 164, 183, 185, 188, 204, 279
Thipa, Allan, 269
Thorne, J. Albert, 127–30, 181, 255, 277
Tilowa, Henry, 216
tobacco, 19, 155, 188, 257
Tonga, 214
tracheotomy, 208, 211
trade unionism, 272
translation, 22, 77–8, 91–101, 186, 235–8, 242–3, 276
tribalism, 10
Tswana, 7

Ubuntu, 279
Uganda, 14
United Kingdom. See Britain
United States, 107, 127, 255–6
Universities' Mission to Central Africa, 20, 36, 40, 88, 90–1, 109, 114, 149, 169

Vail, Leroy, 80
Venn, Henry, 12

Walker, John, 43, 47, 54
war, 66, 140, 142, 257, 263
Watch Tower, 257
Watson, David, 229
Werner, Alice, 169–70
West Indies, 127
Westminster Abbey, 1
White settlers, 10, 140, 187–90, 201, 212, 220, 224, 229, 233, 239, 245, 257–8, 260, 268
White supremacy, 6, 16, 126, 189, 259–60

Index

White, Landeg, 20
Whittinghame Parish, 52
Wilberforce, William, 128
Williams, George, 57
Williams, Rowan, 275, 277
Winter, Johannes, 8
witchcraft, 86, 90, 113, 116, 153–4
Wolof, 102
World Christianity, 279

Xhosa, 56

Yao, 18, 20–1, 34–7, 59, 65, 84, 112–13, 117–18, 120, 122, 132, 140–1, 207, 214, 265

Zambesi Industrial Mission, 241, 254
Zambesi river, 137, 139, 179
Zambia, 18, 21, 253
Zanzibar, 37, 105, 140, 216
Zimbabwe, 135
Zomba, 140, 214, 246, 252, 257
Zulu, 18, 21, 67, 117